Cities, Politics, and Policy

Cities, Politics, and Policy
A Comparative Analysis

Edited by
John P. Pelissero
Loyola University Chicago

CQ PRESS

A Division of Congressional Quarterly Inc.
Washington, D.C.

CQ Press
1255 22nd Street, N.W., Suite 400
Washington, D.C. 20037

(202) 729-1900; toll-free, 1-866-4CQ-PRESS (1-866-427-7737)

www.cqpress.com

♾The paper used in this publication meets the minimum requirements of the American National Standard for Information Sciences—Permanence of Paper for Printed Library Materials, ANSI Z39.48-1992.

Printed and bound in the United States of America

06 05 04 03 02   5 4 3 2 1

Typeset and designed by Mid Atlantic, Linthicum, Maryland
Cover design by Naylor Designs

Library of Congress Cataloging-in-Publication Data

Cities, politics, and policy : a comparative analysis / edited by John P. Pelissero.
    p. cm.
Includes bibliographical references and index.
ISBN 1-56802-686-2 (alk. paper)
    1. Municipal government--United States. 2. Urban policy--United States. I. Pelissero, John P. II. Title.
    JS331 .C54 2003
    320.8'5'0973--dc21   2002015014

*To
Paula*

Contents

Part III: Policy Outputs and Outcomes

Tables and Figures

Tables

Figures

Preface

America's cities, for better or worse, have long been the dwelling places of choice for American residents. Today, 226 million people—a full 80 percent of the U.S. population—live in metropolitan areas, with 85 million people residing in the central cities. This country's urban population outnumbers the entire populace of every other country except for two—China and India. Needless to say, this is an exciting and important time to study cities, politics, and policy. America's cities and urban areas today are more socially diverse than ever; they are also better managed and, as a result of their continued growth and expansion, infinitely more complex.

Consider a few examples. New demographic and social forces have dramatically changed urban areas and their politics and policies. New residents, issues, and urban movements have caused significant shifts in the patterns of political participation. Since 1990, 13 million immigrants have come to the United States, contributing to a 17 percent increase in the number of urban residents. As a consequence, we have seen a dramatic rise in cultural conflicts in cities as diverse as Portland, Oregon, and Gary, Indiana. New battles are being fought over rights for women, gays, and various racial and ethnic groups. Civic controversies abound in cities over school choice, metropolitan tax-base sharing, abortion clinics, and benefits for domestic partners.

Each of these debates has given rise to greater political action at the ballot box and in the streets of our cities. Racial and ethnic groups eager to make substantial policy changes in their communities are working to extend their political incorporation in city governing circles. Houston, Texas, and Des Moines, Iowa, have elected their first black mayors. Austin, Texas, elected its first Latino mayor in 2001. Chicago has more blacks, Latinos, and Asians heading its city service departments than at any time in the city's history. The distribution of political power in cities is shifting the policy outcomes in many urban areas. New-style mayors and city councils are charting new directions for politics and policies from New York to Los Angeles. Most recently, our cities have been challenged to meet the increasing needs of their populations as they struggle to maintain a sense of security in the wake of terrorist threats. Our cities—once the dependents of national and state governments—are now heavily interdependent and exist in a complex intergovernmental environment. The goal of this collection is to enhance students' understanding of this new environment.

Cities, Politics, and Policy: A Comparative Analysis addresses recent trends in a comprehensive manner. It presents current findings from the thriving field of urban politics on each of the major topics of urban research, such as political participation, power, urban government institutions, and public policy. Each chapter orients students in the key areas of study (how city councils work, how political participation in cities has changed over time), synthesizes the current state of urban research in the field, and then gives a preview of the research agenda for the next decade. Throughout the book the authors use systems analysis to help students connect the environment in which urban politics takes place to the political processes, actors, and institutions of city government. The systems model allows us to describe the formation of urban politics as well as to explain the outcomes of political interactions in the city. The book's comparative perspective draws heavily upon empirical works— both case studies and cross-sectional research on U.S. cities. We show that our theories of urban politics are solidly based on the extensive collection of case studies that have long been the primary research vehicles for understanding cities. But the contributors to this volume have also relied upon cross-sectional studies of multiple cities across the nation and across time. Moreover, readers will see that these scholars have provided an insightful look not only into what we know about city politics and policy but also into areas of urban democracy that need further study. The approach and thoroughness of this book make it an ideal choice as a textbook for an undergraduate urban politics course or as a companion volume in upper-division undergraduate and graduate courses in urban politics.

Acknowledgments

I am indebted to the many people who have supported the writing and publication of this work. First are the contributors to this volume. Each is a recognized leader in political science and a scholar who has made a profound impact on the discipline. I am grateful that they were willing to take the time to produce these wonderful essays. I had originally hoped that David R. Morgan, my mentor and friend from the University of Oklahoma, would join me as coeditor of the book. Although Dave retired before I could move this project forward, I appreciate his guidance of my vision for the book. I thank my colleagues and administrators at Loyola University Chicago who encouraged me to complete this book and who provided the resources that helped make it possible. Jim Krueger, a Loyola graduate student, helped with research and editing. The team at CQ Press has been invaluable, beginning with Brenda Carter, who embraced the idea behind this book, convinced the press that it was worth doing, and then provided the professionals who helped me complete the volume. I am grateful for the assistance of my development editor, Elise Frasier, who helped to clarify and focus the writing for this book. I also thank Charisse Kiino, acquisitions editor; Janet Wilson and Molly Lohman, copyeditors; Belinda Josey, production editor; James Headley, sales manager; and Rita Matyi, marketing manager. Finally, I owe a debt of gratitude for patience and understanding to my family. My wife, Paula, and our children, Carolyn and Steven, offered the encouragement and love that allowed me to finish this work. They deserve special thanks.

J. P. P.
Chicago, Illinois

Contributors

David N. Ammons is professor of public administration and government and director of the Master of Public Administration Program at the University of North Carolina at Chapel Hill. His works include *Tools for Decision Making: A Practical Guide for Local Government* (2002), *Municipal Benchmarks: Assessing Local Performance and Establishing Community Standards,* 2d ed. (2001), and other books on local government management. He consults with public sector units on organizational and management concerns, including performance measurement, bench-marking, and productivity improvement.

Richard D. Bingham is professor of public administration and urban studies and senior research scholar at the Levin College of Urban Affairs at Cleveland State University. His current research interests include economies of urban neighborhoods and modeling urban systems. He has written widely in the fields of economic development and urban studies. His latest books include *Evaluation in Practice* (2002), with Claire Felbinger; *The Economies of Central City Neighborhoods* (2001), with Zhongcai Zhang; *Industrial Policy American Style* (1998); and *Dilemmas of Urban Economic Development,* edited with Robert Mier (1997). He is founding editor of *Economic Development Quarterly.*

Robert E. England is professor of political science at Oklahoma State University. He graduated from the University of Oklahoma with an M.P.A. and a Ph.D. in political science in 1982. His primary areas of research include public administration, minority politics, and urban politics and administration. His research has appeared in a number of scholarly journals. He is the coauthor, with David R. Morgan and John P. Pelissero, of *Managing Urban America,* 5th ed. (1999).

Timothy B. Krebs is assistant professor of political science at the University of New Mexico. His research interests include urban politics, city council policymaking, and urban campaigns and elections. His most recent research on campaign fund-raising in Chicago and Los Angeles city council elections appeared in *Social Science Quarterly* (September 2001). He is currently studying the effect of press coverage, issue positions, and attack speech on candidates' fundraising in the 2001 Los Angeles mayoral election.

J. Eric Oliver is associate professor of political science at the University of Chicago. He is the author of *Democracy in Suburbia* (2001) and numerous articles on political participation, suburbanization, and racial attitudes. He is currently writing books on the relationship between racism and racial segregation and on the politics of America's obesity epidemic. He is also working on a multiyear study of voting in suburban elections funded by the National Science Foundation.

John P. Pelissero is professor and chair of political science at Loyola University Chicago. He specializes in urban and state politics and also teaches and writes on Chicago politics. He has published dozens of articles on urban and state politics in political and social science journals, including, most recently, *Urban Affairs Review* and the *American Journal of Political Science*. He is currently working on a book about Chicago politics and a new edition of *Managing Urban America* (1999), with David R. Morgan and Robert England.

Dianne M. Pinderhughes is professor of political science, Afro-American studies, and women's studies at the University of Illinois at Urbana-Champaign, where she has been a member of the faculty since 1984. Pinderhughes directed the Department of Afro-American Studies from 1987 to 1990 and from 1991 to 2000. She published *Race and Ethnicity in Chicago Politics* (1987). Her current research, "The Evolution of Civil Rights Organizations in the Twentieth Century: The Case of Black Politics," investigates the ways in which civil rights and especially black organizations have created the national political infrastructure that has shaped national policy on voting rights laws and politics.

Michael J. Rich is associate professor of political science and director of the Office of University-Community Partnerships at Emory University. He is the author of *Federal Policymaking and the Poor* (1993) and several publications on federalism and a variety of urban public policy topics, including community development, housing and homelessness, crime, and economic development. His current research focuses on community building, neighborhood revitalization strategies, and welfare reform, particularly issues relating to the accessibility of low-income households to job opportunities and related support services.

Elaine B. Sharp is professor of political science at the University of Kansas. Her research interests include urban public policy and governance, urban social conflict, and policing. She recently completed a National Science Foundation–funded research project on city governments' responses to volatile morality issues. Her recent major publications include *The Sometime Connection: Public*

Opinion and Social Policy (1999), *Culture Wars and Local Politics* (1999), and *The Dilemma of Drug Policy* (1994), along with journal articles on urban social conflict in *Urban Affairs Review* and *Political Research Quarterly.*

Lana Stein is professor and chair of the Department of Political Science at the University of Missouri at St. Louis. She is the author of numerous articles and chapters, and her work has appeared in the *Journal of Politics, Political Research Quarterly,* and *Urban Affairs Review.* She is also the author of *St. Louis Politics: The Triumph of Tradition* (2002) and *Holding Bureaucrats Accountable* (1991), as well as the coauthor of *City Schools and City Politics* (1999).

Robert M. Stein is Lena Gohlman Fox Professor of Political Science and dean of the School of Social Sciences at Rice University. He is the coauthor of *Perpetuating the Pork Barrel* (1995) and the author of *Urban Alternatives* (1990). His current research focuses on metropolitan governance and distribution of federal assistance to metropolitan area governments.

Clarence N. Stone is professor emeritus in the Department of Government and Politics at the University of Maryland and Research Professor of Public Policy and Political Science at the George Washington University. His most recent book is a coauthored work on urban school reform, *Building Civic Capacity* (2001). He is currently a member of School Communities that Work, the Annenberg Institute's national task force on the future of urban districts, and studies urban school reform while pursuing research on the politics of poverty.

Kenneth K. Wong is professor in the Department of Leadership, Policy, and Organizations and the Department of Political Science at Vanderbilt University. He also serves as the associate director of the Peabody Center for Education Policy. He has published widely in the areas of federalism, urban and state politics, policy implementation, and educational reform. He currently serves as president of the Politics of Education Association, whose national membership consists of professors in school policy and politics.

1 The Political Environment of Cities in the Twenty-first Century

John P. Pelissero

American cities and urban areas are perhaps the most exciting venues for politics. National elections and political processes, as well as state politics, certainly capture the attention of citizens and the media, but in cities people find the greatest opportunities to directly participate in politics. Here political campaigns are waged door to door, as candidates and groups seek support from residents of their neighborhoods. Communities organize to fight city hall and band together to promote issues ranging from crime prevention to environmental protection, from school reform to tax reform. City residents can talk directly to their mayor or city council member, and they can attend meetings of the school board or public housing authority. Opportunities to run for local offices abound. In cities one will know the bureaucrats who deliver services, from the neighborhood police officer to the solid waste collectors to a health inspector. The "retail" nature of local politics is accessible and engaging. Indeed, face-to-face contact with local politicians, government officials, and bureaucrats gives local politics the comfortable feel of interacting with a neighborhood retailer. It is also filled with opportunities for conflict when alternative values compete with one another for the benefits afforded by urban governments. Cities, their leaders, and institutions must therefore have the capacity to manage conflict and provide the quality of local governance that all of their citizens expect. At the beginning of a new century, the ability of our cities to meet this challenge has evolved, with transformations within the very "system" of urban politics.

When the twentieth century began, cities and their governments did not share fine reputations. Progressive municipal reformers and muckraking journalists condemned the corrupt political bosses and parties that ran cities for their own political and personal gain. City governments were marked by significant operational inefficiency and were often incapable of managing the multiple service functions required to serve growing populations. The municipal reform movement heavily influenced ideas among urban scholars of the early 1900s. They adopted the reformist prescriptions for better urban governance and promoted restructuring of urban governments in an effort to rid them of the overt influence of "politics" (Hays 1964).

By the 1950s it had become clear to urban scholars that "politics" was no less apparent in reformed governments than it was in those that had preceded them (Lineberry and Masotti 1976, 2). Rather than attempting to change the system of politics in cities, many urbanists began to examine the nature of politics in cities and to explain their findings with social science theories. Thus began the era of behavioral studies of cities, in which case studies and survey research were conducted to test theories about urban politics. This research of the 1950s and 1960s was characterized by a debate over who had political power in cities. Although the debate was not convincingly resolved, it forced scholars to consider new issues of access, influence, and representation in cities. This gave way to an interest in understanding the nature of political relationships among citizens, leaders, and institutions in an urban system.

The late 1960s and 1970s were a period of "crisis" in urban America. From civil unrest to political protest, from rising crime rates to declining city revenues, urban areas were forced to confront a host of national problems that took root within the boundaries of central cities and suburbs. The responses of cities to this crisis were many. Some cities changed their structure of government to become more responsive to citizens and develop more efficient ways to deliver services. Political processes were opened to racial and ethnic minorities, who began to be incorporated into political and policymaking systems. New relationships were forged between the national and city governments to enhance the flow of federal money to help cities deal with their problems. Cities also considered new ways to finance their governments, often moving away from general taxation and toward more user fees for local services and programs.

In the 1980s cities began a significant period of redevelopment in response to declining tax bases, as residents and businesses continued to exit central cities for the expanding suburbs, and northern cities lost population and their economic base to growing urban areas of the South and West. This marked the beginning of a phase in which urban economic development became an overriding issue. Cities were forced to become more competitive, vying with one another for population and economic growth. By the 1990s it appeared that many urban areas had succeeded in responding to the changing economic system. In many instances, central cities were experiencing a new period of growth, as they became attractive locales for business development, gentrification of older neighborhoods, and tourism. Many city governments "reinvented" their style of governing and management of services to increase the benefits to residents and visitors.

Cities enter the twenty-first century in a strong position. They have a better capacity to govern. Their economic base is stronger. They are attractive venues for conventions, tourism, and world commerce. Leaders and institutions of city government have become more inclusive and responsive. Urban schools have improved, as a result of the implementation of school governance reforms.

Nonetheless, problems and conflict persist in America's urban areas. The federal government has curtailed its financial support. State governments mandate new policies for cities but do not provide additional funding to pay for them. Some central cities have not recovered from the economic and social crises that afflicted them in the 1960s. Public schools in central cities are still not as attractive to middle- and working-class families as are those in the suburbs. Despite gains in representation in city and school governing circles, many racial and ethnic minorities still lack full incorporation in urban politics.

What we know about cities, politics, and policy at the start of the twenty-first century is due in large part to the careful research of urban scholars, including those who have contributed to this book. Examining the urban political system from a comparative perspective, in which ideas are tested among many diverse cities and urban areas, scholars have developed our theoretical understanding of cities. The purpose of this book is to place in a contemporary context the major areas of inquiry into urban politics. The field of urban politics demands an anthology that is current and covers the major topics of research, including political participation, power, urban government institutions, intergovernmental politics, and urban and suburban policy. The book uses systems analysis to explore the environment of cities and how it affects patterns of political participation, power distribution, leadership, decision making, and policy implementation. The material is presented from a comparative perspective that emphasizes knowledge derived from empirical works—both case studies and cross-sectional research on U.S. cities. Each chapter has a thorough discussion of key topics, noting how research approaches to these topics have changed over time. These chapters have been developed to tell the reader what we know to be true about cities and to show how the research of the past has informed our knowledge of cities today. The authors synthesize the current state of urban research and highlight the research agenda for the next decade. This collection is the first work in many years that provides comprehensive coverage of urban politics in an anthology that can serve as a primary text or as a supplement to other urban textbooks. We begin with an overview of the system of urban politics.

The Systems Model of Urban Politics

In *The Political System,* David Easton (1953) began to develop an influential theoretical framework that facilitated an understanding of politics, including urban politics. He applied the open systems models of natural science to the political world, showing that political systems, like natural systems, are open to influences from their environments. The environment is viewed as one that shapes the political process—in which "authoritative decision-makers" respond to inputs, transforming them into political and policy outputs (Easton 1965a, 1965b).

Figure 1-1 presents a model of the urban political system. The open systems framework includes a conceptual scheme of the key components of the model. In broad

Figure 1-1 Urban Political Systems Model

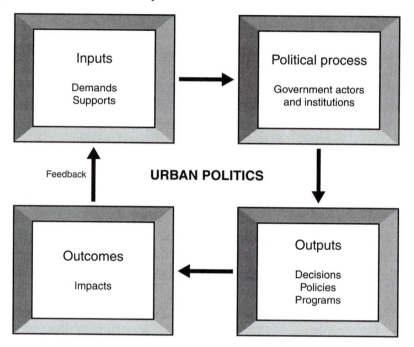

terms, we theorize that the urban political system is composed of *inputs* from the political environment that are channeled into the *political process*. The political process is the essence of deciding the "authoritative allocations of values" (Easton 1965b, 348). The result of the decision makers' processing of inputs yields *outputs*. The impact of these concrete decision outputs of political actors produces a set of *outcomes* that send information back into the environment. The process is best viewed as a continuous stream of *feedback* to the environment that may result in the alteration and creation of inputs that keep cycling in the system.

The Environment of Urban Politics: System Inputs

Political inputs are drawn from the environment of cities. Easton's model describes two varieties of inputs: demands and supports. Actions of individuals and groups produce demands, whereas conditions and resources in a city's environment provide support for political and policy processes and actions.

Demands

Demands are made by individuals and groups who have a stake in the urban political process. This would include action by individuals who function as demand makers, such as citizens, residents, taxpayers, and visitors. Acting on their own and not viewed as part of an organized movement, individual demand makers may contact government institutions or officials in person or in writing to express their views on public issues.

Demands also come from groups of organized citizens and potential groups that can influence the political process. Interest groups made up of individuals with a common interest or characteristic are active demand makers in the urban context. This may include business-related groups, labor organizations, neighborhood groups, racial and ethnic groups, environmentalists, and taxpayer organizations. Each attempts to influence the political process through information, requests, or mobilization of its membership (Berry, Portney, and Thomson 1993; Galaskiewicz 1981; Rich, Giles, and Stern 2001; Schumaker and Getter 1983).

Political parties and local caucuses represent another type of group that makes demands in the system. Although the influence of political parties waned after the adoption of key municipal reforms (nonpartisan elections and the appointment of city managers) (Erie 1988; Rosenstone and Hansen 1993), party organizations continue to be important demand makers in many large cities (Hawley 1973; Krebs 1998). For example, Chicago has held nonpartisan elections for city council since the 1930s. Nonetheless, the city's Democratic Party has dominated the political process in all respects, and nearly every city council member over the past twenty-five years has been a Democrat.

In most cities, major political parties are not directly involved in city government politics, but local parties or a caucus may have active roles in the system. Many reformed governments, seeking ways to replace the political parties' role in recruiting candidates to run for local office, created formal or informal means for local parties and caucuses to assume this responsibility. Some cities, such as Dallas, operated through a Citizens' Charter Association to recruit city council candidates who would support the system of government and its pro-business values (Elkin 1987). Many cities have formal "slate making" organizations to select and promote a slate of candidates for local offices (Fraga 1988). A complete discussion of the ways in which citizens and groups participate as demand makers in urban politics is provided in chapters 3 and 4.

Urban regimes constitute another variety of demand maker in the urban system. As explained in chapter 5, these governing coalitions include key actors from the environment who cooperate with local officials in the development of public policy. Regimes provide demands to the political process and support local institutions and officials, thereby shaping public decisions. Regimes, sometimes viewed as the governing coalitions of cities, afford a window on the makeup of the power structure, which is a powerful determinant of public policy. Some regimes have pro-business orientations, such as those in Atlanta or Dallas (see Stone and Sanders 1987). Others may have their base of support among interests in neighborhoods and community groups with a progressive political agenda, such as those in Berkeley (Clavel 1986), Chicago in the 1980s (Bennett 1993), or San Francisco (DeLeon 1992). The variations are extensive (see Logan, Whaley, and Crowder 1997) and are reviewed in chapter 5.

A final component of the demand environment is the media. Because of its ability to set the public agenda though its coverage of news, issues, and politics, the media are also a demand maker in the urban setting. Metropolitan television and radio stations use their resources to report and analyze issues of concern to urban residents. Newspapers are key inputs to the political process through both reporting urban news and editorializing on issues in their opinion sections. The growth of newer media, particularly cable systems and the Internet, has caused exponential increases in demands being filtered through the political processes of cities. E-mail and Web sites offer easier ways to communicate demands to local decision makers. As a recent national survey revealed, more cities are developing communications plans to respond to the new demands brought about by technological developments (Norris and Demeter 1999; ICMA 2002b)

Supports

The other types of inputs to the political system are supporting conditions for action. These supports are drawn from the political environment and contain both active and latent components. Active support is elicited from the overt behavior of the populace, such as voting in city elections and paying one's local taxes. Overt support for the local political system allows local decision makers to act with legitimacy and confidence. In contrast, withholding active support (for example, not voting in city elections or challenging local tax assessments) can undermine the ability of local actors and institutions to carry out government service. It can also erode the stability of the local political system. Active support works in concert with demand makers to stimulate action from the political system.

Latent support for government action is drawn from four major types of environments that exist as subsystems of the local political environment: physical, socioeconomic, political culture, and intergovernmental. These subenvironments contain passive and covert elements of support for the system.

The *physical environment* of cities includes aspects of the local climate, geography, and the built environment—those structures within the city limits. Each in its own way supports certain kinds of actions by local government. For example, climatic conditions that include extreme temperatures in summer and winter, snow and ice, rain and floods create an environment that supports government action. Cities must be prepared to provide the needy with refuge from extreme temperatures, such as warming or cooling centers. Cities will acquire snow removal equipment, salt to combat ice on roads, and warning sirens for dangerous storm conditions. The actors and institutions of city government undertake these actions because the physical environment supports policy action. The same can be said for geography. Cities must adjust their services and programs to reflect their geographical setting. Hence, bridges are needed over rivers, marine patrols are required for lakes, and recreation policies are developed for forests, beaches, and parkland. Finally, cities must respond to the built environment. This includes public infrastructure such as roads, sidewalks, subways, airports, and sewers. Public buildings, museums, and sanitation plants are built by cities and other local governments to support a local populace and commercial activity. As cities determine the density, height, location, and type of construction, they also must develop policies to support the built environment. Land-use plans, zoning ordinances, building and fire codes, and inspection services to ensure the general health and safety of the buildings and their occupants are among the ways cities respond to this need. In general, the physical environment supports certain actions by local decision makers, even in the absence of demands or demand makers. In effect, the political system's actors draw their policy cues from supporting conditions in the environment.

Support is also drawn from the latent *political culture.* Robert Alford (1968, 265) defined cultural factors as the "value commitments of groups within the community as a whole, expressed through laws and policies." Culture can also be viewed as representing the underlying attitudes in a community about the proper role and scope of government action. One can presume that the behavior of government actors and institutions mirrors the underlying value system of the community. Political scientists have tried many ways to measure this value system. For example, Oliver P. Williams and Charles R. Adrian (1963) did comparative case studies of four cities. They found that local history helped cement the existing political culture of an area and that culture was a major factor in determining policy differences across communities. James Q. Wilson and Edward C. Banfield (1964, 1971) gave us the often-maligned ethos theory. They argued that cities have two fundamental political value systems—public regarding and private regarding, each associated with different ethnic and income groups. One ethos could dominate politics in a city, or the two value systems could be competing for dominance. The public-regarding ethos tended to be associated with middle-class, white Anglo-Saxon Protestants (WASPs) and Jews who were interested in having government serve a unitary or common good in the community. The private-regarding ethos was more individualistic in nature and was associated with the working class and poor European ethnics. This culture was commonly linked to political machines in cities and the private interests of their supporters. Although research on this theory was subjected to much criticism and found little empirical verification, it is still a useful dichotomy of competing cultures in cities.

Daniel Elazar's (1966) research on political culture in states has been applied to the study of urban political culture (Elazar 1970). He found three dominant political cultures in states. A moralistic political culture is associated with the northern stream of European immigrants whose values led to pursuit of the public interest. The role of government in a community with a moralistic culture is to develop policies that favor the common good. Minneapolis is often described as a city that embodies this culture. Cities with an individualistic political culture share many of the characteristics of the private-regarding ethos of Wilson and Banfield. Politics is a competitive market environment in which government's role is limited to fostering a healthy marketplace and politicians seek office for material gains for themselves and their supporters. Chicago may be a good example of this type of culture. Finally, the traditionalistic political culture views government's role as part of the social and economic power structure of a community. The hierarchy in a city's economic and social structure is also reflected in government. In effect, government, like society, is a tool of the elites. Many southern cities, including Atlanta, are thought to reflect this culture.

Political culture supports policies that are consistent with the dominant values of the community. In many ways, the actors and institutions of city government will reflect the underlying political culture in their policy actions. Elaine Sharp (1999) offers an excellent analysis of the role of culture in city policymaking in a series of case studies on moral controversies in cities. However, local political culture is often difficult to measure, a fact that has been borne out by the controversy surrounding the Elazar or Wilson and Banfield typologies. Most researchers rely upon proxy measures that are related to political culture. These have included the form of city government, voting patterns, and socioeconomic characteristics of cities. The latter is such an important explanatory variable in city politics that it is recognized as a third subenvironment.

The *socioeconomic environment* is the most broad-ranging of the supporting environments for city politics and policy. Assessing the literature on this topic, David R. Morgan and Samuel Kirkpatrick (1972) concluded: "More extensive research has been done on the effects of socioeconomic factors on local politics than on the other major environmental components" (p. 38). This statement has proved to be valid in the past thirty years, during which urban systems research has widely explored the profound socioeconomic effects on politics and policy. This environmental support in the urban system includes the demographic, social, and economic characteristics of the population and the character of the local economy.

City politics and policy are driven, in part, by the makeup of the population. How many people reside in the city? How densely populated is it? Larger, more densely grouped populations will provide conditions that support certain types of action by local governments. These may well be different from the actions of cities with smaller, more scattered residential populations.

The characteristics of the population are also important to understanding the behavior of actors and institutions in the political system. Elderly and young populations warrant different types of programs. White European ethnic residents have been shown to have political objectives that differ from those of African American, Latino, or Asian populations (see, for example, Browning, Marshall, and Tabb 1997). New immigrants and long-term residents have different needs. Religious affiliations of residents contribute to the development of different political cultures and support divergent policy actions (see Button, Rienzo, and Wald 1997). The ratio of male to female residents affects political action and also supports different policy preferences.

The economic characteristics of the population provide support for action to address the needs of the disadvantaged or the opportunities presented by significant wealth. Communities with populations that have a higher median income level will support policies that differ from those with a high level of family poverty. Higher unemployment causes a local government to pursue policies that are not necessarily warranted in a community with full employment. Education also affects the political system. Communities with a better-educated population will have a different style of politics, participation, and policy outputs from that of a community whose adult population has lower educational attainment.

Finally, the economic condition of the community is a support for certain government activity. The politics and policies in a system are going to be affected by the nature of the community's economic base (for example, commercial vs. residential), health of the local economy, value of real property, employment opportunities, and development, redevelopment, or reinvestment in the community. Related to this is the nature of a community's housing stock, the degree of racial and income integration in neighborhoods, and the possibilities for growth in the residential sector. The role of the local economy in city politics is discussed in chapter 10.

The final subenvironment that supports action in a political system is the *intergovernmental environment*. This refers to the mix of governments and governmental levels that are present in the area of a city. The typical city operates within an environment that includes the national government, state government, and other local governments, including counties, townships, school districts, special districts, and other cities. The more complex the intergovernmental mix of an area, the more challenging it is for a local government to act (Park 1997). In effect, other governments and their programs operating in the environment of a city condition the political and policy options for local action. In many instances, a city cannot operate in an independent fashion but rather must coordinate its political processes and policy decisions with the web of other governments in the same area (Dreier, Mollenkopf, and Swanstrom 2001; Peterson 1981).

The complexity of the urban intergovernmental subenvironment can be seen in the data on the distribution of governments in a city. Table 1-1 shows the census of

Table 1-1 Governments in the United States

Type	Number	Change in 1990s (%)
Federal	1	0
State	50	0
County	3,043	0
Municipal	19,372	0.5
Township	16,629	−0.2
Independent school district	13,726	−4.8
Special district	34,683	9.9
Total	87,504	2.9

Source: U.S. Bureau of the Census (1999), *1997 Census of Governments, vol. 1, Government Organization.* (Washington, D.C.: U.S. Government Printing Office), 3.

governments in the United States at the end of 1999 (U.S. Bureau of the Census 1999). In addition to the federal and state governments, over 87,400 local governments are operating, an increase of nearly 3 percent since 1992. This includes 19,372 *municipal,* or city governments—a number that was relatively stable throughout the 1990s. Among the four other types of local governments shown in Table 1-1, county and township governments have been relatively stable in number, whereas school districts and special districts have experienced a significant degree of change over the past decade.

A *county* is a subdivision of a state, and county government is the administrative arm of state government in local areas. County governments are found throughout the United States, except in Delaware, the District of Columbia, and Rhode Island. Traditionally the most important form of local government in this country, county governments today are usually just a political-administrative division of the state government. The state must keep records of births, deaths, and marriages; establish a system of justice and law enforcement; maintain roads and bridges; collect taxes; conduct voter registration and elections; and provide for public welfare and education. To make these responsibilities easier to carry out, states have generally entrusted their administration to local courthouses—the seat of county government in the United States.

According to the Census Bureau, *township* is the proper classification for 16,629 governments that are located in only twenty states. Townships include general-purpose governments called "towns" in New York, "plantations" in Maine, "locations" in New Hampshire, and "townships" in twelve other Mid-Atlantic and North Central states. Unlike municipalities, which are usually organized to serve population concentrations, this is not a factor in the creation of town and township governments (U.S. Bureau of the Census 1999, vi).

Public education in this country is a state government responsibility, but the operation of public schools and teaching of students are entrusted to 13,726 *school districts*. Although about 1,400 city or county governments run schools as a division of their governments, the vast majority of schools are under the control of independent school districts with their own governing boards. The number of independent school districts dropped by nearly 5 percent in the 1990s, a continuation of the process of school consolidation that began earlier in the twentieth century. Chapter 12 presents an overview of the organization of school districts and the efforts to reform urban schools.

Special districts are defined as "independent, limited-purpose governmental units (other than school districts), which exist as separate entities with substantial administrative and fiscal independence from general-purpose local governments" (U.S. Bureau of the Census 1999, vii). This classification includes a wide variety of local districts (for example, parks, natural resources, housing), public authorities, boards, and government corporations; special district units of government can be found in every state. During the past two decades special districts have been the fastest-growing form of local government in the United States. There were 34,683 in 1997, almost a 10 percent change from 1992. The largest number of special districts (6,982) are established to administer functions related to natural resources (for example, drainage and flood control, soil conservation, and irrigation). Other popular functional needs that give rise to these districts include fire protection (5,601), housing and community development—including public housing authorities (3,469), water supply (3,409), sewerage (2,004), and cemeteries (1,655). The variety of special district functions is further reflected in the establishment of special governments to operate public hospitals, parks, libraries, highways, health facilities, and airports. And whereas 93 percent are responsible for only one function of government, over 2,500 districts were created to operate more than a single function.

General-purpose governments are sometimes unable, or their officials are unwilling, to assume responsibility for a new service. New suburban communities need services, often before they are incorporated. The wide range of service needs can often be fulfilled by a multiple-function special district that might provide trash collection, sewerage and water needs, fire protection, and streets with lights, as well as a number of other services. The multiple functions managed by such districts have led some writers to call them "urban fringe districts" (Perrenod 1984). Fiscal considerations, including debt management, have frequently been at the root of creating special-purpose government. Many park districts in Illinois, for example, were established to overcome state-imposed debt limitations on municipalities. Special-purpose governments are often found to be more flexible and have a unique ability to keep very talented employees. As Walsh (1978, 7, 234) points out, compared with other public institutions, they "provide stronger in-

Figure 1-2 Local Governments Serving Chicago

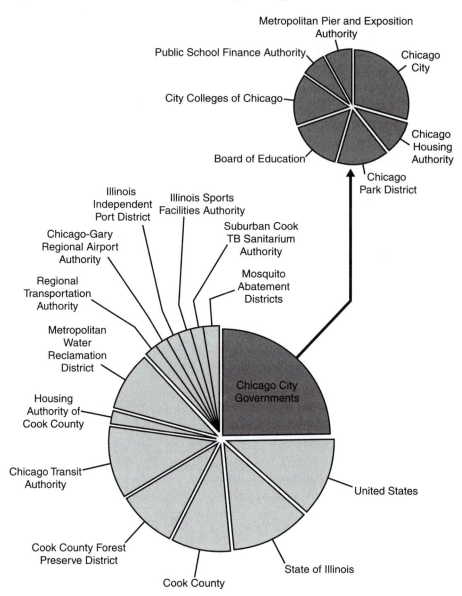

centives for productivity and performance" and, in many ways, "are run like private businesses." Special districts are able to take advantage of economies of scale, particularly in services that are capital intensive and part of the physical infrastructure. Commonly, the districts are more centrally organized and therefore more efficient than general-purpose governments in providing services.

If one envisions the intergovernmental subenvironment for a typical city in a metropolitan area, it is likely to include at least one county, several other cities (perhaps more than 100 in a large metro area), some townships, an independent school district, and several special districts. This complexity may be made clearer by examining the intergovernmental environment of Chicago. Figure 1-2 shows the various local governments serving Chicago residents, in addition to the wider view of intergovernmental service providers for a typical resident. Chicago has a city government and separate governments to handle schools, parks, transit, public housing, community colleges, school finance, and tourism, all of which are supported by Chicago taxpayers. These governments are nested within an even more complex intergovernmental setting in which at least thirteen other levels and types of government are operating. And this does not include more than 120 other municipal governments in the suburbs and their related schools and special districts. In fact, the Chicago metropolitan area encompasses thirteen counties in three states (Illinois, Indiana, and Wisconsin).

The intergovernmental environment can be viewed as one that supports and restricts the options for local governments. Cities are required to function interdependently in this environment. They must coordinate their policies and ordinances with one another, consider one another's taxing policies, and confront the spillover effects of one another's programs and residents. For example, neighboring city governments, as well as their counties and states, must coordinate traffic policies to ensure safe driving conditions on highways and streets that intersect one another's boundaries. The annual tax rate for a city government is often established after consideration of the expected tax rate change in the school district, county, and special districts serving the same taxpayers. An increase in one unit's tax rate may prevent another unit from increasing its rate for the same year. And if one community decides to have a popular amusement venue, cities must confront the effects this will have on traffic, noise, and quality of life in their own community. The importance and complexity of the intergovernmental subenvironment are covered in chapter 2.

Structure of City Governments and Authoritative Decision Making

A municipal corporation or municipality is the formal name given to city governments by state constitutions and statutes. Municipalities are chartered by state governments to serve as general-purpose governments at the local level. Until 1875, the legislatures of most states wrote and granted the charters for cities and had to approve any change in the structure of city governments, which subjected them to the whims of state legislators. However, in 1875 Missouri implemented a constitutional change that allowed cities to write their own charters and change them without the state legislature's permission. Today this practice, known as *home rule,* is widely used to organize and modernize city governments. Some form of home rule is available to city governments in forty-eight states (Berman 1999, 49).

The municipal charter is a basic element of the political process. It can be viewed as a fundamental statement of the rules of the political game in a city. That is, along with the federal and state constitutions, a municipal charter frames the nature of politics, the process of governance, and the parameters for policymaking. Charters will contain provisions on the boundaries of the city, the structure of city government, its powers and policy responsibilities, methods of financing the government, and key aspects of political participation for residents. If citizens want to change the charter, they may do so by means of a charter referendum.

Forms of City Government

Municipal charters establish the structure of government. In doing so, these legal documents shape the roles played by different institutions of city government. Each city will have a city council—the legislative branch of government. The executive branch will be headed by a mayor or city manager, who will be responsible for running the daily affairs of the city. The executive branch includes the municipal bureaucracy, which implements policies and delivers services. The political and policymaking roles performed by city councils, mayors, city managers, and bureaucrats will vary with the form of government used.

Historically, many local communities in the United States operated under a form of direct democracy—the *town meeting* form of government. In this arrangement, all adults of voting age in a community gathered once a year to make public policy, such as passing new local laws, approving a town budget, and electing a small number of residents to serve as government officials for the year. As the populations of cities grew and the issues facing city governments became more complex, the town meeting proved inadequate for governing an urban place. Less than five percent of cities with populations over 2,500 use this form of government today (ICMA 2002a). Three forms of government are more commonly employed in cities at the start of this century.

Mayor-Council Government. This is the typical form of city government. Under this structure, residents elect a mayor and a city council to represent them. City charters have produced two variations on this form that reflect alternative allocations of power for the mayor and city council. In the strong-mayor form, shown in Figure 1-3, more power is vested in the mayor's position than in the city council. The council adopts public policies, whereas the mayor is responsible for policy implementation. But the mayor's authority goes beyond this simple separation of powers. The mayor is a true chief executive, with almost complete control over the administration of

Figure 1-3 Strong Mayor-Council Form of Government

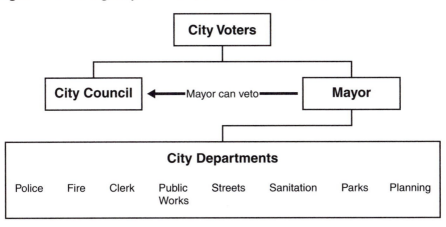

government and public services. The mayor appoints and dismisses all department managers and directs the operations of the city bureaucracy. The mayor is the prime actor when it comes to formulating and initiating public policies, including those that will require city council approval. Chief among the policy powers of the mayor is the development and implementation of the city budget, a document that is subject to at least pro forma approval by the council. Also, strong mayors can veto actions of the city council. Cities that use the strong-mayor form include Denver, New York, and Philadelphia.

The weak-mayor form is displayed in Figure 1-4. This system of governance vests most of the power in the city council, which directs the activities of the city bureaucracy. The mayor serves as the presiding officer at city council meetings and is the ceremonial

Figure 1-4 Weak Mayor-Council Form of Government

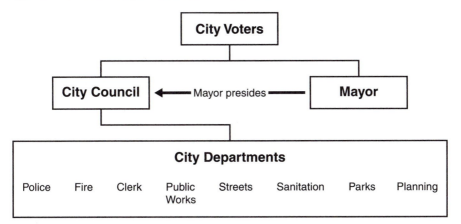

Figure 1-5 Council-Manager Form of Government

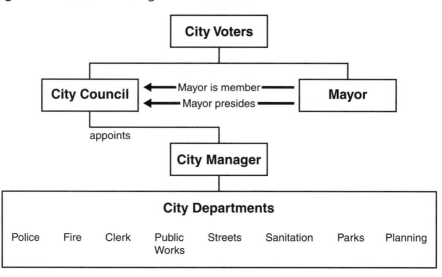

head of city government. Most mayor-council cities use the weak-mayor form. Small cities with 10,000 or fewer residents (of which there are many) are more likely to have a weak mayor charter. Cities that use this form include Madison, Wisconsin; Minneapolis; Seattle; and, formally, Chicago (where mayors have exercised stronger powers than the council in most of the past fifty years). The powers of mayors are discussed in chapter 6.

Council-Manager Government. Municipal reform groups at the turn of the twentieth century advocated a new style of municipal government that would be less political and more efficient. In 1913 Dayton, Ohio, became the first city in the United States to adopt the council-manager form of government. In this form, shown in Figure 1-5, voters choose a city council and may choose a mayor, who often serves as both presiding officer and voting member of the council. The council is responsible for political and policy decisions. The implementation and administration of the council's actions are placed in the hands of an appointed city manager, who is expected to carry out policy with the city bureaucracy. More than one-third of cities use this form of government, including major cities such as Dallas, Kansas City, Phoenix, and San Diego. City managers are the subject of chapter 8.

Commission Government. A very small percentage of cities, less than 3 percent, still rely upon an earlier reformed organization for city governance. The commission form, first adopted by Galveston, Texas, in 1901, following the devastation caused by a hurricane, is designed to integrate, not separate, executive and legislative functions. Voters elect a panel of city commissioners, each of whom serves as both a legislator and an executive. These legislators make public policy just like city council members in the other two forms of government. But each member is also elected as a commissioner of a functional area of city government (for example, public safety), and bureaucrats report to a single commissioner. Little is written about commission governments today, but students of urban politics should understand their organization. Among the few cities still using a commission government are Chattanooga, Tennessee; St. Petersburg, Florida; and Vicksburg, Mississippi.

The Impact of Reform

When reformers advocated change in the organizational structure of city government—first with the commission system and later with the council-manager plan—they sought to improve its effectiveness and efficiency. Municipal reformers hoped to remove politics from city government as much as possible, creating a style of governance that embraced the best practices of successful businesses. A list of common goals for reform would include the following:

- Separating politics from the administration of government
- Strengthening executive powers and leadership
- Replacing partisan ballots with nonpartisan elections
- Electing city council members at large, not from wards
- Reducing the number of elected officials
- Separating local elections from state and national contests
- Establishing a merit-based civil service

How successful were the reformers? Like many efforts to improve governance, success is in the eyes of the beholder. The one reform that has been embraced by most cities is the nonpartisan ballot. City residents have accepted the reformers' argument that partisan differences do not extend to the provision of municipal services. Contending that there is no difference between a Republican way and a Democratic way to pave a street, reformers wanted voters to know the policy views of individuals running for local office, not the parties' views. Today, over 75 percent of cities hold nonpartisan elections for city council and mayor. The choice of ballot type is not without consequences (Schaffner, Streb, and Wright 2001). Research on this topic is discussed in chapter 7.

Although not intended to be controversial, the at-large method of representation for city council seats has been at the center of many political and judicial battles for decades. Traditionally, city council members represented a district or ward of the city—a practice that permitted the ward-based machine bosses to control elections and try to create public policies that were good for individual wards rather than for the city as a whole. Reformers advocated at-large elections, with all members of the city council chosen by voters across the city. These at-large representatives would not create public policies to benefit only their own neighborhoods, since they would have to answer to all of the city's voters. A majority of cities use at-large elections today. However, an unintended consequence of at-large representation is that minority group members have had difficulty gaining election to the city council. Cities that employ district elections have a greater degree of representational equity for African Americans and Latinos on city councils (Welch and Bledsoe 1988, 12–15). A broad discussion of this issue and the arguments on both sides are discussed in chapter 7.

Other electoral changes have been adopted more quietly because they have drawn little attention. Strengthening the powers of the executive—be it the mayor or a city manager—required eliminating many other executives who had been subject to election. Instead of having voters choose a long list of "row officers"—executives who head functional areas of city government—most executive posts were converted to appointive positions that would be under the direct control of the chief executive. This change was implemented with the so-called short ballot, on which local voters would choose their city council members, mayor, and perhaps a few other executives such as the city clerk and treasurer. Similarly, many cities adopted new election schedules that do not coincide with the dates of national and state elections. City elections are commonly held in off years and in the spring or summer (rather than November) to permit voters to focus on city issues and candidates. An unintended effect of this change, however, has been to reduce turnout for local elections. An average national election can yield a 50 percent or higher turnout, whereas city elections held apart from national contests tend to have fewer than 25 percent of eligible voters participating (Hajnal, Lewis, and Louch 2002; Karnig and Oliver 1983; Welch and Bledsoe 1988).

The biggest change advocated by reformers was an attempt to separate politics from administration. Politics was to be the realm of policymaking, done by the peoples' representatives on the city council. Here the important value choices would be made about which of many alternative policies would be adopted. It was expected that city councils would manage conflict in the community by having vigorous debates on the appropriate services and programs for the city. If residents were dissatisfied with the results of these decisions, the electoral process would permit a change in council membership and the advancement of a new set of values for consideration.

Once the political decision had been made, however, the implementation of policy would be the responsibility of a strong executive. Ideally, a city manager, with the help of a capable civil service, would implement the policy choices of the city council in the best way possible. Professionalism, efficiency, and effectiveness would be the benchmarks for executing city policy. Politics was not to enter into the calculus for how programs

Figure 1-6   Mission-Management Separation with Shared Responsibility for Policy and the Administration

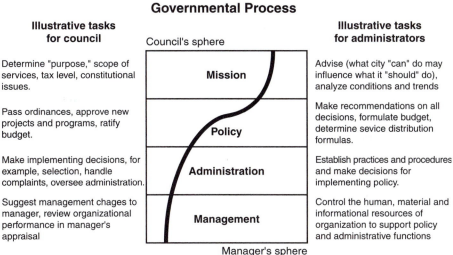

Dimensions of Governmental Process

Illustrative tasks for council	Council's sphere	**Illustrative tasks for administrators**
Determine "purpose," scope of services, tax level, constitutional issues.	**Mission**	Advise (what city "can" do may influence what it "should" do), analyze conditions and trends
Pass ordinances, approve new projects and programs, ratify budget.	**Policy**	Make recommendations on all decisions, formulate budget, determine sevice distribution formulas.
Make implementing decisions, for example, selection, handle complaints, oversee administration.	**Administration**	Establish practices and procedures and make decisions for implementing policy.
Suggest management chages to manager, review organizational performance in manager's appraisal	**Management**	Control the human, material and informational resources of organization to support policy and administrative functions

Manager's sphere

Source: James H. Svara, "Dichotomy and Duality: Reconceptualizing the Relationship Between Policy and Administration in Council-Manager Cities," *Public Administration Review* 45 (January–February 1985): 228. Reprinted with permission from *Public Administration Review* © by the American Society for Public Administration.

would be implemented or services delivered to city residents. Policy choices would be in the hands of the political actors—the city council—whereas administration devoid of political consideration would be the responsibility of the manager.

As James Svara (1985) has carefully explained, the politics-administration dichotomy is more complex than reformers may have envisioned. A better understanding of the operating relationships in cities today indicates that they are closer to a model that Svara characterizes as the "dichotomy-duality model." Figure 1-6 is Svara's new model of the relationships between councils and executives. He argues that the governmental process has four dimensions, each with a different set of relationships between the council and the executive.

According to Svara (1985), mission is a political process in which the broad purposes of city government and the scope of city services, taxes, and benefits are determined. Developing a mission is a council sphere of activity, with the manager providing advice to assist in the decision making. Policy is the dimension wherein the programs, ordinances, and budgets that will fulfill the city's mission are approved. As another political process, policy is a responsibility shared by the council and manager, with the former adopting policy that has been recommended by the latter. The shared responsibility reflects an understanding that the typical part-time city council will need to rely upon the professional advice of the full-time manager when considering policy options that best meet the city's mission. The manager's sphere also has both separate and shared processes. Administration is where the executive develops the implementing procedures for the policies that have been adopted. The council shares in administration by making decisions that shape the scope of implementation and provides oversight of the executive branch. Management is the dimension of city governance in which the manager establishes the resources needed to run the day-to-day affairs of city government. It includes management of human resources and budgets and acquisition of the information, technology, and materials required to run the municipal corporation in a professional manner. Although the council may oversee this process and suggest change, it is largely a manager's responsibility (Svara 1985, 224–228).

This ideal model of the dimensions and responsibilities is different from the simplicity of the politics-administration dichotomy but is generally thought to be a more accurate depiction of the operating dimensions of the process. The dichotomy-duality model will deviate from the ideal type under circumstances in which councils are dominant, strong mayors are present, or council and manager have developed a pattern of conflict that causes each to interfere in the other's sphere of influence (Svara 1985, 228–230). The relationships among city councils, mayors, and city managers are described in detail in chapters 6, 7, and 8.

Urban System Outputs, Outcomes, and Feedback

The authoritative decision makers of the urban political system convert the demands and supports from the environment into outputs. That is, binding decisions and implementing actions of urban decision makers are considered system outputs (Easton 1965b, 350–351). Knowing that outputs will have varying impacts requires that we distinguish outputs from outcomes in our discussion of the system model. And the type of outcome—be it a positive, negative, or neutral impact—will provide feedback information to the environment, where new demands and supporting conditions will develop. Each of these system components is explained below.

Policy Outputs

The actions taken by the urban political system's actors and institutions in response to system demands and supports produce the outputs of the process (Figure 1-1). These outputs include decisions, programs, policies, and regulations that are approved by city officials. A decision that results in the adoption of a municipal law is known as an *ordinance*. In most instances, ordinances are approved by the city council, and their adoption is part of the formal legitimation of municipal policy. For example, when a city council adopts a program to recycle refuse or approves the annual budget or tax rate, it has made policy. But policy outputs also stem from actions of executives. Mayors can issue executive orders that do not require formal council approval but carry the same authority as an ordinance. This could be an order setting aside a portion of city contracts for minority and female contractors, or an ethics order that applies to all employees under the mayor's authority. City managers and bureaucrats make decisions on daily service delivery that are designed to guide implementation of policy. For example, they decide how many police officers to assign to a district, or which areas of the city will be among the first to receive community development funds. Regardless of the source of policy adoption, each constitutes a formal policy output. These outputs are the binding decisions and implementing plans of the political actors and institutions and, according to Easton (1965a), should be distinguished from policy outcomes (discussed below), which are the consequences of policy outputs.

Developing distinct labels for public policy has been the subject of some research and debate in political science. Building upon broad work in American politics, Morgan and Kirkpatrick (1972) suggest that urban policies may fall into two areas—rewards and deprivations. "*Rewards* consist of the goods and services which a person might receive or be able to receive from his government" (p. 19). Most urban services, city infrastructure, and public programs covering everything from police and fire protection to city streets and sewers to urban schools and public health facilities could be categorized as rewards. "*Deprivations* . . . would not only include taxes to pay for government services but also such things as regulations and restrictions imposed by local authority to maintain public order and protect the peace" (p. 19). These are not always mutually exclusive categories. As Morgan and Kirkpatrick observe, a reward like good streets is also subject to a speed limit and traffic controls that deprive citizens of the liberty to drive at will in order to ensure safety and public order.

Another well-known typology of public policies was developed by Theodore Lowi (1964). He classified domestic policies into three types: distributive (policies available for the common good, such as water and sewers), redistributive (programs that reallocate resources from those who have them to those who are needy, such as subsidized housing programs), and regulatory (policies to induce behavior that will be in the public interest, such as fire codes and zoning ordinances). Contemporary writing on urban policy types by Paul Peterson (1981) has been the subject of much debate among urban scholars for two decades. Peterson argues that urban policy can be divided into three varieties and that not all types are in the interest of a city. Developmental policies are designed to advance the economic base and fiscal health of a city. Urban policymakers should be pursuing these policies, including economic and community development policies that provide rewards to businesses. Allocational policies are somewhat akin to Lowi's distributive category; they are designed to provide the basic daily services needed in a community, such as refuse collection, police patrols, street maintenance, water distribution, and fire protection. According to Peterson, without good allocational programs, a city cannot promote sound developmental policies. The third type of policy is redistributive, and Peterson contends that cities should avoid adopting these programs. He argues that redistributive policies are beyond the capacity of many cities, which would incur too many costs with their adoption (programs that could not be funded because of the portion of the budget going to redistributive programs). Redistribution should be the responsibility of the national or state governments, according to Peterson's articulation of federalism.

Urban scholars have critiqued Peterson's political economy thesis (for example, Stone and Sanders 1987), contending that cities cannot pursue a monolithic policy of development, but his typology has been employed in many output studies in urban politics (for example, Schneider 1989; Stein 1990). It has provided a framework for the analysis of urban policies and explanations for policy adoption in cities.

Policy Outcomes

As shown in Figure 1-1, the adoption of a policy is the output of system action. But each output will have some sort of consequence. The effects of the policy output yield a policy outcome that is shaped by the implementation of the adopted policy. One way to view policy outcomes is to look for the intended and unintended, positive, neutral, or negative impacts of the policy. On the one hand, the impact of the policy may be entirely consistent with the policy that had been formally adopted by the city council. It may indeed result in the positive change sought by decision makers that was intended to address demands and supports in the system. However, a policy may possibly have unintended consequences. Because the outcomes may not be consistent with the intentions of the policy adopters, the result could be no effect or even a negative impact on the issue being addressed. For example, to reduce the number of traffic accidents at a busy intersection, a city council may adopt a policy that reduces the speed limit to twenty-five miles per hour on the intersecting streets. The police department must implement and enforce this policy. After a few months, an evaluation of the outcomes of this policy change may show that the number of accidents has been significantly reduced. Hence, a positive policy outcome has apparently occurred. However, more detailed analysis may reveal the development of a new problem—an unintended consequence—if traffic congestion has increased due to the reduced speed limit. This outcome will have to be addressed by the council and the executives. It will also be important for the council to know if the police department enforced the new speed limit, or if the mere presence of police with speed radar devices caused motorists to slow down. In this instance, the police could be enforcing a somewhat higher speed limit, and their random enforcement may be the cause of the policy outcome—not the policy as adopted (and intended) by the city council.

The role of the implementer of the policy output is crucial to the actual policy outcome. Here the municipal bureaucracy has a profound effect on the possible outcome (Levy, Meltsner, and Wildavsky 1974; Lineberry 1977; Lipsky 1980; Meier 2000). If the bureaucrats implement and administer the program as intended by the city council or mayor, for example, then the likelihood of an outcome consistent with legislative or executive intent may be enhanced. On the other hand, if the bureaucrats veer from the program's intent, they have the power to shape an outcome that may be very different from the adopters' goals. Occasionally, this may be done to improve the likelihood of success—an option that may be necessary if a policy was adopted with flawed assumptions. Nonetheless, the urban bureaucracy has a preeminent role in the consequences of policies. As such, when evaluating policies to assess their outcomes, it is critical to know both the intention of the policy adopted and the process used in implementing the policy.

Chapter 8 looks at the important role of the bureaucracy in policy outcomes. Important policy output and outcome areas are examined in later chapters. These include city finance policies (chapter 9), economic development policies (chapter 10), urban services (chapter 11), and public schools (chapter 12).

Feedback

The final assumption in the open system model of urban policy is that the outcomes yield feedback information to the system. This is a key component in the model. The positive and negative, intended and unintended effects of a policy are known to be channeled back to the environment, where they will affect future demands and supports and new political process actions. Obviously, if the impact of a policy is positive, the demands or supports that arose to advance a policy through the process will no longer be active on this issue. Policymakers will not be responding to environmental inputs related to this issue. However, if the issue has not been resolved because the policy outcomes are negative or neutral, then the inputs will continue to stimulate further actions to develop a new policy. As in the traffic example above, a city council and the bureaucracy would be involved in reviewing the feedback information on policy outcomes related to the policy adopted to address accidents and would adjust future policies based upon feedback. In Easton's (1965a) view, feedback is part of a healthy dynamic process that is necessary in a system that must constantly adapt and transform itself to deal with the changing issues, inputs, and outcomes of the political process.

Approaches to Urban Analysis

Many scholars have used the systems approach as a framework for the analysis of city politics and policy. It has proved to be a useful way of thinking about the interrelationships of actors, institutions, and the environment of cities. Systems analysis has been a component of urban research for more than forty years and has been applied to a variety of research designs (see DeLeon 1997). Most of the research can be classified as either case studies or survey research.

Case Studies

One common design used to study cities is the case study. In a typical example, researchers focus their study on one city and employ structured methods of data collection and interpretation to develop and test theories of urban politics. Intensive observational designs have been used in some of the classic case studies of cities. For example, many of the early studies of community power were case studies in which researchers often lived in the community, interviewed residents and experts, analyzed data on local government, and observed the play of local politics. Among these case studies of single cities are those on "Middletown" (Muncie, Indiana); (Lynd and Lynd 1929, 1937), Atlanta (Hunter 1953), New Haven (Dahl 1961), and Chicago (Banfield 1961). Later research on urban regimes and growth machines pursued similar intensive studies of cities, including Atlanta (Stone 1989), Cleveland (Swanstrom 1985), and Houston (Feagin 1988). Recent case studies that have successfully employed political concepts to explain politics or policies in cities have included Chicago (Grimshaw 1992), Los Angeles (Sonenshein 1993), St. Louis (Stein 1991), and San Antonio (Rosales 2000).

An enhancement of the case study approach is the comparative method, in which multiple cities are studied or independent case studies are launched in several cities, employing similar methods and research questions. Early examples of comparative case studies of urban political processes would include Williams and Adrian's classic study, *Four Cities* (1963), in which the anonymity of their cases was preserved; the study of community power in four cities over a period of time by Agger, Goldrich, and Swanson (1964); and Wilson and Banfield's (1964) study of Chicago and Cleveland. Among the best-known comparative studies are the Bay Area research projects that examined multiple cities in the San Francisco area to reveal the importance of institutions to political processes (for example, Eulau and Prewitt 1973; Eyestone 1971; Loveridge 1971; Prewitt 1970). The comparative case study approach has been used to extend our theories of many areas of city politics, including citizen participation in policymaking (Berry, Portney, and Thomson 1993), political parties (Erie 1988), urban regimes (Stone and Sanders 1987; Ferman 1996), minority group political incorporation (Browning, Marshall, and Tabb 1984), racial and ethnic politics (Browning, Marshall, and Tabb 1997), school politics (Portz, Stein, and Jones 1999; Stone 1998; Stone, Henig, Jones, and Pierannunzi 2001), and moral controversies in cities (Sharp 1999), among many others. Comparative case studies have been used to further our knowledge about institutions, including mayors (Ferman 1985; Fuchs 1992), city councils (Heilig and Mundt 1984; Hero 1997), and urban bureaucracy (Mladenka 1981; Osborne and Gaebler 1992).

Survey Research

Another approach in which the systems model has been a common theoretical thread is survey research, such as the comparative cross-sectional study of cities. Researchers began collecting data on a large number of cities and used statistical techniques to assess the determinants of politics or public policies in those cities. Terry Nichols Clark developed the Permanent Community Sample for this purpose (Clark 1968; Clark and Ferguson 1983). Many researchers examined similarly populated cities (for example, all central cities of Metropolitan Statistical Areas, such as New York, Los Angeles, Chicago, and Atlanta) or cities with populations of 25,000 or more). The volume of books and research articles using cross-sectional data is too extensive to adequately synthesize here. A number of excellent works have collected and summarized the importance of these studies to the advancement of theory building in urban politics (see, for example, Morgan and Kirkpatrick 1972; Welch and Bledsoe 1988; Vogel 1997).

In more recent years, the development of new statistical methods and greater availability of datasets on cities have led to more analysis conducted over time. Computers, advanced statistical software programs, and Web-based datasets have increased the opportunities for performing comparative time-series analysis of urban political and policy changes. Some examples of this approach include David R. Morgan and John P. Pelissero's (1980) study of the impact of municipal reform; research on mayors by Harold Wolman and colleagues (Strate, Wolman, and Melchior 1993; Wolman, Strate, and Melchior 1996); bureaucratic policy changes by Kenneth Mladenka and colleagues (Mladenka 1989; Kerr and Mladenka 1994); and studies of city councils, including structural evolution (Waste 1989) and electoral campaign changes (Krebs 1998). The chapters that follow present a fine overview of survey research using both cross-sectional and time-series designs.

Comparing Politics and Policy in Cities

The contributors to this volume have undertaken comprehensive syntheses of the major themes of urban politics and policy, classic and contemporary scholarship in each major area, reviews of the prevailing theories and methods of comparative analysis, and a presentation of the issues that confront cities and urban areas at the start of the twenty-first century. The original essays found in this volume are designed not only to give students a general overview of the field but also to provide the necessary preliminary tools to think about future research. No other recent anthology has attempted to do for urban politics what a similar collection of essays assembled by Virginia Gray, Russell Hanson, and Herbert Jacob (1999) has done for students of state politics.

The Political Environment of Cities

The first set of essays addresses the political environment of cities—the inputs to the system of urban politics and policy.

In chapter 2, "The Intergovernmental Environment," Michael Rich reviews the complex set of interrelationships that have evolved in the intergovernmental environment of cities. Rich shows that as our system changed from one of dual federalism to a much more complex pattern of intergovernmental relations—which Wright (1982) called "overlapping authority"—and independent cities became enmeshed in a web of metropolitan governments, the task of governing cities became more challenging. The mix of counties, cities, school districts, and special district governments in urban areas forces twenty-first–century cities to address issues such as fragmentation, sprawl, shared finances, and coordinated interlocal policymaking. Federal and state governments control many aspects of cities' fiscal policies and complicate local governance with mandates for compliance with national or state laws.

Chapter 3, "Political Participation in Cities," written by Elaine Sharp, covers a wide spectrum of demand makers in the urban political system. Sharp synthesizes the extant literature on both individual and group participation in city politics. As individuals, citizens can participate in elections, contact public officials, and express opinions on public issues. Political parties, campaign organizations, neighborhood organizations, interest groups, social movements, and protests are among the group-based or collective demand-making options for city residents. As Sharp notes, not all methods of participation are equally effective for all citizens. Many factors within the urban system affect civic activities; fair representation of interests must be balanced against bias; and the influence of citizens and groups varies with structural features of the system.

In chapter 4, "Urban Racial and Ethnic Politics," Dianne Pinderhughes discusses the changing pattern of what is also called urban minority politics in cities, showing how social and political exclusion led to protest movements that eventually gave way to political incorporation by way of the ballot box. She looks at how these groups convey their demands in cities and how the political system responds to them, emphasizing the changes that have occurred in demands by non-European immigrants who have migrated to urban areas. Pinderhughes begins to reevaluate our theories of group politics in light of the distinctive experiences of African Americans and the first generations of Latinos and Asians in our cities.

An additional element of the urban environment that has had a profound impact on city governance is the power and influence derived from the socioeconomic and structural features of an urban system. In chapter 5, "Power and Governance in American

Cities," Clarence Stone takes the reader beyond the historical debate among scholars of community power, wherein elitism and pluralism were twin pillars of scholarship. In more recent work of his own and of others, he shows the importance of a new understanding of power relationships among actors from the environment and the government of cities. The theory of urban regimes and their pivotal role in shaping city politics and policy is at the heart of this chapter. As Stone demonstrates, having the "power to" affect urban policy is often more important than the formally assigned "power over" urban government.

Authoritative Decision-making Institutions

The political process of authoritative decision-making institutions and actors in city government is the subject of the next set of chapters. Lana Stein delineates the role of mayors in chapter 6, "Mayoral Politics." Reminding the reader of the importance of mayors to authoritative decision making in the political process, Stein shows how their powers and impact vary with the form of city government. She is able to demonstrate the challenges facing mayors and the potential for a successful run in today's large cities by synthesizing the extant literature of mayoral biographies, case studies, and comparative works. This chapter is linked to the power relationships described by Stone in chapter 5, wherein mayors are both leaders and subjects of urban regimes with vast potential for success as agents of change.

The importance of legislatures to the authoritative allocation of values in the urban political system is the focus of chapter 7, "City Councils." Timothy Krebs and John Pelissero evaluate the varying powers and role orientations of councils under alternative structural arrangements. Representation of the local citizenry has been the subject of much debate in the electoral systems used for city councils. As this chapter illustrates, the structural features of city government are critical to the fair representation of interests, the power of the council, and the adoption of municipal policy by these legislative bodies. The authors show why structural and electoral components of cities will be the focus of research on city councils for some time.

In chapter 8, "City Managers and the Urban Bureaucracy," Robert England highlights the theoretical basis for professional city management in his discussion of the central role played by managers and bureaucrats in determining the shape of city policy and the delivery of urban services. He offers a comprehensive look at the political and policy roles of the administrative branch of city government and discusses how a new style of public management has now become essential to successful city operations.

Policy Outputs and Outcomes

The policy outputs and outcomes of urban systems are the topics covered in the final chapters. Robert M. Stein reviews the basic features of the most important of urban outputs—city budgets—in chapter 9, "The Politics of Revenue and Spending Policies." He describes the balance that must be constructed between a city's revenue sources and the scope of municipal service functions. In many ways, all other urban outputs flow from the decisions that are made on taxes and spending in each annual budget. Stein synthesizes the abundant comparative research on municipal finances and demonstrates the importance of the urban environment to city fiscal policies. He constructs a theoretical model for understanding municipal fiscal policies that builds upon community power and political economy perspectives of urban policy. Moreover, he provides a clear picture of the internal demands for spending and the external constraints on resources that characterize city finances in the twenty-first century.

Closely linked to city finances is the environment for local economic development. In chapter 10, "Economic Development Policies," Richard Bingham assesses the emphasis on these policies that characterized city governments in the last two decades of the twentieth century. He demonstrates the effects of external forces on cities' economic foundations and how the global economy has forced cities to compete with one another for businesses that will generate jobs and income. As Bingham notes, however, the success of economic development programs is often difficult to gauge, yet most cities continue to pursue such strategies.

In chapter 11, "Urban Services," David Ammons tackles the wide-ranging scope of urban services. The adoption and delivery of urban service programs are at the heart of operating any city. Ammons shows the importance of the bureaucracy to service policy outcomes and how cities have experimented with new ways to improve the efficiency, effectiveness, and responsiveness of services. He illustrates how today's cities have begun to reinvent themselves to provide better quality and management of important day-to-day services.

The final two chapters take a special look at two areas of scholarship that are important to understanding the politics of any urban area—public schools and the suburban component of metropolitan area politics. In chapter 12, "The New Politics of Urban Schools," Kenneth Wong looks at school districts as institutions engaged in providing one critical policy in cities—the delivery of public education. He reviews the organization of independent school districts and discusses why the reform of urban schools has become the central feature of education policy. Increasingly, the very independence of big-city schools is being challenged not only by their own failure to demonstrate that they can successfully educate pupils but also by the subsequent intent of mayors to take control of schools and make them a centerpiece for urban reform.

In Chapter 13, "Suburban and Metropolitan Politics," Eric Oliver discusses how metropolitan areas and suburban cities transformed urban politics in the twentieth century. He describes how suburban politics and policies differ from those of large cities but also shows the emerging pattern of urbanism that characterizes suburbs today. The challenge now facing urban areas is centered on ways to allow large cities and diverse suburbs to coexist in a system of improved metropolitan governance.

Conclusion

The original essays in this volume reflect a serious attempt on the part of the authors to place urban politics in a twenty-first–century context. By looking at cities from a comparative perspective, these contributors are able to show where cities have been and what challenges confront them in a new century. Importantly, the following chapters also demonstrate how political science has contributed to and will continue to add to a valid understanding of the state of urban politics in the United States. Clearly, our fundamental knowledge of cities, politics, and policy has been formed by case study and survey research spanning more than half a century. The field has evolved from fairly normative prescriptions of what it was believed cities ought to be at the turn of the twentieth century to valid social science theories of the nature of urban politics and policy at the start of another century.

The experts who have written on the major topics of urban politics and policy in this volume have updated our knowledge in each major area of city politics. They have shown the importance of understanding the urban political system as we craft future research. The significance of cities in the American system of governance is clear in their reviews of the literature in each area. Moreover, their conclusions reflect the positive developments made by institutions, leaders, and city residents that provide hope for good governance of urban areas in the future. It is our collective goal that this book will be a beginning, a solid basis for new research and inquiry into the state of urban politics and policy in the twenty-first century.

Suggested Readings

Banfield, Edward, and James Q. Wilson. 1963. *City Politics*. Cambridge: Harvard University Press. A classic work that helped to refocus urban scholarship on political behavior and political processes instead of the institutional aspects of urban reformism.

Dahl, Robert A. 1961. *Who Governs? Democracy and Power in an American City*. New Haven: Yale University Press. This classic case study of New Haven advanced the argument for a pluralist understanding of city politics.

Dreier, Peter, John Mollenkopf, and Todd Swanstrom. 2001. *Place Matters: Metropolitics for the Twenty-first Century*. Lawrence: University Press of Kansas. This book argues that cities and regions cannot solve the fundamental urban problem of place-based inequalities by themselves, largely due to the fact that these inequalities are the result of state and federal policies that distort market forces.

Easton, David. 1965. *A Systems Analysis of Political Life.* New York: Wiley. This book is the completion of an influential three-volume series on applying systems analysis to the empirical study of politics that has guided urban research for decades.

International City/County Management Association. *The Municipal Year Book.* Washington, D.C.: ICMA. This annual volume presents the latest information on city government organization, finances, and emerging issues.

Orfield, Myron. 2002. *American Metropolitics: The New Suburban Reality.* Washington, D.C.: Brookings Institution Press. A careful look at the political environment in the twenty-five largest metropolitan areas in the United States and the continuing disparities between central cities and suburbs and the emerging diversity of suburbs.

Peterson, Paul. 1981. *City Limits.* Chicago: University of Chicago Press. This book provided what was then an important new thesis on urban politics and policy, in which cities have a unique "self-interest" that focuses on policies that develop their economy, preventing them from pursuing redistributive social services.

Stone, Clarence N., and Heywood T. Sanders, eds. 1987. *The Politics of Urban Development.* Lawrence: University Press of Kansas. A collection of original essays on regime formation in a variety of cities, which offers an alternative to Peterson's thesis on urban policies.

Urban Issues: Selections from *The CQ Researcher.* 2001. Washington, D.C.: CQ Press. A collection of articles on such contemporary issues as immigration, school vouchers, and affordable housing in America's cities, also including a discussion of historical trends, new reports, and alternative perspectives on each issue.

References

Agger, Robert E., Daniel Goldrich, and Bert E. Swanson. 1964. *The Rulers and the Ruled: Political Power and Impotence in American Communities.* New York: Wiley.

Alford, Robert R. 1968. "The Comparative Study of Urban Politics." In *Social Science and the City,* ed. Leo F. Schnore, 263–302. New York: Praeger.

Banfield, Edward C. 1961. *Political Influence.* New York: Free Press.

Bennett, Larry. 1993. "Harold Washington and the Black Urban Regime." *Urban Affairs Quarterly* 28 (March): 423–440.

Berman, David R. 1999. "State-Local Relations: Authority, Finance, and Regional Cooperation." *The Municipal Yearbook, 1999.* Washington, D.C.: International City/County Management Association, 47–61.

Berry, Jeffrey M., Kent E. Portney, and Ken Thomson. 1993. *The Rebirth of Urban Democracy.* Washington: Brookings Institution Press.

Browning, Rufus P., Dale Rogers Marshall, and David H. Tabb. 1984. *Protest Is not Enough.* Berkeley: University of California Press.

——— 1997. *Racial Politics in American Cities.* 2d ed. New York: Longman.

Button, James W., Barbara A. Rienzo, and Kenneth Wald. 1997. *Private Lives, Public Conflicts: Battles over Gay Rights in American Communities.* Washington, D.C.: CQ Press.

Clark, Terry Nichols. 1968. "Community Structure, Decision-Making, Budget Expenditures, and Urban Renewal in Fifty-one American Communities." *American Sociological Review* 33 (August): 576–593.

——— and Lorna Ferguson. 1983. *City Money.* New York: Columbia University Press.

Clavel, Pierre. 1986. *The Progressive City.* New Brunswick, N.J.: Rutgers University Press.

Dahl, Robert. 1961. *Who Governs? Democracy and Power in an American City.* New Haven: Yale University Press.

DeLeon, Richard E. 1992. *Left Coast City: Progressive Politics in San Francisco, 1975–1991*. Lawrence: University Press of Kansas.

———— 1997. "Research Methods in Urban Politics and Policy." In *Handbook of Research on Urban Politics and Policy in the United States*, ed. Ronald E. Vogel, 17–30. Westport, Conn.: Greenwood Press.

Dreier, Peter, John Mollenkopf, and Todd Swanstrom. 2001. *Place Matters: Metropolitics for the Twenty-first Century*. Lawrence: University Press of Kansas.

Easton, David. 1953. *The Political System*. New York: Knopf.

———— 1965a. *A Framework for Political Analysis*. Englewood Cliffs, N.J.: Prentice-Hall.

———— 1965b. *A Systems Analysis of Political Life*. New York: Wiley.

Elazar, Daniel J. 1966. *American Federalism: A View from the States*. New York: Crowell.

———— 1970. *Cities of the Prairie: The Metropolitan Frontier and American Politics*. New York: Basic Books.

Elkin, Stephen L. 1987. "State and Market in City Politics: Or, the 'Real' Dallas." In *The Politics of Urban Development*, ed. Clarence Stone and Heywood Sanders, 25–51. Lawrence: University Press of Kansas.

Erie, Steven. 1988. *Rainbow's End: Irish-Americans and the Dilemmas of Urban Machine Politics 1840–1985*. Berkeley: University of California Press.

Eulau, Heinz and Kenneth Prewitt. 1973. *Labyrinths of Democracy: Adaptations, Linkages, Representation, and Policies in Urban Politics*. Indianapolis: Bobbs-Merrill.

Eyestone, Robert. 1971. *The Threads of Public Policy: A Study in Policy Leadership*. Indianapolis: Bobbs-Merrill.

Feagin, Joe R. 1988. *Free Enterprise City: Houston in Political and Economic Perspective*. New Brunswick, N.J.: Rutgers University Press.

Ferman, Barbara. 1996. *Challenging the Growth Machine*. Lawrence: University Press of Kansas.

———— 1985. *Governing the Ungovernable City: Political Skill, Leadership and the Modern Mayor*. Philadelphia: Temple University Press.

Fraga, Luis R. 1988. "Domination Through Democratic Means: Nonpartisan Slating Groups in City Electoral Politics." *Urban Affairs Quarterly* 23 (June): 528–555.

Fuchs, Ester R. 1992. *Mayors and Money: Fiscal Policy in New York and Chicago*. Chicago: University of Chicago Press.

Galaskiewicz, Joseph. 1981. "Interest Group Politics from a Comparative Perspective." *Urban Affairs Quarterly* 16 (March): 259–280.

Grimshaw, William. 1992. *Bitter Fruit: Black Politics and the Chicago Machine, 1931–1991*. Chicago: University of Chicago Press.

Gray, Virginia, Russell L. Hanson, and Herbert Jacob, eds. 1999. *Politics in the American States*. 7th ed. Washington: CQ Press.

Hajnal, Zoltan, Paul Lewis, and Hugh Louch. 2002. *Municipal Elections in California: Turnout, Timing, and Competition*. San Francisco: Public Policy Institute of California.

Hawley, Willis D. 1973. *Nonpartisan Elections and the Case for Party Politics*. New York: Wiley.

Hays, Samuel P. 1964. "The Politics of Reform in Municipal Government in the Progressive Era." *Pacific Northwest Quarterly* 55 (October): 157–189.

Heilig, Peggy, and Robert J. Mundt. 1984. *Your Voice at City Hall*. Albany: State University of New York Press.

Hero, Rodney E. 1997. "Latinos and Politicos in Denver and Pueblo, Colorado: Differences, Explanations, and the 'Steady-State' of the Struggle for Equality." In *Racial Politics in American Cities*. 2d ed., ed. Rufus P. Browning, Dale Rogers Marshall, and David H. Tabb, 247–258. New York: Longman.

Hunter, Floyd. 1953. *Community Power Structure: A Study of Decision Makers.* Chapel Hill: University of North Carolina Press.

International City/County Management Association. 2002a. "Form of Government." http://www.icma.org/issueintersections/formofgovt.cfm.

———— 2002b. "Telecommunications in Local Government Survey Results." http://www.icma.org.

Karnig, Albert, and Walter B. Oliver. 1983. "Decline in Municipal Voter Turnout." *American Politics Quarterly* 11 (October): 491–505.

Kerr, Brinck, and Kenneth R. Mladenka. 1994. "Does Politics Matter? A Time-Series Analysis of Minority Employment Patterns." *American Journal of Political Science* 38 (November): 918–943.

Krebs, Timothy B. 1998. "The Determinants of Candidates' Vote Share and the Advantages of Incumbency in City Council Elections." *American Journal of Political Science* 42 (July): 921–935.

Levy, Frank, Arnold Meltsner, and Aaron Wildavsky. 1974. *Urban Outcomes: Schools, Streets, and Libraries.* Berkeley: University of California Press.

Lineberry, Robert L. 1977. *Equality and Urban Policy: The Distribution of Municipal Public Services.* Beverly Hills, Calif.: Sage.

———— and Louis H. Masotti. 1976. "The New Urban Politics." In *The New Urban Politics,* ed. Robert L. Lineberry and Louis H. Masotti, 1–15. Cambridge, Mass.: Ballinger.

Lipsky, Michael. 1980. *Street-Level Bureaucracy: Dilemmas of the Individual in Public Services.* New York: Russell Sage.

Logan, John R., Rachel B. Whaley, and Kyle Crowder. 1997. "The Character and Consequences of Growth Regimes: An Assessment of Twenty Years of Research." *Urban Affairs Review* 32 (May): 603–630.

Loveridge, Ronald O. 1971. *City Managers in Legislative Politics.* Indianapolis: Bobbs-Merrill.

Lowi, Theodore J. 1964. "American Business, Public Policy, Case Studies, and Political Theory." *World Politics* 16 (July): 677–715.

Lynd, Robert S., and Helen M. Lynd. 1929. *Middletown.* New York: Harcourt Brace and World.

———— 1937. *Middletown in Transition.* New York: Harcourt Brace and World.

Mladenka, Kenneth R. 1981. "Citizen Demands and Human Services: The Distribution of Bureaucratic Response in Chicago and Houston." *American Journal of Political Science* 25 (November): 693–714.

———— 1989. "Blacks and Hispanics in Urban Politics." *American Political Science Review* 83 (March): 165–191.

Meier, Kenneth J. 2000. *Politics and the Bureaucracy.* 4th ed. New York: Harcourt.

Morgan, David R., and Samuel A. Kirkpatrick, eds. 1972. *Urban Political Analysis: A Systems Approach.* New York: Free Press.

Morgan, David, and John Pelissero. 1980. "Urban Policy: Does Political Structure Matter?" *American Political Science Review* 74 (December): 999–1006.

Norris, Donald F., and Lori A. Demeter. 1999. "Information Technology and City Governments." *The Municipal Year Book, 1999.* Washington: ICMA, 10–19.

Osborne, David, and Ted Gaebler. 1992. *Reinventing Government: How the Entrepreneurial Spirit Is Transforming the Public Sector.* Reading, Mass.: Addison-Wesley.

Park, Keeok. 1997. "Friends and Competitors: Policy Interactions between Local Governments in Metropolitan Areas." *Political Research Quarterly* 50 (December): 723–750.

Perrenod, Virginia M. 1984. *Special Districts, Special Purposes: Fringe Governments and Urban Problems in the Houston Area.* College Station: Texas A&M University Press.

Peterson, Paul. 1981. *City Limits.* Chicago: University of Chicago Press.

Prewitt, Kenneth. 1970. *The Recruitment of Political Leaders: A Study of Citizen-Politicians.* Indianapolis: Bobbs-Merrill.

Portz, John, Lana Stein, and Robin R. Jones. 1999. *City Schools and City Politics: Institutions and Leadership in Pittsburgh, Boston, and St. Louis.* Lawrence: University Press of Kansas.

Rich, Michael J., Michael W. Giles, and Emily Stern. 2001. "Collaborating to Reduce Poverty: Views from City Halls and Community-Based Organizations." *Urban Affairs Review* 37 (November): 184–204.

Rosales, Rodolfo. 2000. *The Illusion of Inclusion: The Untold Political Story of San Antonio.* Austin: University of Texas Press.

Rosenstone, Steven J., and John Mark Hansen. 1993. *Mobilization, Participation, and Democracy in America.* New York: Macmillan.

Schaffner, Brian F., Matthew Streb, and Gerald Wright. 2001. "Teams Without Uniforms: The Nonpartisan Ballot in State and Local Elections." *Political Research Quarterly* 54 (March): 7–30.

Schneider, Mark. 1989. *The Competitive City: The Political Economy of Suburbia.* Pittsburgh: University of Pittsburgh Press.

Schumaker, Paul, and Russell Getter. 1983. "Structural Sources of Unequal Responsiveness to Group Demands in American Cities." *Western Political Quarterly* 36 (March): 7–29.

Sharp, Elaine B., ed. 1999. *Culture Wars and City Politics.* Lawrence: University Press of Kansas.

Sonenshein, Raphael J. 1993. *Politics in Black and White: Race and Power in Los Angeles.* Princeton: Princeton University Press.

Stein, Lana. 1991. *Holding Bureaucrats Accountable: Politicians and Professionals in St. Louis.* Tuscaloosa: University of Alabama Press.

Stein, Robert M. 1990. *Urban Alternatives: Public and Private Markets in the Provision of Local Services.* Pittsburgh: University of Pittsburgh Press.

Stone, Clarence N. 1989. *Regime Politics: Governing Atlanta 1946–1988.* Lawrence: University Press of Kansas.

——— ed. 1998. *Changing Urban Education.* Lawrence: University Press of Kansas.

Stone, Clarence N., and Heywood T. Sanders, eds. 1987. *The Politics of Urban Development.* Lawrence: University Press of Kansas.

Stone, Clarence N., Jeffrey R. Henig, Bryan D. Jones, and Carol Pierannunzi. 2001. *Building Civic Capacity: The Politics of Reforming Urban Schools.* Lawrence: University Press of Kansas.

Strate, John, Harold Wolman, and Alan Melchior. 1993. "Are There Election-Driven Tax-and-Expenditure Cycles for Urban Governments?" *Urban Affairs Quarterly* 28 (March): 462–479.

Svara, James H. 1985. "Dichotomy and Duality: Reconceptualizing the Relationship between Policy and Administration in Council-Manager Cities." *Public Administration Review* 45 (January–February): 221–232.

Swanstrom, Todd. 1985. *The Crisis of Growth Politics: Cleveland, Kucinich, and Challenge of Urban Populism.* Philadelphia: Temple University Press.

U.S. Bureau of the Census. 1999. *1997 Census of Governments.* Vol. 1, *Government Organization.* Washington, D.C.: U.S. Government Printing Office.

Vogel, Ronald K., ed. 1997. *Handbook of Research on Urban Politics and Policy in the United States.* Westport, Conn.: Greenwood Press.

Walsh, Annmarie H. 1978. *The Public's Business.* Cambridge: MIT Press.

Waste, Robert J. 1989. *The Ecology of City Policymaking.* New York: Oxford University Press.

Welch, Susan, and Timothy Bledsoe. 1988. *Urban Reform and Its Consequences.* Chicago: University of Chicago Press.

Williams, Oliver P., and Charles R. Adrian. 1963. *Four Cities: A Study in Comparative Policy Making*. Philadelphia: University of Pennsylvania Press.

Wilson, James Q., and Edward C. Banfield. 1964. "Public-Regardingness as a Value Premise in Voting Behavior." *American Political Science Review* 58 (December): 876–887.

———— 1971. "Political Ethos Revisited." *American Political Science Review* 65 (December): 1048–1062.

Wolman, Harold, John Strate, and Alan Melchior. 1996. "Does Changing Mayors Matter?" *Journal of Politics* 58 (February): 201–223.

Wright, Deil S. 1982. *Understanding Intergovernmental Relations*. 2d ed. Monterey: Calif: Brooks/Cole.

2 The Intergovernmental Environment

Michael J. Rich

The two most important attributes of the American political system—federalism and separation of powers—constitute an intergovernmental context that presents numerous challenges and opportunities for urban policymaking. The diffusion of power and authority in metropolitan areas is especially salient for central city governments, which often face a disproportionate share of problems and a shortage of resources and authority to respond to them. Thus, in order to more fully understand contemporary urban policymaking, one must extend the scope of inquiry beyond the formal institutions of city government and examine the variety of means federal, state, and other local governments can employ to limit or expand the actions city officials can take to address important problems. Two recent examples, from Buffalo and Atlanta, illustrate the complexity of urban problem solving and emphasize the importance of looking at urban issues within an intergovernmental context.

On December 19, 1996, the New York State Court of Appeals handed down a decision requiring the Buffalo board of education to implement a 1990 contract agreement with its teachers that compelled the district to provide as much as $200 million in back pay—a staggering amount for a school district and a city government both facing serious fiscal crises (Scott 1998). The Buffalo school district, unlike those in most urban areas, is fiscally dependent, meaning that it does not have its own taxing authority and must instead raise revenues through contributions from the city, state, and federal governments. Faced with a strong possibility that the school district would have to declare bankruptcy, city, school, and union officials began negotiations, guided by the state courts, and eventually agreed on a figure of $73 million. To finance the agreement, the school district was able to arrange a $45 million no-interest loan from the state and a modest increase in the city's contribution to the school budget.

In 1998 the U.S. Environmental Protection Agency ruled that, owing to Atlanta's poor air quality, it would withhold all federal highway money to the region. The funds were to be suspended until the region developed a transportation plan that would bring the metropolitan area into compliance with federal clean air standards, as established by the Clean Air Act of 1990 (Ehrenhalt 1999). To respond to this crisis, Roy Barnes, Georgia's newly elected governor, pushed for the creation of the Georgia Regional Transportation Authority (GRTA) during the state's 1999 legislative session.

The new agency, whose design was crafted by a blue-ribbon panel assembled by the Metropolitan Atlanta Chamber of Commerce, was given extensive powers over the thirteen metropolitan Atlanta counties located within the nonattainment area. These powers included the authority to review and approve (or veto) transportation plans and projects proposed for the area, to design and operate public transit within the region, and, perhaps most significant, to review major development activities such as shopping malls and large subdivisions that might have an adverse impact on the region's traffic and water and air quality. If local governments refused to accept GRTA's rulings about the compliance of their development proposals with regional and state plans, the new superagency could withhold public money for transportation improvements.

As the examples illustrate, despite the efforts of federal and state policymakers over the past two decades of devolution to bring government decision making closer to the people, local governments in urban areas—particularly in central cities—operate in an increasingly complex intergovernmental environment in which federal, state, and local agencies can frequently limit the actions cities take or, alternatively, mandate certain actions. In addition, many metropolitan areas have experienced unprecedented growth in terms of population, land area, and government organizations over the past two decades. (More than eight out of ten Americans now live in metropolitan areas.) As a result, issues involved in crafting an effective governance strategy for managing that growth have assumed center stage in many communities.

This chapter summarizes a variety of means by which federal and state governments influence the actions of local governments in urban areas, particularly central city governments. As the chapter will illustrate, there are four primary sets of policy tools through which external influence is brought to bear on city governments: (1) authority/discretion regarding issues of local governmental organization and structure; (2) authority/discretion regarding the powers of local governments to tax, spend, and borrow; (3) federal and state mandates; and (4) federal and state court rulings and judicial interventions in the operation of local agencies. The chapter concludes with a brief discussion of several analytic frameworks for examining urban policymaking in an intergovernmental context and offers a few observations on areas ripe for future research.

Government Organization and Structure

Perhaps the single most important fact about the American federal system is the diversity of local governments. As discussed in chapter 1, the most recent census of governments, conducted in 1997, enumerated more than 87,000 local governments, including 3,043 counties, 19,372 municipalities, 16,629 townships and towns, 13,726 school districts, and 34,683 special districts. How these governments are organized within metropolitan areas, as well as the power and authority they have been granted by their respective states, provides the foundation for the urban political environment. The mix of local governments, their functional responsibilities, and their fiscal and regulatory powers provide both the context within which public issues arise and the venues for which those demands can be vetted.

Most important, it should be emphasized that local governments did not spring up automatically, nor were they in existence when the nation's communities were settled. Rather, as Nancy Burns (1994, 3) notes, "Americans continually create new local governments—new cities and new special district governments. Over the course of the past 350 years, Americans have formed almost 50,000 cities and special districts. The reasons they have done so and the arrangements that have enabled them to succeed illuminate the place of local government in American politics, point to the importance of boundaries and politics that these citizens have created, and describe the values that they have embedded in these new institutions." Burns's observation on the determinants of local government organization builds on the earlier work of Daniel Elazar (1984), who argued that political culture is a primary factor shaping the diversity of political structure and action in the American states. Elazar presented an intricate mosaic of the United States, noting different preferences for what government should do and how public action should be carried out and linking them to three primary political cultures (and several subcultures composed of combinations of these three) that could be traced back to the sociocultural differences of the settlers who founded the first communities in America. Differences in the number and type of local governments across urban America can thus be linked in part to differences in the values and political culture of residents of different states and metropolitan areas. Stephens and Olson (1979), for example, identified fourteen different "systems of local government" in the United States, ranging from the simplest in Hawaii (state/county) and Alaska (state/municipal) to the most complex (New Jersey, New York, Pennsylvania, and Wisconsin), where all five types of local government are present.

Overall, the median number of local governments in U.S. metropolitan areas is about 200, meaning that about half of the metropolitan areas have more than 200 local governments and about half have fewer than that number. There are nearly 1,500 local governments in the Chicago metropolitan area, tops among all U.S. metropolitan regions. The Pittsburgh, Philadelphia, and Houston metropolitan areas all have more than 800 local governments. In contrast, there are fewer than 100 local governments in metropolitan Miami, Baltimore, Charlotte, and Memphis. The density of local governments, whether measured in terms of population or land area, also varies widely. Generally, metropolitan areas in the Northeast and Midwest tend to have a greater number of local governments than their counterparts in the South or West have.

As Table 2-1 illustrates, the mix of local governments is also quite diverse across metropolitan areas, both within and across regions. For example, the Atlanta and Boston metropolitan areas have roughly the same number of local governments, and their distribution by type is relatively comparable, except that there are twenty county governments in metropolitan Atlanta as compared with three in metropolitan Boston. Moreover, county governments in Boston (as well as throughout the New England states) generally administer only the courts, whereas county governments in metropolitan Atlanta are major service providers. Comparing Atlanta and Houston, we find a much greater number and density of local governments in metropolitan Houston than in metropolitan Atlanta, although the Atlanta region has more general purpose local governments (counties, cities, towns), whereas Houston has more than 700 special purpose governments, compared with about 150 in Atlanta. It is important to note that these different preferences for the type of local government are not simply due to differences in state–local relations. Compare Pittsburgh and Philadelphia, for example. While the population of metropolitan Philadelphia is more than twice as large as that of metropolitan Pittsburgh, there are more than twice as many local governments per 10,000 residents in the Pittsburgh area as there are in metropolitan Philadelphia.

State–Local Relations

The extent of discretionary authority given to local governments also varies considerably across states. The degree of local government autonomy is determined by how much discretion state governments grant in four basic areas: (1) structure (form of government, internal organization); (2) function (service responsibilities); (3) fiscal (taxing, spending, borrowing); and (4) personnel (number and type of employees and employment conditions).

The U.S. Advisory Commission on Intergovernmental Relations (1981) developed a composite measure of local government discretionary authority based on these four types of authority for all local governments in a state, as well as separate scores for each type of local government. The study found that most states do not grant discretionary authority to local governments uniformly; the state rankings varied, depending on whether they were based on an overall composite score for all types of local governments or on a score for only cities or only counties. According to the U.S. ACIR study, the ten states granting the most discretionary authority to city governments (ranked from highest to lowest) were Texas, Maine, Michigan, Connecticut, North Carolina, Oregon, Maryland, Missouri, Virginia, and Illinois. The ten states granting the least discretionary authority (ranked from lowest to highest) were New Mexico, Vermont, Idaho, West Virginia, Nevada, New York, South Dakota, Rhode Island, Massachusetts, and Indiana. No apparent pattern emerges from these rankings,

Table 2-1 Local Governments by Number and Type in Selected Metropolitan Areas, 1997

Metropolitan area	Land area (sq. mi.)	1996 population (thousands)	Number of Local Governments					Governments per 10,000 residents
			Total	Counties	Cities and towns	Special districts	School districts	
Northeast								
Baltimore[a]	2,619	2,502	81	6	20	55	0	0.32
Boston[a]	1,836	3,209	260	3	106	129	22	0.81
New York[a]	1,145	8,643	201	3	80	65	53	0.23
Philadelphia[a]	3,870	4,953	845	8	354	296	187	1.71
Pittsburgh	4,637	2,379	858	6	412	334	106	3.61
Midwest								
Chicago[a]	5,103	7,734	1,456	9	455	662	330	1.88
Cleveland[a]	2,718	2,233	345	6	200	55	84	1.54
Minneapolis	6,061	2,765	519	13	331	97	78	1.88
St. Louis	6,396	2,565	788	11	300	357	120	3.07
South								
Atlanta	6,150	3,541	263	20	107	109	27	0.74
Houston[a]	5,961	3,792	802	6	79	669	48	2.12
Memphis	3,013	1,078	92	5	40	41	6	0.85
Miami[a]	1,955	2,076	36	1	27	6	2	0.17
West								
Denver[a]	3,755	1,867	430	4	31	378	17	2.30
Los Angeles[a]	4,070	9,128	378	1	88	196	93	0.41
Phoenix	14,470	2,747	215	2	32	105	76	0.78
Portland[a]	5,019	1,759	282	6	56	163	57	1.60
Total								
All metro areas > 1 million	254,490	132,355	15,844	295	5,540	6,902	3,000	1.20
All metro areas	707,211	211,231	35,024	780	12,915	15,310	6,019	1.66
Total United States	3,538,624	263,256	87,453	3,043	36,001	34,683	13,726	3.32

Source: Calculated from U.S. Bureau of the Census, *1997 Census of Governments, Vol. 1, Government Organization.* (Washington, D.C.: U.S. Government Printing Office, 1999).

[a] Primary metropolitan statistical area. All other areas are metropolitan statistical areas.

although the least discretionary authority tends to be granted to smaller states with a large proportion of the population living in nonmetropolitan areas.

Despite these variations in organization and structure, state–local relations in the United States are dominated by the legal doctrine known as Dillon's Rule. In 1868 Judge John F. Dillon of the Iowa Supreme Court, then the nation's leading expert on municipal law, ruled: "Municipal Corporations owe their origin to and derive their powers and rights wholly from the legislature. It breathes into them the breath of life, without which they cannot exist. As it creates, so it may destroy. If it may destroy, it may abridge and control" (quoted in Krane, Rigos, and Hill 2001, 10).

For more than one hundred years, local governments have been seeking greater autonomy or "home rule" from their state governments. Beginning in 1875, when Missouri wrote its constitution and included a provision permitting the drafting of municipal charters, an alternative paradigm known as home rule emerged to challenge the predominant doctrine of Dillon's Rule. As Krane, Rigos, and Hill (p. 2) note in their comprehensive volume on the subject, "In general terms the ideal of home rule is defined as the ability of a local government to act and make policy in all areas that have not been designated to be of statewide interest through general law, state constitutional provisions, or initiatives and referenda." The authors cite three basic types of home rule: (1) structural (power to create a new local government or to allow an existing government to expand or annex its territory); (2) functional (choice in determining the mix and level of services to provide); and (3) fiscal (ability to determine how a local government raises its revenues).

Krane, Rigos, and Hill found that over the years state governments have been more willing to grant home rule authority to municipal governments (forty-seven states) than to county governments (forty states). They also report that states have been more willing to grant broader discretion to local governments in determining their structure and function than in setting their fiscal policies.

While most state governments have granted some type of home rule authority, states continue to play a major role in regulating the activities of their local governments. A 1993 U.S. ACIR study compared state laws in 1978 and 1990 in six major areas: form of government, annexation and consolidation, local elections, administrative operations and procedures, financial management, and personnel management. Overall, the study examined more than 200 local functional and procedural areas; in about half of these areas (47 percent) the number of states legislating on the topic increased from 1978 to 1990, whereas in about one-third of the topic areas (32 percent) the number of states legislating decreased. States were most likely to increase their legislative activity regarding local governments in areas pertaining to financial management (twenty-seven states) and personnel management (twenty-nine states).

Implications of Local Government Organization

The variations in local government organization and structure that affect politics and policy in the nation's metropolitan regions have many implications. One theme that has captured the attention of scholars for some time is whether the proliferation of local governments in metropolitan areas has adverse consequences on the governance of these areas and the quality of life of their residents. Some scholars claim that the political fragmentation of metropolitan areas has made it nearly impossible to address a wide range of urban problems. For example, Campbell and Sacks, writing in 1967, concluded their study of metropolitan America by stating that "the conventional wisdom in the metropolitan field stresses the necessity for the total reorganization of the governments of these areas. The argument is that the present governmental fragmentation and overlapping in metropolitan areas makes it impossible for what is otherwise a social and economic unit to rationally attack the problems that more and more tend to be area-wide rather than merely jurisdiction-wide." Nearly thirty years later David Rusk (1995, 47), former mayor of Albuquerque, New Mexico, drew essentially the same conclusion, backed by a bevy of lessons and strategies to demonstrate his point: "[F]ragmentation of local government reinforces racial and economic segregation. Rivalry among jurisdictions often inhibits the whole area's ability to respond to economic challenges."

Empirical studies of the debate over government organization in metropolitan areas have found support for both the reform and the status quo positions. Morgan and Mareschal's (1999) study analyzed data from ninety-seven large metropolitan areas and found that government structure had only modest effects on social, economic, and racial outcomes. They used three different measures of fragmentation (number of municipalities, central city's share of metropolitan area population, and change in central city land area) and examined their effects on three separate dependent variables (central city–suburban income disparity, fiscal health of the core community, racial segregation). Morgan and Mareschal found that the fragmentation measures had no effect on income disparities, a modest effect but in the wrong direction on fiscal health, and strong effects on racial segregation. They conclude, however, that "it would be overly simple, of course, to assume that a reduction in the proliferation of perimeter jurisdictions would substantially reduce racial segregation in U.S. metropolitan areas. That massive problem is far too intractable. The relationship between fragmentation and black isolation does remind us, though, that municipal boundaries are not inconsequential. They have abundant social meaning" (p. 591).

Rusk's analysis, though largely confined to seven pairs of metropolitan areas, found similar results on racial segregation. He also noted, however, that elastic cities (those with the political and legal tools to expand their territory) were much better off in terms of fiscal health and city–suburban income disparities than were their nonelastic counterparts in fragmented metropolitan areas.

Stephens and Wikstrom (2000, 169), in another recent study, examined the evidence on metropolitan reform (that is, "elimination of political and government fragmentation in metropolitan areas"), as well as the public-choice perspective that defends the fragmented or polycentric character of metropolitan areas (for example, Ostrom, Tiebout, and Warren 1961). Stephens and Wikstrom conclude that "we do not believe that there is currently a crisis or breakdown in the governmental structure of our metropolitan areas; the formal and informal system of metropolitan governance, although it may be assailed as chaotic, confusing, crazy-quilt, or simply incomprehensible to the average citizen, is seemingly viable and far from broken. In a collective sense, the bewildering structural array of general-purpose and special-purpose governments splashed across the usual metropolis are largely responding to and meeting the varied service needs of the citizenry, with the less fortunate, to some extent, falling outside this deft generalization."

This brief review of three current studies of government organization in metropolitan areas shows mixed support for the metropolitan reform agenda. These findings are due, in part, to the varied emphasis given in the studies to the different values that regionalism and metropolitan governance can promote. As Benjamin and Nathan (2001, 256) pointed out, regionalism's three core values—social equity, governmental efficiency, and economic competitiveness—often conflict with one another, and "the various ways these core values are prioritized produce different and distinct approaches to the delicate political act of balancing regionalism with realism." Thus, one's support for a regional or metropolitan governance strategy is likely to depend to a great extent on which of these three core values one would like to emphasize.

Fiscal Federalism

One of the most complex public policy topics to untangle is that of fiscal federalism, particularly as it applies to urban areas. The way that local governments in the American federal system arrange for, pay for, and provide services is intricately intertwined (see, for example, Break 1980; Aronson and Hilley 1986; Ostrom, Bish, and Ostrom 1988; Savas 2000). Only a handful of the functions that city governments typically provide are ones in which the city plays a dominant role in arranging, financing, and delivering the service (for example, police, fire, parks and recreation, libraries, sanitation, utilities). For most other services, particularly those in the areas typically associated with urban problem solving, city governments are partners with the state and/or federal governments and with special districts and authorities. Examples include elementary and secondary education, housing and community development, workforce development, transportation, environmental protection, health and hospitals, and a variety of social programs.

State Aid to Cities

In their extensive study of the fiscal health of central cities, Helen Ladd and John Yinger (1991) pointed out that states provide financial assistance to their cities through two primary means—institutions and grants. By institutions, Ladd and Yinger referred to such practices as allowing city governments access to specific revenue sources, as well as establishing the rates they may set and any exemptions they may grant (for example, property, income, and sales taxes). Fiscal institutions also include laws and provisions that establish service responsibilities (and levels of service), as well as those that set limits on how much debt a city can issue (and by what means and for what purpose). In addition, states provide direct assistance to city governments in various ways. State aid may include unrestricted grants, shared revenues, or grants for specific purposes such as education, welfare, or affordable housing. In addition, some states may distribute some (or all) of its local aid on an equalizing basis (larger grants for poorer cities), whereas others may emphasize per capita distributions.

Ladd and Yinger found that state assistance to central cities varies in form in different states and even in different cities in the same state. They used a standard set of measures to compare the fiscal health of seventy-one central cities to ensure that the variations could be attributed to the underlying structural factors influencing the city's ability to provide services to its residents, and not the budgetary choices made by city officials. These measures included the revenue-raising capacity of the city, the amount it must spend to provide services of average quality, and the balance between its revenue-raising capacity and expenditure requirements.

One of their most important findings was that states did more through fiscal institutions than through grants-in-aid to assist cities in the poorest fiscal condition. Ladd and Yinger determined that state grants and fiscal institutions combined to eliminate about two-thirds of the differences in standardized fiscal health across cities between 1972 and 1982, and that about four-fifths of this equalizing effort was accomplished through institutional assistance.

Table 2-2 reports data from the U.S. Census Bureau's 1998–1999 survey of city government finances and shows that state aid to selected cities ranged from a low of less than 5 percent of general revenue in Atlanta, Dallas, and St. Louis to nearly half or more in Boston, Baltimore, and Detroit. Overall, state aid to cities averaged about 16 percent (median, 10.8 percent) of general revenue for the 230 cities and townships with populations of 100,000 or more included in the survey.

However, the proportion of a city's general revenues made up of state aid can be deceptive and does not necessarily indicate that one state is more responsive to the needs of its big cities than another is. In most cities, the amount of state aid received is largely driven by the state–local distribution of service responsibilities. For example, ten cities (Lowell, Mass.; Syracuse, N.Y.; Springfield, Mass.; Buffalo, N.Y.; New Haven, Conn.; Yonkers, N.Y.; Detroit, Mich.; Bridgeport, Conn.; Hartford, Conn.; and Worcester, Mass.) received more than half of their general revenues from state governments. All ten cities had a comparable proportion of their general expenditures earmarked for education, health, and welfare programs.

Table 2-2 shows support for this pattern, as cities with higher proportions of state aid tend to spend a greater proportion of their revenues on education and aid to the poor than do cities that receive less state aid.[1] The importance of this finding is that in many cities state aid goes to agencies outside the city government (for example, independent school districts, public hospital authorities, transit authorities, county welfare departments) that directly serve city residents, whereas in some cities state aid for these services goes directly to the city governments responsible for providing the services. One must therefore exercise extreme caution in comparing the relative responsiveness of state governments to needy cities (see, for example, Stein 1981; Pelissero 1984; Stein and Hamm 1987; Rich 1993, 128–131).

In addition to examining the amount of state aid to local governments, it is also important to look at the actions states have taken to limit taxing and spending. In 1978, voters in California approved passage of Proposition 13, which reduced property taxes by about 57 percent. The measure limited tax rates to no more than 1 percent of property value and prohibited increases in assessed valuations by more than 2 percent per year unless the property was sold. In addition, Proposition 13 required that all state tax increases be approved by at least a two-thirds vote of the state legislature and that local tax rates could not increase unless they were approved by a popular vote (Fox n.d.). Over the next two years, voters in forty-three states adopted new limitations on property taxes or authorized new property tax relief measures (Stansel 1994). The revolt also spread to other taxes. Stansel reports that between 1978 and 1982, fifteen states reduced income taxes, ten indexed their personal income taxes, seven eliminated gift taxes, and six repealed their inheritance taxes. Also, during this same time period twenty states instituted limits on spending.

The tax revolt that swept the country over the past three decades is popularly perceived as a citizen-led effort made possible through the use of ballot-box democracy tools such as the initiative and referendum. However, Hoene (2001) points out that "state legislatures have been just as likely to limit local property taxes through statutory constraints on rate limits, levies and assessment practices." He notes that the majority of tax and expenditure limitations adopted since 1978 have been the result of legislative actions, including forty of the fifty-seven approved in the November 2000 elections. He adds that these actions have resulted in a dramatic decline in property tax revenues, which dropped from 56 percent of municipal own-source revenues in 1962 to 29 percent in 1997. Among the consequences of the decline in these revenues have been a shift in the tax burden to lower-income households as a result of greater use of regressive revenue sources such as sales taxes and user charges, greater volatility of local revenues to fluctuations in economic conditions, and increased fiscal strain on many public school districts.

Federal Aid to Cities

One of the most important domestic policy developments over the past forty years has been the creation of a complex set of federal fiscal policy instruments. Most prominent have been grants-in-aid, which have increased from $7 billion in 1960 to nearly $300 billion in 2000. During this same period federal grants as a percentage of total federal outlays doubled, rising from 7.6 percent in 1960 to 15.9 percent in 2000. Today federal grants account for about a quarter of every dollar spent by state and local governments, down slightly from a peak of 30.4 percent in 1980.

A grant-in-aid is the payment of funds from one level of government (for example, federal) to another (state and/or local), generally for a specified purpose, with "strings," or conditions attached and often requirements for matching funds from the recipient jurisdiction (U.S. ACIR 1978). Examples of strings include both procedural requirements (for example, environmental review, equal opportunity, citizen participation) and substantive ones (restricting the use of funds to certain types of programs or activities). The grant-in-aid has evolved over time to become a fairly flexible policy instrument that has enabled the federal government to pursue a wide variety of objectives, including stimulating action at the state and/or local level where none had existed before, guaranteeing a minimum level of service, promoting equalization of resources by targeting assistance to needy jurisdictions, and encouraging innovative responses to important public problems, to name but a few (Wright 1968).

Federal grants-in-aid have several characteristics that affect the degree of flexibility recipient governments will have in carrying out activities (U.S. ACIR 1978). Traditionally, grants have been classified as either categorical grants (spending limited to a specific category or purpose) or block grants (spending permitted at the discretion of the recipient government within a broad range of activities such as housing and community development, job training, or health). General-purpose grants, such as the general revenue-sharing program that operated between 1972 and 1986 (Nathan, Manvela, and Calkins1975; Nathan and Adams 1977; Wallin 1998), have the fewest restrictions and typically require only that funds be spent for government purposes.

Grants also differ in how they are awarded. Project grants are awarded on a discretionary basis by federal departments and agencies, based on an application and review process. Formula grants are distributed on the basis of a legislatively prescribed formula or an administrative regulation to all jurisdictions entitled to assistance (those that meet the requirements as defined in the program's authorizing statute).

A third important characteristic of grant programs is whether they involve payments to jurisdictions (state and local governments) or to individuals (for example, medical care, public assistance, housing support), though the latter generally involve state and local governments as administering entities for individual benefit programs. In fiscal 2000, payments to individuals represented about two-thirds of all federal grant outlays (64.1 percent), which was nearly double their share in 1980 (35.7 percent). Other important features are whether the recipient government must contribute matching funds to the program, maintain its existing level of spending in the program area (maintenance of effort), and/or meet specified planning, coordination, and public participation requirements, such as conduct one or more public hearings and/or establish a citizen advisory committee.

Richard Nathan (1983, 48), an astute observer of the behavior of state and local governments under various federal grant-in-aid programs, notes that "a grant-in-aid is the product of a political bargaining process, not just in Washington where the grant is created, but also at the state and local levels where it is executed. The best way to think about this process is that there is a horizontal policy bargaining process, which consists of decision making about policy goals and instruments for the country as a whole, and a vertical dimension, involving the way in which a particular grant is defined and executed by individual recipient jurisdictions. The larger the grant, the more important it is to consider both dimensions."

A study by the U.S. General Accounting Office (1996) identified 633 separate grant-in-aid programs, of which 617 (97.5 percent) were categorical programs and sixteen were block grants. According to the GAO study, the categorical programs accounted for 75 percent of fiscal year 1994 obligations, and the block grant programs represented 25 percent. Almost 90 percent of federal funds were distributed through formula grant programs in fiscal 2000, about the same as fiscal 1987. Only two-thirds of federal funds were distributed by formula in fiscal 1975 (U.S. GAO 1987).

Table 2-3, which updates a recent analysis by Mollenkopf (1998), reports the distribution of federal grant outlays for urban assistance by program category for 1978 (the high-water mark in federal grant outlays), for 1992 (the last year of the Reagan–Bush era), and for 2000 (the last year of the Clinton administration). Emphasis is warranted on several important points regarding the changing character of federal aid during this period and the implications of those changes for city governments.

Table 2-2 Finances of Selected City Governments, 1998–1999 (in millions of dollars)

	1999 Population (thousands)	Percentage of General Revenue From			Percentage of General Expenditures For		
		State government	Federal government	Own sources	Education	Aid to poor[a]	Education and poverty
Dallas	1,076	2.1	3.8	94.0	0.0	4.4	4.4
Denver	499	9.3	1.5	89.2	0.0	14.0	14.0
Seattle	537	8.2	4.5	86.6	0.0	6.5	6.5
St. Louis	339	4.3	9.8	85.8	0.0	11.5	11.5
Atlanta	404	0.9	5.4	85.6	0.0	0.8	0.8
Los Angeles	3,598	9.0	6.9	81.4	0.3	4.6	4.9
Cleveland	496	13.9	7.4	78.7	0.0	12.4	12.4
Chicago	2,802	18.3	7.7	74.0	0.0	9.9	9.9
Phoenix	1,198	21.5	6.7	69.6	0.9	4.6	5.5
San Francisco	746	30.9	6.5	62.4	2.3	28.5	30.8
New York	7,420	33.1	4.7	62.0	25.5	32.1	57.6
Philadelphia	1,436	28.5	10.2	58.2	0.0	32.7	32.7
Boston	555	45.4	3.2	51.3	33.5	13.3	46.8
Milwaukee	578	42.1	9.0	48.7	0.0	14.9	14.9
Baltimore	646	46.3	5.5	45.5	39.3	9.4	48.7
Detroit	970	53.2	8.5	37.7	42.5	7.9	50.4
Memphis	604	35.5	2.3	33.2	50.6	2.5	53.1
Mean	315	15.8	4.9	76.7	5.9	10.0	15.9
Median	176	10.8	4.5	81.0	0.0	7.6	8.9

Source: U.S. Bureau of the Census, *Government Finances, 1998–1999*, Table 4 (Washington, D.C.: U.S. Government Printing Office, 2000).

Note: Cities are ranked by percentage of general revenues from own sources. Means and medians are based on municipal and township governments with populations of 100,000 or more (*n* = 230).

[a] Aid to poor includes expenditures for public welfare, hospitals, health, and housing and community development.

First, as noted in more detail elsewhere (Nathan 1987; Caraley 1992; Rich 1993; Conlan 1998), the Reagan–Bush era resulted in a significant restructuring of the composition of federal grant-in-aid programs. Payments to jurisdictions—primarily city governments—were cut sharply, while payments to individuals—primarily Medicaid—substantially increased. Overall, while total federal grant outlays increased by about 13 percent between 1978 and 1992 (in constant dollars), payments to individuals more than doubled. As Table 2-3 indicates, during this period grant outlays for infrastructure (except highways) were cut by half; general fiscal assistance was essentially eliminated; and substantial cuts were sustained in the community services and social services block grants and employment and training programs. At the same time, federal outlays for assistance to needy individuals increased by 122 percent, with the sharpest gains recorded in the Medicaid, WIC (supplemental nutrition for women, infants, and children), and Earned Income Tax Credit programs.

Second, while the Clinton administration restored funding for several existing grant programs that provided aid to jurisdictions and added a few new ones, federal outlays for grant programs providing assistance to or through city governments and agencies in fiscal 2000 were about 14 percent less (in constant dollars) than the figure reported for fiscal 1978. Between 1992 and 2000, federal grant outlays for infrastructure (52.2 percent) and social services (43.6 percent) increased faster than outlays for payments to needy individuals (31.1 percent). Major increases in grant funding during the Clinton years took place in the areas of public and low-income housing (238 percent), assistance to the homeless (438 percent), and justice assistance and law enforcement (376 percent). Funding for programs traditionally popular during Democratic administrations, such as education for the disadvantaged (18 percent), environmental protection (–3 percent), and employment and training services (–26 percent), grew more slowly than the overall trend or continued to decline, although at a slower rate than during the Reagan–Bush years.

Third, and perhaps most important, although total federal grant outlays in fiscal 2000 were nearly 50 percent greater (in constant dollars) than in fiscal 1978, the vast majority of federal urban assistance today is not being administered by city governments or local agencies traditionally aligned with city hall (for example, school districts, public housing authorities, transit authorities, airports, employment and training agencies). Indeed, only three of the thirty-one largest federal grant programs in fiscal 2001 provided funds directly to city governments (Community Development Block Grants, HOME Investment Partnership, and Community-Oriented Policing Services). Overall, the share of federal outlays for urban assistance directed to city governments or local agencies declined from 51 percent in 1978 to 24 percent in 2000. Thus, much of the federal aid reaching city residents—in the form of payments to needy individuals—is being provided in most instances through county departments and agencies.

This disconnect between place-oriented programs, which tend to be administered by city government agencies, and people-oriented programs, generally under the control of state and county agencies, poses a formidable challenge for many urban areas that seek to foster a more comprehensive approach to addressing problems of persistent poverty and neighborhood decline. Although this disconnect is by no means a new development, the implications of the assignment of functional responsibilities and authority at the local level has been intensified by recent shifts in the composition of federal grant outlays.

Some mayors have moved to capitalize (politically as well as economically) on the new federal grant environment. In 2000, for example, Chicago Mayor Richard Daley launched the creation of Mayor Daley's Earned Income Tax Credit Outreach Initiative, a citywide outreach campaign designed to educate Chicago taxpayers about the federal EITC and encourage them to file for the credit. According to a Brookings Institution analysis (Berube and Forman 2001), more than 262,000 Chicago residents brought $430 million into the city in 1998 through EITC tax refunds. Mayor Daley maintains that as much as an additional $100 million could be brought to the city and its neighborhoods if every eligible Chicago resident filed for an EITC credit.

Federal grants-in-aid have received the most attention, but other federal fiscal policy instruments such as loans, loan guarantees, and tax credits also have important implications for city governments. For example, the Economic Development Administration, the Farmers Home Administration, the Small Business Administration, and the U.S. Department of Housing and Urban Development all administer a variety of programs that provide loans and loan guarantees to assist local communities in attracting and retaining businesses and promoting economic development. The Empowerment Zones and Enterprise Communities Program and the subsequent Renewal Communities initiative have extended a variety of tax credits to selected cities to help stimulate business development and job creation in distressed neighborhoods. The Low Income Housing Tax Credit is the nation's major means of financing affordable rental housing.

The federal government has also played an important role in state and local finance by exempting the interest earned on state and local bonds from income-tax liability, saving state and local governments billions of dollars in interest charges they would have had to pay at market rates. However, as nontraditional tax-exempt debt began to mount and federal deficits rose in the early 1980s, Congress began to reconsider the tax-exempt status of state and local bonds. Beginning in the mid-1970s, the use of municipal bonds expanded beyond traditional infrastructure purposes to include new, private purpose tax-exempt borrowing such as industrial revenue bonds to subsidize the cost of business development and expansion (in effect, passing the interest subsidy on to private businesses and developers); mortgage revenue bonds to subsidize the interest costs of first-time home buyers; and pollution control bonds to assist businesses in complying with environmental requirements. By the mid-1980s, general obligation debt constituted only about 25 percent of the tax-exempt market, down from about 65 percent at the end of the 1960s (Sbragia 1996, 168). One study reported that private purpose tax-exempt borrowing accounted for nearly 60 percent of all tax-exempt debt issued in 1983 (Sbragia 1996, 172).

While Congress had previously placed caps on the volume of tax-exempt debt that could be issued and also tightened restrictions on the public purposes to which such debt was directed, several major pieces of legislation were enacted in the 1980s, culminating in the Tax Reform Act of 1986, which placed significant constraints on the use of tax-exempt financing by local governments. The 1986 legislation established a volume cap on the total amount of tax-exempt borrowing that states and localities could undertake for private purposes and entirely eliminated some forms of this borrowing (for example, industrial parks, sports stadiums, convention centers, nongovernmental office buildings, and most parking facilities). Sbragia (1996, 192) reports that the 1989 cap was set at $14.4 billion for all state and local government private purpose, tax-exempt borrowing, whereas the total amount of borrowing for these purposes in 1984 was $66 billion.

Regulatory Federalism

Another important policy tool used by federal and state governments to influence the actions of local governments is regulation (U.S. ACIR 1984). Although the grant-in-aid has been the primary means by which the federal government has sought to encourage state and local governments to pursue national policy objectives, Nivola (1999) points out that rising federal deficits and fiscal retrenchment during the 1980s led to a shift toward more regulatory approaches that did not involve the direct expenditure of federal funds (Figure 2-1). By the beginning of the 1990s, the term mandates had become widespread in domestic policy discourse, and state and local government officials were mobilizing to seek relief from the burden of unfunded mandates.

Mandate is actually a general term used to refer to a wide variety of regulatory tools that higher levels of government (federal and state) can use to shape or restrict the actions of lower levels of government (state and local). A 1984 study by the U.S. Advisory Commission on Intergovernmental Relations identified four types of mandates:

1. *Direct Orders.* These mandates require state or local government action under the threat of criminal or civil penalties for noncompliance. Examples include the Equal Employment Opportunity Act of 1972, which prohibits job discrimination by state and local governments on the basis of race, color, religion,

Table 2-3 Federal Outlays for Urban Assistance, Fiscal 1978–2000 (in thousands of 1996 dollars)

Program category	1978	1992	2000	Percentage Change		
				1978–1992	1992–2000	1978–2000
To or through city governments and local agencies						
Infrastructure						
Community and economic development	14,018	3,803	5,055	-72.9	32.9	-63.9
Urban mass transportation	4,690	3,922	4,894	-16.4	24.8	4.3
Public and low-income housing	1,528	2,642	8,930	72.9	238.0	484.4
Highways[a]	13,512	16,651	23,411	23.2	40.6	73.3
Airports	1,243	1,833	1,509	47.5	-17.7	21.5
Environmental protection	7,048	3,331	3,244	-52.7	-2.6	-54.0
Subtotal	42,039	32,181	47,043	-23.4	46.2	11.9
Subtotal minus highways	28,527	15,531	23,632	-45.6	52.2	-17.2
General fiscal assistance[b]	19,589	861	813	-95.6	-5.6	-95.8
Social services						
Community and social services	8,174	4,735	4,193	-42.1	-11.4	-48.7
Justice assistance and law enforcement	1,245	931	4,426	—	375.5	—
Education for the disadvantaged	5,896	6,720	7,911	14.0	17.7	34.2
School improvement programs	644	1,492	3,122	131.9	109.2	385.1
Special education, vocational education	2,028	3,384	5,711	66.9	68.8	181.6
Children and family services, child care, foster care	2,475	7,202	13,798	191.0	91.6	457.6
Substance abuse and mental health	1,338	1,949	1,795	45.7	-7.9	34.1
Employment and training	10,181	4,366	3,252	-57.1	-25.5	-68.1
Subtotal	31,980	30,779	44,208	-3.8	43.6	38.2
To needy individuals concentrated in cities[c]						
Medicaid	23,618	74,364	109,602	214.9	47.4	364.1
Supplemental security disability income	11,676	18,900	27,429	61.9	45.1	134.9
Welfare (AFDC/TANF)	14,138	16,558	17,074	17.1	3.1	20.8
Food stamps	12,161	24,997	17,004	105.6	-32.0	39.8
Child nutrition, WIC	6,713	9,528	12,225	41.9	28.3	82.1
Housing assistance (certificates, vouchers)	6,477	17,859	15,569	175.7	-12.8	140.4
Earned income tax credit	1,948	8,053	24,258	313.3	201.2	1145.1
Subtotal	76,730	170,259	223,162	121.9	31.1	190.8

Source: *Budget of the United States Government, FY 2003, Historical Tables*, Tables 10.1, 11.3, 12.3 (Washington, D.C.: U.S. Government Printing Office, 2000).

[a] Most highway aid is not spent within city boundaries.

[b] Includes antirecession fiscal assistance, general revenue sharing, and impact aid.

[c] Includes payments to state and local governments to finance benefits paid to individuals.

Figure 2-1 Federal Discretionary Budget Outlays and Off-Budget Cost of Federal Regulatory Mandates, 1977–2000

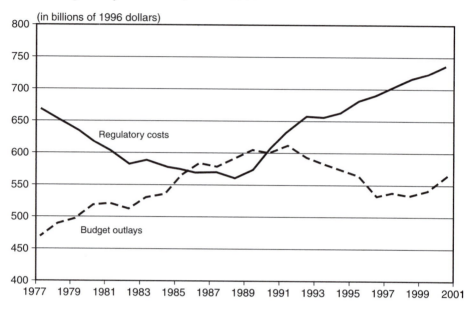

Source: U.S. Small Business Administration, Office of the Chief Counsel for Advocacy, *The Changing Burden of Regulation, Paperwork, and Tax Compliance on Small Business: A Report to Congress,* Washington, D.C., October 1995, Table 3; *Budget of the United States Government, Historical Tables* (Washington, D.C.: U.S. Government Printing Office, 2002).

gender, and national origin, and the Americans with Disabilities Act of 1990, which requires all public buildings and facilities to be accessible to all persons with physical disabilities.

2. *Crosscutting Requirements.* These mandates apply to all or many federal agencies and their assistance programs. Examples include the nondiscrimination provisions of the Civil Rights Act and requirements for an environmental impact statement called for by the National Environmental Policy Act. In short, these are examples of the strings that are attached to the receipt of federal aid.

3. *Crossover Sanctions.* These are mandates that threaten the termination or reduction of aid provided under one program if the requirements of another program have not been met. Like crosscutting requirements, these mandates are tied to federal grant-in-aid programs. In this sense, the penalty crosses over from one program to another. For example, the Education for All Handicapped Children Act of 1975, as amended, authorizes the federal government to withhold funding

from other federal education programs to schools that do not provide educational services appropriate to the needs of children with disabilities.

4. *Partial Preemption.* These mandates establish national standards but delegate administration to state or local governments if they adopt standards equivalent to the national ones. Examples include the Water Quality Act of 1965, the Clean Air Act amendments of 1970, and the Occupational Safety and Health Act of 1970.

In a 1998 study on the subject, Posner added two additional types of mandates:

1. *Total Preemption.* These mandates totally prohibit state and local governments from taking action in a particular area. Examples include preemption of state and local governments placing restrictions on cigarette advertising.

2. *Major Program Specific Grant Conditions.* These requirements are attached to major federal grant programs that mandate significant fiscal and policy actions by recipient governments as a precondition for receiving aid. For example, the U.S. Department of Housing and Urban Development requires the reduction of lead-based paint in all housing receiving federal assistance, as mandated by the Lead-Based Paint Poisoning Prevention Act of 1982, as amended.

When the first major wave of federal mandates were enacted in the 1960s and 1970s in such areas as civil rights, education, and the environment, it was generally felt that many federal grant programs provided assistance for meeting these requirements. Some, for example, noted that General Revenue Sharing was created in part to compensate state and local governments for the rise in regulatory action. Nonetheless, state and local officials complained of the federal government's unfunded mandates. New York City mayor (and former congressman) Edward Koch (1980, 542), for example, wrote in 1980 of the "maze of complex statutory and administrative directives [that] has come to threaten both the initiative and the financial health of local governments throughout the country." Koch noted that New York City "is driven by 47 federal and state mandates. The total cost of meeting these requirements over the next four years will be $711 million in capital expenditures, $6.25 billion in expense-budget dollars, and $1.66 billion in lost revenue."

As Posner (1998) recounts, concerns about unfunded mandates accelerated in the early 1990s, culminating in a National Unfunded Mandates Day, held in 1993 to publicize the fiscal impacts of unfunded mandates on state and local governments. The U.S. Advisory Commission on Intergovernmental Relations had issued a report that year indicating that Congress had passed more regulatory legislation during the 1980s than in the 1970s (quoted in Posner 1998, 8). A year later, in 1994, the Republican Party included mandate relief as one of the planks of its Contract with America, and in 1995 Congress passed the Unfunded Mandates Reform Act. The act had two primary purposes: first, to ensure that Congress had adequate information about the likely fiscal impacts of mandates before making a decision to impose them; and second, to encourage the national government to provide the necessary funding to meet the costs of federal mandates (U.S. CBO 2001).

A report by the Congressional Budget Office (2001) found that the Unfunded Mandates Reform Act has been successful in achieving its objectives. During the first five years following enactment of the reform legislation, the percentage of bills with intergovernmental mandates, whose costs were estimated to exceed $50 million (the statutory threshold for a detailed cost estimate), declined steadily, and only two out of eleven bills were enacted into legislation. The CBO report also found that in several instances legislators revised their proposals to lower the estimated costs of complying with the federal mandate before enacting them.

Mandates do not come from Washington alone. State governments are also a significant source of unfunded mandates, and, like many other matters, a state's penchant for imposing mandates varies widely. For example, Berman (2002) notes that a study of Ohio estimated that about one in twelve laws passed in that state imposed an unfunded mandate on local governments, whereas a similar study in Tennessee found that one in four laws imposed an unfunded mandate. A 1994 study by the National Conference of State Legislatures reported that local government officials found most troublesome the state mandates issued in the areas of personnel policies (state-established wage levels, hours or working conditions, retirement benefits), environmental standards, service levels, and tax base exemptions (for example, exemption of business inventories from local property tax base, exemption of food and medicine from local sales tax; Radatz 1996, 5).

Although firm estimates of the costs of unfunded state mandates are difficult to come by, one recent study estimated that unfunded mandates in Connecticut accounted for half of all municipal expenditures (Berman 2002, 49). In 1972, California became the first state to provide reimbursement provisions for certain types of state mandates. Currently, some type of mandate restraint program exists in twenty-eight states, with thirteen states providing full reimbursement for all mandates (Radatz 1996). Ten of the twenty-eight states with mandate restraint programs adopted their programs in 1990 or later.

Judicial Federalism

Over the past three decades, there have been several notable developments involving the federal courts and local governments (U.S. ACIR 1986). Two such developments warrant emphasis because of their impact on the intergovernmental context. First, the U.S. Supreme Court has considered a number of cases concerned with the balance of power between the federal government and the states (and, by implication, local governments). Similarly, state supreme courts have been called upon to settle disputes about the proper balance of authority and autonomy between state and local governments. Second, the courts have become an increasingly popular venue for policy advocates to seek redress through litigation. As Charles M. Haar (1996) notes, "Over the past two decades, courts have been drawn more and more into the reorganization of public institutions that are failing in their designated missions."

A factor contributing to the increased litigation involving state and local governments during the past three decades was the increasing complexity of the domestic policy environment. The intricate interconnections among federal, state, and local governments were manifested in patterns of government organization, financing, and regulatory activities, as summarized above. For example, the U.S. Advisory Commission on Intergovernmental Relations (1993) summarized the reach of federal courts on the actions of state and local governments, noting that during calendar year 1994 the federal courts handed down 3,500 decisions involving state and local governments that were related to more than 100 different federal laws (Radatz 1996).

Interpreting Federalism: The Supreme Court and State and Local Governments

One of the distinctive features of the American federal system is the existence of concurrent powers shared by the national and state governments. Throughout the nation's history the U.S. Supreme Court has been called upon to interpret the Constitution to determine whether a specific governmental action was more appropriately the province of the national government or of the states (or, by extension, localities). As Wise and O'Leary (1992, 560) point out, "Federalism analysis is inherently complex because the courts cannot and do not rely on one basis in the Constitution to decide issues of the relative powers of the federal and state governments but rather must choose and assess tradeoffs among different sections of the Constitution and various principles of constitutional interpretation." These include, for example, the Necessary and Proper Clause, the Commerce Clause, the Supremacy Clause, the Taxation and Spending Clauses, and the Tenth (rights reserved to the states), the Eleventh (suits against the states), the Fourteenth (due process, equal protection), and the Fifteenth (voting rights protections) Amendments.

Federalism cases can be traced back to the early years of the nation. (For example, in the 1819 decision *McCulloch v. Maryland*, the Supreme Court established the doctrine of implied national powers and the principles of national supremacy.) Since the

1970s, a number of important federalism cases have been brought before the Supreme Court. As Wise and O'Leary (1992, 570) observed, based on their review of Supreme Court cases during this period, the trend has generally been toward shifting power from state and local governments to Congress and federal agencies. The authors conclude that "taken together, these cases have increased the constraints on state and local government decision makers and have affected their abilities to administer programs, to initiate adaptive changes, and to deal with groups who see their interests better represented in federal, rather than state or local, policies."

Beginning in the 1990s, the Supreme Court issued a series of rulings that have encouraged a shift in policymaking away from the federal government and toward state (and local) governments through constitutional interpretations that lend strength to a states' rights position. As Lens (2001) points out, a consequence of this shift is that it is now more difficult for the federal government to enact progressive legislation. Several cases decided by the Court, for example, have overturned federal laws that would have required state and local governments to take actions in specific policy areas. Among these are the disposal of nuclear waste (*New York v. United States,* 1992), gun control in schools (*United States v. Lopez,* 1995), background checks for weapons purchasers (*Printz v. United States,* 1997), and violence against women (*United States v. Morrison,* 1999).

Federal District Courts and Local Governments

Although the actions of the federal district and appellate courts have received less scholarly attention than the Supreme Court has, they continue to play an important (and perhaps more frequent) role in urban politics (Rose 1988). Exceptions include Joseph Cooper's (1988) comparative study of remedial decrees issued by federal district judges in the areas of schools, prisons, housing, employment, and mental health facilities, and two excellent case analyses of the federal courts and subsidized housing—the Gautreaux case in Chicago (Rubinowitz and Rosenbaum 2000) and the Mount Laurel cases in New Jersey (Haar 1996).

Federal judges in dozens of cities across the country have appointed special masters to oversee a wide variety of local government departments and agencies, including schools, police departments, public housing authorities, jails and prisons, mental health agencies, homeless shelters, and the like. In some cities, such as Los Angeles and New York, there may be multiple judicial orders in effect concurrently.

One reporter recently quipped that the voters of Los Angeles "would be better served if they appointed a Grand Master of Consent Decrees," as opposed to electing a new mayor. A consent decree is a voluntary agreement between the parties that settles a lawsuit before it goes to trial. Kathleen Connell, who ran for mayor in 2001, noted that "we're becoming a city run by federal consent decrees. We're the only city

I know of that operates like a ward of the federal courts. I don't feel like a ward of the state as much as one of the Tweedy farm hens in 'Chicken Run.' It seems like all our elected leaders have gone on holiday" (Robison 2001).

The above quote was in reference to a spate of consent decrees in Los Angeles that included the following:

- Since 1974, the Los Angeles Fire Department has been under a consent decree requiring recruits to the department to live within the city limits.
- In 1986, the city's Bureau of Sanitation agreed to a consent decree with the U.S. Environmental Protection Agency to end a lawsuit concerning pollution of Santa Monica Bay. City officials agreed to undertake $2 billion in improvements to the Hyperion sewage treatment plan to comply with the terms of the decree.
- In 1993, the Los Angeles County Sheriff's Department signed a consent decree ending a long-running class action suit that alleged sexual harassment and discrimination in the department's hiring practices. The decree required the department to spend $2.5 million to improve working conditions and promotion opportunities for women.
- In 1996, the Los Angeles Unified School District signed a consent decree to end a class action suit filed by a parent who charged her daughter had been wrongfully held back a grade (twice) because she had been denied enrollment in a special education program. School officials estimate the decree may cost as much as $69 million a year when fully implemented.
- Also in 1996, the Metropolitan Transit Authority signed a consent decree that required the MTA to cease transporting passengers in older, overcrowded, poorly maintained buses. The agency estimates the cost of the decree will reach more than $730 million by 2004, including the cost of acquiring and operating new buses, legal fees, and salary for the special master.
- In December 1996, the City Council and the American Civil Liberties Union entered into a consent decree concerning hiring and promotion practices in the Los Angeles Police Department. City officials estimate it will cost $35 million over the next eighteen years to comply with the hiring and promotion of women and minority police officers called for by the decree.
- In November 2000, the city entered into a consent decree with the U.S. Department of Justice that would put the city's police department under court order to implement a series of reforms designed to eliminate a "pattern or practice" of civil rights abuses by LAPD officers. Under the terms of the decree, the department will be required to collect and report data to determine the extent of racial profiling and to install a computer system to track performance evaluations, complaints, disciplinary actions, and other matters pertaining to the department's officers (Daunt 2001).

New York City also has a number of judicial orders, many of them dating back two decades or more, that direct the activities of several municipal agencies. For example, New York City officials agreed in 1981 to a consent decree to end a lawsuit brought by the Coalition for the Homeless that required the city to provide free shelter for all homeless men. Ross Sandler and David Schoenbrod (1994) report that since the case was originally filed in the late 1970s, the number of homeless single adults seeking shelter has more than tripled (from two thousand to seven thousand) and, despite the fact that the city spends approximately $20,000 per year to shelter each of them, "most observers agree that conditions in the shelters are terrible." A primary reason for this, according to the authors, is the court order that constrains the city's ability to make changes to the shelter system. Sandler and Schoenbrod also note that "the court continues to manage the city's shelter system in exquisite detail, right down to the number of toilets and showers each shelter is required to have." They add that a preliminary study by Mayor Rudolph Giuliani's administration estimated that the city uses a quarter of its tax revenues to comply with the ten largest decrees and mandates.

State Supreme Courts and Local Governments

State supreme courts have also been active over the past twenty-five years, issuing numerous rulings to apply newly amended provisions of state constitutions to a number of important issues concerning state–local relations (Tarr 1994). The U.S. Advisory Commission on Intergovernmental Relations (1993) noted that several significant rulings were issued by state supreme courts between 1978 and 1992. These concerned, among others, the capacity of local governments to sue the state, the constitutionality of local or special legislation, immunity, and interlocal cooperation. Although the U.S. ACIR (1993, 58) concluded that "the patterns of state supreme court opinions exhibit a striking continuity with the historical ambivalence toward the policy of local self-government," it did find several instances in which state supreme courts issued rulings that affirmed or advanced the autonomy of local governments. For example, state high courts in New York, Colorado, Utah, and Massachusetts, issued decisions during the study period that held that "local government units possess at least a minimal attribute of structural autonomy—i.e., the capacity to have constitutional rights and to invoke them against infringing state agencies and instrumentalities" (U.S. ACIR 1993, 51). The U.S. ACIR study also noted that many states had issued rulings that interpreted home-rule powers as giving the upper hand to local governments on matters pertaining to local government structure and procedure. However, the study also reported that a number of states had rejected similar claims based on home-rule authority, frequently by ruling that state activity—direct or tangential—permitted preemption of a home-rule charter or ordinance.

Analytic Frameworks: Understanding City Politics in the Intergovernmental Context

As this chapter has indicated, the federal and state governments have many policy tools to broaden or limit the policy choices that city governments can make, and these tools are combined and interconnected in a variety of intricate combinations across the local government landscape. This section summarizes some of the major analytic frameworks that have been employed to understand the dynamics of urban policy-making in an intergovernmental context.

As Thomas Anton (1989, 19) argues in his analysis of American federalism, "Efforts to impose some alternative intellectual order on this large and diverse group of governments has exposed the enormous difficulty of stating generalizations that are not subject to endless qualification—except, of course, for the truism that politics and policy 'differ from state to state.'" He adds that "some scholars have reacted to the size and complexity of our system by rejecting the existence of comprehensible patterns of activity that can be defined, described, and understood. For them, federal politics is so varied that patterns seldom emerge, or if they do, they seldom last long enough to explain very much." Anton argues for a different approach, maintaining that "patterns do exist and they can be described." The key, he states, is to "focus our attention on the behavior of public officials," and the "observation of behavior must be guided by analytic concepts appropriate to the task of discovering behavioral patterns within masses of particular details."

This section provides a brief overview of some of the more important analytic frameworks that have been used in studying urban politics and policy in the American federal system. Much of the early urban politics scholarship was based on a pluralism paradigm. As Judge (1995, 13) notes, "[P]luralism has been remarkably influential in the study of urban politics. If anything, given the developments within pluralism itself and among its critics, there is the danger that in the 1990s 'we are all pluralists now.'" He adds that while "there is little agreement to the defining characteristics of 'pluralism,'" the "'core' or 'principal tenets' of urban pluralism" would include, among others, such characteristics as fragmented or dispersed power, dispersed inequalities, different outcomes across policy areas due to differences in the composition of actors, decision-making processes, and the distribution of power. Much of the urban scholarship from the 1950s to the 1970s focused on questions of political power and who exercised it in urban communities, spawning a debate between pluralists, who maintained that power was dispersed, and elitists, who held that power was exercised by a small group of community leaders (see, for example, Polsby 1980). The scholarship defining that debate, however, largely looked at the city in isolation and failed to incorporate the ways in which state and/or federal actions influenced the outcomes and distributional impacts of local decisions.

As federal grant-in-aid programs began to proliferate in the 1960s and continued to rise in importance during the 1970s, when many of the Nixon administration's New Federalism programs distributed an increasing amount of federal aid directly to city governments, scholars began to pay more attention to intergovernmental politics, especially those revolving around the implementation of federal programs (Pressman and Wildavsky 1984; Pressman 1975). Much of this scholarship, however, tended to focus almost exclusively on the role of mayors and their entrepreneurial uses of federal resources. Some scholars, such as Jeffrey Pressman (1975), recognized that "by stimulating mobilization and organization in the black community, federal programs have thus helped to alter the political landscape of the city." However, that influence was largely confined to what Pressman (p. 15) called "pseudo-arenas," where bargaining "involves no meaningful changes for the participants and does not have an impact on the outside world." Scholars from the federalism and intergovernmental relations field also embraced the pluralist, bargaining paradigm (see, for example, Derthick 1970; Ingram 1977; Hale and Palley 1981; Brown, Fossett and Palmer 1984), although this research was also largely shaped by the notion of separate arenas of federal programs and city politics.

In a very important and controversial work, Paul Peterson (1981, 210) argued that city politics was limited politics and pointed out that "the contentious aspects of local politics consist, in the main, of petty disputes over patronage, ethnic appointments, and service delivery." Peterson's thesis was that economic limits (the inability of cities to control the movement of labor and capital) trump all others, and therefore cities could never be effective agents for pursuing redistributive policies that seek to improve the well-being of disadvantaged residents. Peterson maintained that because of these limits there was—and needed to be—a clear separation of functions across levels of government that relegated city politics to an irrelevant arena.

Much of the urban scholarship that followed Peterson's influential work was built around what Stone (1987, 5) described as "the dual theme that local politics matters and that politics is shaped by the division of labor between state and market," leading Stone to conclude that "how the governing coalition is constituted and what kind of accommodation it represents are centrally important questions." The publication in 1989 of Stone's *Regime Politics* spawned the ascendancy of a political economy approach to the study of urban politics, with an emphasis on understanding "the informal arrangements that surround and complement the formal workings of governmental authority." But much like the earlier community power studies, the urban regime paradigm has largely examined cities from an internal perspective and focused on business–government relations. When external actors are brought into the analysis, they are typically used to illustrate the ability of mayors to mobilize external resources to carry out projects consistent with the interests and needs of the urban regime, much as the pluralists and elitists had done two decades ago.

In their detailed study of politics and policy outcomes in ten California cities over two decades (1960 to 1980), Browning, Marshall, and Tabb (1984) developed a more integrative approach that weaves together issues of federalism and urban politics. Their analysis of the struggle of blacks and Hispanics for equality demonstrates how intervention of the federal courts as well as federal and state agencies affected policy outcomes in the communities they studied. Moreover, they found that intervention of higher-level governments was neither consistent across cities nor consistent in the direction of the position taken. Browning, Marshall, and Tabb (1984, 148) found, for example, "Whereas black activists tried to use the courts to force Vallejo to allocate more city services to black residents, courts were used to pull the city of Berkeley in the opposite direction. . . . Whereas in Vallejo the authority of HUD was engaged to obtain representation of blacks on city boards, HUD in the late seventies scolded and threatened Berkeley with defunding of several programs, charging that the city gave too much autonomy to citizen boards or was spending more grant funds on social services than regulations permitted."

Thomas Anton further develops this synthesis of local politics and federalism with his concept of benefits coalitions. According to Anton (1989, 30), "Government in the American sense is not some abstract essence, but an agency created to do something for specific groups of people." He adds that "a benefits coalition, accordingly, can be defined as any association of individuals, often representing other individuals, who mobilize to develop, support, and implement government benefit programs." The types of benefits governments distribute, Anton notes, are numerous and include economic benefits (the promotion of economic well-being through tax and spending decisions), juridical benefits (assignment of rights and obligations), as well as symbolic benefits. Anton argues that the system works through the organization of interests into coalitions that have horizontal and vertical components: "Coalitions that are strong enough at one level of government to achieve their desired benefits operate primarily at that level. Coalitions that are too weak to achieve the desired benefits at one level, however, have other options. By seeking allies at higher or lower levels, these coalitions can gain sufficient strength to achieve some or all of the benefits they seek—often in the form of financial grants from a higher- to a lower-level unit (p. 97)."

The benefits coalition approach that Anton advocates allows one to view a very dynamic process in which the composition of coalitions frequently shifts and generally includes participants from multiple levels of government. The importance of this observation is that the fault lines in American urban politics are not necessarily ones that divide power between state and market or by level of government (for example, nation v. state, nation v. city, state v. city), but revolve around interests and the manner in which those interests seek to mobilize governments to respond to their needs and concerns.

Much recent urban scholarship has focused on issues of regionalism and metropolitan land-use reform, particularly as it pertains to smart growth and attempts to rein in urban sprawl (Lewis 1996; Savitch and Vogel 1996; Orfield 1997; Katz 2000). Although Anton's development of the benefits coalition framework may seem more fitting for an analysis of federal social programs, it also has salience for current debates about metropolitan land use. Indeed, as Margaret Weir (2000) observed, one of the key ingredients of the successful adoption of metropolitan-oriented policy initiatives has been the existence of a regional bipartisan coalition. Similarly, Rusk (1999) views building regional coalitions as a key part of a winning strategy for saving urban America.

Conclusion

This chapter has shown that the intergovernmental context has important implications for the decision-making processes and policy outcomes of local governments in urban areas. No longer can we view city politics as an isolated politics, nor can we view federal programs as separate or pseudo-arenas that have little lasting impact on local decision-making processes and the distribution of benefits. Rather, much of what city governments do, whether in policy domains where they are the primary service provider or those in which service provision is shared among different levels of government, is influenced by public officials and institutions at higher levels of government. Also, the opportunities for the exercise of that influence have increased, both in number and type.

As we try to more fully understand the implications of the contemporary intergovernmental context for urban policymaking, several issues are ripe for further investigation and inquiry. Three are briefly summarized below.

First, with the demise of the U.S. Advisory Commission on Intergovernmental Relations in 1996, there is no central repository of data and trends on the American federal system. Although it is widely recognized that a number of developments over the past decade have greatly altered the character of the intergovernmental context—devolution, mandates, increased judicial activism, shifts in the composition and nature of local public spending—the loss of the U.S. ACIR has made it more difficult not only to compare the present with the past but also to compare experiences across selected communities. We need to know more about how developments such as these have affected local governments and the impact of these influences on policy outcomes at the local level.

Second, the increased salience of regional and metropolitan issues concerning topics such as growth and land use, poverty and social policies, and financial disparities suggests the need for further work to examine the dynamics of regional problem solving. While a few areas have received a great deal of attention (for example, Portland, Oregon; Minneapolis–St. Paul; and New York), we need more studies that examine the relationships among government structure and functions, policy tools, and policy outcomes in a greater number of metropolitan areas.

Third, more attention needs to be directed to understanding the consequences and implications of judicial intervention in the operation of local departments and agencies. As discussed above, Los Angeles and New York City have signed several consent decrees that have turned over control of a number of local agencies to the courts and their appointed masters.

If we are to better understand the dynamics of governance in the nation's urban centers, we need to expand the scope of our inquiry to more fully incorporate the intergovernmental context. As this chapter has demonstrated, that context has become more deeply entwined with local institutions and processes and is likely to continue to play a significant role in the resolution of important urban policy issues.

Suggested Readings

Benjamin, Gerald, and Richard P. Nathan. 2001. *Regionalism and Realism: A Study of Governments in the New York Metropolitan Area.* Washington, D.C.: Brookings Institution Press. Using the New York tri-state region as a critical case, the authors describe three different values that can be used to promote equity, efficiency, and competitiveness—and the trade-offs among these competing values that policymakers must balance in crafting effective metropolitan strategies for addressing regional issues.

Burns, Nancy. 1994. *The Formation of American Local Governments.* New York: Oxford University Press. A comprehensive analysis of the creation of local governments—principally municipalities and special districts—and the impacts of these new institutions on local politics. Burns argues that private interests—primarily developers and businesses—have used the creation of local governments to institutionalize racial segregation, maintain low taxes, and gain access to new services.

Dreier, Peter, John Mollenkopf, and Todd Swanstrom. 2001. *Place Matters: Metropolitics for the Twenty-first Century.* Lawrence: University Press of Kansas. This book argues that cities and regions cannot solve the fundamental urban problem of place-based inequalities by themselves, largely because these inequalities are the result of state and federal policies that distort market forces. The authors outline the sources of urban inequalities, identify needed policies, and provide guidance on a political strategy for overcoming city–suburban disparities.

Haar, Charles M. 1996. *Suburbs Under Siege: Race, Space, and Audacious Judges.* Princeton: Princeton University Press. This book focuses on the role of the New Jersey Supreme Court and the development of its Mount Laurel doctrine, which struck down the practice of exclusionary zoning and required suburban municipalities to provide a range of housing choices. The book examines the role of judges and special masters and their strategies for designing remedies and monitoring compliance in communities.

Stephens, G. Ross, and Nelson Wikstrom. 2000. *Metropolitan Government and Governance: Theoretical Perspectives, Empirical Analysis, and the Future.* New York: Oxford University

Press. A comprehensive overview of local and metropolitan governance and its relationship to the larger intergovernmental context. The authors describe a variety of different theoretical perspectives for examining these issues and provide illustrations drawn from case studies of major reforms that highlight the strengths and weaknesses of different approaches to metropolitan problems.

References

Anton, Thomas J. 1989. *American Federalism and Public Policy: How the System Works.* New York: Random House.

Aronson, J. Richard, and John L. Hilley. 1986. *Financing State and Local Governments,* 4th ed. Washington, D.C.: Brookings Institution Press.

Beer, Samuel H. 1977. "A Political Scientist's View of Fiscal Federalism." In *The Political Economy of Fiscal Federalism,* ed. Wallace E. Oates, 21–48. Lexington: Lexington Books.

Benjamin, Gerald, and Richard P. Nathan. 2001. *Regionalism and Realism: A Study of Governments in the New York Metropolitan Area.* Washington, D.C.: Brookings Institution Press.

Berman, David R. 2002. "State–Local Relations: Authority, Finances, Cooperation." In *The Municipal Year Book 2002.* Washington, D.C.: International City/County Management Association.

Berube, Alan, and Benjamin Forman. 2001. "Rewarding Work: The Impact of the Earned Income Tax Credit in Greater Chicago." Washington, D.C.: Brookings Institution, Center on Urban and Metropolitan Policy, EITC Series (November).

Break, George F. 1980. *Financing Government in a Federal System.* Washington, D.C.: Brookings Institution Press.

Brisbin, Richard A., Jr. 1998. "The Reconstitution of American Federalism? The Rehnquist Court and Federal–State Relations, 1991–1997." *Publius: The Journal of Federalism* 28 (winter): 189–215.

Brown, Lawrence D., James W. Fossett, and Kenneth T. Palmer. 1984. *The Changing Politics of Federal Grants.* Washington, D.C.: Brookings Institution Press.

Browning, Rufus P., Dale Rogers Marshall, and David H. Tabb. 1984. *Protest Is Not Enough: The Struggle of Blacks and Hispanics for Equality in Urban Politics.* Berkeley: University of California Press.

Burns, Nancy. 1994. *The Formation of American Local Governments: Private Values in Public Institutions.* Ann Arbor: University of Michigan Press.

Campbell, Alan K., and Seymour Sacks. 1967. *Metropolitan America: Fiscal Patterns and Governmental Systems.* New York: Free Press.

Caraley, Demetrios. 1992. "Washington Abandons the Cities." *Political Science Quarterly* 107 (spring): 1–30.

Conlan, Timothy. 1998. *From New Federalism to Devolution: Twenty-five Years of Intergovernmental Reform.* Washington, D.C.: Brookings Institution Press.

Cooper, Phillip J. 1988. *Hard Judicial Choices: Federal District Court Judges and State and Local Officials.* New York: Oxford University Press.

Daunt, Tina. 2001. "Consent Decree Gets Federal Judge's OK." *Los Angeles Times,* June 16, part 2.

Derthick, Martha. 1970. *The Influence of Federal Grants.* Cambridge: Harvard University Press.

Dommel, Paul R., and Associates. 1982. *Decentralizing Urban Policy: Case Studies in Community Development.* Washington, D.C.: Brookings Institution Press.

Ehrenhalt, Alan. 1999. "The Czar of Gridlock." *Governing* (May): 20–27.

Elazar, Daniel J. 1984. *American Federalism: A View from the States,* 3d ed. New York: Harper and Row.

Fox, Joel. n.d. "Proposition 13: A Look Back." Howard Jarvis Taxpayers Association. Available at http://www.hjta.org.

Haar, Charles M. 1996. *Suburbs Under Siege: Race, Space, and Audacious Judges.* Princeton: Princeton University Press.

Hale, George E., and Marian Lief Palley. 1981. *The Politics of Federal Grants.* Washington, D.C.: Congressional Quarterly Press.

Hoene, Chris. 2001. "History, Voters Not Kind to Property Tax." *Nation's Cities Weekly,* May 14. Available at http://www.nlc.org.

Ingram, Helen. 1977. "Policy Implementation through Bargaining: The Case of Federal Grants-in-Aid." *Public Policy* 25 (fall): 499–526.

Inman, Robert P., and Daniel L. Rubinfeld. 1997. "Rethinking Federalism." *Journal of Economic Perspectives* 11 (fall): 43–64.

Judge, David. 1995. "Pluralism." In *Theories of Urban Politics,* ed. David Judge, Gerry Stoker, and Harold Wolman, 13–34. Thousand Oaks, Calif.: Sage.

Katz, Bruce, ed. 2000. *Reflections on Regionalism.* Washington, D.C.: Brookings Institution Press.

Koch, Edward I. 1980. "The Mandate Millstone." *Public Interest* 61 (fall): 42–57.

Krane, Dale, Platon N. Rigos, and Melvin B. Hill, Jr. 2001. *Home Rule in America: A Fifty-State Handbook.* Washington, D.C.: CQ Press.

Ladd, Helen F., and John Yinger. 1991. *America's Ailing Cities: Fiscal Health and the Design of Urban Policy.* Baltimore: Johns Hopkins University Press.

Lens, Vicki. 2001. "The Supreme Court, Federalism, and Social Policy." *Social Service Review* 75 (June): 318–336.

Lewis, Paul G. 1996. *Shaping Suburbia: How Political Institutions Organize Urban Development.* Pittsburgh: University of Pittsburgh Press.

Mollenkopf, John. 1998. "Urban Policy at the Crossroads." In *The Social Divide: Political Parties and the Future of Activist Government,* ed. Margaret Weir, 464–505. Washington, D.C.: Brookings Institution Press.

Morgan, David R., and Patrice Mareschal. 1999. "Central-City/Suburban Inequality and Metropolitan Political Fragmentation." *Urban Affairs Review* 34 (March): 578–595.

Nathan, Richard P. 1978. "The Outlook for Federal Grants to Cities." In *The Fiscal Outlook for Cities: Implications of a National Urban Policy,* ed. Roy Bahl, 75–92. Syracuse: Syracuse University Press.

———— 1983. "State and Local Governments Under Federal Grants: Toward a Predictive Theory." *Political Science Quarterly* 98 (spring): 47–57.

Nathan, Richard P., Allen D. Manvel, and Susannah E. Calkins. 1975. *Monitoring Revenue Sharing.* Washington, D.C.: Brookings Institution Press.

Nathan, Richard P., and Charles F. Adams, Jr. 1977. *Revenue Sharing: The Second Round.* Washington, D.C.: Brookings Institution Press.

Nathan, Richard P., Fred C. Doolittle, and Associates. 1987. *Reagan and the States.* Princeton: Princeton University Press.

Nivola, Pietro S. 1999. *Laws of the Landscape: How Policies Shape Cities in Europe and America.* Washington, D.C.: Brookings Institution Press.

Oates, Wallace E. 1977. "An Economist's Perspective on Fiscal Federalism." In *The Political Economy of Fiscal Federalism,* ed. Wallace E. Oates, 3–20. Lexington, Mass.: Lexington Books.

———— 1999. "An Essay on Fiscal Federalism." *Journal of Economic Literature* 37 (September): 1120–1149.

Orfield, Myron. 1997. *Metropolitics: A Regional Agenda for Community and Stability*. Washington, D.C.: Brookings Institution Press.

Ostrom, Vincent, Charles M. Tiebout, and Robert Warren. 1961. "The Organization of Government in Metropolitan Areas: A Theoretical Inquiry." *American Political Science Review* 55 (December): 831–842.

Ostrom, Vincent, Robert Bish, and Elinor Ostrom. 1988. *Local Government in the United States*. San Francisco: Institute for Contemporary Studies Press.

Pelissero, John P. 1984. "State Aid and City Needs: An Examination of Residual State Aid to Large Cities." *Journal of Politics* 46 (August): 916–935.

Peterson, Paul E. 1981. *City Limits*. Chicago: University of Chicago Press.

Peterson, Paul E., Barry G. Rabe, and Kenneth K. Wong. 1986. *When Federalism Works*. Washington, D.C.: Brookings Institution Press.

Polsby, Nelson W. 1980. *Community Power and Political Theory*, 2d ed. New Haven: Yale University Press.

Pressman, Jeffrey L. 1975. *Federal Programs and City Politics: The Dynamics of the Aid Process in Oakland*. Berkeley: University of California Press.

Pressman, Jeffrey L., and Aaron Wildavsky. 1984. *Implementation*, 3d ed. Berkeley: University of California Press.

Posner, Paul L.1998. *The Politics of Unfunded Mandates: Whither Federalism?* Washington, D.C.: Georgetown University Press.

Radatz, Clark G. 1996. "Funding State and Federal Mandates." Madison: State of Wisconsin, Legislative Reference Bureau, Informational Bulletin 96-3.

Rich, Michael J. 1993. "Riot and Reason: Crafting an Urban Policy Response." *Publius: The Journal of Federalism* 23 (summer): 115–134.

———— 1993. *Federal Policymaking and the Poor*. Princeton: Princeton University Press.

Robison, Jane. 2001. "Henpecked! L.A. Officials Play Chicken with the Courts," *Daily News of Los Angeles*, February 4.

Rose, Jerome G. 1988. "Waning Judicial Legitimacy: The Price of Judicial Promulgation of Urban Policy." *Urban Lawyer* 20 (summer): 801–839.

Rubinowitz, Leonard S., and James E. Rosenbaum. 2000. *Crossing the Class and Color Lines: From Public Housing to White Suburbia*. Chicago: University of Chicago Press.

Rusk, David. 1995. *Cities Without Suburbs*, 2d ed. Baltimore: Johns Hopkins University Press.

———— 1999. *Inside Game/Outside Game*. Washington, D.C.: Brookings Institution Press.

Sandler, Ross, and David Schoenbrod. 1994. "Government by Decree—The High Cost of Letting Judges Make Policy." *City Journal* 4 (summer): 54–62.

Savas, E. S. 2000. *Privatization and Public–Private Partnerships*. New York: Chatham House.

Savitch, H. V., and Ronald K. Vogel. 1996. *Regional Politics: America in a Post-City Age*. Thousand Oaks, Calif.: Sage.

Sbragia, Alberta M. 1996. *Debt Wish: Entrepreneurial Cities, U.S. Federalism, and Economic Development*. Pittsburgh: University of Pittsburgh Press.

Scott, Esther 1998. "A Time of Reckoning: Crisis in the Buffalo Public School System." Cambridge: Harvard University, Kennedy School of Government Case Program, C15-98-1406.0.

Stansel, Dean. 1994. "Taming Leviathan: Are Tax and Spending Limits the Answer?" *Policy Analysis* 213 (July). Available at http://www.cato.org.

Stein, Robert M. 1981. "The Targeting of State Aid: A Comparison of Grant Delivery Mechanisms." *Urban Interest* 3 (Special Issue): 47–59.

Stein, Robert M., and Keith Hamm. 1987. "A Comparative Analysis of the Targeting Capacity of State and Federal Intergovernmental Aid Allocations: 1977–1982." *Social Science Quarterly* 68 (September): 447–465.

Stephens, G. Ross, and Gerald W. Olson. 1979. *Passthrough Federal Aid and Interlevel Finance in the American Federal System.* Kansas City, Mo.: University of Missouri–Kansas City. Quoted in U.S. Advisory Commission on Intergovernmental Relations, "State and Local Roles in the Federal System." Washington, D.C.: ACIR, Report A-88, April 1982.

Stephens, G. Ross, and Nelson Wikstrom. 2000. *Metropolitan Government and Governance: Theoretical Perspectives, Empirical Analysis, and the Future.* New York: Oxford University Press.

Stone, Clarence N. 1987. "The Study of the Politics of Urban Development." In *The Politics of Urban Development,* ed. Clarence N. Stone and Heywood T. Sanders, 3–22. Lawrence: University Press of Kansas.

——— 1989. *Regime Politics: Governing Atlanta, 1946–1988.* Lawrence: University Press of Kansas.

Tarr, G. Alan. 1994. "The Past and Future of the New Judicial Federalism." *Publius: The Journal of Federalism* 24 (spring): 63–79.

Tiebout, Charles M. 1956. "A Pure Theory of Local Expenditures." *Journal of Political Economy* 64 (October): 416–424.

U.S. Advisory Commission on Intergovernmental Relations. 1978. *Categorical Grants: Their Role and Design.* Washington, D.C.: ACIR, Report A-52.

——— 1981. *Measuring Local Government Discretionary Authority.* Washington, D.C.: ACIR, Report M-131.

——— 1984. *Regulatory Federalism: Policy, Process, Impact and Reform.* Washington, D.C.: ACIR, Report A-95.

——— 1986. *A Framework for Studying the Controversy Concerning the Federal Courts and Federalism.* Washington: ACIR, Report M-149.

——— 1993. *State Laws Governing Local Government Structure and Administration.* Washington, D.C.: ACIR, Report M-186.

U.S. Congressional Budget Office. 2001. *CBO's Activities Under the Unfunded Mandates Reform Act, 1996–2000.* Washington, D.C.: U.S. Congressional Budget Office.

U.S. General Accounting Office. 1987. *Grant Formulas: A Catalog of Federal Aid to States and Localities.* Washington, D.C.: U.S. GAO, Report HRD-87-28.

——— 1996. *Federal Grants: Design Improvements Could Help Federal Resources Go Further.* Washington, D.C.: GAO, Report AIMD-97-7.

U.S. Small Business Administration. 1995. *The Changing Burden of Regulation, Paperwork, and Tax Compliance on Small Business: A Report to Congress.* Washington, D.C.: Office of the Chief Counsel for Advocacy, U.S. Small Business Administration.

Wallin, Bruce A. 1998. *From Revenue Sharing to Deficit Sharing: General Revenue Sharing and Cities.* Washington, D.C.: Georgetown University Press.

Weir, Margaret. 2000. "Coalition Building for Regionalism." In *Reflections on Regionalism,* ed. Bruce Katz, 127–153. Washington, D.C.: Brookings Institution Press.

Wise, Charles, and Rosemary O'Leary. 1992. "Is Federalism Dead or Alive in the Supreme Court? Implications for Public Administrators." *Public Administration Review* 52 (November–December): 559–572.

Wright, Deil S. 1968. *Federal Grants-in-Aid: Perspectives and Alternatives.* Washington, D.C.: American Enterprise Institute.

Note

1. This relationship also held for all 230 cities included in the Census Bureau's survey of government finances. The correlation between the percentage of general revenues from state aid and the percentage of general expenditures on education and aid to the poor was .68.

3 Political Participation in Cities

Elaine B. Sharp

Political participation refers to those activities through which ordinary citizens become involved in the public life of the community. As the following sections show, political participation encompasses a broad array of activities. Indeed, the diversity of forms of local participation distinguishes it from participation in governmental affairs at the national level.

This does not necessarily mean that there is widespread engagement in all forms of participation at the local level. Voter turnout rates, for example, are notoriously low, even in comparison with the limited voter turnout rates in presidential and congressional elections that have come to characterize U.S. politics in the past twenty years. However, voting is but one of the forms of participation that we will consider, and citizen involvement in other forms is arguably at least as important, if not more so.

Significance of Political Participation

Political participation is significant for many reasons. In several respects, it has implications for the quality of governance. The level of participation in the public life of the community and the distribution of citizens who take part determine who will represent the public's interests as elected officials. They also shape the quality of decision making in government because of the information that involved citizens convey to public officials about their needs, concerns, and interests. In addition, political participation can directly assist government officials in the implementation of public policy. Police officials, for example, often claim that the members of their force cannot do their job alone. When citizens take an active part by participating in "block watch" programs that organize the community to be on the alert for suspicious activity and to be informed about how to report it, the job of enhancing community safety is made that much easier. Finally, proponents of citizen participation often claim that engagement in the public life of the community is important in that it allows individuals to more fully develop as authentic citizens (Pateman 1970). That is, participation itself provides a learning experience about the needs and circumstances of others and about the qualities of leadership, compromise, and tolerance that are necessary in a democratic society. In the process, participation replaces the alienation of the disconnected individual with a sense of empowerment.

Perhaps the most influential thesis in recent years concerning the benefits of participation comes from the work of Robert Putnam, who argues that participation fosters the development of "social capital," which is critical for problem solving in democratic societies and also a key to economic success. By social capital, Putnam means the "social networks and the norms of reciprocity and trustworthiness that arise from them" (Putnam 2000, 19). According to Putnam, in communities that are characterized by "dense networks of reciprocal social relations," where individuals are involved in a variety of cross-cutting venues for social involvement, expectations develop about taking turns and mutual obligation ("norms of reciprocity"), and individuals learn that their fellow citizens can be counted on. The result is that it is easier to solve problems in communities with a substantial stock of "social capital."

Research on political participation at the local level has focused on three key issues: (1) factors affecting citizen involvement in civic affairs, (2) bias vs. representativeness, and (3) empowerment vs. co-optation. The first of these issues stems in part from an underlying concern about the extent of political participation, whether rates of involvement in public affairs have dropped to levels unbefitting a democratic society. By implication, this takes us to a concern with the factors affecting political participation: the reasons for its decline, or why it is more prevalent in some settings than in others. The second issue concerns the extent to which there are significant differences in who participates—differences that may exacerbate inequalities across politically relevant subgroups of the population, thus leading to a biased political system. The third issue has to do with the impact of political participation: whether citizen empowerment is effective in altering governance outcomes, or, by contrast, whether it is an empty exercise through which public officials can legitimize their actions without genuinely taking into account the input of citizens.

There are important links between these issues. In particular, some explanations for the variation in the extent of political participation have important implications for the representativeness of the political system. If differences in wealth or social status account for differences in political participation (with the more privileged taking part to a greater extent than the less privileged), we have isolated not only one cause of political participation but also identified an important bias. Note also that the issue of bias versus representativeness is based on the assumption that political participation has an impact. If participation did not affect "who gets what" in local politics, much of the concern about a participatory bias would disappear.

These three issues serve as the key themes of this chapter, which elaborates on the research on several specific forms of political participation at the local level. In addition to providing a description of each form of political participation and evidence of their respective prevalence, the following sections will indicate what is known about the factors affecting participation, the biases with respect to who engages in each form of participation, and the consequences or impacts of each form of participation.

Electoral Participation

One of the most important forms of participation for citizens in a representative democracy is voting. Closely related forms of electoral involvement include campaigning for a candidate and making campaign contributions. Yet we know relatively little about voting and electoral participation in city elections. In contrast with the voluminous and sophisticated research literature devoted to the factors affecting voter participation and choice of candidates in national elections, the research on local voting is quite small and typically is more focused on aggregate outcomes of particular electoral contests than it is on microlevel analyses of the voting behavior of individual citizens. This insufficient attention to voters in local elections is almost certainly due to lack of data, for no established mechanism exists for getting information on local voting behavior that is equivalent to the National Election Study's (NES) large-scale, random-sample surveys of the citizenry in presidential and congressional election years. Occasionally, however, a national sample survey of citizens for a broader study of participation does include information on voting at the subnational level. The research base on local voting consists of the latter, combined with case studies of particular local election contests.

One essential finding about participation in city elections is that the rate of voter turnout for them is low compared with the turnout for national elections. Using a random sample national survey conducted in 1967, Verba and Nie (1972, 31) found that 47 percent of respondents claimed that they always voted in local elections, as compared with 72 percent who claimed that they regularly voted in presidential elections. Verba, Schlozman, and Brady's (1995) analysis of a late 1980s telephone survey of an unusually large random sample of the public allows us to update that finding. Consistent with the well-known decline in voter participation in the United States since the 1960s (Rosenstone and Hansen 1993), Verba, Schlozman, and Brady find lower voter turnout rates in the late 1980s for both national and local elections than the Verba and Nie study did. Indeed, the decline in voter turnout appears to be even worse at the local level than at the national level; only 35 percent of respondents indicated that they always vote in local elections, compared with 58 percent who make that claim with respect to national elections (1995, 72).

Although these figures provide a sense of the relatively low rate of citizen involvement in local elections generally, there is evidence of higher voter turnout in some elections in some cities, as well as evidence of considerable variation in levels of electoral involvement in different cities. Pelissero, Krebs, and Jenkins (2000, 757), for example, report that the voter registration rate in Chicago "was near 81% in the first two elections held in the 1990's," and that the turnout rate in Chicago was 47 percent in the primary election held in 1991 and 45 percent in the general election. Similarly, Ardrey (1993, 123) reports a turnout of 53 percent in Cleveland's 1989 mayoral election. Turnout rates such as these underscore two key factors influencing electoral participation at the local level: race and the structure of governing institutions.

Political Parties, Machines, and Other Factors Affecting Participation

It is clear that institutional arrangements associated with "reformed" government, such as at-large election of city council members, nonpartisan elections, and the replacement of directly elected mayors with professionally credentialed, appointed city managers, have come at a price. Turnout in local elections is typically lower in cities with such reform-style institutions than it is in cities with unreformed governing institutions (Ross and Levine 1996, 195). There are various ways of understanding why this is so. Because professionalized council-manager government depoliticizes local governance, it may create a context in which electoral politics seems less significant. Similarly, when council members are elected at large, fewer citizens are likely to be as knowledgeable about the candidates as they would be if these office seekers were from their own neighborhood. Moreover, the absence of a high-profile race for a strong mayor at the top of the ticket removes much of the election's interest value.

Machine Politics

Perhaps most important, by squeezing political parties out of the electoral process, reform government removes the institution that has historically been of key significance in mobilizing potential voters for participation in elections (Rosenstone and Hansen 1993). Prior to the reform era, in many cities political parties were key to the development of machine politics. This arrangement was characterized by a strong, hierarchically organized, party-based system that controlled nominations to public office, using a network of party loyalists who were mobilized on the basis of material rewards. These rewards involved "patronage-jobs, contracts, inside information . . . and exceptions and partiality in the administration of the law" (Stone 1996, 448). Party loyalists, functioning as precinct leaders at the neighborhood level, were in turn responsible for cementing residents' ties to the party by providing them with an array of helpful services and contacts and ultimately for getting out the vote for the party on election day. This mobilizing function enhanced the voting participation of those connected to the party. Hence, political machines, although often criticized for their graft and corruption, have also often been credited with bringing new immigrant groups into the political process and providing avenues for economic mobility, based on jobs and other material benefits.

However, it is important to note that recent scholarship has conditioned our understanding of the role of political machines. In particular, Stephen Erie (1988) counters what he calls the "rainbow theory" of machine politics, which posits that although the Irish were the "main beneficiaries of machine politics," political machines were multiethnic coalitions in which a variety of new immigrant groups experienced political incorporation and avenues for social and economic mobility (p. 5). Instead, based upon a historical analysis of machine politics in eight cities, Erie shows convincingly that urban political machines "did not incorporate immigrants other than the Irish" (p. 6), in large part because so few material benefits were available that they had to be largely reserved for the Irish and were only selectively provided to later-arriving immigrant groups. Therefore, political machines must be understood as having mobilized electoral participation in an ethnically selective fashion. As an example, Erie notes that although 88 percent of the naturalized Irish were registered to vote in the 1896 presidential election in Boston, only 25 percent of naturalized Italians and 39 percent of Russian-born citizens were registered to vote (p. 95). As Stone concludes, some early political machines in special circumstances tried to get new immigrants quickly naturalized and politically incorporated, but that was an exception to the rule; more generally, "machines have preferred a small and controllable electorate over a large and unpredictable one" (1996, 453).

Only later, when the original Irish-dominated political machines experienced challenges from reform organizations, did the resulting competition for votes lead them to extend benefits to and mobilize the voting of newer ethnic and minority groups (Stone 1996, 453). And even in the later, post-depression years of mature political machines, there is evidence that they held some ethnic groups at arm's length despite their vote potential. For example, Polish Americans remained largely independent of the political machine in Chicago during Mayor Richard J. Daley's consolidation of the machine in the 1950s and also long afterward, because its Irish leaders provided no more than symbolic rewards to the Poles (Inglot and Pelissero 1993).

These caveats about the pre-reform role of political parties indicate that, even when at their strongest, as organized political machines, the parties directly mobilized high levels of electoral participation selectively on the basis of ethnic group. To the extent that political machines are linked with high levels of voter turnout, it may well be due to the machine's mobilization of its supporters in combination with the counter-mobilization efforts of opposing parties.

The decline of most big-city political machines has been accompanied by a broader decline in the official role of political parties in cities. In the wake of the reform movement that began in the first decade of the twentieth century, numerous cities adopted nonpartisan elections, in which neither party appears on the ballot. However, even in cities that officially have ballot nonpartisanship, party-like structures have emerged. In their comparative case analysis of four cities in Texas, Davidson and Fraga (1988, 374) detail the activity of these "slating groups," which are "organizations not formally connected to national parties but which, like those parties, nominate a list of candidates identified with a name such as 'Citizens for Good Government.'" Although these slating organizations were highly successful in getting their candidates elected, there is no evidence that they mobilized the electorate to higher levels of voting. Rather, they tended to flourish in southwestern cities, where at-large elections and other elements of reform were put together in a distinctive pattern of "big city political reform" that used overt restrictions on electoral participation (such as requiring registration far in advance of elections or re-registration for each municipal election, siting polling places in locations inconvenient for the poor and racial minorities, and even using poll taxes and literacy tests) to generate an electorate that was biased toward the Anglo middle class (Bridges 1997) and business interests.

Race

It is also important to note that race is a factor shaping urban electoral participation in several respects. For one thing, race affects the level of electoral participation, but in somewhat complex ways. A substantial line of research on voting in national elections has established that there is a systematic bias in voter turnout, with racial minorities and socioeconomically disadvantaged individuals less likely to vote than are whites and advantaged individuals (Verba, Schlozman, and Brady 1995, 190, 233; Calvo and Rosenstone 1989). Although there is less research to confirm this at the local level, what does exist supports the notion of systematic bias in contemporary big-city elections. For example, in a study designed primarily to assess the impact of Asian American immigration on electoral participation in Chicago, Pelissero, Krebs, and Jenkins (2000, 762–763) find that in each of two contemporary elections in Chicago the precinct turnout rate was lower in precincts with the higher percentages of the population that were African American, Hispanic, and Asian American, even after income was taken into account.

Race thus appears to matter in the sense of shaping levels of participation, with racial minorities being less likely to vote. But this general finding is altered when we consider the importance of mobilization on the basis of race. As exemplified by higher-than-usual turnout rates for some city elections, it is evident that in key election contests in U.S. cities featuring African American candidates for mayor, turnout rates can be unusually high, either because racial minorities are energized to support a minority candidate or because white voters turn out in unusually large numbers to try to prevent the election of a minority candidate, or for both reasons. This is dramatically illustrated by Summers and Klinkner's (1991) study of the 1989 election of John Daniels as New Haven's first black mayor. Average voter turnout in the predominantly black wards studied was only 30 percent in the general election immediately prior to the 1989 contest, but more than doubled to 61 percent in the 1989 election. Similarly, average voter turnout in the predominantly white wards studied was about 43 percent in the 1987 general election but shot up to 63 percent in the 1989 election.

This points to the other key role of race in electoral participation. Race not only shapes levels of electoral participation but also strongly influences how the individual votes, at least in elections where candidates of different races vie against each other. Prior to 1990, the conventional wisdom was that African American candidates were limited in their capacity to gain office because white voters were unwilling to support them. A study of mayoral elections held between the late 1960s and 1983 provides empirical evidence of this view, noting that white support for black candidates was never even as much as 25 percent, and sometimes was less than 10 percent of the white electorate (Henry 1987). Other research also illustrates the "intensity of race as a basis for electoral choice" on both sides in mayoral elections featuring minority candidates (Perry 1991, 185).

The elections of 1989, however, showed the success of a number of African American candidates for mayor in cities that were predominantly white. In these elections the candidates downplayed race-specific issues in ways that succeeded in diminishing the usual racial polarization of the electorate. This has sparked a substantial round of research on "deracialization," that is, minority candidates' use of racially neutral campaign strategies and racial crossover voting in the electorate (Perry 1991; McCormick and Jones 1993). Although the tone of that research was initially optimistic, the continuing significance of race as a basis for electoral choice, even when minority candidates use a deracialization strategy, is evident from research such as Longoria's (1999) study of Milwaukee's mayoral and circuit judge elections of 1996. Both contests involved competition between a white candidate and a black candidate. Longoria finds that although the circuit judge contest involved racialized rhetoric whereas the mayoral campaign did not, racial voting patterns were nevertheless more pronounced in the latter contest. Longoria interprets the result as showing the subtle way in which racial considerations can be embedded in an ostensibly deracialized campaign and the smaller likelihood of racial crossover voting in contests for offices that are symbolically more significant.

Effects of Bias

The biases or factors shaping electoral participation, as noted, give strong reasons for concern. If electoral participation is diminished in cities that have reform structures, an important tool for maintaining the accountability of governments in those communities is weakened. Socioeconomic and, even more importantly, racial differences in voting propensity at the local level have even more problematic implications, although the nature of those implications depends upon one's expectations concerning the outcomes of voting power. First, the diminished level of voting by racial minorities, combined with racialized patterns of vote choice, suggests very limited success for minority candidates and lowered expectations of minority groups, in the sense that a member of their group can win office. There are also negative implications from the perspective of those who presume that a racial or ethnic minority can translate its voting power into material benefits for individuals in the group.

Recent study has shown that political machines offered less in the way of economic benefits, even to white ethnic groups, than once had been thought (Erie 1988), and that the strategic considerations that prevented these older minority groups from receiving benefits would also now apply to minority groups' expectations of wangling benefits from a political regime based on a "rainbow coalition" of minority voting blocs. Generally, lower levels of electoral participation by any group presumably translate into less responsiveness to their needs and preferences because elected officials have less incentive to give them priority. Finally, the durability of racial voting patterns suggests that, beyond any difficulties that are implied in building rainbow coalitions, such voting patterns reflect and underscore the interracial competition and conflict that are a part of urban life in many American cities, which can sometimes lead to violent confrontations.

Citizen-Initiated Contacts with Public Officials

When citizens contact elected or appointed public officials to make requests, complain about services, or convey their policy preferences, they are engaging in an important form of participation that is typically referred to as citizen-initiated contacting. The earliest research on citizen-initiated contacting indicated that it includes two varieties of participation: (1) contacting with a particularized referent, that is, concerning problems relevant only to the individuals and their households, and (2) general-referent contacting, that is, issue-based contacts on matters more broadly relevant for the community (Verba and Nie 1972). Particularized contacting is typically viewed as a narrow, purely self-interested act that is unlikely to be related to community problem solving or of wider social significance, whereas general-referent contacting is typically viewed as a more civically conscious act that is more like other forms of political participation.

The most useful source for gauging the extent to which American citizens engage in this form of political participation at the local level is Verba, Schlozman, and

Brady's (1995) national sample study. They report that, although contacting is a little less than half as prevalent as self-reports of voting, it is nevertheless one of the most common acts of political participation. Twenty-four percent of the sample said that they had engaged in issue-based (general referent) contacting of a local official in the previous year, and 10 percent reported a particularized contact of a local official. The issue-based contacts were most commonly about school issues or taxes, while the particularized contacts were most commonly about basic human needs, such as a missed trash pickup (p. 72).

Research on factors affecting citizen-initiated contacting has generated considerable controversy, especially about the role of socioeconomic status. On the one hand, several studies, typically based on survey research in case study cities, have shown that the higher an individual's socioeconomic status (SES), the more likely that person is to engage in contacting (Vedlitz and Veblen 1980; Sharp 1982). This is usually referred to as the standard socioeconomic model of participation. However, occasionally a study based on survey research finds just the reverse, that contacting is slightly more likely among the least advantaged (Vedlitz, Dyer, and Durand 1980) (a curvilinear model), and still other studies find no relationship at all between SES and contacting (Zuckerman and West 1985; Sharp 1986). To complicate matters further, Jones, Greenberg, Kaufman, and Drew (1977) have documented an unusual pattern to the relationship between social well-being and contacting, showing that the greatest propensity to contact local officials comes from middle-class neighborhoods, whereas both the most advantaged and the least advantaged neighborhoods generate fewer contacts. This model results in a pattern similar to a parabola and may appear as such: ∩.

Several factors may account for these conflicting findings and help us to sort out what they tell us. First, some studies distinguish between particularized and general-referent contacting, while others do not. On theoretical grounds, we should expect that general-referent contacting would, like other forms of political participation, be positively associated with SES because wealthier and better-educated citizens have more resources for participation, such as knowledge about city government and greater confidence in their capacity to communicate effectively with public officials. In contrast, because particularized contacting involves immediate personal problems rather than civically conscious activity, we should expect it to be affected by the need for governmental assistance rather than the resources that typically shape political participation. In fact, those studies that carefully make the distinction between these two forms of contacting find precisely this pattern (Traut and Emmert 1993; Sharp 1984). Furthermore, socioeconomically distinctive patterns of need and resources for participation constitute the theoretical basis for the parabolic model reported by Jones, Greenberg, Kaufman, and Drew (1977), who note that the need for governmental assistance is negatively associated with SES, while "awareness"—meaning the resources for participation mentioned above—is positively associated with SES. Consequently, in lower-status areas, there is ample need but insufficient awareness to mobilize citizens for contacting, whereas in high-status areas there is ample awareness but not enough need for such mobilization. Hence, we should not be surprised that contacting overall is most prevalent in middle-class areas, because they are the only areas having sufficient levels of both need and awareness.

Another explanation for the welter of confusing findings concerning SES and contacting is the difference in research methodology used by various scholars. In particular, the model used by Jones and colleagues resulted from research using governmental data on the volume of citizen contacts received from various neighborhoods; this model has not been found in any of the published research based on surveys that asked individual citizens about their contacts with government officials. More generally, Coulter (1992) notes that research based on surveys typically finds either a positive relationship between SES and contacting or no relationship, whereas research based on government records typically finds either a negative relationship or the parabolic relationship.

Yet another explanation for the conflicting findings has to do with the sorts of additional explanatory variables that researchers bring to bear in attempting to account for variations in citizen-initiated contacting. Some studies have shown the importance of political efficacy (Sharp 1982; Traut and Emmert 1993); others have found that race is an important factor, with whites being more likely to engage in contacting officials than are blacks or Hispanics (Thomas 1982; Hero 1986; Verba and Nie 1972; Traut and Emmert 1993). By contrast, Zuckerman and West's study (1985, 119) of contacting in several different countries is based on the premise that it is "the result of a relationship, of an existing political bond, not a personal characteristic, such as education, income, efficacy, or need." Their study finds that the individual's political ties—the extent to which they are active in political parties and election campaigns—are the key predictor of the propensity for contacting; however, no variables measuring education, income, efficacy, or need are included in the study. Still other researchers have emphasized contextual factors that might stimulate citizens' participation rather than the individual characteristics that have been emphasized so far. Clingermayer and Feiock (1994) explore this possibility, at least for contacts about economic development, in a survey of a random sample of city council members in large American cities. They find that several contextual factors are important, including the extent of media attention to the issue, issue salience, and the diversity of groups that are part of the council member's electoral coalition.

As a result of the conflicting findings, it is impossible to give a completely definitive assessment of socioeconomic bias in contacting. However, two of the three models (the curvilinear model and the standard model of a positive SES relationship) and the vast majority of the contacting studies overall suggest that people with lower SES lag in this form of participation. This, combined with the consistent finding concerning race and contacting, suggests that the same sort of bias that is found in voting behavior also occurs with respect to contacting.

The implications of this bias are greatest, of course, if contacting has significant consequences in urban communities. Research on contacting has largely focused on the causes rather than the consequences of this form of participation. But we do know that city services are distributed on the basis of "bureaucratic decision rules" (Lineberry 1977; Jones 1980; Jones, Greenberg, Kaufman, and Drew 1978), and that one of the most common of these rules is to allocate resources for problem solving on the basis of citizen complaints. Such contacts are, after all, a form of information, free of the costs the bureaucracy would have to incur if it were to scan for problems and for information on the perceived importance of those problems to citizens. To the extent that the city's attention to delivery of services is directed on the basis of citizen-initiated contacts, resource allocation will be biased in the same fashion as is involvement in this form of participation.

Interest Group Participation

In a claim that has since drawn much criticism, Peterson (1981) once described urban politics as "groupless" politics. Although many of the organized interests that are prominent in national-level politics are indeed less consistently visible on the local government scene, a diverse array of groups is active in urban politics. That includes, of course, business groups (such as Chambers of Commerce, downtown business-owner organizations, and development-project coalitions) whose existence and importance are very commonly acknowledged in the urban politics literature. In addition to business interests, however, both private and perhaps more especially public-sector labor organizations are frequently key players in municipal politics. Regaldo (1991), for example, shows that organized labor was a key component in former Los Angeles mayor Tom Bradley's political base. Based upon surveys with thirty public and private-sector labor unions, Regaldo (p. 90) finds that virtually all of the unions not only formally endorsed Bradley but also actively engaged in "monetary assistance, rank-and-file membership electoral mobilization, member precinct mobilization (which includes everything from phone banking and house-to-house canvassing by precinct to briefing the press), and voter registration drives." Similarly, DeLeon's (1992) case study shows that even though the importance of labor unions as an interest group in San Francisco politics has declined since the early 1970s, labor cannot be counted out of the city's politics. The political significance of organized labor, especially municipal employee unions, clearly will not be the same in all cities. In some places, employee unions are constrained by weaker collective bargaining laws. In addition, research has documented that the extent to which municipal employee unions can affect wage rates and employment levels depends upon the form of government. In a study of public-sector compensation and employment rates in U.S. cities with populations of at least 25,000, Mehay and Gonzalez (1994, 388) found that "municipal employees tend to have greater influence over employment conditions in cities with district elections, and this power tends to be enhanced when employees are unionized."

Faith-based organizations also are politically important groups at the local level. A case study of nonprofit organizations as political actors confirms this with respect to BUILD, a citywide coalition of church and labor groups in Baltimore. Noting, however, that the churches "are the strength behind BUILD," Hula, Jackson, and Orr (1997, 469–470) document how the coalition was able to promote its agenda successfully by challenging private-sector financial institutions and demanding that mayoral candidates sign on to their agenda before they would provide electoral support. Similarly, a recent study of the politics of school reform acknowledges that in Detroit "churches are perhaps the most important community-level organization in the city" because church leaders frequently are involved in the building of coalitions, and churches "frequently function as arenas for political debate and election campaigns" (Henig, Hula, Orr, and Pedescleaux 1999, 106–107).

Churches have also been recognized as significant interest organizations with respect to issues involving morality. One study reports that cities that have adopted gay rights ordinances have significantly lower levels of evangelical Protestants in their church going population and noticeably higher levels of liberal Protestants—a finding that reflects the policy positions on this issue taken by various church denominations (Button, Rienzo, and Wald 1997, 81). Evangelical Protestant churches have been openly opposed to homosexuality, whereas liberal Protestant denominations such as Episcopalians, Friends, the United Church of Christ, and especially Unitarians have "taken public positions welcoming gays and lesbians"; Unitarian churches in Cincinnati announced that they were "hate-free zones" and vigorously endorsed the gay rights ordinance being considered by the city government (Button, Rienzo, and Wald, p. 91). Churches have also been significantly involved in other morality issues, such as opposition to pornography and other forms of sexually explicit entertainment (Sharp 2002) and the mobilization of abortion-clinic protests (Clarke 1999).

Citizen involvement in such groups is therefore a key form of urban political participation to explore. Generalizing about this form of citizen involvement, however, is difficult because of the sheer diversity of groups and the fact that some types of groups have been studied more extensively than others. This section focuses on neighborhood organizations, for which there is the most substantial research base.

Political involvement of several other types of groups will be discussed later in this chapter. For example, single-issue morality groups, because of their basis in social movements and the character of their activities, will be discussed in the section on protest as a form of political participation.

Neighborhood Organizations

Even within the category of groups whose participation is focused on neighborhood-level concerns, there is some diversity. The most commonly studied forms are the homeowners' association, a voluntary association of residents of neighborhoods where homeownership predominates, and tenant associations, for residents who are renters. Another form of neighborhood-based association is the Community Development Corporation (CDC), an organization that is legally incorporated, with a board of directors drawn from various elements of the community, and is typically devoted to housing development and job creation. CDCs are sometimes offshoots of traditional homeowners' or tenants' associations. In Minneapolis, for example, some neighborhoods have a citizen participation organization that also serves as the CDC for the neighborhood, while others have a CDC that is distinct from the neighborhood's citizen participation organization (Goetz and Sidney 1997, 493). A distinction should also be made between grass-roots neighborhood associations, formed by citizens as a result of one or more of the mobilizing issues discussed below, and government-initiated neighborhood associations, created when city governments attempt to set up a formal structure for city-wide citizen participation. In St. Paul, for example, city officials divided the community into seventeen district councils elected by residents of each area. Each district council is given a community organizer, paid for by city government, who is delegated various zoning-related powers and has influence on capital expenditures affecting the neighborhood (Berry, Portney, and Thomson 1993).

Participation in neighborhood groups is actually multifaceted, incorporating a number of the specific forms of participation outlined elsewhere in this chapter. In their study of over 100 neighborhood associations in Columbus, Ohio, for example, Mesch and Schwirian (1996) find that virtually all associations contacted public officials by phone or mail and participated in public hearings; the vast majority organized programs designed to solve problems of crime or neighborhood beautification through collaborative efforts with public authorities. More than two-thirds of Columbus's neighborhood associations even engaged in organizing petition drives, a form of electoral activity.

Evidence concerning levels of citizen participation in neighborhood organizations is derived from two kinds of studies: national sample survey research on modes of citizen participation and survey-based evidence from case studies of neighborhood organization activity in particular cities. With respect to the former, Verba, Schlozman, and Brady's study (1995, 63) reveals that only 12 percent of respondents were affiliated with an organization specifically identified as a neighborhood or homeowners' organization. Of course, citizen participation at the neighborhood level may be construed more broadly than involvement with formal, neighborhood-based organizations. Verba, Schlozman, and Brady (p. 72) also asked respondents whether they "worked with others on local problems" and whether they had an active membership in a "community-problem solving organization." Just over one-third (34 percent) of respondents indicated that they had engaged in such informal problem solving, and 34 percent indicated membership in a problem-solving organization. The case study evidence is consistent with these findings of low levels of involvement with neighborhood organizations. In a study of Cincinnati, which has long had a practice of officially incorporating neighborhood-level involvement in city governance, Thomas (1986, 45) found very low levels of citizen participation; somewhere between 3.3 percent and 12.6 percent of the population was involved with their neighborhood council. Berry, Portney, and Thomson (1993) draw upon case study evidence from neighborhood organizations in five cities where local government has made a major effort to enhance neighborhood organization involvement in local governance, comparing them with a group of ten cities with similar demographic characteristics. Pooling responses for all fifteen cities, they find that only 6 percent of citizens participated in a citizen group or neighborhood association more than once a month; another 5.2 percent did so about once a month; and another approximately 10 percent participated less than once a month (p. 77).

The evidence concerning citizen participation in CDCs is more limited, but that which exists suggests an even more restricted level of citizen involvement in these organizations, perhaps in large part because CDCs are not necessarily structured to invite mass citizen involvement. Based on a survey of community-based development organizations functioning in the El Paso area, Fredericksen and London (2000) report that less than half of the organizations (44 percent) showed evidence of community support in the form of either informal access to the CDC board of directors or "straw poll" input concerning organizational priorities; and they found that less than half of the CDCs even allowed citizen participation in the selection of members of the board of directors.

There is a substantial consensus about the factors affecting the emergence of neighborhood groups as institutions. That consensus emphasizes (1) the importance of governmental policies that require or enable citizen participation, such as the requirements for citizen participation attached to various federal grant programs and the efforts of some cities to create or build upon neighborhood-level organizations as venues for citizen input into community affairs, and (2) the significance of external threats to the neighborhood as a motivator for grass-roots–initiated activism at the neighborhood level. Development projects or land uses that are undesirable, such as highway projects that disrupt the neighborhood, housing or commercial plans that would displace residents or change the character of the neighborhood, and even un-due concentrations of liquor stores (Sonenshein 1996) are well-documented exam-ples of threats to a neighborhood that have engendered its mobilization. In their study of more than seventy functioning neighborhood organizations in the Albany, New York, region, Logan and Rabrenovic (1990, 77–80) found that about half of the or-ganizations were initially formed in response to proposed land-use changes that the neighborhood opposed, and that the threat of land-use development was the most commonly cited issue of concern to urban and especially suburban neighborhood as-sociations.

Research on patterns of participation in neighborhood organizations reveals some of the same bias that has been observed with respect to voting behavior and contact-ing. In particular, a number of studies have shown that citizen participation in neigh-borhood organizations, perhaps especially those established as part of a city government effort to have a city-wide system of participation, is much more exten-sive in middle- and upper-class neighborhoods than it is in poor neighborhoods and less extensive in neighborhoods where racial minorities predominate than it is in nonminority neighborhoods (Schwirian 1983; Goetz and Sidney 1997). Similarly, Fredericksen and London's (2000) study of El Paso CDCs reports that, relative to the population of El Paso as a whole, whites were overrepresented on both the boards and the staffs of the CDCs, while Latinos were underrepresented. Thomas (1986) reports the "usual socioeconomic bias" in neighborhood organization participation in Cincinnati, where better-educated and higher-income individuals are more likely to participate. However, he finds that, contrary to the usual bias, "Cincinnati's blacks, de-spite having on the average much lower socioeconomic status than the city's whites, are more inclined to report council membership" (p. 46).

Alex-Assensoh's (1998) study of participation in four poor neighborhoods in Columbus, Ohio, also offers a contrasting perspective to the "usual bias," which also underscores the importance of the social context for participation. Black residents of concentrated poverty neighborhoods, those with 40 percent or more of the residents with incomes below the poverty line, were *more* likely than whites in similar neigh-borhoods to have attended community meetings; and black residents of both low poverty and concentrated poverty neighborhoods were more likely than whites in corresponding neighborhoods to have worked to solve community problems (pp. 91–94). Similarly, Berry, Portney, and Thomson (1993, 86–87) report that among cit-izens in the lowest socioeconomic group, blacks are *overrepresented* in the top three categories of the index of community participation (which is based upon items such as participating in a citizen group or neighborhood association), while nonminorities are underrepresented.

Our knowledge of the functioning and impact of neighborhood groups and other residentially based community organizations is largely based on case studies focusing on a single such organization, or a limited number of them, in a particular city. Partly for that reason, there are conflicting findings regarding the effectiveness of this form of citizen participation. But an even more important reason for the conflicting findings is that different authors have different standards concerning what is required for a neighborhood organization to have impact or to be effective. Tullos (1995, 517) explicitly acknowledges the problem of differing standards or expectations for group effectiveness in her study of citizen participation in Boston's development policy. She concludes, however, that neighborhood-based community groups in that city "achieved their goals" in battles over development in the 1960s and 1970s, that these early efforts set the stage for more recent efforts by community groups, and that in the primary case that she examines citizens succeeded in transforming an objectionable project into one more acceptable to the neighborhood.

There is, in fact, a considerable body of research, based on case studies of individual cities, community organizations, or controversies, that indicates equally positive results concerning the effectiveness of neighborhood organizations, while illustrating the diverse criteria for effectiveness that are used. Chan (1997), for example, reports on a CDC in Washington, D.C., that accomplished a variety of goals that the author deemed important. Specifically, the CDC relies upon residents who volunteer their time to leverage (or acquire) pro bono hours of assistance from a law firm—an arrangement that has empowered the CDC to get rid of crack houses, fight police corruption, and clean up a local playground. Logan and Rabrenovic (1990, 91) suggest that neighborhood organizations are highly effective, based on the fact that 80 percent of organization leaders whom they surveyed claimed that their organization had been either "very" or "moderately" successful in achieving their goals in the previous year; 89 percent thought that the organization had been "very" or "moderately" successful in dealing with the challenge that had sparked the formation of the organization.

Other research based on data from a larger number of neighborhood associations, but still within a single case study city, begins from the premise that there is variation in the effectiveness of neighborhood associations and attempts to account for this. In their study of over 100 neighborhood associations in Columbus, Ohio, Mesch and Schwirian (1996) measured effectiveness, based on neighborhood association presidents' assessments of one indicator of organizational process—the extent to which residents were "more aware of neighborhood issues" as a result of the association's activities—and one indicator of results—the extent to which the association "has an influence in major decisions affecting the neighborhood" (p. 475). They found that neighborhood associations are more likely to be judged effective on these grounds if they are in areas higher in socioeconomic status, with high levels of homeownership and long-term residency, if they are facing threats in the form of unwanted land-use developments, if the organization is complex (with a larger number of members and specialized roles for them, such as a newsletter producer), and if the organization is involved in coalition partnerships with other neighborhood associations. They found that racial composition of the neighborhood is not a relevant factor; when these other factors are taken into account, neighborhood associations in black neighborhoods are no less likely to emerge as effective.

Berry, Portney, and Thomson (1993) tackle the question of the effectiveness of neighborhood organizations in a fashion that improves upon the limitations of single-city case studies and addresses the dilemma of conflicting standards for gauging effectiveness by employing a broad array of criteria derived from the literature on citizen participation. The result is a mixed and highly nuanced set of findings. When evaluated in terms of their capacity to enhance citizen involvement in the community, neighborhood organizations did not fare well. The level of citizen participation in the five cities studied was no greater than that in the comparison cities, nor were the neighborhood organizations in the study cities able to overcome the usual bias of lesser participation among the disadvantaged and minorities. The results are also disappointing with respect to the agenda-setting capacity of these organizations, in that they were credited with initiating only 10 percent of the policy proposals considered by local government.

There are more encouraging results with respect to the ability of neighborhood organizations to shape policy outcomes. Decisions that they preferred were made on half of the issues they had initiated—a batting average better than that of other policy initiators (p. 141). In addition, cities with higher levels of citizen participation generated policy outcomes that were a better match with citizen preferences (p. 153). On the other hand, Berry, Portney, and Thomson (pp. 142–145) acknowledge that, despite neighborhood opposition, business interests got their way on the most significant issues, involving large-scale development projects. The most positive results concerning the impact of these neighborhood-based organizations, however, have to do with matters that are relevant to Putnam's theme of social capital. Based upon surveys of residents of the neighborhoods, Berry, Portney, and Thomson are able to show that participants in these organizations are less likely to feel politically powerless than are other citizens (pp. 204–205), and that a higher level of participation through these neighborhood organizations is linked to a stronger sense of community (p. 238), a higher level of trust in government (p. 251), and greater knowledge of local politics and government (p. 273).

This major study of the impact of neighborhood organizations, in the best-case scenario of cities that empower such organizations, cannot prove that their involvement produced the various outcomes. Lurking behind each finding is the possibility that the alleged outcome actually caused the citizen participation—that is, those with a greater knowledge of local politics are more likely to be drawn into participatory activities or that those with stronger feelings of political powerlessness are therefore less likely to participate. Despite this limitation and the mixed results, the study does provide some important evidence that neighborhood organizations, at their best, can be highly effective in a variety of senses.

Protest and Social Movement Participation

Protest as a form of citizen participation may be defined as any behavior by which individuals attempt to influence government by publicly calling attention to grievances. Two features of this definition are worthy of special note. First, unlike citizen-initiated contacting, where people communicate directly with officials in order to provide information on their needs, demands, or requests, protest is distinguished by publicly visible action designed to put pressure on governing officials by evoking the sympathies of broader audiences. Tactics such as marches, rallies, demonstrations, and picketing, rather than letter writing or phone calls, are the stuff of protest behavior. Many analysts include violent action such as rioting among the activities considered to be protest behavior. With respect to urban politics especially, an important line of research on the "race riots" in American cities that occurred in the 1960s and more recently constitutes a key piece of our understanding of protest.

Second, although protest can be an individualistic act, as when a lone person pickets outside city hall, it is more typically a group phenomenon. Indeed, a voluminous literature, largely based on case studies and historical analysis, reveals the dynamics of how social movements such as those concerned with civil rights, environmentalism, women's issues, and gay rights are especially effective in mobilizing citizen involvement in protest activity. These movements have been studied primarily by scholars interested in their role in politics and governance at the nation-state level. However, a substantial line of recent research shows the importance of the local level (1) as an arena for such activities, as when city officials are confronted with maintaining social order during major anti-abortion demonstrations, and (2) the importance of city government as a direct target of protest activity, as when gay rights activists agitate for the adoption of city ordinances protecting them against discrimination (Bailey 1998; Button, Rienzo, and Wald 1997; Sharp 1996, 1997, 1999).

Protest is a relatively rare political act (Oberschall 1992, 2). Verba, Schlozman, and Brady's study (1995, 51–52) found only 6 percent of respondents reporting that they had attended a protest, march, or demonstration in the previous two years—a figure that encompasses protest activity regardless of the level of government at issue. For this reason, and because protest can include violent action and perhaps even political revolution, it is often considered quite distinct from all other forms of citizen participation. It is "extraordinary politics," according to Charles C. Euchner (1996).

Because protest is such a rare political act, there is relatively limited research on the types of individuals who engage in protest and on other factors affecting patterns of involvement in protest. As Conway (2000, 177) notes, "Only a few studies have examined participation in and support for unconventional political activity in the United States, and hardly any of them have been based on data from national samples." In addition, attempting to understand the factors shaping protest participation is complicated by several other considerations. One of them is the diversity of phenomena that within the concept of protest. Garden-variety picketing of city hall by a neighborhood group opposed to the siting of a landfill in their area and anti-abortion demonstrations in cities such as Wichita and Denver during Operation Rescue's heyday may both be construed as protest, but they differ greatly in terms of the number of participants and the degree of disruptiveness and violent action involved. Hence, case study research that provides insights on the one may or may not be appropriately generalized to the other. Second, research relevant to protest has been done at both the individual level and the group, or social movement level, but the results from one level of analysis are not useful for the other level. In particular, the individual characteristics that make some types of people more likely than others to engage in protest do not help explain the emergence and decline of social movements that foster protest, because the latter "are collective, involving the coordination of many people and groups—not just the individual motivations of members" (Euchner 1996, 67). The review that follows deals with these challenges by including research and theory from both levels of analysis, based on the assumption that individual-level research and theory are most useful in specifying who protests and why, while group-level research and theory are most useful in specifying the structural conditions most conducive to political protest. Research on the full range of protest behaviors, including riots, is considered, while leaving aside the assessment of generalizability across forms of protest.

With respect to individual-level factors, protest is sometimes described as a form of political participation distinctive to the disadvantaged. From this point of view, protesters are "outsiders" to the policy process, lacking the political resources and access necessary for more conventional forms of lobbying. This would lead us to expect that the disparities in participation that have been observed in other forms of participation would be reversed and that protest would be more prevalent among those with lower incomes and less education than among more socioeconomically advantaged individuals. Similarly, although racial disparities in participation are not as consistent as SES disparities and sometimes are simply an artifact of SES differences (Alex-Assensoh 1998), the preceding review of other forms of participation has shown that blacks and Hispanics typically are less likely to be involved in conventional forms of citizen participation such as voting and contacting city officials. Once again, then, the "outsider" perspective on protest would suggest a reversed pattern of higher levels of participation among racial minorities.

With respect to race, there is evidence to support this expectation. Verba, Schlozman, and Brady (1995, 233) find that African Americans are more likely than whites to have engaged in protest, and Latinos are nearly as likely as whites to report involvement in protest. Surprisingly, however, the empirical research does not support the "outsider" view's expectation of greater protest participation among the have nots. Verba, Schlozman, and Brady's study of patterns of participation in the United States finds that those with higher incomes are twice as likely to have engaged in protest activity as those in the lowest-income category (p. 190). Ron Inglehart (1990, 316) finds much the same thing for the United States and several other advanced industrial nations, noting that the finding that "those who are materially best off, protest most" is very much at odds with traditional models of politics, which posit that "social protest is based on the working class, while those with better jobs and higher income normally support the status quo."

Several factors help to make sense of the irony that better-off individuals protest more than disadvantaged individuals. Most obviously, the rise of so-called new social movements, espousing such causes as environmentalism, women's rights, gay rights, and animal rights, have mobilized individuals who are far from socioeconomically disadvantaged. This is in stark contrast to the early civil rights movement in the United States, which activated very poor and otherwise politically inert African Americans in the South, and the follow-up period of protest and disorder in northern cities, which mobilized many poor African Americans.

But this does not really explain why causes appealing to advantaged individuals have emerged and become the subjects of successful protest organizing. Inglehart (1990) offers an explanation in his culture-shift theory. Those who come of age, he posits, at a time of economic scarcity such as the Great Depression or of threats to national security such as World War II will have "materialist" values, giving priority to such matters as fighting rising prices, maintaining economic growth and a stable economy, fighting crime, and having a strong defense. In contrast, those who come of age at a time of prosperity and security will have "post-materialist" values, taking economic security for granted and giving priority to freedom of speech, individual participation, and personal growth. Given their values, post-materialists would be expected to be more prone to protest participation. Indeed, Inglehart's study shows that people with post-materialist values are about two and a half times as likely to engage in two or more types of protest than are those with material values (p. 313). More importantly, Inglehart's theory suggests that those who came of age in the relative prosperity and security of the post–World War II period (and are therefore disproportionately socioeconomically well off) will nevertheless be ripe for social movement mobilization and protest activity.

Inglehart's theory also provides some perspective on another individual-level factor that is associated with protest activity—age (Conway 2000, 177). The findings that older individuals are less likely to engage in protest are sometimes interpreted as revealing a universal tendency for such people to become more conventional and less willing to engage in obstreperous behavior. But Inglehart's work reminds us that *cohort* effects may be more important than mere *age*. In other words, the individuals who are older, by the standards of contemporary research, constitute a group that collectively shared the experience of growing up during a period of economic scarcity and insecurity and hence developed materialist values; the individuals who are younger constitute a group or cohort that grew up in a period of prosperity and hence developed post-materialist values and the propensity for protest behavior that is associated with those values.

As noted above, we can also glean information on the factors shaping political protest from research that focuses on the conditions leading to the successful emergence of social movements that are the engines for so much protest activity. The earliest research in that genre was based on mass society theory, which holds that movements arise whenever there is a breakdown of the intermediary groups (such as conversation groups at the workplace and social groups in the community) that normally provide political information and an avenue for individuals to discuss politics in settings that help discourage extremist responses (Baer and Bositis 1993). When large organizations and the mass media become more important and intermediary groups are weak, individuals can be reached through demagogic appeals and are ripe for revolutionary mobilization. This research perspective, which views social movements as potentially dangerous and destructive, was based upon historical analysis of the mass movements that were implicated in the emergence of fascism in Europe. The implications for contemporary analysis lie primarily in the connection to Putnam's ideas about social capital. Putnam's emphasis on the importance to communities of a rich network of local groups that allows citizens to develop norms of trust and reciprocity, his critique of the way in which the mass media, especially television, has contributed to the erosion of civic engagement at the local level, and his concerns about the damaging effects this has on a democracy are all reminiscent of writing in the genre of mass society theory.

Taken to the extreme, this perspective would suggest not only that social movements are most likely to emerge at times and in places where local intermediary groups are weakened relative to the mass media, but also that such social movements would have negative consequences, ranging from the failure of local problem-solving efforts to the emergence of violent protest behavior. However, it is important to note that Putnam does not unequivocally make this interpretation. Instead, he acknowledges that genuinely grass-roots social movements can "both embody and produce social capital," while simultaneously acknowledging that other social movements are really nationally based organizations with full-time professional staffs relying on the contributions of "checkbook" members to generate resources that can be used for "manipulating the mass media so as to influence public opinion" (p. 153). And, as Baer and Bositis note (p. 162), mass society theory has been contradicted by empirical research such as Sears and McConahay's (1973) study of involvement in the Watts riot in 1965. Contrary to the expectations of mass society theory, riot participants tended to be more involved in the community, not socially disconnected individuals isolated from intermediary groups.

Other research on social movements is rooted in a theoretical framework emphasizing their emergence as a response to group grievances and the capacity of the group's leadership to give voice to those grievances and build a sense of attachment, or group consciousness, among its members. In stark contrast to mass society theory, this "group consciousness" theory (Baer and Bositis, 165) stipulates that social movements are more likely to emerge at times or in places where there are strong social or communal groups upon which the movement can build. What has come to be called "identity politics" is crucial to this interpretation of social movements; racial, ethnic, gender, and sexual characteristics that are core elements of an individual's identity are also powerful elements for building group consciousness rooted in that identity, particularly if triggering events crystallize grievances long endured by the group. The emergence of the modern gay rights movement, for example, is frequently traced to the 1969 Stonewall riots in New York City, when patrons of a gay bar actively resisted being harassed by the police department. While this event sparked a gay rights movement nationwide, that movement is "local rather than national in focus" (Baer and Bositis, p. 184), and its strength in any particular city is a function of the extent to which a strong local network of gay social and communal organizations exists (Bailey 1998).

Although research in this genre that is most relevant to urban politics in the United States is typically based on qualitative case studies or historical analysis, other research is also relevant to it. Perhaps the most notable example, Browning, Marshall, and Tabb's (1984) quantitative case analysis of ten cities in California, actually provides some evidence that can be interpreted as contrary to the theory. In their assessment of the causes of protest activity, for example, they found that several factors that would be logical indicators of minority grievance, such as socioeconomic inequality of minority groups in comparison with the white population and the dominant political coalition's resistance to minority-group preferences, were not predictors of greater levels of minority protest. If anything, they found the reverse; minority protest activity was greater where there was less socioeconomic inequality and where whites were more supportive of black leaders' agenda. Similarly, some of the earliest empirical work on protest in American cities (Eisinger 1973) found that protest was more likely in communities with institutional arrangements that were more accessible to minority groups (mayor-council government) and in communities with public policies favorable to the demands of racial minorities, such as the hiring of minority police officers.

On the other hand, some quantitative, cross-national research indicates that income inequality is a key predictor of the development of protest and revolutionary social movements (Muller and Seligson 1987, as cited in Euchner 1996, 73). And other elements of Browning, Marshall, and Tabb's analysis are consistent with group-consciousness theory. In particular, they find (pp. 92–93) that the size of the minority population is by far the most important predictor of the extent of protest activity, and they interpret this finding to mean that substantial protest tends to occur in cities with large enough minority populations to have the social and political groupings that are the key building blocks for group consciousness. Research on race riots in U.S. cities in the 1960s and in more recent years is also consistent with the social-consciousness theoretical perspective, in that it emphasizes how these events were triggered by the grievances of African Americans in northern urban centers (Sears 1994).

Contemporary research on social movements relies heavily on yet a third theoretical perspective. Resource mobilization theory maintains that social movements emerge whenever entrepreneurs from outside an affected group take a leadership role to leverage resources necessary for group mobilization (McCarthy and Zald 1973). From this perspective, social movements and the protest they foster are dependent upon the distribution of resources that can be accessed, such as foundation support, law firms willing to provide pro bono services, church-related support, and government grants (Baer and Bositis 1993, 163), as well as upon entrepreneurial leaders motivated to put such resources to work. It should be noted that from this theoretical perspective, the extent to which a group experiences grievances or has a strong sense of group consciousness is not particularly relevant for understanding where and when protest movements will emerge. Rather, such groups constitute *potential* social movements, activated only through the mobilization of resources by outside brokers.

Research on protest movements devoted to various decency issues is highly consistent with resource mobilization theory. In a ground-breaking case study of the introduction of controversial new ordinances regulating pornography in Indianapolis and Minneapolis, Downs (1989) reports how prominent feminist theorists brought in legal expertise and national visibility to stoke a local movement to treat pornography as an abrogation of women's rights. Cress and Snow (1998), in a study of social movements of the homeless in eight American cities, document a broad array of resources (in terms of money, labor, and moral legitimacy) that were mobilized by these movements and show that 75 percent of them were derived from external sources (p. 82).

With respect to the impact or consequences of protest, a number of interpretations suggest that the mobilization of mass protest in American cities has had substantial policy consequences. Much of this type of analysis is based upon historical analysis of the race-related urban disorders of the 1960s. Frances Fox Piven and Richard A. Cloward generated a line of work suggesting that disruptive protest can be a potent vehicle for the poor to get policy attention from an otherwise unresponsive capitalist welfare state. More specifically, they concluded that the political volatility of blacks in northern urban centers caused the emergence of "a series of federal service programs directed to the ghetto" (Piven 1974, 320). More recently, Gale (1996) has generated similar findings with respect to the policy impact of both the 1960s riots and the Los Angeles riots of 1992. Based on careful analysis of historical materials, Gale concludes that just as targeted urban aid programs such as Model Cities were the government's response to "urban interracial mob violence in the 1960's," so also was the federal government's urban enterprise zone/empowerment zone program of targeted aid a response to the more recent riots.

Still other analysts emphasize that social movements have been successful in gaining governmental responsiveness and policy reform by using a combination of protest tactics, electoral mobilization, and interest-group lobbying. Dufour (1998), for example, uses a case study of the gay and lesbian rights movement in Chicago to show how that movement, which is well known for high-profile protest activities such as marches and demonstrations, achieved policy responses such as the city's adoption of nondiscrimination and hate-crime ordinances protecting gays and lesbians through a process of electoral mobilization. Browning, Marshall, and Tabb offer an even more highly developed theory and set of empirical findings about the connections between protest, electoral mobilization, and policy success. They argue that the protest activity of blacks and Hispanics did effectively put some pressure on city governments, resulting in minority hiring, the institution of civilian police review boards, minority representation on other boards and commissions, and city contracts with minority businesses. However, they find that protest was most important when it set the stage for electoral mobilization that led to the inclusion of racial minorities in the cities' dominant electoral coalitions. Such "incorporation" is a far more important predictor of policy responsiveness to minority interests.

Conclusion

When viewed from a systems perspective, the various forms of citizen participation reviewed in this chapter play an interesting dual role. On the one hand, citizen participation is a classic system input. When citizens vote, contact city officials about services, participate in neighborhood organizations, or engage in protest activity, they are providing both the demands and the resources (for example, information and volunteer problem-solving efforts) that are crucial inputs to the political process. If urban political systems are to be responsive, it will be responsiveness to these inputs. The key problem here is the bias in these system inputs. As we have seen, the level of involvement in each form of citizen participation is lower among the disadvantaged and usually among racial minorities as well. To the extent that this is the case, responsiveness to these participatory inputs will lead to policy bias.

Historically, both the federal and city governments have initiated a variety of efforts to counteract these racial and class-based differentials in citizen participation; these include the establishment of ombudsman offices that "level the playing field" for citizens to contact city officials with complaints and requests (Sharp 1986) and the federal government's requirement for citizen participation in urban redevelopment programs. This takes us to government's role in facilitating citizen participation, which is to say, viewing citizen participation as an output of the governmental process.

Much research suggests that when citizen participation is an intended outcome, as it is when government produces programs designed to enhance citizen involvement, especially among the disadvantaged, the results can be quite disappointing. However, it is important to note that enhanced citizen participation can be an unintended output as well. For example, some research on urban schools suggests that school choice programs actually contribute to the levels of parental involvement in voluntary organizations (Schneider, Teske, Marschall, Mintrom, and Roch 1997). Although many critics have charged that school choice programs will fail because they assume a greater level of parental knowledge and involvement than can be found in many urban neighborhoods, this research suggests that "government policies that enhance choice over public goods can increase the capacity of the citizen/consumer to act as a responsible, involved citizen" (p. 91). In a quite different vein, Schneider and Ingram (1997) argue that the very design of public policies can be damaging to participatory democracy. In particular, they argue that policies that define people as being deserving but weak "dependents" will lead those individuals to become politically passive, and policies that define people as undeserving and weak will alienate them and cause them to eschew conventional forms of political participation.

As these various lines of research suggest, citizen participation as an unintended outcome of what government does has both a positive and a negative face. Governmental policies designed for other purposes may yield an unexpected bonus in the form of enhanced levels of involvement in voluntary organizations, or they may systematically deactivate the participatory potential of certain groups. More generally, acknowledgment that citizen participation is both an input and an output of governmental decision making is an important antidote to naiveté. It reminds us that the demands upon and the support for government are, for better or worse, partly shaped by government itself.

Suggested Readings

Baldassare, Mark, ed. 1992. *The Los Angeles Riots.* Boulder: Westview Press. This edited volume provides a variety of interpretations of urban protest in its most violent form.

Berry, Jeffrey M., Kent E. Portney, and Ken Thomson. 1993. *The Rebirth of Urban Democracy.* Washington, D.C.: Brookings Institution. An in-depth analysis of neighborhood organization–based citizen participation in cities that have made major commitments to enhancing such participation.

Henig, Jeffrey R., Richard C. Hula, Marion Orr, and Desiree S. Pedescleaux. 1999. *The Color of School Reform.* Princeton: Princeton University Press. A richly detailed story of school reform in urban areas that illustrates the range of stakeholders involved and the way in which their participation (or the lack thereof) affects the success of reform efforts.

Putnam, Robert D. 2000. *Bowling Alone: The Collapse and Revival of American Community.* New York: Simon and Schuster. This book provides the most comprehensive statement of Putnam's enormously influential work on both the causes and consequences of declining civic involvement and social capital.

Rosenstone, Steven J., and John Mark Hansen. 1993. *Mobilization, Participation, and Democracy in America.* A broad overview and important interpretation of trends in participation in the United States.

Sharp, Elaine B., ed. 1999. *Culture Wars and City Politics.* Lawrence: University Press of Kansas. This edited volume focuses on a special category of local governance—the highly charged morality issues such as gay rights and control of abortion protest—that occasionally confront urban officials and illustrates the participation of various stakeholder groups in this area of governance.

References

Alex-Assensoh, Yvette M. 1998. *Neighborhoods, Family, and Political Behavior in Urban America.* New York: Garland.

Ardrey, Saundra C. 1993. "Cleveland and the Politics of Resurgence: The Search for Effective Political Control." In *Dilemmas of Black Politics*, ed. Georgia A. Persons. New York: HarperCollins, 109–127.

Baer, Denise L., and David A. Bositis. 1993. *Politics and Linkage in a Democratic Society.* Englewood Cliffs, N.J.: Prentice Hall.

Bailey, R.W. 1998. *Gay Politics, Urban Politics: Identity and Economics in the Urban Setting.* New York: Columbia University Press.

Berry, Jeffrey M., Kent E. Portney, and Ken Thomson. 1993. *The Rebirth of Urban Democracy.* Washington, D.C.: Brookings Institution.

Bridges, Amy. 1997. "Textbook Municipal Reform," *Urban Affairs Review* 33 (September): 97–120.

Browning, Rufus, Dale Rogers Marshall, and David H. Tabb. 1984. *Protest Is Not Enough*. Berkeley: University of California Press.

Button, James W., Barbara A. Rienzo, and Kenneth Wald. 1997. *Private Lives, Public Conflicts: Battles over Gay Rights in American Communities*. Washington, D.C.: CQ Press.

Calvo, Maria Antonia, and Steven J. Rosenstone. 1989. *Hispanic Political Participation*. San Antonio: Southwest Voter Research Institute.

Chan, Edgar S. 1997. "The Co-Production Imperative." *Social Policy* 27 (spring): 62–68.

Clarke, Susan. 1999. "Ideas, Interests, and Institutions Shaping Abortion Politics in Denver." In *Culture Wars and Local Politics*, ed. Elaine B. Sharp, 43–62. Lawrence: University Press of Kansas.

Clingermayer, James C., and Richard C. Feiock. 1994. "Campaigns, Careerism, and Constituencies: Contacting Council Members About Economic Development Policy." *American Politics Quarterly* 22 (October): 453–468.

Conway, M. Margaret. 2000. *Political Participation in the United States*. Washington, D.C.: CQ Press.

Coulter, Philip B. 1992. "There's a Madness in the Method: Redefining Citizen Contacting of Government Officials." *Urban Affairs Quarterly* 28 (December): 297–316.

Cress, Daniel M. and David A. Snow. 1998. "Mobilization at the Margins: Organizing by the Homeless." In *Social Movements and American Political Institutions*, ed. Anne N. Costain and Andrew S. McFarland, 73–98. Lanham, Md.: Rowman and Littlefield.

Davidson, Chandler, and Luis Ricardo Fraga. 1988. "Slating Groups as Parties in a 'Nonpartisan' Setting." *Western Political Quarterly* (June): 373–391.

DeLeon, Richard Edward. 1992. *Left Coast City*. Lawrence: University Press of Kansas.

Downs, Donald. 1989. *The New Politics of Pornography*. Chicago: University of Chicago Press.

Dufour, Claude. 1998. "Mobilizing Gay Activists." In *Social Movements and American Political Institutions*, ed. Costain and McFarland, 59–72.

Eisinger, Peter. 1973. "The Conditions of Protest Behavior in American Cities." *American Political Science Review* 67 (March): 11–28.

Erie, Steven. 1988. *Rainbow's End: Irish-Americans and the Dilemmas of Urban Machine Politics, 1840–1985*. Berkeley: University of California Press.

Euchner, Charles C. 1996. *Extraordinary Politics: How Protest and Dissent Are Changing American Democracy*. Boulder: Westview Press.

Fredericksen, Patricia, and Rosanne London. 2000. "Disconnect in the Hollow State: The Pivotal Role of Organizational Capacity in Community-Based Development Organizations." *Public Administration Review* 60 (May): 230–239.

Gale, Dennis E. 1996. *Understanding Urban Unrest*. Thousand Oaks, Calif.: Sage.

Goetz, Edward G., and Mara Sidney. 1997. "Local Policy Subsystems and Issue Definition: An Analysis of Community Development Policy Change." *Urban Affairs Review* 32 (March): 490–512.

Henig, Jeffrey R., Richard C. Hula, Marion Orr, and Desiree S. Pedescleaux. 1999. *The Color of School Reform*. Princeton: Princeton University Press.

Henry, Charles P. 1987. "Racial Factors in the 1982 California Gubernatorial Campaign: Why Bradley Lost." In *The New Black Politics*, 2d ed., ed. Michael B. Breston, Lenneal J. Henderson, and Paul L. Puryear, 76–94. New York: Longman.

Hero, Rodney E. 1986. "Explaining Citizen-Initiated Contacting of Government Officials: Socioeconomic Status, Perceived Need, or Something Else?" *Social Science Quarterly* 67 (September): 626–635.

Hula, Richard C., Cynthia Y. Jackson, and Marion Orr. 1997. "Urban Politics, Governing Nonprofits, and Community Revitalization." *Urban Affairs Review* 32 (March): 459–489.

Inglehart, Ronald. 1990. *Culture Shift in Advanced Industrial Society.* Princeton: Princeton University Press.

Inglot, Tomasz, and John P. Pelissero. 1993. "Ethnic Political Power in a Machine City: Chicago's Poles at Rainbow's End." *Urban Affairs Quarterly* 28 (June): 526–543.

Jones, Bryan D. 1980. *Service Delivery in the City.* New York: Longman.

Jones, Bryan D., Saadia R. Greenberg, Clifford Kaufman, and Joseph Drew. 1977. "Bureaucratic Response to Citizen Initiated Contacts: Environmental Enforcement in Detroit." *American Political Science Review* 71 (March): 148–65.

———— 1978. "Service Delivery Rules and the Distribution of Local Government Services: Three Detroit Bureaucracies." *Journal of Politics* (May): 332–368.

Lineberry, Robert L. 1977. *Equality and Urban Policy.* Beverly Hills, Calif.: Sage.

Logan, John R., and Gordana Rabrenovic. 1990. "Neighborhood Organizations: Their Issues, Their Allies, and Their Opponents." *Urban Affairs Quarterly* 26 (September): 68–94.

Longoria, Thomas Jr. 1999. "The Impact of Office on Cross-Racial Voting." *Urban Affairs Review* 34 (March): 596–603.

McCarthy, John D., and Mayer N. Zald. 1973. *The Trends of Social Movements in America.* Morristown, N.J.: General Learning Press.

McCormick II, Joseph, and Charles E. Jones. 1993. "The Conceptualization of Deracialization: Thinking Through the Dilemma." In *Dilemmas of Black Politics,* ed. Persons, 66–84.

Mehay, Stephen L., and Rodolfo A. Gonzalez. 1994. "District Elections and the Power of Municipal Employee Unions." *Journal of Labor Research* (fall): 387–397.

Mesch, Gustavo S., and Kent P. Schwirian. 1996. "The Effectiveness of Neighborhood Collective Action." *Social Problems* 43 (November): 467–484.

Muller, Edward N., and Mitchell A. Seligson. 1987. "Inequality and Insurgency." *American Political Science Review* 81 (June): 425–451.

Oberschall, Anthony. 1992. *Social Movements: Ideologies, Interests, and Identities.* New Brunswick, N.J.: Transaction.

Pateman, Carole. 1970. *Participation and Democratic Theory.* Cambridge: Cambridge University Press.

Pelissero, John P., Timothy B. Krebs, and Shannon Jenkins. 2000. "Asian-Americans, Political Organizations, and Participation in Chicago's Electoral Precincts." *Urban Affairs Review* 35 (July): 750–769.

Perry, Huey L. 1991. "Deracialization as an Analytical Construct in American Urban Politics." *Urban Affairs Quarterly* 27 (December): 181–191.

Peterson, Paul. 1981. *City Limits.* Chicago: University of Chicago Press.

Piven, Frances Fox. 1974. "The Urban Crisis: Who Got What, and Why?" In *The Politics of Turmoil,* ed. Richard Cloward and Frances Fox Piven, 314–351. New York: Vintage.

Putnam, Robert D. 2000. *Bowling Alone: The Collapse and Revival of American Community.* New York: Simon and Schuster.

Regaldo, James A. 1991. "Organized Labor and Los Angeles City Politics." *Urban Affairs Quarterly* 27 (September): 87–108.

Rosenstone, Steven J., and John Mark Hansen. 1993. *Mobilization, Participation, and Democracy in America.* New York: Macmillan.

Ross, Bernard H. and Myron A. Levine. 1996. *Urban Politics.* 5th ed. Itasca, Ill.: F. E. Peacock.

Schneider, Anne, and Helen Ingram. 1997. *Policy Design for Democracy.* Lawrence: University Press of Kansas.

Schneider, Mark, Paul Teske, Melissa Marschall, Michael Mintrom, and Christine Roch. 1997 "Institutional Arrangements and the Creation of Social Capital: The Effects of Public School Choice." *American Political Science Review* 91 (March): 82–93.

Schwirian, Kent P. 1983. "Urban Spatial Arrangements as Reflections of Social Reality." In *Remaking the City: Social Science Perspectives on Urban Design*, ed. John S. Pipkin, Mark E. LaBory, and Judith R. Blau, 121–147. Albany: State University of New York Press.

Sears, David O., and John B. McConahay. 1973. *The Politics of Violence.* Boston: Houghton Mifflin.

Sears, David O. 1994. "Urban Rioting in Los Angeles: A Comparison of 1965 with 1992." In *The Los Angeles Riots,* ed. M. Baldassare, 237–254. Boulder: Westview Press.

Sharp, Elaine B. 1982. "Citizen-Initiated Contacting of Government Officials and Socioeconomic Status: Determining the Relationship and Accounting for It." *American Political Science Review* 76: 109–115.

———— 1984. "Citizen Demand-Making in the Urban Context." *American Journal of Political Science* 28 (November): 654–670.

———— 1986. *Citizen Demand-Making in the Urban Context.* Tuscaloosa: University of Alabama Press.

————1996. "Culture Wars and City Politics: Local Government's Role in Social Conflict." *Urban Affairs Review* 31 (July): 738–758.

———— 1997. "A Comparative Anatomy of Urban Social Conflict." *Political Research Quarterly* 50 (June): 261–280.

———— ed. 1999. *Culture Wars and City Politics.* Lawrence: University Press of Kansas.

———— "Local Government and the Politics of Decency." Paper presented at the 2002 Annual Meetings of the Southwestern Social Science Association. New Orleans, Louisiana, March 27–30. (forthcoming in *Social Science Quarterly*).

Sonenshein, Raphael J. 1996. "The Battle over Liquor Stores in South Central Los Angeles." *Urban Affairs Review* 31 (July): 710–728.

Stone, Clarence N. 1996. "Urban Political Machines: Taking Stock." *PS: Political Science and Politics* 29 (September): 446–451.

Summers, Mary E., and Philip A. Klinkner. 1991. "The Daniels Election in New Haven and the Failure of the Deracialization Hypothesis." *Urban Affairs Quarterly* 27 (December): 202– 215.

Thomas, John C. 1982. "Citizen-Initiated Contacts with Government Agencies: A Test of Three Theories." *American Journal of Political Science* 26: 504–522.

———— 1986. *Between Citizen and City: Neighborhood Organizations and Urban Politics in Cincinnati.* Lawrence: University Press of Kansas.

Traut, Carol Ann, and Craig F. Emmert. 1993. "Citizen-Initiated Contacting: A Multivariate Analysis." *American Politics Quarterly* 21 (April): 239–254.

Tullos, Janice K. 1995. "Citizen Participation in Boston's Development Policy: The Political Economy of Participation." *Urban Affairs Review* 30 (March): 514–537.

Vedlitz, Arnold, James Dyer, and Roger Durand. 1980. "Citizen Contacts with Local Governments: A Comparative View." *American Journal of Political Science* 24: 50–67.

Vedlitz, Arnold, and Eric Veblen. 1980. "Voting and Contacting: Two Forms of Political Participation in a Suburban Community." *Urban Affairs Quarterly* 16: 31–48.

Verba, Sidney, and Norman H. Nie. 1972. *Participation in America: Political Democracy and Social Equality.* New York: Harper and Row.

Verba, Sidney, Kay Lehman Schlozman, and Henry E. Brady. 1995. *Voice and Equality: Civic Volunteerism in American Politics.* Cambridge: Harvard University Press.

Zuckerman, Alan S., and Darrell M. West. 1985. "The Political Bases of Citizen Contacting: A Cross-National Analysis." *American Political Science Review* 79: 117–131.

4 Urban Racial and Ethnic Politics

Dianne M. Pinderhughes

As a field, urban politics explores the legislative, executive, and administrative activities of the many forms of government present in most large urban metropolitan areas. Education, housing, economic development, criminal justice, fiscal affairs, transportation, the environment, and health care are only a few areas in which urban governments are active. Political attitudes, partisan identification, and party politics form in part at the local level. As new groups arrive they bring new issues to the political system. Communicating with public officials is a vital part of urban public policy and urban politics. If people are unable to elect representatives of their own group, or if incumbents do not understand their constituents, the urban setting faces fundamental challenges. When the needs and interests of different populations are not absorbed into the political system, congestion, conflict, riots, and rebellions follow. As urban disorder and unrest in the 1960s and 1990s demonstrated, equitable (or inequitable) management of urban policy areas and smooth (or bumpy) daily operations affect local—and even national—security and stability (Judd and Swanstrom 1994; Palley and Palley 1977).

Racial and ethnic politics (or minority politics, as it is sometimes called) covers a range of areas vital to urban politics. Racial and ethnic groups play a role in every aspect of American government, including electoral participation and voting rights; legislative, executive, and judicial institutions; and partisan and policy issues. In this sense the study of racial and ethnic politics is similar to urban politics. But there are differences. Urban politics focuses on the institutional and geographic dimensions of politics and of the specific character of racial and ethnic group interactions with the urban setting. The study of racial and ethnic groups requires an understanding of the legal, economic, and historical patterns of these groups' entry into and engagement with the American political system. Understanding the groups' experiences in the larger American context is different from understanding specific encounters in one or several cities.

The most important starting point for any discussion of these issues is definitions. What is the meaning and significance of the term minority politics? Groups categorized by this definition are expected to be literally in the minority, to be less able to express their interests in the rough-and-tumble political arena because they are a small proportion of the population. The legal framework of immigration law historically incorporated preferences for citizens from European nations, making blacks, Asians, Latinos, and other non-European groups a challenge to the political dominance and leadership of European immigrants and their descendants.

Since each of the major racial or ethnic groups entered American society within distinct legal and political frameworks, their participation in American politics tends to show different patterns of substantive issues and controversies. Because African Americans arrived as slaves without legal standing as citizens, political participation and economic standing continue as issues in their political agenda in the twentieth and twenty-first centuries. Affirmative action and reparations are examples of two such issues. Asian Americans were allowed to become citizens for the first time as recently as the mid-twentieth century, making their acceptance as U.S. citizens and their participation in electoral politics a continuing challenge. Latinos represent a wide range of nationalities even though they are characterized as a single group. Some Latinos in the Southwest are descended from precolonial settlers who were forced to give up their land and comply with the American legal and property ownership systems. Expropriation of property—and its political consequences—had a powerful impact on the Latino populations in the Southwest. But Puerto Ricans, for example, are citizens whose nation of origin sits outside the U.S. mainland and is not fully included in its system of political representation.

The terms blacks, Latinos, and Asians are shorthand for a large number of nationality groups that arrive from myriad countries. Mexicans, Cubans, Dominicans, Puerto Ricans, Colombians, and more—all become Latinos in the United States. The Japanese, Indians, Chinese, Cambodians, Filipinos, Vietnamese, and others become Asian Americans. African Americans are distinguished by the long period of political acculturation they underwent during centuries of enslavement. Multiple nationalities, cultural groups, and language groups gradually formed a relatively unified group unique to North America, one with which most African Americans strongly identify (Dawson 1994). Two things strengthened this identity: slavery and laws that limited immigration by blacks from Africa, South America, or the Caribbean. Less than one percent of blacks admitted annually during the late nineteenth and most of the twentieth centuries were from these three areas. The African American population grew by immigration only slightly for a century and a half. It is only in recent decades that blacks have been admitted into the United States in larger numbers, opening the possibility of increasing ethnicity among African Americans.

Thus, I prefer the phrase racial and ethnic politics to minority politics, because the former has no meaning in relation to the groups' size or implied subordination in the national hierarchy. Although this phrase does not necessarily limit the groups in question to Latinos, Asian Americans, and African Americans—Europeans also fit—for the purposes of this chapter I will limit my discussion to non-European groups. The chapter will cover four main areas: a brief introduction to major developments in racial and ethnic politics, a review of theoretical developments, an examination of methodological issues related to urban racial and ethnic politics, and proposed subjects on an agenda for future study in the field.

Urban racial and ethnic politics raises questions as to how groups convey their demands and how the political system responds to them. The institutional structures built around European immigrants faced substantial stresses from African Americans during the tense 1960s and 1970s when African Americans demanded political access and responsiveness. The migration experiences, homeland ties, and economic base of Asians and Latinos reflect sharply different political patterns than those of blacks and whites. How urban governments and racial and ethnic groups manage the efforts of dizzying numbers of new and old groups to seek and hold power is the subject of this chapter.

Developments in Racial and Ethnic Politics

This section traces the arrival and movement into the urban political arena in the mid-twentieth century of blacks followed by Latinos and Asians in the last decades of the century.

Slavery and Immigration Policy

The legacy of racial slavery affects political participation by African Americans. African Americans are descendants of populations brought by force to U.S. shores; their legal status placed them paradoxically inside and outside of the American political system. Though slaves were counted as property before the Civil War and not extended the right to vote, they were included among the population of the southern states, boosting the South's numbers to ensure the region dominated the electoral college. Afterward slaves became citizens without full citizenship, unable to stabilize their participation in electoral politics or to secure their economic rights. When blacks began to migrate out of the rural South and into urban areas in the industrial North and West and the commercial South in the twentieth century, their presence still generated considerable controversy and conflict.

The legacy of slavery poses one kind of problem to political participation. Immigration policy poses another. Early twentieth-century immigration policy limited entry to people from European nations, and when even those numbers grew too large legislators revised the policies to substantially deny entry to all immigrants for forty-five years after World War I. The United States substantially reformed its immigration policy in the 1950s and 1960s. The creation of citizenship for Asians in the 1950s and the removal of immigration quotas for non-Europeans in 1965 brought large numbers of new racial and ethnic groups into the country and introduced new issues of language and cultural difference and new debates about what it meant to be American. In this era, though large cohorts of immigrants constructed whole language and cultural environments as they settled into American life—building new Korean and Mexican commercial areas and enhancing older Chinese ones—popular expectations continued to demand that new groups subject themselves to the "melting pot," or the idea of total assimilation. Research showed, however, that total assimilation was at best an extended process and at worst pure fiction (Glazer and Moynihan 1973; Torres 1995).

These changes in immigration policy—and new changes in the economy, such as the out-migration of skilled, high-wage jobs and the increase in low-wage service jobs—attracted increasing numbers of Mexicans and Central and South Americans to the U.S. labor market. Today the black and European urban political leadership faces a new era of contestation as Latinos, Asian Americans, West Indians, and South Americans of any race enter the urban arena, opening new opportunities and dangers for urban political environments already challenged once by black political demands.

The political legacy of slavery and problematic immigration policies make racial and ethnic politics an important challenge to the American political system. Most often these challenges appear first in the urban political arena because racial and ethnic groups tend to settle in large metropolitan areas.

Political Participation

Since Latinos and Asians have been active politically for a much shorter time, their impact on the urban political environment is still in its early stages. In the second half of the twentieth century changes in agricultural production pushed—and production demands pulled—large numbers of blacks (then referred to as Negroes) out of the rural South and into northern and western urban settings for the first time. Though blacks had begun to migrate during World War I, their movement accelerated substantially during the economic depression of the 1930s and in response to the economic demands of World War II in the 1940s. Political scientists explored the politics of European and black minority groups in American cities from a variety of perspectives. Early on, political scientists hypothesized that blacks would assimilate into the political system in much the same way European ethnic groups were assumed to have done, and therefore blacks were not studied separately, or were not expected to be politically distinct (Dahl 1961, 59; Wolfinger 1970; Parenti 1970). Other political scientists, such as James Q. Wilson (1960), concentrated on Negro politics in Chicago with a theoretical framework limited to their posture toward white political authority, emphasizing protest and bargaining and thereby missing the greater political differences within the group (McClain and Garcia 1993; Pinderhughes 1987).

The arrival of large numbers of blacks to cities in the North in the 1950s and 1960s created tension and led to urban crises associated with urban renewal, education and desegregation, public order, and poverty. The federal urban renewal program of the 1950s and 1960s was widely perceived as a strategy for the removal of blacks from central city areas. Black neighborhoods in cities where the program was implemented were frequently demolished and reconstructed (Rossi and Dentler 1961). Strategies to address the de facto racial segregation in urban schools included planned desegregation and busing in a range of cities. Urban white political leaders such as Mayor Richard Daley in Chicago and local communities such as South Boston resisted school desegregation policies initiated by the federal government (Crain 1969). In other cases black communities challenged the education system's failure to educate their children, experimenting with grassroots programs such as community control of neighborhood schools (Gittell and Berube 1969; LaNoue and Smith 1973).

Finally the federal government, responding partially to the riots, disorders, and unrest of the 1970s, created programs to address poverty. These programs, however, had no coherent strategy to end poverty (Greenstone and Peterson 1973; Moynihan 1970).

The urban politics literature followed these developments closely and placed racial and ethnic group politics at the center of their observations—and hence at the center of American politics—in the 1960s and early 1970s (Rossi and Dentler 1961; Banfield 1968; Piven and Cloward 1971).

To a certain extent the centrality of racial and ethnic groups to urban politics was unavoidable. Urban politics centered around the struggle for power as new racial groups demanded socioeconomic reform from a system led by white Anglo-Saxon Protestants or descendants of early-twentieth-century European immigrants. The tensions of the civil rights movement began in southern cities such as Baton Rouge and continued in Montgomery, Birmingham, and elsewhere in the 1950s and early 1960s. The conflicts and tensions in northern and western cities accelerated faster than either urban or national governments could respond to them and exploded into the riots of the 1960s and early 1970s. The intersection of these northern and southern regional developments was probably best symbolized by the 1965 Los Angeles riots, which began in Watts in August just weeks after President Lyndon Johnson signed the Voting Rights Act, the legislative high-water mark of the civil rights era. The 1965 voting rights legislation committed the federal government to reaffirming constitutional protections of African Americans' right to vote. Southern states, counties, and towns were required to allow the federal government to monitor and regulate registration procedures, the conduct of elections, and any changes in election laws where black electoral participation was low and where any prerequisites had been used as barriers to black voting in the past.

After urban political unrest began in the 1960s, the Johnson administration's War on Poverty created institutional channels linking the energies of protest around racial and economic concerns to local, state, and national governments. Studies of rent strikes among the poor in New York City and analysis of the operations of the Office of Economic Opportunity addressed some of the governmental efforts and social movement efforts to introduce reform. The studies weren't explicitly about minority groups or their politics, but they were nonetheless about the politics in which minority groups were deeply involved and often on the front lines of protest that ultimately resulted in some change (Lipsky 1970; Moynihan 1970).

This period of unrest and civil disturbances was followed by electoral firsts; blacks began to compete for and win election to political office in larger numbers. Blacks had been elected to city council and state legislative office in modest numbers from early in the century, but these seats were won especially in urban districts where blacks were heavily concentrated. By the 1960s and 1970s blacks began to seek greater power in legislative, executive, and administrative positions as mayors, school superintendents, judges, and members of Congress (Gosnell 1967; Henderson 1972; Preston, Puryear, and Henderson 1982, 1987; Pinderhughes 1987). As citywide leader, the role of mayor symbolized a power not previously held by blacks in urban political life. The literature on black mayors considered the impact of the new enfranchisement, measured the effectiveness of black mayors, and evaluated whether black residents were better off under the new black leadership. Some of those first elected included Mayor Kenneth Gibson of Newark, New Jersey, and Mayor Richard Hatcher of Gary, Indiana, in the 1960s and later Mayor Harold Washington in Chicago in 1983 and Mayor David Dinkins in New York City in 1989 (Bush 1984; Mollenkopf 1997; Grimshaw 1992). In the 1970s and particularly in the 1980s, voting rights policy began to reshape northern electoral politics as the courts accepted the constitutionality of single-member districts where blacks had difficulty winning election to office in at-large elections (Karnig and Welch 1980; Parker 1990).[1]

Racial and ethnic group politics as a subset of urban politics was defined for the first decades after World War II primarily in terms of black Americans. Because of Nathan Glazer and Daniel Patrick Moynihan's focus on New York City, their exploration of assimilationist possibilities included a more diverse range of groups, comparing the experiences of "Negroes, and Puerto Ricans" with the earlier European immigrants, "Jews, Italians, and Irish" (1973). These groups' selection as study subjects grasped the real complexity of New York and prefigured the urban immigration patterns that followed in other cities in the 1970s and 1980s. Increasing numbers of Latinos, Asians, and immigrants from a variety of nations began to settle in American urban areas. Coastal cities where these populations concentrated, such as Los Ange-les, Miami, New York, and Washington, D.C., experienced a new wave of violence and disorders in the 1980s and 1990s.

In the 1960s and 1970s the FBI created a Counterintelligence Program (Cointel-pro) that cooperated with state and local authorities in targeting gangs, civil rights groups, and other groups deemed left wing or in any way a threat to the status quo. The NAACP, Martin Luther King, the Black Panthers, and Chicago's Blackstone Rangers were among those subject to surveillance (Blackstock 1976; Garrow 1983). In the 1980s and 1990s police harassment came to national attention after a series of beatings of blacks and Latinos by Los Angeles and Miami police ignited riots and mul-tiracial conflict. When a trial of Los Angeles police officers charged in the beating of Rodney King, which had been captured on videotape, resulted in acquittal, the 1992 Los Angeles riots spread across much of the city. Surveillance of blacks, Latinos, and Asians—known as racial profiling—became a strategy for control used by local and state police (Smith and Tarallo 1995). Several state legislatures began to require police to record racial identity for these encounters to gather evidence of racially discrimi-natory profiling.[2]

While Latino and Asian populations increased substantially in the 1970s, 1980s, and 1990s, several factors complicated these groups' ability to elicit responses from urban governments. Both populations included multiple-nationality groups, with Asians divided by language as well as country of origin. American immigration poli-cies had limited continuing entry from Asian and South American countries so that existing populations distinguished themselves from recent arrivals.

Political participation, communication, electoral politics, and political representa-tion are significant issues for the new racial and ethnic groups. This was vividly demonstrated in the 1992 Los Angeles riots when Asian businesses recognized they had no direct access or regular means of communication with Mayor Bradley's office or with the police department. The contrast with black Los Angeles, which had far fewer businesses but had representatives in the mayor's office, city council, county board of supervisors, and the state and congressional delegations, could not have been more marked (Jackson 1991; Saito 1998).

The expansion of Latino and Asian populations challenged the capacity of urban governments to respond along a number of dimensions. The 1975 extension of the Voting Rights Act of 1965 required governmental jurisdictions to provide election materials—including ballots in languages other than English—when the popula-tion reached a minimum threshold and where literacy rates were lower than the na-tional average. But information was not necessarily available in the language of every new group, nor was material available in all service areas. More directly, agen-cies did not necessarily have employees able to converse in several languages. In many cases popular movements attacked these policies, instead supporting "English only" policies.

By the end of the century immigration reform and the Voting Rights Act increased the policy complexities that urban governments faced; they had just begun to address new responsibilities after the arrival of black Americans from the rural South. New populations with new languages and new problems generated additional policy demands (Jackson and Preston 1991; McClain and Stewart 1995; Kim 2000; Jennings 1994).

Also toward the end of the century many of the policy innovations that had sprung from the racial crises and tensions of the 1960s and 1970s encountered political and social backlash and legal challenges. School desegregation, voting and redistricting strategies, and even affirmative action lost political support and faced challenges in the courts. President Johnson's War on Poverty was ridiculed as a failure, and the Democratic Party was blamed for creating cities with attractive social welfare benefits, also known as "welfare magnets." Democrats also faced criticism for attempting to address racial and economic problems through public sector programs. Welfare was one of a number of "wedge" issues used to polarize voters and undermine popular support for such Democratic programs as the War on Poverty, affirmative action, and civil rights initiatives. Increased interest in the significance of class and the characterization of the underclass helped solidify the expectation that liberal political reform would be unable to remedy intractable racial problems (Barnett and Williams 1986; Drake and Holsworth 1996; Edsall and Edsall 1991; Peterson 1990; Wilson 1980; 1987).

Although by the 1990s racial and ethnic politics had become a central part of urban politics, economic changes on the international level—namely the expansion of large corporations onto a global scale—shifted the geographic competition for space in metropolitan regions from the suburban edges of cities (to which middle- and upper-class and ethnic whites had fled after World War II) back to downtown. Whereas blacks had complained of whites abandoning cities in the 1970s and 1980s, by the 1990s black and Latino neighborhoods encountered new residents who were young, upwardly mobile, and not black. Competition for land in closer proximity to large public and private cultural and social institutions gradually transformed the economic dynamics that had driven down the values of central city properties in the 1960s and 1970s (Squires 1989).

In those decades, as civil rights legislation and urban black coalitions generated greater electoral participation and elected public officials in substantial numbers, uncontested black control of American cities seemed a possibility. But the changes in immigration policy that occurred in the same year as the passage of the Voting Rights Act gradually reconfigured the urban population. For example "[i]n 1980 South-Central Los Angeles, which for decades had been the heart of the city's African American neighborhoods . . . was 90 percent native black; in 1990 it was 50 percent Latino" (Jones-Correa 2000, 150). By the beginning of the new century economic gentrification and black displacement had become real issues in cities. A mix of demographic changes and governmental and market forces eventually reconstructed neighborhoods, replacing blacks with new racial and ethnic groups and in some cases reclaiming the inner city for economic elites. Blacks moved to the suburbs, Latinos immigrated from a variety of countries in the hemisphere, and urban populations diversified as immigrants arrived from all over the world. Chicago, Detroit, Baltimore, Washington, D.C.—seemingly on the verge of becoming predominantly black in the 1960s and 1970s—looked much different by the end of the century.

Urban racial and ethnic politics, no longer dominated by either white or black majorities, will in the twenty-first century be a balance of competing racial and ethnic group politics. Nationalities from across the globe have made the urban political process one in which a variety of new groups will again be developing political values, shaping political goals, and building institutions for political mobilization and communication within the urban political system. Koreans, Dominicans, Mexicans, Haitians, Chinese, Puerto Ricans, Vietnamese, Colombians, Indians, Irish, Cambodians, and Russians are some of the groups that constitute a significant presence in American urban areas. As cities have grown more diverse, Peter Dreier, John Mollenkopf, and Todd Swanstrom suggest that increasing economic inequalities, accompanied by geographic segregation, could turn into political crises for urban areas. "The fundamental reality is one of growing economic segregation in the context of rising overall inequality . . . although growing economic inequality is bad, it is greatly worsened by growing economic segregation" (Dreier, Mollenkopf, and Swanstrom 2001, 12). As economic divisions divide populations within racial and ethnic groups as well as between racial groups, urban politics will become increasingly complex.

Theoretical Developments: Paradigms and Approaches

Some of the paradigms that have defined urban racial and ethnic politics in the past half century encompass numerous theoretical debates. This section will review only a few, including elite and pluralist theory, electoral participation and political attitudes, racial and ethnic group dynamics, policy studies, regime theory, and social capital and civil society. The study of elite and pluralist theory explored questions about the centralization of power and authority in American life after the 1950s. As African Americans, Latinos, Asians, and other groups have entered urban areas, scholars have measured their political attitudes and examined their participation in electoral politics and political parties. Urban politics has also studied whether racial and ethnic groups promote their individual group interests or the conditions under which they compete with or collaborate with other groups.

Policy studies is a subfield in which political scientists concentrate on specialized policymaking arenas. In this we'll see what impact racial and ethnic groups have on urban policymaking. Regime theory lays out the stability of political alliances over time and shows the significance of this stability in understanding the role of racial and ethnic groups in particular cities' policymaking. The institutional capacities of American groups has become a subject of particular interest in the past decade. Understanding the specific meaning of this concept in urban political environments and applying it to different racial and ethnic groups is an endeavor of many students of urban politics.

Elite and Pluralist Theory

Elite and pluralist theory centers on the concentration of political power in American public life and whether all groups routinely make demands and extract resources from the political system. Research on Atlanta, Georgia, in the 1950s emphasized the significance of political authority and the consolidation of resources and cooperation between the economic and political leadership in the city. As the de facto economic capital of the southern United States, Atlanta reflected the socioeconomic and political infrastructure that had grown out of the southern economy based on slavery. It is within this context that the strongest findings on the power of political elites and the stability of political regimes have been made.

Research that concentrated on northern industrial cities in the 1960s and 1970s, by contrast, emphasized decentralized political structures and the absence of political and economic integration of power. Studies of the North looked at the broad distribution of power and the expectation that distinctive political interests could organize, articulate their interests, introduce those concerns into the political system, and win substantive and equitably distributed resources in a range of policy areas. These pluralist theories reflected a postwar vision of American democratic values at a time when political and economic interests were, if anything, increasing their capacity to exercise authority. For most of the period pluralists' emphasis on the relative accessibility of the political system was directly contradicted by the conflicts new groups encountered as they attempted to participate in electoral politics.

These studies established the pluralist framework that dominated the assumptions of openness and decentralization many scholars brought to their work on urban politics and racial and ethnic politics for decades. Scholars of black politics and later Latino and Asian American politics tended to take a more critical view of the pluralist perspective, because they found more resistance than access. Marguerite Barnett analyzed the distinctions between black politics and racial and ethnic participation in racial and urban public policy in the 1960s and 1970s (1976). Pluralist perspectives had already begun to wane by the late 1970s and 1980s when the first research on Latinos and Asian Americans began (Dahl 1961; Banfield and Wilson 1963; Wilson 1960, 1995).

The earliest scholars of black politics explicitly challenged the assumptions of pluralist theory. Mathew Holden divided his pathbreaking analysis into two separate volumes. *The Politics of the Black Nation* (1973a) and *The White Man's Burden* (1973b) took the view that these two nations, white and black, reflected distinct moral communities. Holden explored the contours of each group and thereby challenged basic pluralist assumptions about the American political system's capacity for openness and political assimilation. But he also attacked some of the black separatist and revolutionary alternatives proposed. A symposium edited by Joseph McCormick published in *The National Political Science Review* revisited Holden's work on the twenty-fifth anniversary of its publication (2001). The review essays concluded that Holden's analysis more than stood the test of time and remains, according to Robert Smith, "the single best treatment of black politics" (Smith 2001, 4). Ernest Patterson's study of black city politics in St. Louis claimed to be the first book on big city politics published from a black perspective (1974). In 1967 Hamilton and civil rights activist Stokeley Carmichael published *Black Power,* which challenged the stability and wisdom of pluralism, political assimilation, and political coalitions. Later Charles V. Hamilton (1972) explored political leadership roles in his study of black preachers.

A number of studies during the 1970s and 1980s, often critical of pluralism, explored the first large generation of blacks elected to political office and their impact on the black and urban political environment. Later research surveyed black elected officials and concluded that there had been significant improvements in the volume of black political representation in public office in the 1970s, although racial inequality had not been eliminated. These authors reported on the factors associated with higher rates of election to office and greater influence on public policy. The most important factors were "socioeconomic characteristics" (income, education and occupation), "organizational [resources], media [resources], and other resources" (Karnig and Welch 1980, 148). Mack Jones (1972) emphasized the distinctions between ethnic/assimilationist politics and black politics and, according to McClain and Garcia (1993), attempted to "redirect . . . research in black politics away from the use of traditional political science frameworks and toward . . . alternative[s]. . . ." (p. 252); Nelson and Meranto 1977; Persons 1993; Preston 1976; Preston, Puryear, and Henderson 1987; Starks and Preston 1990).

Huey Perry, by contrast, is one of the few scholars of black politics to have touted the strength of pluralism. Perry (1991) argued for deracialization, a perspective that deemphasizes the prominence of racial strategy in the electoral arena. Perry and

Wayne Parent (1995) grounded their edited collection on the role of blacks in the American political system on the importance of pluralist theory. More often, however, students of black politics have emphasized the power of race in American urban racial and ethnic politics (Walton 1972, 1985; Walton, McLemore, and Gray 1990).

Recent research has focused on Asian American politics in urban areas, showing that Asians are more likely to form coalitions with Anglos than with Latinos or blacks. Research has also explored conflict between black customers and Asian shopkeepers, studied Asian electoral possibilities in Los Angeles, and studied Asians' political influence through financial contributions. Asians and Latinos have low levels of electoral participation; they also have a range of nationality groups with important differences in political attachment (Henry 1994; Umemoto 1994; Nakanishi 1991; Brackman and Erie 1995; Waldinger 1995; Kim 2000).

Arab Americans have settled in cities such as Cleveland and Detroit, where Lebanese Syrians, Iraqis, and Palestinian Jordanians constitute the largest groups, and Los Angeles, which has a large number of Iranians (Schopmeyer 2000). In Detroit Lebanese business owners and their black customers experience tensions similar to those between Koreans and blacks in Brooklyn and Los Angeles (David 2000, 156–157, 165–173).

Electoral Participation and Political Attitudes

Surveys of African American and Latino political attitudes are based on national rather than urban samples, although the population is concentrated in urban areas. Studies of electoral participation and political attitudes balance tensions between the larger discipline that treats political attitudes as grounded in individual behavior and racial and ethnic politics, which emphasizes group behavior. The research on black and Latino political participation explores the importance of the group and group identity in the development of political ideas and values and in the relationship of those views to the political system (Dawson 1994, 2001; de la Garza, DeSipio, Garcia, Garcia, and Falcon 1992).

Hanes Walton has written on a variety of subjects in black politics, and his book *Invisible Politics* (1985) is highly useful. Walton explores electoral and nonelectoral politics and argues that black politics includes a wider range of participation than the most conventional manifestations of support for the political system: elections.

The National Black Election Studies, conducted by James Jackson and his colleagues at the University of Michigan, laid the foundations for other examinations of black political attitudes. Patricia Gurin, Shirley Hatchett, and James Jackson's *Hope and Independence* (1989), Katherine Tate's *From Protest to Politics* (1993), and Michael Dawson's *Behind the Mule* (1994) are based on these surveys. Tate examines the political attitudes of black voters who participated in national elections in the 1970s and 1980s as they moved away from protests and demonstrations and into routinized electoral politics. Dawson discusses the dimensions of black linked-fate, that is, the idea that the experience of the individual is linked to the fate of the group, as an intellectual opening for exploring the strengths and weaknesses of group identity among African Americans (1994). Dawson also examines the range of philosophical perspectives within black political attitudes (2001).

Rodolfo de la Garza, Louis DeSipio, F. Chris Garcia, John Garcia, and Angelo Falcon and Harry Pachon and Louis DeSipio developed a model for conducting surveys of Latino public opinion. De la Garza and colleagues' Latino National Political Survey (1992) found in the late 1980s that Latinos did not view themselves in terms of a pan-Latino identity but as distinct nationality groups of Mexicans, Puerto Ricans, and Cubans. Pachon and DeSipio (1994) surveyed the political values of Latino immigrants (McClain and Garcia 1993, 261). Falcon found that Latinos increasingly in the 1980s and 1990s served as a swing voting bloc in urban elections (McClain and Garcia 1993, 263).

Racial and Ethnic Group Dynamics: Single Group vs. Coalition Politics

Early research in single group and coalition politics tended to focus on black efforts to overcome white resistance to their political participation. As the rate of black population growth in urban areas stabilized in the 1980s and 1990s, the total number of new racial and ethnic groups grew and their proportion in the population expanded. Accordingly, scholars began to study opportunities for biracial and coalition politics. These studies were especially prominent among researchers who had previously concentrated on a single racial or ethnic group, and among a new generation of scholars (Jackson and Preston 1991; Jennings 1994; Marable 1994; Rich 1996; DeSipio 1996; McClain and Stewart 1995; Alex-Assensoh and Hanks 2000).

When Latinos began to participate in electoral politics, they collaborated with blacks. But by the 1980s "the policy preferences of . . . blacks and Latinos diverged" (McClain and Garcia 1993, 269). Blacks and Latinos have divided over such policies as the English Only Movement (which lobbies for English to be the official language of government), employer sanctions for hiring undocumented workers, and immigration reform, thereby making local coalitions, through which the two groups might dominate the urban scene, unstable or unlikely. Research on California introduced to the rest of the country biracial coalitions and the importance of black and Latino political incorporation (Browning, Marshall, and Tabb 1984, 1990, 1997; Sonenshein 1993).

Other researchers, such as Ira Katznelson and William Nelson, developed their comparison from a different perspective, studying urban racial politics in the United States and Britain. Katznelson (1973) published a broad historical comparison that examined the context in which black urban politics had evolved in each country.

More recently Nelson (2000) explored the relations among black political activists in Boston and Liverpool. Amy Freedman studied Chinese political participation in Indonesia, Malaysia, Monterey Park (California), and New York City. She found that Chinese communities participate when mobilized by elites in systems open to electoral participation and through the influence of "individual networking and group mobilization" (2000, 183).

Policy Studies

Understanding the effect of racial and ethnic political participation on public policy formation has been a consistent theme in the research on urban politics. This section concentrates on poverty, class, and the underclass and economic development and affirmative action. These two broad categories overlap to some degree.

Poverty, Class, and the Underclass. The post–World War II urban politics literature was dominated by the controversies arising from poverty, the immigration of many blacks and later Latinos, and problems with the urban economic infrastructure as production relocated from center city areas to the suburbs, then to the South and Southwest, and eventually out of the country altogether. Much of the literature concentrated on conflicts arising from government's efforts to address these problems in the community action program, an offshoot of federal antipoverty efforts. Stanley Greenberg surveyed the residents of five poor black neighborhoods in Philadelphia, Detroit, and Atlanta; Appalachian whites in Hamilton, Ohio; and Mexican Americans in San Jose, California, using standard surveys, in-depth interviews, and longer observations to understand how they grappled with poverty and economic deterioration (1974). More recently, Yvette Alex-Assensoh (1998) revisited these issues to examine political behavior among the underclass in the 1990s (Greenstone and Peterson 1973).

Literature on housing segregation and its impact on the underclass takes another perspective on these problems. In the 1970s scholars proposed housing integration as a solution to the racial and economic problems of the era, and by the 1990s they were arguing that the failure to address segregated urban communities had led to the development of an underclass (Downs 1973; Massey and Denton 1993). In the 1980s William Wilson (1980; 1987) introduced class (and the concept of the underclass more specifically) as a subject of importance for black policy. The concept of the underclass was widely adopted and proved influential throughout the social sciences and partisan politics in theorizing on late twentieth-century urban policy. Would cities, with their substantial welfare programs, attract members of the underclass? Did Latino society have an underclass? (Peterson 1990; Moore and Pinderhughes 1993). These were just two of the questions examined in the literature that evolved from Wilson's work.

Although the concept of the underclass and the language used to describe this population remain controversial, Wilson has indelibly shaped the urban politics literature in this area.

Economic Development and Affirmative Action. Understanding the implications of local, state, and national economic policy introduced new perspectives on racial and ethnic politics and policy. Ester Fuchs (1992) compared the leadership roles of the mayors of New York City and Chicago in formulating fiscal policy for the two cities. During this period New York and other cities faced grave fiscal crises, and studies of the institutional politics associated with urban financial management helped frame another of the policy arenas in which racial and ethnic groups compete. Case studies described how private business interests dominated public-private partnerships and supported economic redevelopment in twelve cities in the decades after World War II (Squires 1989). Neighborhood groups encountered differing successes as they resisted conventional economic development and progrowth policies in Chicago and Pittsburgh; Chicago's political organization limited the effectiveness of neighborhood interests by constraining their impact on government decision making (Ferman 1996).

Research on affirmative action in Richmond and Atlanta revealed that the policy's implementation had had limited success. Studies of Richmond's municipal affirmative action contracting policies showed relatively modest accomplishments, with only a few black businesses receiving the bulk of the contracts. Federal court decisions recently eliminated these policies. Atlanta's accomplishments have also been modest (Drake and Holsworth 1996; Orfield and Ashkinaze 1991). Separate studies of wealth showed little or no change in the relative proportions of wealth holdings by blacks and whites in recent decades: blacks hold less than 1 percent of the value of wealth held by whites, although relative income has changed (Oliver and Shapiro 1995; Conley 1999). Although neither study focused specifically on urban residents, the studies are valuable in outlining the interrelationship between race and economic well-being.

Case studies in the 1980s and 1990s illustrated the transformation of the Los Angeles political economy and the attendant shifts in its demographic profile. A city once dominated by European Americans became an international city with a majority of Latinos, Asians, and African Americans. Marta Lopez-Garza and David Diaz view this transition through several lenses: women in the global economy, economic issues in southern California, political and social shifts, consideration of racism and group identity, and policy arenas. Ivan Light and Edna Bonacich conducted a detailed study of the economic standing of Koreans in Los Angeles during the first fifteen years after immigration reform made the nation more accessible to Asians. Light and Bonacich studied Korean entrepreneurs and the international forces that shaped their decisions to move to a new economic location (Light and Bonacich 1988; Lopez-Garza and Diaz 2001).

Regime Theory and Social Capital

The concepts of regime theory and social capital (the institutions, relationships, and norms that shape the quality and quantity of a society's social interactions), introduced and developed roughly in the past decade, bring political science and the urban racial and ethnic politics literature full circle to the earlier work on power in Atlanta. The terminology is different, but the subject of the research resonates powerfully with Floyd Hunter's (1953) emphasis on power and has been used to explore the institutional character of urban policymaking and of racial and ethnic groups. Social capital and civic capacity bring back some of the foundational work on the importance of group-based political and social institutions. Clarence Stone and his colleagues define civic capacity as involving problem solving in the public sector, whereas social capital addresses private behavior. (Stone, Henig, Jones, and Pierannunzi 2001, 4–5; Orr 1999, 6; Putnam 1995) While these are distinct areas, urban politics has begun to look more carefully at detailed institutional developments to understand the acquisition and operation of power, whether in public sector policymaking or in the evolution of private social capital in specific racial or ethnic groups.

Atlanta's governing arrangements can be characterized as a regime. Regime is the word used by Clarence Stone to characterize the relationships between political and business leaders in Atlanta that endured across a half-century and several different mayors and that survived the transition from white to black leadership. Regimes "are dynamic, not static, and regime dynamics concern the ways in which forces for change and forces for continuity play against one another. . . . Understanding Atlanta's urban regime involves understanding how cooperation can be maintained and continuity can prevail in the face of so many possibilities for conflict" (Stone 1989, 9). The character of racial policy that evolved in Atlanta was crucial to the formation of the urban regime. Whites gave up racial segregation in exchange for economic success and growth. The black community contributed its electoral support, participated directly in the political leadership, and a "tiny group" of black businesses got to participate in economic policymaking (Stone 1989, 159). Stone's work has reframed urban research in recent decades, and a number of urban scholars have used his concept of political regimes as a foundation for their work. Former Chicago city councilman Dick Simpson used roll call analysis of the Chicago City Council to track the development of several political regimes that have cropped up during the council's lifespan (2001). And Barbara Ferman adapted Stone's concept of political regimes to compare the differing outcomes of competition over economic development in Chicago and Pittsburgh (1996).

A series of studies in educational policy combines the concept of urban regimes with social capital. Over more than a century, Baltimore's black community created a complex black civil society with significant social capital, became more involved in the public sector, and participated in the educational system (Orr 1999; Putnam 1995, 2000). Scholars used the related concept of civic capacity as a theoretical framework for organizing their studies of educational reform in cities, most of which have had significant racial and ethnic populations (Stone 1998; Stone, Henig, Jones and Pierannunzi 2001, 59, 60). The proportion of nonwhite students in public schools in 1990 was much higher than the proportion of nonwhite school-age children in the total population in all eleven cities studied. In other words, although 25 percent of children in Boston's public schools were white, 45 percent of the school-age population was white and 60 percent of the city's total population was white. This means that the other 20 percent of white students were in private schools (Stone, Henig, Jones, and Pierannunzi 2001, 72). Stone and his colleagues argue for understanding the historical patterns behind the development of the cities and their racial and ethnic groups' ability to develop social capital and therefore to participate in public sector policy-making as critical factors in the success of school reform.

A review of theoretical paradigms shows that the prominence of pluralist theory, emphasizing decentralized and accessible urban politics, has been replaced by theories of political regimes and the development of social capital. Blacks, Latinos, and Asians arrived in American cities through distinct socioeconomic pathways, but all have faced challenges in gaining access to and influencing the urban political system. In contrast to blacks, Latinos and Asians face differences in language and nationality and are very recent arrivals. And blacks, unlike Asians and to a lesser degree Latinos, have relatively homogeneous patterns of partisan identification and political values. Research on racial and ethnic group dynamics shows that blacks and Latinos have shifted from periods of policy agreement into greater policy conflict. Poverty and class are still salient issues that have become increasingly divisive in recent decades. Economic elites have dominated urban economic redevelopment, and affirmative action was not effective in helping black middle-class interests participate routinely in city contracting. Regime theory facilitated the exploration of institutional relationships in the public sector and focused on understanding how similar business and government relationships survived over time. Social capital focused on the private sector and the development and character of institutional relationships within specific racial and ethnic groups.

Research Methodology

Urban politics is a large and complex area of study. Cities tend to have specific characteristics that developed from their relatively unique sociodemographic and cultural patterns. Scholars seek to understand each city's or sets of cities character through multiple rather than singular research methodologies and strategies. Racial and ethnic groups, given their distinct origins within the American context, are not easily aggregated into a single minority group category. Scholars of the groups tend to have a strong preference for contextual analyses, institutional development, and specific details of a group's political life as well as quantitative evidence accumulated through demographic data, survey research, and aggregate information.[3] Thus scholars of urban racial and ethnic politics use a variety of qualitative and quantitative evidence.[4] In recent decades other political science fields have accepted the significance of contextual data, in which survey data collected at the individual level is put into the socioeconomic context within which the individual functions (Leighley 2001).

Urban research on racial and ethnic group politics tends to involve greater complexity than studies from other fields in American politics. The work is systematic and the methods consistent, but the authors have a commitment to the specifics of the institutional and group-related developments that distinguish this area from its counterparts. Scholars of urban racial and ethnic politics have tried to develop behavioral hypotheses by comparing several groups within a single city, comparing racial and ethnic politics in several cities, and comparing such systemic interactions as political incorporation, civic and social capacity, and substantive policy outputs (like education) in a number of cities (Gosnell 1967; Bunche 1928; Browning, Marshall, and Tabb 1990; Orr 1999; Stone 1989; Persons 1993; DeLeon 1997).

The urban politics literature often focuses on description, laying out the dimensions within which a group functions. While the penchant for description might seem atheoretical or even antitheoretical in some evaluations of research methodology, the relatively short time span in which the racial and ethnic groups most prominent in the urban literature have participated in urban politics makes description a foundation for the development of theory.

African Americans have been a significant presence in urban areas for most of U.S. history, but their ability to participate in all aspects of urban politics has been a twentieth-century phenomenon. Gosnell and Bunche wrote important studies of black political participation in Chicago using census information, statistics, interviews, surveys, and maps (Gosnell 1967; Bunche 1928).

Groups that have spent less time in the urban scene present greater theoretical, empirical, and methodological challenges to scholars. In establishing evidence for patterns of immigration and naturalization (Pachon and DeSipio 1994), citizenship, political attitudes, partisan identification (de la Garza, DeSipio, Garcia, Garcia, and Falcon 1992; Garcia 1988), voting and political contacting, public policy influence, and regional patterns of political evolution, researchers are required to take many different directions (Barrera 1979). Similarly, case studies can examine complex and provocative events, such as when a Korean shopkeeper in Los Angeles named Soon Ja Du shot and killed LaTasha Harlins, a black customer (Umemoto 1994). A volatile exchange between a Korean owner and a Haitian customer resulted in a long, highly politicized economic boycott in Brooklyn (Kim 2000). Studies of electoral empowerment of Asians in Los Angeles (Brackman and Erie 1995; Nakanishi 1991; Saito 1998) have helped us understand the political frameworks within which Asian Americans participate in American politics. Understanding how racial and ethnic groups function in the political system—independently and in competition with one another—requires extensive and continuing empirical observation and comparison across a variety of types.

Two patterns may be evident from the most recent research in urban racial and ethnic politics. First there may be changes in the patterns of research team construction. Research on racial and ethnic groups in cities was previously conducted alone or by pairs of researchers. Some well known examples include Edward Banfield and James Q. Wilson (1963), Nathan Glazer and Daniel Patrick Moynihan (1970), Francis Fox Piven and Richard Cloward (1971), Joel Aberbach and Jack Walker (1973), Dennis Judd and Todd Swanstrom (1994), J. David Greenstone and Paul Peterson (1973), Albert Karnig and Susan Welch (1980), and Paula McClain and Joseph Stewart Jr. (1995). Larger groups of scholars are now collaborating on more complex projects with life cycles as long as a decade (Dreier, Mollenkopf, and Swanstrom 2001; Browning, Marshall, and Tabb 1997; Stone, Henig, Jones, and Pierannunzi 2001). Research on the Latino National Political Survey (de la Garza, DeSipio, Garcia, Garcia, and Falcon 1992) and the National Black Election Studies (Gurin, Hatchett, and Jackson 1989) has also included larger research groups.

Why the shift from pairs of researchers to groups? First, the complexity required to develop and analyze large databases combined with the range of methods typically used in the urban field may lead to more collaboration among scholars. These complex studies promise to provide more detailed comparisons of political involvement across larger numbers of cities and more detailed analyses of policy areas. Second, since much of urban politics research—particularly that on racial and ethnic politics—takes place at ground level and close to the event, some work has developed in several research phases. First generation or primary research captures the political developments and makes a first effort at theory building and hypothesis testing. A second generation of research reviews and integrates several decades of primary research developments and the first-stage theories developed from them. In the past decade scholars have reviewed a half century of research on the accumulation of political power by blacks and whites in Atlanta, evaluated the intersection of black and Latino political incorporation in a range of cities, and revisited research on race in black and white America first published a quarter century ago (Stone 1989; 1998; Dreier, Mollenkopf, and Swanstrom 2001; Browning, Marshall, and Tabb 1984, 1990, 1997; McCormick 2001). These studies have a perspective on past and present developments in racially complex urban contexts.

Future Agenda

The future for urban racial and ethnic politics is an exciting one. Definitions of racial and ethnic identity, urban politics and globalization, methodological challenges, twenty-first century America, and security issues in the wake of the September 2001 terrorist attacks on the United States constitute some new areas of research in the field.

Definitions of Racial and Ethnic Identity

The demographic changes that the nation, and especially urban centers, have faced in the past fifteen years challenge scholars to observe the laboratory that is outside their university windows. Just as the pluralist and assimilationist literature of the 1960s had to be reevaluated in light of the distinctive experiences of African Americans and the first generations of Latinos and Asians, the increased density and complexity of twenty-first century American urban populations will require reconsideration of our definitions of racial and ethnic populations.

Some of the research will depend on the interactions among contemporary urban groups. How Haitians, Mexicans, Vietnamese, Cambodians, Chinese, Native Americans, Puerto Ricans, Hmong, Colombians, and the many other populations that now reside in our urban areas meet and cooperate, marry, compete, and challenge each other politically and economically will shape our changing definitions of group identity and political participation. Whether the American conception of blacks as a singular, ethnically undivided racial group, for example, will evolve into a fully developed racial ethnicity will be of particular theoretical and political interest. Whether participation and identification will continue along lines of country of origin, or whether the newest groups will reframe their values into identities related to American values—such as blacks have done and Asians and Latinos may be doing—is a subject for continued observation. Continued examination of race and ethnicity and the political significance of those definitions will be crucial for the urban research literature (Smith and Tarallo 1995).

Urban Politics and Globalization

The definition of urban politics in the context of globalization is a second important issue. Diminishing boundaries between nation states, hastened by the enhancement of communication, and the increasing need for labor will give urban politics an international focus. This will also allow for a broader perspective on the accomplishments of the past quarter-century in American racial and ethnic politics (McCormick 2001; Persons 1993).

Methodological Challenges

More sophisticated analysis of racial and ethnic groups will be required. A review of the urban racial and ethnic literature reveals that scholars frequently use multiple methods, and combine an array of quantitative and qualitative research strategies. Urban scholars are also particularly interested in the importance of contextual analysis.

Twenty-first Century America

Recent research has set an important agenda for twenty-first century studies of racial and ethnic politics. Dreier, Mollenkopf, and Swanstrom (2001) argue very effectively for reasserting cities' important status in American public life and for managing relationships between racial and ethnic groups and their location in metropolitan urban and suburban areas differently. These political scientists have challenged the urban research field and the political system to come to terms with racial and ethnic political issues, such as segregation and poverty, still unresolved after the past half-century of American political conflicts. Treating power and authority as a problem of metropolitan America as a whole, rather than limiting discussion and debate to the political boundaries that divide city from suburb, forces a very different approach than the one we are used to.

Mid-twentieth-century policy assumptions in transportation, education, and the economy have "supersized" metropolitan America far beyond its early twentieth-century boundaries, and these assumptions challenge our capacity for long-term economic stability. Without smart growth the costs of living—for individuals, single families, and the nation as a whole—will be jeopardized. The problems of poverty, housing, transportation, economic inequality, and urban and racial representation permeate the wealthiest suburbs and the least attractive neighborhoods in our cities. Developing a strategy for solving these problems will require a metropolitan perspective.

Security Issues

It is too early to grasp the meaning of the terrorist attacks of September 11, 2001, for urban racial and ethnic politics. However, the realization that cities are vulnerable to violent attacks—whether by airplanes, anthrax, or suicide bombers—is troubling. Metropolitan areas' economic, cultural, educational, and political assets make them attractive and vulnerable targets. Most of our racial and ethnic populations are concentrated in dense urban locations.

Most of the conceptual planning in the wake of September 11 has taken place at the national level, or at best in top-down discussions between national and metropolitan leaders. Discussion of protection strategies needs to develop at the metropolitan level and among racial and ethnic institutional leaders. Scrutiny of the diverse population now residing in American cities may increase, and civil liberties and civil rights could be jeopardized in the scramble for enhanced security. Debates about racial profiling in the context of homeland security make the safety of racial and ethnic groups a serious concern. The increasing diversity we have gradually come to take for granted as our cities grow more dynamic and exciting may be challenged as society emphasizes and redefines the meaning of homeland security.

Conclusion

The groups on which this chapter focuses—blacks, Asians, and Latinos—have challenged the entrenched political system. Today urban bureaucracies—dominated by blacks, especially in northeastern industrial cities—and political leaders must respond to the newer Latino and Asian populations.

The relatively stable patterns of governmental interaction in cities and the failure to effectively address the economic well-being of blacks or even to stabilize a network of black corporate relationships through affirmative action or government contracting raise continuing challenges of economic stability for the urban polity. Asian Americans have established an array of businesses in their first generation, but this economic involvement has not been balanced by comparable electoral participation. Whether the varying nationality groups of Asians and Latinos will consolidate around stronger group identities, and whether blacks will respond to the arrival of new black ethnic groups with a weakened sense of group identity, will be fascinating to observe. Given the substantially different composition of the polity that the past third of a century has brought to American cities, the regimes that have been stabilized in Atlanta, the recent reconfiguration of the Chicago regime, and California's cities in which black and Latino political incorporation were successful a generation ago confront the possibility of political instability. Research on political incorporation in California cities, and analysis and application of it to cities outside of California, show that American cities face greater volatility as the racial and ethnic complexity of the urban population increases. Cities are no longer biracial; they are multiracial political entities in which whites will increasingly be in the minority.

Urban racial and ethnic research draws on a range of qualitative and quantitative methodologies, as well as different types of research teams. Case studies, interviews, aggregate and census data, survey research, biographies, and ethnographies conducted by individuals, pairs, and large complex research teams offer myriad approaches.

The urban racial and ethnic research agenda is a crowded one. Some unresolved policy issues remain from the last century, including poverty relief, racial issues, and the physical growth of cities. New issues such as globalization and terrorism and security open urban policy to new dimensions of planning and interaction. Understanding all of these areas will also require continued attention to how information on urban racial and ethnic politics is collected and interpreted.

The challenge for urban racial and ethnic politics research in the early twenty-first century, therefore, is not just to plan the study of a new generation of European immigration and the politics evolving from it, but to create a foundation for understanding new experiences of political participation. Because of immigration restrictions, Dominicans, Cambodians, Koreans, and Colombians have resided in American cities for a generation or less, so they are unlikely to repeat the patterns of European immigrants who arrived in urban areas in the late nineteenth century. There is no prior research available for comparison with contemporary residents of urban America, who exist in unprecedented volume, geographic range, and number of nationalities. Urban racial and ethnic politics faces an exciting and dynamic new era.

Suggested Readings

de los Angeles Torres, Maria. 1999. *In the Land of Mirrors: Cuban Exile Politics in the United States.* Ann Arbor: University of Michigan Press. This work is a complex examination of the meaning of politics and lives lived between the United States and Cuba. It moves racial and ethnic politics beyond an assimilationist framework.

Cohen, Cathy J. 1999. *The Boundaries of Blackness: AIDS and the Breakdown of Black Politics.* Chicago: University of Chicago Press. Cohen explores how New York City's black community leaders addressed the needs of black gays, lesbians, and bisexuals. She explains how the black media nationwide and in New York discussed and framed the AIDS problem as the disease began to spread.

Dreier, Peter, John Mollenkopf, and Todd Swanstrom. 2001. *Place Matters: Metropolitics for the Twenty-First Century.* Lawrence: University Press of Kansas. This book argues for a reconsideration of twentieth-century urban solutions and recommends a metropolitan strategy for dealing with America's increasing physical and economic segregation.

Jackson, Byran O., and Michael B. Preston. 1991. *Racial and Ethnic Politics in California.* Berkeley: IGS Press, Institute of Governmental Studies, University of California, Berkeley. This collection of readings introduces the issues faced by California's increasingly heterogeneous population a decade before other U.S. regions and cities.

Kim, Claire Jean. 2000. *Bitter Fruit: The Politics of Black-Korean Conflict in New York City.* New Haven: Yale University Press. Kim's meticulous investigation of the Red Apple Boycott explains how multiracial, multiethnic groups struggled to extract political and economic standing from New York City's leaders during the administration of David Dinkins, New York's first black mayor.

Stone, Clarence N. *Regime Politics: Governing Atlanta 1946–1988.* 1989. Lawrence: University Press of Kansas. Stone's study of Atlanta's politics integrates a conceptual explanation of biracial competition for power with a convincing theory of political regimes.

References

Aberbach, Joel D., and Jack L. Walker. 1973. *Race in the City: Political Trust and Public Policy in the New Urban System.* Boston: Little, Brown.

Alex-Assensoh, Yvette M. 1998. *Neighborhoods, Family, and Political Behavior in Urban America.* New York: Garland.

Alex-Assensoh, Yvette, and Lawrence Hanks, eds. 2000. *Black and Multiracial Politics in America.* New York: New York University Press.

Banfield, Edward C. 1968. *The Unheavenly City.* Boston: Little, Brown.

Banfield, Edward C., and James Q. Wilson. 1963. *City Politics.* New York: Vintage Books.

Barnett, Marguerite Ross. 1976. "A Theoretical Perspective on Racial Public Policy." In *Public Policy for the Black Community: Strategies and Perspectives,* ed. Marguerite Ross Barnett and James A. Hefner, 1–54. New York: Alfred Publishing.

Barnett, Marguerite Ross, and Linda Faye Williams. 1986. "Affirmative Action and the Politics of the Contemporary Era." In *Readings on Equal Education,* vol. 9, *Education Policy in an Era of Conservative Reform,* ed. Marguerite Ross Barnett, Charles C. Harrington, and Philip V. White, 36–92. New York: AMS Press.

Barrera, Mario. 1979. *Race and Class in the Southwest: A Theory of Racial Inequality.* Notre Dame, Ind.: University of Notre Dame Press.

Blackstock, Nelson. 1976. *Cointelpro: The FBI's Secret War on Political Freedom.* New York: Vintage Books.

Brackman, Harold, and Steven P. Erie. 1995. "Beyond Politics by Other Means? Empowerment Strategies for Los Angeles Asian Pacific Community." In *The Bubbling Cauldron: Race, Ethnicity, and the Urban Crisis,* ed. Michael Peter Smith and Joe R. Feagin, 282–303. Minneapolis: University of Minnesota Press.

Browning, Rufus, Dale Rogers Marshall, and David Tabb. eds. 1984. *Protest Is Not Enough: The Struggle of Blacks and Hispanics for Equality in Urban Politics.* Berkeley: University of California Press.

———. eds. 1990. *Racial Politics in American Cities.* New York: Longman.

———. eds. 1997. *Racial Politics in American Cities.* 2d ed. New York: Longman.

Bunche, Ralph J. 1928. "The Negro in Chicago Politics." *National Municipal Review* 18 (May): 261–264.

Bush, Rod, ed. 1984. *The New Black Vote: Politics and Power in Four American Cities.* San Francisco: Synthesis Publications.

Carmichael, Stokeley, and Charles V. Hamilton. 1967. *Black Power: The Politics of Liberation in America.* New York: Vintage Books.

Conley, Dalton. 1999. *Being Black, Living in the Red: Race, Wealth, and Social Policy in America.* Berkeley: University of California Press.

Crain, Robert L. 1969. *The Politics of School Desegregation: Comparative Case Studies of Community Structure and Policy Making.* Garden City, N.Y.: Vintage.

Dahl, Robert. 1961. *Who Governs?* New Haven: Yale University Press.

David, Gary C. 2000. "Behind the Bulletproof Glass: Iraqi Chaldean Store Ownership in Metropolitan Detroit." In *Arab Detroit: From Margin to Mainstream,* ed. Nabeel Abraham and Andrew Shryock, 151–180. Detroit: Wayne State University Press.

Dawson, Michael C. 1994. *Behind the Mule: Race and Class in African-American Politics.* Princeton: Princeton University Press.

———. 2001. *Black Visions: The Roots of Contemporary African-American Political Ideologies.* Chicago: University of Chicago Press.

DeLeon, Richard. 1997. "Research Methods in Urban Politics and Policy." In *Handbook of Research on Urban Politics and Policy in the United States,* ed. Ronald E. Vogel, 17–30. Westport, Conn.: Greenwood Press.

DeSipio, Louis. 1996. *Counting on the Latino Vote: Latinos as a New Electorate.* Charlottesville: University Press of Virginia.

Downs, Anthony. 1973. *Opening Up the Suburbs: An Urban Strategy for America.* New Haven: Yale University Press.

Drake, Avon W., and Robert D. Holsworth. 1996. *Affirmative Action and the Stalled Quest for Black Progress.* Urbana: University of Illinois Press.

Dreier, Peter, John Mollenkopf, and Todd Swanstrom. 2001. *Place Matters: Metropolitics for the Twenty-first Century.* Lawrence: University Press of Kansas.

Edsall, Thomas Byrne, and Mary D. Edsall. 1991. *Chain Reaction: The Impact of Race, Rights, and Taxes on American Politics.* New York: Norton.

Ferman, Barbara. 1996. *Challenging the Growth Machine: Neighborhood Politics in Chicago and Pittsburgh.* Lawrence: University Press of Kansas.

Freedman, Amy L. 2000. *Political Participation and Ethnic Minorities: Chinese Overseas in Malaysia, Indonesia, and the United States.* New York: Routledge.

Fuchs, Ester R. 1992. *Mayors and Money: Fiscal Policy in New York and Chicago.* Chicago: University of Chicago Press.

Garcia, F. Chris, ed. 1988. *Latinos and the Political System.* Notre Dame, Ind.: University of Notre Dame Press.

Garrow, David J. 1983. *The FBI and Martin Luther King, Jr.* New York: Norton.

de la Garza, Rodolfo, Louis DeSipio, F. Chris Garcia, John A. Garcia, and Angelo Falcon. 1992. *Latino Voices: Mexican, Puerto Rican, and Cuban Perspectives on American Politics.* Boulder: Westview Press.

Gittell, Marilyn, and Maurice Berube. 1969. *Confrontation at Ocean Hill-Brownsville.* New York: Praeger.

Glazer, Nathan, and Daniel P. Patrick Moynihan. 1970. *Beyond the Melting Pot: The Negroes, Puerto Ricans, Jews, Italians, and Irish of New York City,* 2d ed. Cambridge: MIT Press.

Gosnell, Harold. 1967. *Negro Politicians.* Chicago: University of Chicago Press.

Greenberg, Stanley B. 1974. *Politics and Poverty: Modernization and Response in Five Poor Neighborhoods.* New York: Wiley.

Greenstone, J. David, and Paul E. Peterson. 1973. *Race and Authority in Urban Politics: Community Participation and the War on Poverty.* Chicago: University of Chicago Press.

Grimshaw, William. 1992. *Bitter Fruit: Black Politics and the Chicago Machine 1931–1991.* Chicago: University of Chicago Press.

Gurin, Patricia, Shirley Hatchett, and James Jackson. 1989. *Hope and Independence.* New York: Russell Sage.

Hamilton, Charles V. 1972. *The Black Preacher in America.* New York: Morrow.

Henderson, Lenneal J., ed. 1972. *Black Political Life in the United States: A Fist as the Pendulum.* San Francisco: Chandler.

Henry, Charles P. 1994. "Urban Politics and Incorporation: The Case of Blacks, Latinos and Asians in Three Cities." In *Blacks, Latinos and Asians in Urban America: Status and Prospects for Politics and Activism,* ed. James Jennings, 17–28. Westport, Conn.: Praeger.

Holden, Mathew. 1973a. *The Politics of the Black Nation.* New York: Chandler.

———— 1973b. *The White Man's Burden.* New York: Chandler.

Hunter, Floyd. 1953. *Community Power Structure.* Chapel Hill: University of North Carolina Press.

Jackson, Byran. 1991. "Racial and Ethnic Voting Cleavages in Los Angeles Politics." In *Racial and Ethnic Politics in California,* ed. Byran Jackson and Michael B. Preston, 193–220. Berkeley: IGS Press, Institute of Governmental Studies, University of California at Berkeley.

Jackson, Byran, and Michael B. Preston, eds. 1991. *Racial and Ethnic Politics in California.* Berkeley: IGS Press, Institute of Governmental Studies, University of California at Berkeley.

Jennings, James, ed. 1994. *Blacks, Latinos, and Asians in Urban America: Status and Prospects for Politics and Activism.* Westport, Conn.: Praeger.

Jones, Mack H. 1972. "A Frame of Reference for Black Politics." In *Black Political Life in the United States: A Fist as the Pendulum,* ed. Lenneal Henderson, 7–20. San Francisco: Chandler.

Jones-Correa, Michael. 2000. "Immigrants, Blacks, and Cities." In *Black and Multiracial Politics in America*, ed. Yvette M. Alex-Assensoh and Lawrence J. Hanks, 133–164. New York: New York University Press.

Judd, Dennis R., and Todd Swanstrom. 1994. *City Politics: Private Power and Public Policy*. New York: HarperCollins College Publishers.

Karnig, Albert K. and Susan Welch. 1980. *Black Representation and Urban Policy*. Chicago: University of Chicago Press.

Katznelson, Ira. 1973. *Black Men, White Cities: Race, Politics, and Migration in the United States, 1900–30, and Britain, 1948–68*. New York: Oxford University Press.

Kim, Claire Jean. 2000. *Bitter Fruit: The Politics of Black-Korean Conflict in New York City*. New Haven: Yale University Press.

LaNoue, George R., and Bruce L. R. Smith. 1973. *The Politics of School Decentralization*. Lexington, Mass.: Lexington Books.

Leighley, Jan. 2001. *Strength in Numbers? The Political Mobilization of Racial and Ethnic Minorities*. Princeton: Princeton University Press.

Light, Ivan, and Edna Bonacich. 1988. *Immigrant Entrepreneurs: Koreans in Los Angeles, 1965–1982*. Berkeley: University of California Press.

Lipsky, Michael. 1970. *Protest in City Politics Rent Strikes, Housing, and the Power of the Poor*. Chicago: Rand McNally.

Lopez-Garza, Marta, and David R. Diaz, eds. 2001. *Asian and Latino Immigrants in a Restructuring Economy: The Metamorphosis of Southern California*. Stanford: Stanford University Press.

Marable, Manning. 1994. "Building Coalitions among Communities of Color: Beyond Racial Identity Politics." In *Blacks, Latinos, and Asians in Urban America: Status and Prospects for Politics and Activism*, ed. James Jennings, 29–44. Westport, Conn: Praeger.

Massey, Douglas S., and Nancy A. Denton. 1993. *American Apartheid: Segregation and the Making of the Underclass*. Cambridge: Harvard University Press.

McClain, Paula D., and John A. Garcia. 1993. "Expanding Disciplinary Boundaries: Black, Latino and Racial Minority Group Politics in Political Science." In *Political Science: The State of the Discipline II*, ed. Ada W. Finifter, 247–279. Washington, D.C.: American Political Science Association.

McClain, Paula D., and Joseph Stewart Jr. 1995. *"Can We All Get Along?" Racial and Ethnic Minorities in American Politics*. Boulder: Westview Press.

McCormick, Joseph, ed. 2001. "Symposium: *The Politics of the Black 'Nation': A Twenty-Five Year Retrospective." National Political Science Review* 8: 1–71.

Mollenkopf, John. 1997. "New York: The Great Anomaly." In *Racial Politics in American Cities*, ed. Rufus Browning, Dale Rogers Marshall, and David Tabb, 97–115. New York: Longman.

Moore, Joan, and Raquel Pinderhughes, eds. 1993. *In The Barrios: Latinos and the Underclass Debate*. New York: Russell Sage Foundation.

Moynihan, Daniel Patrick. 1970. *Maximum Feasible Misunderstanding: Community Action in the War on Poverty*. New York: Free Press.

Nakanishi, Don T. 1991. "The Next Swing Vote? Asian Pacific Americans and California Politics." In *Racial and Ethnic Politics in California*, ed. Byran O. Jackson and Michael B. Preston, 25–54. Berkeley: IGS Press, Institute of Governmental Studies, University of California at Berkeley.

Nelson, William E. Jr. 2000. *Black Atlantic Politics: Dilemmas of Political Empowerment in Boston and Liverpool*. Albany: State University of New York Press.

Nelson, William E. Jr., and Philip J. Meranto. 1977. *Electing Black Mayors*. Columbus: Ohio State University Press.

Oliver, Melvin, and Richard Shapiro. 1995. *Black Wealth, White Wealth: A New Perspective on Racial Inequality*. New York: Routledge.

Orfield, Gary, and Carole Ashkinaze. 1991. *The Closing Door: Conservative Policy and Black Opportunity*. Chicago: University of Chicago Press.

Orr, Marion. 1999. *Black Social Capital: The Politics of School Reform in Baltimore, 1986–1998*. Lawrence: University Press of Kansas.

Pachon, Harry, and Louis DeSipio. 1994. *New Americans by Choice: Political Perspectives of Latino Immigrants*. Boulder: Westview Press.

Palley, Marian Lief, and Howard Palley. 1977. *Urban America and Public Policies*. Lexington, Mass.: D. C. Heath.

Parenti, Michael. 1970. "Ethnic Politics and the Persistence of Ethnic Identification." *The Ethnic Factor in American Politics*, ed. Brett W. Hawkins and Robert A. Lorinskas, 63–78. Columbus, Ohio: Merrill.

Parker, Frank R. 1990. *Black Votes Count*. Chapel Hill: University of North Carolina Press.

Patterson, Ernest. 1974. *Black City Politics*. New York: Dodd, Mead.

Perry, Huey, ed. 1991. "Exploring the Meaning and Implications of Deracialization in African-American Urban Politics: A Minisymposium." *Urban Affairs Quarterly* 27 (December): 63–78.

Perry, Huey, and Wayne Parent, eds. 1995. *Blacks and the American Political System*. Gainesville: University Press of Florida.

Persons, Georgia, ed. 1993. *Dilemmas of Black Politics: Issues of Leadership and Strategy*. New York: HarperCollins College Publishers.

Peterson, Paul E. 1990. *Welfare Magnets: A New Case for a National Standard*. Washington, D.C.: Brookings Institution.

Pinderhughes, Dianne M. 1987. *Race and Ethnicity in Chicago Politics: A Reexamination of Pluralist Theory*. Urbana: University of Illinois Press.

Piven, Francis Fox, and Richard A. Cloward. 1971. *Regulating the Poor: The Functions of Public Welfare*. New York: Vintage Books.

Preston, Michael B. 1976. "Limitations of Black Urban Power: The Case of Black Mayors." In *The New Urban Politics*, ed. Louis Massotti and Robert Lineberry. Cambridge: Ballinger: 111–130.

Preston, Michael, Paul Puryear, and Lenneal Henderson, eds. 1982. *The New Black Politics: The Search for Political Power*. New York: Longman.

——— 1987. *The New Black Politics: The Search for Political Power*. 2d ed. New York: Longman.

Putnam, Robert D. 1995. "Bowling Alone: America's Declining Social Capital." *Journal of Democracy* 6 (January): 65–78.

——— 2000. *Bowling Alone: The Collapse and Revival of American Community*. New York: Simon and Schuster.

Rich, Wilbur. 1989. *Coleman Young and Detroit Politics: From Social Activist to Power Broker*. Detroit: Wayne State University Press.

——— ed. 1996. *The Politics of Minority Coalitions: Race, Ethnicity, and Shared Uncertainties*. Westport, Conn.: Praeger.

Rossi, Peter, and Robert Dentler. 1961. *The Politics of Urban Renewal: The Chicago Findings*. New York: Free Press.

Saito, Leland T. 1998. *Race and Politics: Asian Americans, Latinos, and Whites in a Los Angeles Suburb*. Urbana: University of Illinois Press.

Schopmeyer, Kim. 2000. "A Demographic Portrait of Arab Detroit." In *Arab Detroit: From Margin to Mainstream*, ed. Nabeel Abraham and Andrew Shryock, 61–92. Detroit: Wayne State University Press.

Simpson, Richard. 2001. *Rogues, Rebels and Rubber Stamps: The Politics of the Chicago City Council from 1893 to the Present*. Boulder: Westview Press.

Smith, Michael Peter, and Bernadette Tarallo. 1995. "Who Are the Good Guys? The Social Con-struction of the Vietnamese 'Other'." In *The Bubbling Cauldron: Race, Ethnicity, and the Ur-ban Crisis*, ed. Michael Peter Smith and Joe R. Feagin, 50–76. Minneapolis: University of Minnesota Press.

Smith, Robert C. 2001. "The Politics of the Black 'Nation': Significance and Context of the Book." In "Symposium: *The Politics of the Black 'Nation':* A Twenty-five Year Retrospective," ed. Joseph McCormick. *National Political Science Review* 8: 4–5.

Sonenshein, Raphael J. 1993. *Politics in Black and White: Race and Power in Los Angeles.* Prince-ton: Princeton University Press.

Squires, Gregory D. 1989. *Unequal Partnerships: The Political Economy of Urban Redevelopment in Postwar America.* New Brunswick: Rutgers University Press.

Starks, Robert T., and Michael B. Preston. 1990. "Harold Washington and the Politics of Reform in Chicago: 1983–1987." In *Racial Politics in American Cities*, ed. Rufus P. Browning, Dale Rogers Marshall, and David H. Tabb. White Plains, N.Y.: Longman, 88–107.

Stone, Clarence N. 1989. *Regime Politics: Governing Atlanta, 1946–1988.* Lawrence: University Press of Kansas.

———. ed. 1998. *Changing Urban Education.* Lawrence: University Press of Kansas.

Stone, Clarence N., Jeffrey R. Henig, Bryan D. Jones, and Carol Pierannunzi. 2001. *Building Civic Capacity: The Politics of Reforming Urban Schools.* Lawrence: University Press of Kansas.

Tate, Katherine. 1993. *From Protest to Politics: The New Black Voters in American Elections.* New York and Cambridge: Russell Sage Foundation and Harvard University Press.

Torres, Andres. 1995. *Between Melting Pot and Mosaic: African Americans and Puerto Ricans in the New York Political Economy.* Philadelphia: Temple University Press.

Umemoto, Karen. 1994. "Blacks and Koreans in Los Angeles: The Case of LaTasha Harlins and Soon Ja Du." In *Blacks, Latinos and Asians in Urban America: Status and Prospects for Politics and Activism*, ed. James Jennings, 95–118. Westport, Conn.: Praeger.

Waldinger, Roger. 1995. "When the Melting Pot Boils Over: The Irish, Jews, Blacks, and Kore-ans of New York." In *The Bubbling Cauldron: Race, Ethnicity, and the Urban Crisis*, ed. Michael Peter Smith and Joe R. Feagin, 265–281. Minneapolis: University of Minnesota Press.

Walton, Hanes Jr. 1972. *Black Politics.* Philadelphia: Lippincott.

———. 1985. *Invisible Politics.* Albany: State University of New York Press.

Walton, Hanes Jr., Leslie Burl McLemore, and C. Vernon Gray. 1990. "The Pioneering Books on Black Politics and the Political Science Community, 1903–1965." *National Political Science Review* 2: 196–218.

Wilson, William J. 1980. *The Declining Significance of Race: Blacks and Changing American In-stitutions.* Chicago: University of Chicago Press.

———. 1987. *The Truly Disadvantaged: The Inner City, the Underclass, and Public Policy.* Chicago: University of Chicago Press.

Wilson, James Q. 1960. *Negro Politics: The Search for Leadership.* New York: Free Press.

———. 1995. *Political Organizations.* Princeton: Princeton University Press.

Wolfinger, Raymond E. 1970. "The Development and Persistence of Ethnic Voting." In *The Eth-nic Factor in American Politics*, ed. Brett W. Hawkins and Robert Lorinskas, 101–23. Colum-bus, Ohio: Merrill.

Notes

1. Only one person represented the constituency in single-member districts.

2. New Jersey's state police used racial criteria to target blacks and Latinos on the New Jersey Turnpike, and they had also elicited the cooperation of hotel and motel employees in monitoring behavior.

3. See Rich (1989) for a biography of Mayor Coleman Young of Detroit.

4. See Cohen's recent study of HIV/AIDS (1999), which included a content analysis of black news media.

5 Power and Governance in American Cities

Clarence N. Stone

A recurring issue in urban political science concerns who has power or who governs. For years there has been debate about who is more important, corporate executives or popularly elected representatives. Though schools of thought differed about which is more important, money or votes, both sides assumed that some small body of people ran things.

In recent years, a different understanding has taken hold. In this alternative view, the important considerations are not about who governs but about how governance occurs. Accordingly, we need to know the extent to which various people and organizations work together and the terms on which they cooperate. Power lies not in the hands of some distinct group (who), but rather inheres in *how* people are related. The power structure is not a small body of exceptionally important individuals; power depends on how relationships are structured as the community responds to major issues.

A shift in thinking, from who to how, is no easy matter. People tend to see things in personal terms, to ask questions about who is in charge. Though the term "boss" causes some unease about a potential for abuse of power, people also find comfort in the notion that someone or some group is in control and can fix things if they go wrong. Yet what is comforting and what is realistic are not necessarily the same thing. An ability to fix things depends not only on who comes together but also on the terms of cooperation and how their efforts are combined.

No group is ever all-powerful. Especially in a society that has both popular elections for public office and private control of business investment, there is no central control point. Government is necessary for many problem-solving efforts, but government effort alone is rarely sufficient for making much headway. Business is important, but business executives have neither the capacity nor the inclination to tackle many of society's problems.

The Power to Govern

How, then, does governance occur? Let us start with context. Consider how contemporary society operates. There is no command position from which direction comes, nor is there a ruling class. In many ways, society is loosely joined. Hosts of largely autonomous activities take place, each with its own particular set of rules and guidelines. Many are market-based activities subject to varying degrees of government regulation. Some are government enterprises—bridge and tunnel authorities, water and sanitary districts, as well as police and fire departments and others that provide routine public services. Some activities are neither business enterprises nor government functions, but rest on a voluntary basis. The profit motive operates widely, but nonprofit organizations also hold a significant place. Profit seeking, voluntary cooperation, and regulation are often mixed within the same arena of activity, though one may be more important than the others.

One scholar characterized the local community (the central city itself as well as the metropolitan area overall) as a place in which much of what happens takes place without any overall connection to conscious planning (Long 1958). People go about their daily routines and occupy themselves with activities close at hand, paying little heed to how the overall system operates or how their particular efforts fit into a larger scene.

To be sure, governments do a certain amount of planning and exercise some wide responsibilities, but much of what they do is to respond to breakdowns—react to particular problems. Big businesses like banks and utilities also do a certain amount of planning and overall assessment of trends. Business associations, typically the local Chamber of Commerce, also engage in planning and assessment of trends. Large nonprofit institutions and some social agencies conduct studies and plan as well. But none of these entities, not even the governmental sector, provide comprehensive direction. Government planning, in fact, is often met with a degree of distrust and skepticism. Planning by nongovernmental entities is typically done to further a particular goal, often as a form of advocacy falling far short of being inclusive in the concerns it encompasses. Even some of the planning by government agencies follows narrow functional lines. Transportation planners, for example, may take a metropolitan perspective but pay no special attention to the aims of educators in the region's various school districts. Moreover, though some form of metropolitan planning occurs, it typically carries weak enforcement authority. Indeed, with distrust of government authority widespread, especially in the business sector, planning even within a single unit of government is a relatively weak force.

People are purposeful, but the purposes they seek tend to be specific and immediate. Thus the Chamber of Commerce and the hotel association may be strong and persistent champions of a new convention center, but no one is likely to spend much effort on behalf of a comprehensive plan to combine growth management with transportation planning, combating pollution, and preserving established communities. As one observer noted, the "protagonists of things in particular are well organized and know what they are about; the protagonists of things in general are few, vague, and weak" (Long 1958, 255). Yet social and economic trends sometimes overwhelm "things in particular," and the pursuit of immediate goals is thwarted. Change has unforeseen consequences and may cause growing difficulties.

Governance is the process of identifying and addressing such difficulties. Governance, however, is not a comprehensive form of command and control. Still, it requires a variety of actors to combine their efforts in a common task of problem solving. Cooperation is key.

Cooperation

As a perceptive school superintendent once observed, "Cooperation is an unnatural act."[1] Recognition of a community problem does not guarantee action. The mayor, the police chief, the president of the Chamber of Commerce, and the leader of a neighborhood organization may see a given problem in different ways, or they may attach a varying priority to it. Many things clamor for attention, and not all receive it. Different actors may lack a sense of mutual responsibility to take on a problem, and each may feel that an undivided effort is likely to be ineffective. How, then, does the ability to act together come about?

On community issues, most actions flow through organizations and institutions. Government is often the first place people look to for action on a problem, but other organizations and institutions also control significant resources and may be in a position to play a vital role. If the issue has an economic dimension, business may be a desirable participant. If the issue involves health, hospitals may be enlisted (or may have enlisted themselves). Residential areas may act through neighborhood associations.

People in a local community do not start from scratch every time a new problem emerges. Over time, networks of interaction develop, and these may be altered or expanded and intensified as conditions change. Some positions and individuals in those positions may emerge as especially useful links in bringing people and resources together. Government officials, especially elected officeholders, are often expected to be skillful in bringing people together, working out their differences, and enabling them to join efforts in a common task.

That government controls important resources—principally money, the legal authority to regulate, and special powers such as eminent domain—puts public officials in the center of many interactions. And citizens expect (sometimes unrealistically) public officials to use their resources, contacts, and skills to respond creatively to problems. At the same time, public officials recognize that their resources and capacities are limited. For most complex issues, they need not only to head off damaging opposition but also to enlist the cooperation of other major players.

An obvious example is economic development. If a city is to protect its tax base and provide employment opportunities for its citizens, it needs investment by business. As an inducement for investment, a Chamber of Commerce, for example, may ask the city to develop a festival marketplace downtown and also request increased police patrols in that area. A city council member representing a working-class district might make her support contingent upon an assurance that hotel and restaurant operators will not resist unionization of workers, seeking to ensure that pay is adequate to support a family. A taxpayers' association might insist that downtown businesses pay for increased policing by creating a special tax district consisting only of properties in the central business district. Economic development thus occurs not by the unilateral action of government or business but by recognition that their aims (profit making for business and an expanded employment base for citizens) can be served by acting jointly, while also taking into account the wants of others in the picture.

In somewhat similar fashion, a beleaguered police chief with a rising crime rate and festering friction with the city's African American and Latino communities may develop a program of community-oriented policing in order to seek the cooperation of neighborhood leaders and gain a better understanding of the concerns among the city's people of color. As a complementary effort, the police department might assist citizens in setting up neighborhood watch programs and work with those programs after they are established. For community-oriented policing to be effective, police officers may need to be able to call on other city agencies, such as public works or parks and recreation, to respond to needs in the neighborhood and show that city government is not indifferent to its citizens. In search of better rapport with the citizenry, the police chief might also work with churches and nonprofit agencies to create and operate a police activities league through which after-school sports teams and tutoring sessions could be operated. The police chief might also seek out the local prosecutor's office to join efforts to increase involvement with neighborhoods—going out into the community to talk to citizen about crime issues and listen to their concerns. To increase personal contacts, law-enforcement personnel might also be enlisted to volunteer as tutors or coaches.

With both economic development and crime control, local government has a central part to play but cannot go it alone. The difference between the two examples is that economic development can be pursued with the cooperation of a few major entities, whereas effective crime control calls for interaction with citizens at the grassroots level. In neither case are the authority and resources of the government sector sufficient in themselves to get the job done.

In both cases a common purpose provides a basis around which cooperation can occur, but for energetic problem-solving activity to take place, the various players must make it a priority. And they must have a degree of trust that all will meet their obligations. Trust and a shared priority are easier to establish among a small number of players who interact on a regular basis than among a large number who have little experience dealing with one another. Hence, some issues and circumstances are more likely than others to generate cooperation.

In no case can anyone assume that cooperation is naturally forthcoming. It has to be built and maintained. While public officials and a few others direct much energy and activity into making connections, all urban localities have a tendency toward disconnection, with many autonomous activities coexisting. Most people lead busy lives and concentrate on immediate responsibilities. In large-scale matters, noncooperation is the norm; cooperation is the special case.

Power Over/ Power To

If cooperation is not the natural state of civic life, what about conflict? What about power and domination? Are they the main story? The urban experience suggests not. Conflict is important but not the whole picture.

Often we see power as a matter of contending wills. Players seek to get others to comply with their wishes, but each resists subordination to others. Threats, promises of reward, and deals are the everyday stuff of power as a form of domination—what might be called "power over." The operating assumption is that each player has a distinct set of interests at least partly in conflict with others. As one player uses her or his resources and skills to gain the compliance of others, the others use their resources and skills to resist. A player in a strong position may be able to satisfy many preferences, while a player in a weak position is able to satisfy very few preferences. In this relationship, the former is dominant and the latter subordinate. Often, however, relationships are not one-sided, and the two contenders may reach a compromise. It might take the form of mutual hands-off: Live and let live. Or it might take the form of a bargain: Each party gives up something and gains something in return.

"Power over" is an important phenomenon, and conflict and impasse are frequent occurrences. However, such relationships do not exhaust the realm of power possibilities. Though preferences often conflict, they do not always do so. And preferences can change as new possibilities open up. In the examples given earlier (economic development and law enforcement), cooperation could be built around shared concerns, but only if the key players trusted one another and saw the task as feasible—that the necessary resources and commitments of effort could be forthcoming.

Consider some alternative possibilities. One is a mutual distrust scenario. The police believe that people in communities of color have no broad interest in reducing crime. For their part, citizens of color see the police as racist and interested only in inflicting punishment. In this situation, the police might prefer saturation patrolling and aggressive application of a policy of zero tolerance. Neighborhood leaders oppose this policy and are interested only in establishing a civilian review board. Police come across to neighborhood residents as antagonistic, and residents are reluctant to cooperate with police in investigations of crime.

An alternative scenario might be based on mutual trust. The police see the possibility that neighborhood leaders would respond positively to community-oriented policing. For their part, neighborhood leaders see an opportunity to avoid escalating friction with the agents of law enforcement while bringing about more effective public safety. In this scenario, both police and neighborhood leaders prefer a community-oriented approach. Preferences converge rather than clash. The two parties, police and neighborhood, are not engaged in a contest of wills against one another but, instead, come together around a shared purpose.

To some degree, preferences stem from the situation and how various players see one another and what they believe can be done by conjoining efforts. States of mind about others play an important role. If distrust and wariness prevail, relationships tend toward conflict—and certainly toward noncooperation. If trust and mutuality develop, there is a basis for cooperation. When players come together to take on a task that neither could accomplish singly, they constitute a form of power to achieve a purpose. To distinguish this form of power from "power over" (the capacity to prevail in a contest of wills), we can label it "power to" (Stone 1989).

In some ways, "power to" resembles a bargain achieved under a clash of wills or "power over." The resemblance, in fact, is a reminder that at some stage the two forms of power blend into each other. At another stage the two are quite distinct. For instance, a pure form of "power over" bargaining would be a standoff in which no new purpose is pursued by either player. In some cases, however, what starts off as bargaining opens up a new possibility, and both players embrace it. They may thereby discover that coalition or partnership is fruitful. At the same time, it is important to remember that, because coalition partners are rarely of exactly the same mind, they may engage in bargaining within a partnership arrangement. "Power over" and "power to" thus can coexist and sometimes shade into each other. Note, however, that "power to" always involves two or more parties acting in cooperation with one another in order to accomplish a shared purpose.

Coalition Building and Governance

How does a purpose come to be understood as shared? Operating alone around a fixed set of preferences (an immutable understanding each has of its interest), actors would experience a high level of conflict. Interactions would often take the form of a contest of wills. However, to the extent that preferences are not fixed, interactions can lead to a new understanding of one's interest, and shared purposes have greater room in which to take shape.

A fundamental difference between "power over" and "power to" turns on whether preferences are fixed or malleable enough to allow new possibilities to emerge around which a partnership can form. Sometimes the possibility of a shared purpose emerges from conflict. Take, for example, the experiences in Atlanta, Georgia, and Charlotte, North Carolina. In both cities, white business leaders initially resisted racial change but later came to be champions of desegregation.

In Atlanta, Mayor Ivan Allen, who moved to that office 1962 from the presidency of the Chamber of Commerce, was the first local official in the South to endorse the Civil Rights bill that was being debated in Congress in 1963.[2] Allen's metamorphosis is remarkable. Early in his career, he ran for state office as an unapologetic defender of segregation. Later, as chamber president, he became more pragmatic. In office, charged with the responsibility of governing a city with a large and growing black population in an era of rapid change, he became an avid proponent of racial progress and saw that change as a matter of civic pride. A parallel but less public alteration can be seen in the evolution of the racial position of Robert Woodruff, the long-running and publicity-shy head of Coca-Cola. As chief of a major international corporation, he, too, put aside the racial views that were commonly accepted in that era and became the key figure behind organizing a precedent-setting (for the Deep South of that period) biracial dinner in Atlanta in 1965 to honor Martin Luther King Jr., the recent recipient of the Nobel Peace Prize.

The figure who perhaps best epitomizes racial change is Atlanta's Mayor William Hartsfield. First elected to the office in 1937, Hartsfield was very close to the city's business sector, to Woodruff in particular. In the 1940s, Hartsfield was a vocal critic of the NAACP, calling for its investigation by the House Un-American Activities Committee. Hartsfield was especially vigorous in attacking early proposals for fair-employment legislation. Yet, in office, Hartsfield kept a pragmatic ear open to leaders in the black community as they backed their position with a sizable and growing vote. (At this stage, the relationship was one of bargaining, centered on different preferences.) In the 1950s, as Little Rock, Arkansas, and other southern cities became centers of violent resistance, Hartsfield took pride in Atlanta as "the city too busy to hate." In his farewell address in 1961, making way for Ivan Allen's mayoralty, Hartsfield, at age seventy-one, called for his city to embrace social change and protect racial peace. Hartsfield's evolving preferences marked the emergence of a biracial coalition that rested, at least in part, on a shared embrace of policies and how to pursue them.

Hartsfield and Allen and their business backers had a pragmatic need for African American electoral support, which provided a foundation for further change. Their cumulative experience of interacting with the city's black leadership pushed the process along further. That white leaders played a major role in the governance of the city in a time of volatility solidified the transformation, and civic pride about change displaced an older set of racial preferences. The experience of working in a biracial partnership reshaped the white leadership's understanding of race and drew them into a new set of policy preferences. Though these preferences were not identical to those of Atlanta's black leadership (the city's biracial leadership was a coalition, not a single-minded group), substantial change occurred. Working with the city's African American community, white business and political leaders discovered that in coalition they had a capacity to bring about racial change and that such an effort was a worthy task to pursue. Note that action shaped preferences; fixed preferences did not drive action.

Charlotte's experience parallels that of Atlanta.[3] The city's white business leaders were confronted with a mandatory busing order by a federal judge in 1970. This was not a challenge they sought, but, confronted with the issue and its potentially disruptive consequences for the city and its image, the business leaders (who also provided Charlotte's top political leadership) chose to work with the black community and embrace support from within the religious community for Charlotte-Mecklenberg's massive busing policy. (The school district was and is a consolidated city-county district.) As in Atlanta, successful racial change became a matter of civic pride. Speaking about the emergence of biracial organizing in support of busing, a white clergyman in Charlotte observed that its citizens became "a whole lot better people than we were."[4] And a member of the school board remarked: "We have grown tremendously."[5]

In both Atlanta and Charlotte, white business leaders saw their political position transformed by immersion in a biracial coalition. The new relationships altered policy perspectives as well as obligations. In both cities, business leaders came to value the biracial coalition as a means by which the local community could be governed. The biracial coalition itself took on a value to be protected and preserved. A related example is Denver, Colorado, which has developed a significant form of multiracial politics and in recent years has had both black and Hispanic mayors (Hero 1997). Another striking case is El Paso, Texas, a city with a large Mexican-American population. El Paso is noteworthy for the formation of its Collaborative for Academic Excellence, a coalition bringing together multiple sectors of the community to advocate education reform and make education a priority on the city's agenda (Stone, Henig, Jones, Pierannunzi 2001).

In various cities, we can see that policy preferences do not take shape outside the relationships people build and maintain. Feminist theorists use the concept of "power to" as a way of emphasizing the point that people are not atomized participants in a struggle of each against all others (Hartstock 1983). Relationships shape what we can do and what we want to do. As a concept, "power to" underscores how the relationships we form and maintain guide behavior and shape preferences. In relationships we can do things that we could not do alone, and, as relationships change, the things we want to do alter as well.

"Power To" and Foreclosed Alternatives

"Power to" is about empowerment through coming together; it is about opening up possibilities. However, this process should not be romanticized. Coming together to realize one possibility may also foreclose other possibilities. In Atlanta, when white business leaders and leaders of the city's African American community formed their coalition, the move preempted other options. It put in place political arrangements that favored racial and economic change and worked against maintaining the status quo. The city's whites who preferred the status quo—smaller businesses and small property owners and those less educated and more provincial—found themselves on the outside and unable to mount effective resistance to change.

The alliance of blacks and business, embodied in the slogan "the city too busy to hate," also foreclosed pursuit of class politics. Whatever common interests the city's working-class whites and blacks possessed went undeveloped. Moreover, the mode of bargaining employed—quiet, behind-the-scenes negotiations between elites—provided no channel through which the needs and wants of people of lesser income could be expressed. As the black population grew to become a numerical majority and the coalition dealt with a succession of issues, much activity centered on opening up Atlanta's business and professional life to the city's sizable black middle class. The city's first African American mayor, Maynard Jackson, who was elected in 1973, aggressively pursued minority set-asides for the city's many contracts, especially those involved in building and operating Atlanta's new airport. (Exemplifying the underdevelopment of class politics, Jackson also broke a strike of the city's sanitation workers.) Overall, the Atlanta experience suggests that "power to" is not a means for realizing an infinite number of possibilities; it is about realizing some and forgoing others.

"Power to" involves not only who comes together to form a governing coalition but also the terms on which the coalition operates. These terms facilitate the development of some possibilities but hinder others. Atlanta's biracial coalition has found it much easier to mix the opening up of businesses and professional opportunities for middle-class African Americans with the city's economic development agenda than it has to mix in the expansion of opportunities for the city's sizable lower-income population.

Scholar Bryan Jones (1994) teaches us that complex issues have many aspects, and attention to one aspect may shut out attention to others. That city life is an ecology of autonomous activities is a reflection of our limited ability to see the big picture on an ongoing basis. Because "bounded rationality," or "narrow cognition" is part of the human condition, we simply cannot comprehend all facets of complicated situations at once. Similarly, the coalitions we form and the political arrangements we construct facilitate acting on some possibilities and not others. Thus the combination of formal and informal ways we meet problem-solving challenges—the governing regimes we create—favors pursuit of some possibilities but not others.

The Dynamics of Regime Formation

Although governance is selective in the activities covered, most cities most of the time have a governing coalition. It is made up of a body of people who bring together major institutional capacities and represent significant sectors of the community. In identifying and acting upon an agenda of community problems, this coalition governs. The arrangements through which it governs can be called a city's regime.[6] For example, biracial cooperation is the centerpiece of Atlanta's regime. A regime takes its character not only from who makes up the governing coalition but also from how the coalition members relate to one another.

Governing coalitions do not take shape randomly. They form in response to problem situations and reflect the context in which they take shape. At least four factors are involved in coalition formation: (1) congruent goals, (2) complementary resources, (3) feasible goals and ease of maintenance, and (4) urgency of action and the creative role of leadership.

Congruent Goals

Consider first why city hall/main street coalitions are so widespread, even though there are natural tensions between government and business. Why would companies that populate central business districts turn to local government as coalition partners?

At the end of World War II, cities underwent dramatic economic change. Transportation became less and less rail-centered and more automotive-centered, and manufacturing began to lose ground to a growing service and information economy. To respond to these changes, downtown businesses in many cities came together to pursue programs of redevelopment. Under these programs, land-use patterns would change and new forms of infrastructure would be built. To pursue redevelopment, businesses sought public funds (heavily subsidized by the federal urban renewal and highway programs) and the use of the power of eminent domain (the right to take property, with fair compensation, for public purposes).[7] These plans involved the disruption of many older neighborhoods and caused much controversy.

Why, then, did so many mayors join in a redevelopment coalition? City government, for its part, saw a need to protect its tax base and spark job creation by joining its efforts with those of business. For such a coalition, the particulars behind supporting redevelopment differ, but a general purpose rests on the congruence of particular aims. The coalition's capacity for policy action depends on the meshing of a general purpose with particular and individual goals. Atlanta's biracial coalition represents an enlarged version of the same principle. The city combined an agenda of redevelopment with one of racial change. Though the city underwent considerable political and social turmoil from the 1950s through the 1970s, it embraced and went through a process of change much less turbulent than that occurring in such places as Birmingham, New Orleans, and Little Rock.

Over the same decades, Chicago built a contrasting kind of coalition.[8] Mayor Richard J. Daley centralized that city's ward-based machine politics and worked closely with Chicago businesses to adjust the city to economic change. Initially, Daley relied heavily on the black vote to get into office and hold his position, but he did so by greatly depending on patronage channeled through African American political leaders such as Congressman William Dawson. Operating under the slogan "the city that works," Daley combined redevelopment with an effective delivery of services to Chicago's nonpoor white neighborhoods. "The city that works" built a large amount of high-rise public housing to accommodate its growing African American population, but, as that housing began to age in the 1970s and later, the city paid less and less attention to "making it work."

Under Daley and his immediate successors, the governing coalition in Chicago did not include middle-class blacks and reform-minded whites. The machine maintained complementarity among its core constituencies by avoiding controversial social issues such as desegregated schools and racially integrated neighborhoods. But, over time, Daley's coalition strategy proved increasingly less viable. Support in African American wards declined, deteriorating public housing became a disgrace, and a failing school system attracted growing attention. In 1983, Harold Washington became mayor when he defeated the machine in a crucial election.

The Chicago experience illustrates important points about complementarity. First, coalition unity often rests on a mix of general purposes and highly particular rewards. These rewards may or may not grow directly out of a general purpose. Patronage of the kind Daley provided through Congressman Dawson and other African American political leaders is what may be termed a side payment. It has nothing to do directly with a general purpose (other than maintaining support for the governing coalition and lessening opposition to it), but in some ways it may substitute for a general purpose.

A second lesson of the Chicago experience is that congruent purposes are hard to maintain over a long period of time. Conditions change and the balance of resources shifts. Daley's declining support among black voters as that portion of the electorate grew shows that any given arrangement, though highly stable and resilient in the short run, may give way over the long run. This pattern is termed punctuated equilibrium.

Complementary Resources

Coalitions build around action agendas, not wish lists. To act on an agenda re-quires resources, and these need to be commensurate with a coalition's central policy tasks (Erie 1988; Stone 2001). Indeed, coalitions become necessary because solitary players lack the resources to pursue ambitious goals on their own. The search for needed resources draws players into recognizing interdependent relationships, and interdependence may expand awareness of new facets of a problem.

Atlanta's biracial coalition took shape because black votes became crucial to con-trol of city government. (Note, however, that Atlanta and Chicago represent contrast-ing examples of the terms on which black votes contributed to the governing coalition; in Atlanta black leaders pursued general and particular aims, while in Chicago black membership in the coalition rested almost entirely on side payments.) Redevelopment required the investment resources and skills of the business sector as well as the authority and funds of the public sector. The disestablishment of the Jim Crow system involved both government action and business endorsement, based on a link between economic growth and racial change. Hence, business could not pursue its redevelopment aims without the backing of black voters, and black leaders could more easily pursue racial change if they enjoyed the backing of the city's prominent white business leaders. Pursuit of the overall agenda of change required multiple kinds of resources, and no single group could provide all kinds. Hence, Atlanta's bira-cial coalition rested on the complementary resources that the two principal groups brought to the partnership.

Feasibility

Why do some agendas emerge and hold center stage for long periods of time, while others gain only brief attention and then fade? It is easier to put together and main-tain some coalitions than others. Partners can obtain the needed resources for some purposes more readily than for others. Often, of course, the easiest alternative is sim-ply to go with the status quo. But that path may not be widely appealing. People are purposeful, and the possibility of pursuing a significant goal can be fulfilling (Chong 1991). Moreover, a do-nothing label can be damaging for political leaders or others pursuing a reputation as a community leader. Being on the move has an appeal that standing pat often lacks.

Goal seeking is mediated by feasibility considerations. In other words, people have little appetite for goals that seem unattainable. A mayor coming into office might well have a wide range of policy possibilities in mind but will also realize that not all can be pursued. Of the many groups clamoring for attention, how does a mayor choose whom to court and whom to pass by? Congruent goals are, of course, one consideration, but complementary resources play a major part. Groups such as business control multiple resources—money and credit, investment expertise, access to the media, staff who can be assigned to specific civic projects, and perhaps a reputation for good civic judgment (for example, business endorsement of a bond issue is often deemed a strong plus). Moreover, business is typically organized into active associations, such as the Chamber of Commerce. Individual business executives may play major roles in the United Way, the local arts association, and on the boards of various nonprofits. Business may also be a major force behind the local community foundation. In short, business is a pervasive presence in the civic life of most American cities and therefore a valuable ally in mobilizing a community effort. Action-oriented public officials thus tend to gravitate toward close interaction with business leaders.

Consider a contrasting prospect. A mayor would like to undertake community development in the city's poorest neighborhoods. However, state and federal money for such purposes is often very limited. The neighborhoods may have experienced a decline in the number of businesses and community organizations. Often residents are weakly organized and highly distrustful of city government, based on past experiences of short-lived and ineffective programs. In contrast to collaborating with the business sector, working with low-income neighborhoods confronts the mayor with major obstacles, few readily available resources, and a prospectively long path to visible results. Given that mayors face a short election cycle and in some cases term limits as well, they might predictably be less attracted to coalition partnership with lower-income neighborhoods than with the city's business sector. Feasibility favors alignment with business.

Look at coalition formation from the nongovernmental side. African American leaders in Atlanta chose partnership with business as a means to dismantle the Jim Crow system, and they chose that path over forming a labor union–centered coalition with the white working class, even though Representative Helen Mankin built a nascent alliance around her congressional candidacy in 1946.[9] One calculation in that choice was that in Georgia an alliance built around a labor union component would surely face a hostile environment. Altering the position of Atlanta's African American population would be no easy task in any case, but the most promising path to follow was one of partnership with the city's corporate leadership. Coca-Cola executive Woodruff was no champion of equal rights, but, as head of an international corporation, he could be persuaded to throw his weight behind racial change of a kind consistent with world opinion. Moreover, Woodruff and his business associates in Atlanta had great influence in state affairs. They offered potential leverage that the AFL/CIO could not begin to match.

Both governmental and nongovernmental players have policy interests that guide their searches for coalition partners. Still, these interests can be shaped in different ways, and choices have to be made about what receives primary attention.

Leadership and Urgency of Action

Congruent goals, complementary resources, and feasibility are considerations that bear strongly on the formation of governing coalitions around problem-solving efforts. Yet there is nothing automatic about this process, and little is predetermined. The setting of agendas and the creation of governing arrangements around them are acts of leadership. People are purposeful, but their narrow cognition means that they can perceive and act on situations in a variety of ways. Often they simply draw on local traditions and previous practices to respond to new situations, but on occasion a set of players develop a vision of a new way of governing. Atlanta's biracial coalition drew on some past practices, but it was by and large a radical departure from the city's racial past. In some cases, a crisis gives birth to a new direction. Charlotte's busing decision gave a sense of urgency to the city's civic and business leadership, who had a vision that the community could make it work. That was not inevitable. To a degree, feasibility is in the eyes of the beholder, and one facet of leadership is convincing others that achievement of a goal is doable. Not all would-be leaders are capable of such persuasion. A crisis could be greeted with declining morale and a sense that all is lost, or leadership can use it as a call to action. Crisis itself is partly a matter of how leaders define the situation. What one officeholder sees as an unfortunate but unavoidable reality, another may see as a task to be tackled.

Urgency of action is a complex matter. It turns partly on the gravity of the problem faced, but it may also depend partly on the newness of the problem. A condition that has been around for a long time may give rise to no feeling of urgency because, to many people, it has become a fixture on the social landscape. By contrast, a fresh problem may invite action because it has acquired no sense of inevitability. But urgency of action may also rest on a vision of how to tackle a problem. A long-standing problem may take on a new face if a fresh way of approaching it makes an appearance. Leadership vision is not simply a matter of seeing a problem worthy of tackling; it also involves a plan of attack—a vision of how energy and resources can be mobilized to address a situation.

Martin Luther King Jr. was an eloquent orator, capable of presenting to an audience an inspiring image of the "beloved community," a diverse community living in harmony. King was also a brilliant strategist in waging a struggle against recalcitrant segregationists in Birmingham, Alabama. He used a local stage in the Deep South to gain support for new national legislation and achieve one of the great victories of the civil rights movement. However, later, when he moved north to take on housing conditions and residential segregation in Chicago, King found his efforts thwarted by the shrewd countermoves of Richard J. Daley (Anderson and Pickering 1986; Biles 1995; Cohen and Taylor 2000). Unlike King's Birmingham adversaries, the Chicago mayor avoided confrontation and made paper concessions. What had worked in one setting against one adversary did not work in a new setting with a different adversary. Leadership does not operate in a vacuum, and the building of coalitions does not occur in a context devoid of competition.

Change and Stability

As with the civil rights movement, fundamental change is often initiated by those outside the corridors of official authority. Yet, as King's Chicago experience shows, typically "protest is not enough."[10] Those on the inside are better positioned to have a lasting impact. Conflict and confrontation can raise issues, but, over the long haul, putting pressure on a governing coalition ("power over") may be less effective than incorporation into a governing coalition (achieving a form of "power to"). In the case of the civil rights movement, national legislation altered the local political landscape by providing protection for voting rights and prohibiting racial discrimination. The Community Action and Model Cities programs of the 1960s also put new resources into communities of color and further stirred the urban political scene (Marris and Rein 1982; Jackson 1993).Yet the experience of that time shows how difficult reform is, even with an infusion of new guarantees and new (but quite limited) resources into the local community.

Leaders vary in the problems they see and the gravity they attach to those problems. Hence "throwing the rascals out" and putting new people in office is one way to bring about change. But new faces alone often amount to little. Leaders also vary in their willingness to embrace change and take risks. Most elected officials pursue marginal change and tend to align themselves with elements of the community who have substantial resources. After all, these are the players who can contribute most readily to the governance of the city.

Consider the career of Ed Rendell, Philadelphia's mayor from 1992 to 1999 (Bissinger 1999). Faced with a continuing decline in industrial jobs, Rendell initially sought to bring an overseas company into the city's recently closed shipyard. When that failed, Rendell redoubled his efforts to boost Philadelphia's convention and tourist trade. Yet many of these jobs have modest or low pay, with little capacity to reverse the city's growing problem of poverty. Rendell's boldest move was to avoid bankruptcy by forcing cutbacks in the compensation packages for the unionized municipal work force, a move that received strong approval from Philadelphia's banking community. It was a move born of financial urgency and one supported by the business sector. It showed Rendell to be a realist but hardly a visionary.

Some architects of governing coalitions look beyond what is immediately feasible and beyond the holders of readily available resources; they ask if far-reaching changes can be achieved that will enlarge opportunities and benefits for society's least-advantaged people. Those who take this approach acquire the label of reformer. Their task is risky. They face the formidable challenge of bringing together needed resources, often by what Martin Luther King called "making a way out of no way." This may mean activating people who have been passive. It may involve unifying people who have been divided and even fragmented. It may also entail creating new forms of motivation, of rallying people around the pursuit of worthy civic aims. It may call for elevating social or professional fulfillment and for lessening concern with bread and butter issues. And it may involve getting those with vast resources to view their interests in broad, community terms. Even so, this path has many pitfalls, but its appeal is that, despite the uncertainty of success, attainment would be a lofty and satisfying feat. For this reason, leadership can sometimes make such a path attractive and imbue it with a strong sense of possibility. However, reformers do not populate the political landscape in large numbers. In office, reformers frequently have short tenure, either because they incur defeat or rein in their risk taking to avoid defeat.

Nonetheless, significant reform regimes have made their way onto the urban political scene. Fiorello La Guardia substantially reshaped New York City politics during his twelve years as mayor from 1934 to 1945, pushing aside the Tammany machine and expanding opportunities and services for new elements in New York's population. As mayor of Chicago, Harold Washington also overcame an incumbent machine and began far-reaching reforms, including a new role for the city's neighborhoods. With Washington's untimely death in 1987, barely four years into his mayoralty, his reform regime had a limited run. His successor had neither the vision nor the skill to carry through, but a few reform footprints remained.

La Guardia and Washington represent comprehensive reform regimes. Some reform efforts have a more limited target. In 1991, San Francisco adopted a children's initiative (Proposition J) to make the well-being of those under eighteen a city priority. The impetus for this initiative came from a nongovernmental organization, Coleman Advocates for Children and Youth, which had sought unsuccessfully to get city officials to increase funding for children's programs. Proposition J amended the city charter to mandate that 2.5 percent of the property-tax revenue be set aside to provide expanded services for children and youth. The coalition surrounding this effort started when eighty-five organizations serving children and youth came together to develop a comprehensive agenda. Once they moved from framing an agenda to the initiative and its passage, the mandated pool of money served to rally further support. The mayor at that time, Frank Jordan, at first declined to support the initiative, and for the first few years city hall made little of the opportunity for a new city priority. However, when

Willie Brown became mayor in 1996, the city's Department of Children, Youth, and Families became a catalyst for bringing additional partners into actively pursuing the children's agenda, building on the early support provided by the philanthropic and nonprofit sectors. In particular, the school system became a cooperating partner.

Several facets of San Francisco's experience are notable. The coalition was policy specific and not a comprehensive governing coalition. The initiation of the agenda was outside the mayor's office, though city hall under a subsequent mayor became an important player. The Chamber of Commerce opposed the initiative, as did a major city newspaper and the Republican Central Committee, and the proposition passed with only 54 percent of the vote. But once the new priority was set and the charter amendment proved workable, support became widespread. A renewed Children's Amendment increased funding to 3 percent of the property-tax assessment. In November 2000, it passed overwhelmingly, with most segments of the community giving their endorsement.

As noted, El Paso provides another example of a reform coalition with a policy-specific focus. Created in 1991, the city's Collaborative for Academic Excellence brings together educators, the business sector, a community-based organization especially concerned with parent empowerment, and local elected officials to support school reform. This effort originated at the University of Texas El Paso (UTEP), and it receives significant continuing support from the university and its college of education. The President of UTEP chairs the Collaborative. With a mission-minded staff, the Collaborative promotes professional development, along with such aims as a rigorous curriculum and parent engagement. The city's three urban school districts have had success in raising test scores and winning significant awards. With the cosponsorship of the El Paso Chamber of Commerce, the Collaborative organized a citywide Education Summit in 2000.This resulted in the creation of an array of task forces to continue to highlight the place of education in the local agenda and to mobilize resources behind that agenda.

Seattle provides yet another example of a reform agenda. In this instance, human-capital development is the focus, and both school reform and "second chance" workforce development have gotten substantial attention from the mayor and other elected officials. Though the business sector has been supportive, its role has been minor; initiative has come largely from within the public sector, with significant assistance from the nonprofit sector.

Over time, reform has focused on several targets—sometimes machine politics, at other times the ending of racial segregation and bringing about greater inclusiveness, and at still other times alternative priorities such as children and youth. Some reform efforts aim for a broad transformation of governing arrangements, but sometimes the aim is simply the elevation of a new priority. Across these examples, the role of business varies, ranging from an integral part of the governing coalition to being largely on the sidelines. Although some instances, such as San Francisco's Children's Amendment, represent priorities that business executives may be uncomfortable with, at least at first, reform initiatives can seldom be categorized as antibusiness. Growth-management regulations (as in Portland, Oregon) and development fees (as in Boston) fall closest to the antibusiness side of the ledger, but these are usually found in areas with vibrant economies where the overall well-being of business is not in question. In one of the very few instances in which a mayor launched an antibusiness crusade, Cleveland's Dennis Kucinich encountered heavy opposition and quick defeat. His mayoralty lasted only from 1977 to 1979, and it included a recall election in the middle of that short span.

In summary, effective reform efforts are part of the urban political scene, but they are not widespread. When they do occur, they are often narrow in scope and rarely take an antibusiness form.

Conclusion

Since most people in the local community are usually engaged in immediate and particular tasks, the tackling of community-wide problems—the task of governance—involves special efforts. Standing alone, the authority of government is inadequate. Government commands too narrow a body of resources, and, in any case, governmental authority is often viewed with a degree of skepticism. Hence, government does not equal governance. A city's business sector controls substantial resources and makes an attractive ally, but it, too, lacks a standing-alone capacity to take on community-wide problems. This is also true of other groups and organizations with significant resources. Though government lacks a capacity to govern by itself, it provides mechanisms around which resources cam be gathered and support rallied (as in the case of San Francisco's Children's Amendment).

Resources can take many forms. Money and organization are two of the most obvious, but there are others, including the coercive authority of government to impose regulations and make use of the power of eminent domain. Less obvious are intangible resources in the form of grass-roots cooperation and citizens' engagement in furthering a community aim, such as parent involvement in education or cooperation with agencies of the criminal justice system.

Sometimes resources build strength through cumulative impact and focus. San Francisco's Children's Amendment gathered widespread public support, in part, because diverse organizations came together around a shared agenda. All of this is to say that a community's capacity to address problems is not there for the picking. It has to be created, maintained, and, on many occasions, rejuvenated.

Governance is not a matter of occupying standing positions of power. Instead, it involves creating a set of arrangements through which various elements of the community bring resources to bear in problem-solving tasks. Such a governing regime is not a body of people able and willing to take on any issue brought to its attention. It is better positioned to take on some issues rather than others. At the same time, the interdependent character of the arrangements provides a channel though which members of a coalition can develop a wider and more complex understanding of the issues facing a community. In this way, if the resources and understanding are adequate, new tasks can be undertaken. The embracing of those tasks may even become a matter of civic pride and build cohesion among the coalition members. Nevertheless, over time as new conditions emerge, a governing arrangement may prove to be increasingly less capable of responding effectively. A governing coalition may thus undergo modification or even fundamental reconstitution.

In thinking about governing arrangements, it is useful to see power as more complex than simple "power over" relationships. Not every relationship involves a clash of conflicting wills. "Power to," that is to say, a capacity to pursue goals collectively, grows out of relationships that enable partners to achieve in combination what neither could achieve alone. The process of coming together and protecting a coalition can also bring about new perspectives and even a new sense of responsibility, thus reshaping the outlook and preferences of coalition partners.

"Power to" is not, however, a matter of ever-widening agendas. The human condition of narrow cognition and limited energy means that priorities are set and choices made. The emergence of one alignment may displace others, though this is not necessarily a conscious process. Power is integrally related to the formation of preferences. Some preferences grow out of the immediate situation we are in, but preference is conditioned by feasibility. If a problem seems unyielding, support for tackling it is unlikely to be strong or durable. One element of leadership is to give a course of action a sense of feasibility—to imbue a group with a "we can do it" attitude. This is called vision, because it transcends an everyday understanding of what we can do.

As political beings, people are not locked into conflict over a given set of issues. Interaction directs our attention to new and emerging possibilities. Nevertheless, people are constrained by the circumstances in which they interact. It is easier to pursue goals that can be achieved by bringing together resources already available than it is to pursue goals that require significant new resources and wholly changed relationships. Difference can breed distrust. Those who are disadvantaged and thereby in possession of few immediate resources may also be highly skeptical of the possibilities of change. Reformers thus face the double challenge of persuading some who are advantaged by the existing arrangement to embrace change while convincing those who are disadvantaged that a process of change to which they could contribute is feasible.

Reform is thus beset with obstacles, but a leader who can show ways to overcome or bypass obstacles may be able to build momentum and give reform a sense of feasibility. This is not to say that anything is possible, but it is to say that much depends on what people believe is realizable.

Effective governing arrangements are built through (1) defining purposes and setting an agenda of congruent purposes, (2) mobilizing a complementary blend of resources commensurate with that agenda, and (3) imbuing the effort with a sense of feasibility. There are, however, no predetermined outcomes, and the pursuit of purpose is not a linear process. Although established conditions make some governing arrangements harder to build and maintain than others, leadership can alter the prospects for change. Leaders make us think about our interdependence in fresh ways and thereby widen the world of possibilities. As we consider the nature of power in contemporary society, it is useful to return to the wisdom of Aristotle. People are political animals, and this means that our understanding of social purpose and possibility takes shape in the company of one another.

Suggested Readings

Bizzinger, Buzz. 1997. *A Prayer for the City.* New York: Random House. An inside observer's account of the first term of Edward Rendell, mayor of Philadelphia in the 1990s, when the city faced the possibility of financial insolvency and the virtual certainty of continuing economic decline. It is a compelling account of a major hot spot in big-city politics.

Browning, Rufus, Dale Rogers Marshall, and David Tabb, eds. 2002. *Racial Politics in American Cities,* 3d ed. New York: Longman. Building coalitions in today's multiracial cities is a supreme political test. This collection gives an overview of how these efforts have fared in a wide variety of cities.

Cohen, Adam, and Elizabeth Taylor. 2000. *American Pharaoh: Mayor Richard J. Daley, His Battle for Chicago and the Nation.* Boston: Little, Brown. A carefully researched, no-holds-barred biography of one of Chicago's most important mayors. Among other subjects, it covers the struggle between Daley, the entrenched insider, and Martin Luther King Jr., a master of protest politics in the South but on new and different turf in the urban North.

Erie, Steven. 1988. *Rainbow's End: Irish-Americans and the Dilemma of Urban Machine Politics 1840–1985.* Berkeley: University of California Press. An authoritative treatment of machine politics, showing how the machine evolved over time in response to changes in the nation and its policies. Special attention is given to the importance of resources and the strategic role states can play in establishing terms under which cities operate.

Ferman, Barbara. 1996. *Challenging the Growth Machine: Neighborhood Politics in Chicago and Pittsburgh.* Lawrence: University Press of Kansas. This study of Chicago and Pittsburgh shows how a city's political institutions shape the opportunities for neighborhood groups to enter the political fray and have a policy impact. The book is a good example of combining case studies with comparative analysis.

Stone, Clarence, ed. 1998. *Changing Urban Education.* Lawrence: University Press of Kansas. This collection explores the network of race, civic leadership, and professional education through which school reform must find its way. By spotlighting tangles in the education web, the book shows why reform is unlikely to go very far under apolitical banners like accountability and choice.

References

Allen, Frederick. 1996. *Atlanta Rising.* Marietta, Ga.: Longstreet Press.

Anderson, Alan B., and George W. Pickering. 1986. *Confronting the Color Line.* Athens: University of Georgia Press.

Bennett, Larry. 1993. "Harold Washington and the Black Urban Regime." *Urban Affairs Quarterly* 28 (March): 423–440.

Biles, Roger. 1995. *Richard J. Daley: Politics, Race, and the Governing of Chicago.* DeKalb: Northern Illinois University Press.

Bissinger, Buzz. 1999. *A Prayer for the City.* New York: Vintage.

Browning, Rufus P., Dale Rogers Marshall, and David H. Tabb. 1984. *Protest Is Not Enough.* Berkeley: University of California Press.

Chong, Dennis. 1991. *Collective Action and the Civil Rights Movement.* Chicago: University of Chicago Press.

Cohen, Adam, and Elizabeth Taylor. 2000. *American Pharaoh: Mayor Richard J. Daley His Battle for Chicago and the Nation.* Boston: Little, Brown.

Dowding, Keith. 2001. "Explaining Urban Regimes." *International Journal of Urban and Regional Research* 25 (March): 7–19.

Erie, Steven P. 1988. *Rainbow's End: Irish-Americans and the Dilemma of Urban Machine Politics 1840–1985.* Berkeley: University of California Press.

Ferman, Barbara. 1996. *Challenging the Growth Machine: Neighborhood Politics in Chicago and Pittsburgh.* Lawrence: University Press of Kansas.

Gove, Samuel K., and Louis H. Masotti, eds. 1982. *After Daley: Chicago Politics in Transition.* Urbana: University of Illinois Press.

Green, Paul M., and Melvin G. Holli, eds. 1995. *The Mayors: The Chicago Political Tradition,* rev. ed. Carbondale: Southern Illinois University Press.

Grimshaw, William. 1995. *Bitter Fruit: Black Politics and the Chicago Machine, 1931–1991.* Chicago: University of Chicago Press.

Hartsock, Nancy C. M. 1983. *Money, Sex, and Power.* New York: Longman.

Hero, Rodney E. 1997. "Latinos and Politicos in Denver and Pueblo, Colorado: Differences, Explanations, and The 'Steady-State' of the Struggle for Equality." In *Racial Politics in American Cities,* 2d ed., ed. Rufus P. Browning, Dale Rogers Marshall, and David H. Tabb, 247–258. New York: Longman.

Jackson, Thomas F. 1993. "The State, the Movement, and the Urban Poor." In *The Underclass Debate,* ed. Michael B. Katz, 403–439. Princeton: Princeton University Press.

Jones, Bryan D. 1994. *Reconceiving Decision-making in Democratic Politics.* Chicago: University of Chicago Press.

Keating, Larry. 2001. *Atlanta: Race, Class, and Urban Expansion.* Philadelphia: Temple University Press.

Kleppner, Paul. 1985. *Chicago Divided.* DeKalb: Northern Illinois University Press.

Lauria, Mickey, ed. 1997. *Reconstructing Urban Regime Theory.* Thousand Oaks, Calif.: Sage.

Long, Norton E. 1958. "The Local Community as an Ecology of Games." *American Journal of Sociology* 64 (November): 251–261.

Marris, Peter, and Martin Rein. 1982. *Dilemmas of Social Reform,* 2d ed. Chicago: University of Chicago Press.

Mossberger, Karen, and Gerry Stoker. 2001. "The Evolution of Urban Regime Theory." *Urban Affairs Review* 36 (July): 810–835.

Pomerantz, Gary M. 1996. *Where Peachtree Meets Sweet Auburn.* New York: Simon and Schuster.

Simpson, Dick. 2001. *Rogues, Rebels, and Rubber Stamps.* Boulder: Westview Press.

Smith, Stephen S. *Boom for Whom?* Albany: SUNY Press, in press.

Stone, Clarence N. 1989. *Regime Politics.* Lawrence: University Press of Kansas.

———— 1993. "Urban Regimes and the Capacity to Govern." *Journal of Urban Affairs* 15: 1–28.

———— 2001. "The Atlanta Experience Re-examined." *International Journal of Urban and Regional Research* 25 (March): 20–34.

Stone, Clarence N., Jeffrey Henig, Bryan Jones, and Carol Pierannunzi. 2001. *Building Civic Capacity.* Lawrence: University Press of Kansas.

Stone, Clarence N., and Donn Worgs. "Community Building and a Human-Capital Agenda: The Hampton Story." Unpublished paper.

Notes

1. Quoted in Clarence Stone and Donn Worgs, "Community Building and a Human-Capital Agenda: The Hampton Story," unpublished paper.

2. There are several book-length accounts of Atlanta politics, including: Frederick Allen, *Atlanta Rising* (Marietta, Ga: Longstreet Press, 1996); Larry Keating, *Atlanta: Race, Class, and Urban Expansion* (Philadelphia: Temple University Press, 2001); Gary M. Pomerantz, *Where Peachtree Meets Sweet Auburn* (New York: Simon and Schuster, 1996); and Clarence N. Stone, *Regime Politics: Governing Atlanta, 1946–1988* (Lawrence: University Press of Kansas, 1989).

3. An excellent treatment of Charlotte is contained in Stephen S. Smith, *Boom for Whom?* (Albany, N.Y.: SUNY Press, in press).

4. Quoted in Smith in press.

5. Ibid.

6. The literature on urban regimes is extensive. Works reviewing that literature include: Keith Dowding, "Explaining Urban Regimes," *International Journal of Urban and Regional Research* 25 (March 2001): 7–19; Mickey Lauria, ed., *Reconstructing Urban Regime Theory* (Thousand Oaks, Calif., 1997); Karen Mossberger and Gerry Stoker, "The Evolution of Urban Regime Theory," *Urban Affairs Review* 36 (July 2001): 810–835; and Clarence N. Stone, "Urban Regimes and the Capacity to Govern," *Journal of Urban Affairs* 15 (1993): 1–28.

7. The power of eminent domain can be exercised not only by government (for such purposes as building highways) but also by private utility companies for public purposes such as right of way for power lines.

8. The literature on Chicago is vast. A short list of relevant materials includes: Larry Bennett, "Harold Washington and the Black Urban Regime," *Urban Affairs Quarterly* 28 (March 1993): 423–440; Barbara Ferman, *Challenging the Growth Machine* (Lawrence: University Press of Kansas, 1996); Samuel K. Gove and Louis H. Masotti, eds., *After Daley: Chicago Politics in Transition* (Urbana: University of Illinois Press, 1982); Paul M. Green and Melvin G. Holli, eds., *The Mayors: The Chicago Political Tradition,* rev. ed. (Carbondale: Southern Illinois University Press, 1995); William Grimshaw, *Bitter Fruit: Black Politics and the Chicago Machine, 1931–1991* (Chicago: University of Chicago Press, 1995); Paul Kleppner, *Chicago Divided* (DeKalb: Northern Illinois University Press, 1985); Dick Simpson, *Rogues, Rebels, and Rubber Stamps* (Boulder: Westview Press, 2001); and Adam Cohen and Elizabeth Taylor. *American Pharaoh* (Boston: Little, Brown, 2000).

9. See especially Allen, *Atlanta Rising.*

10. The phrase and an accompanying argument are from Rufus P. Browning, Dale Rogers Marshall, and David H. Tabb, *Protest Is Not Enough* (Berkeley: University of California Press, 1984).

6 Mayoral Politics

Lana Stein

Delineating the role, the powers, or the impact of U.S. mayors is not easy. As Edward C. Banfield noted almost forty years ago, the variations among cities in terms of demographics, economics, governmental structure, and relationship to state government are extensive (Banfield 1963). Hence, generalizing about one aspect—such as the role of a mayor—can be difficult, given the other variables that come into play.

Mayors also present an "*n* of 1," one case at one time in one place, similar to that of governors or presidents. Because cities vary in numerous ways, cross-national or time series quantitative studies concerning mayoral politics are difficult to conduct. Another major emphasis in urban political study in recent years also has worked against analyses of mayoral activity, although it is not quantitative in nature. Urban political economists have produced a significant number of case studies of various cities, in which mayors have frequently been portrayed as handmaidens to business interests. The individual contributions these mayors may have made to policies and projects have not generally been explored in depth.

The role of the individual has taken a back seat in a variety of social science disciplines. Economics and social forces have become more popular (and measurable) foci for a number of researchers. Demonstrating the impact of this trend, the noted historian Gordon Craig (1978) began a study of modern Germany by acknowledging that concentrating on the "prominence of personality" would be considered old-fashioned. Yet how could he write about modern Germany without dwelling on Otto von Bismarck? America's mayors do not rank with the Iron Chancellor, of course, but who could examine Chicago politics without looking at the career of Richard J. Daley? In any major city, whoever holds the position of mayor can make a difference—in citizen mobilization, in policy innovation, in equity—positively or negatively. Although the effects of globalization and demographic change, as well as federal programming, affect all cities, not all react in the same fashion. Municipal structure, political culture, socioeconomics, and characteristics of other governmental sectors impact the well-being of cities. But individual mayors have an influence as well. The increasing number of minority mayors in American cities also raises the question of a different type of impact. Will African American or Hispanic mayors be able to serve their core constituency, and can they redirect municipal priorities? Much attention has been devoted to the election of a particular city's first minority mayor, especially an African American; attention to that mayor's success in office frequently has not been commensurate.

Despite the difficulties in capturing the importance of a mayor or mayors in general, some research highlights differences among mayors of the same city or of two or more metropolises. Interestingly, the role of leadership is being rediscovered in a number of fields and eventually should become a pivotal focus in upcoming urban studies. Dennis Judd, a political economist of long standing, grapples with the issue of urban leadership in a recent article. He notes that "the wellsprings of leadership are to be discovered primarily within the local contours of politics. They do not arise, in some mysterious fashion, from the pressures that cities face" (Judd 2000, 951–961).

This chapter focuses on mayors and their role in urban politics and policymaking. In a systems model that looks at institutions, mayors are part of the political process, composed of actors and institutions that respond to the demands and supporting conditions of the political environment (see Table 6-1). For cities, mayors are the prime actors in the system, although their effect on public policy will be determined, in part, by political structure. The following factors will be considered when assessing the role of a mayor:

- Capacity to govern
- Political economy
- Challenges of nonwhite mayors

The ability to act and to make a difference in politics and policy will be a recurring theme.

Table 6-1   Influences on Mayoral Performance

Exogenous factors	Institutional factors	Internal factors
Demographic	Form of government	Ability to persuade, compromise, negotiate
Economic	Mayoral powers	Cheerleader for city
	Regime makeup	Vision
	Relations with state government	
	Support from federal government	

Government Structure and Mayors

A number of scholars (for example, Banfield and Wilson 1963) trace today's forms of municipal governance to the Progressive reform era. A strong cadre of affluent reformers took umbrage at the corrupt machine politics prevalent in many cities at the end of the nineteenth century. They sought to expunge the partisan political practices they felt were responsible for inefficiency and various forms of corruption. Their enemies were the long ballot, partisan local elections, and council members elected from districts. To Progressives, the nature of the tasks of municipal government, centering principally around housekeeping functions in that era, made a businesslike approach to governance desirable. Progressives also favored a strong executive, initially a mayor with increased powers, and later a city manager. The latter form struck them as analogous to a corporate CEO and a board of directors.

In the 1890s, major U.S. cities resembled one another in their practice of machine politics. After the heyday of Progressive reform (post-1915), the governing institutions of American cities varied widely. The least political structure (in the partisan sense) is the council-manager form, which retains some type of mayoral role. In smaller cities, the mayor frequently can be a member of the city council, who is delegated by his or her peers to perform as official greeter and ribbon-cutter for the city. Over half of the municipalities with populations above 100,000 use the council-manager form. In these larger cities, there may be independently elected mayors, and in some, such as San Antonio and San Jose, the mayors are actively involved in the policymaking process.

The mayor-council form is still dominant in America's very largest cities, although there is considerable variation here as well. Some mayor-council cities have partisan electoral contests, and others do not. Some elect council members from districts, some elect them at large, and a number have a hybrid system. Svara (1990) notes that mayors in mayor-council cities have administrative authority, and residents view them as the people who get things done. However, mayors' statutory power may vary considerably. Strong mayors have "formal powers [that] include control over budget formation and hiring of staff, appointment of members of boards and commissions . . . fill[ing] vacancies in elective offices" (p. 88) and contractual authority. A strong mayor also will be able to veto legislation.

When mayors have fewer of these powers, they are considered to be weak mayors. Administrative authority is often shared by the weak mayor and an estimate board made up of other officials elected citywide or with unelected administrators or commissions. In cities with weak mayor system, the council may have broader fiscal powers. Despite the variations in institutional structure, a mayor has to be able to negotiate and compromise with key players in his or her environment in order to implement an agenda. In the American system of divided government, few elective executives can move forward by fiat. The need to succor other elected officials, representatives of business and labor, and community leaders to achieve objectives is a constant in all cities. An intimate look at this process is provided in Bissinger's (1997) study of Philadelphia mayor Ed Rendell. Rendell succeeded in courting a number of individuals, which helped him put Philadelphia's fiscal house in order. If the mayor's formal powers are greater, he or she may need to stroke a smaller number of egos.

Professionalized government with a citywide focus is advocated by Svara and Banfield and Wilson. This is especially apparent in Banfield and Wilson's discussion of political culture. They view cities that employ machine-style practices as private regarding. Private-regarding cities, in their opinion, emphasize individual rewards such as patronage and neglect the city as a whole (p. 123). On the other hand, public-regarding cities, reformed in nature, look at development needs citywide (especially in the central business district). Public-regarding cities are at a higher level of moral development, according to Banfield and Wilson, who believe that all cities will eventually take the reform path (p. 123). As immigrant groups become more integrated into American society, the need for the private regarding ethos will die out. The Banfield and Wilson typology does not take into account the particular needs of municipal business leaders. Individually tailored rewards can be targeted to a variety of constituencies, including landowners and developers.

Regardless of institutional makeup, mayors need to build networks of support. The cultivation of constituencies that favor their programs takes time and effort. Mayors in all cities seek allies in the business community, a phenomenon that is well covered in the urban political economy literature. A mayor's ability to fashion such alliances is a key to success. The mayor may be able to pull together disparate actors to make projects possible.

Can Cities Be Governed?

In the 1960s, the notion of a mayor as someone helpless to shape significant areas of his or her domain became conventional wisdom. Sayre and Kaufman's (1960) ground-breaking study, *Governing New York,* stated that the impediment appeared to be the burgeoning growth of municipal bureaucracies, where professionals followed their own criteria and successfully resisted political direction. Sayre and Kaufman referred to these bureaus as "islands of functional power." Along with Lowi (1964), they highlighted examples of New York City mayors frustrated in their attempts to shape public health delivery and police protection. In fact, Lowi went on to dub these powerful bureaus the "new machines" (pp. 83–92).

In 1977, Douglas Yates took the idea of mayoral impotence a step further. "Given its present political organization and decision-making processes," he wrote, "the city is fundamentally ungovernable. . . . [T]he urban policymaking system is incapable of producing coherent decisions, developing effective policies, or implementing state or federal programs" (p. 5). Function, fragmentation, and dependency all affected urban governance. Yates maintained that strong mayors such as Chicago's Richard J. Daley and New Haven's Richard Lee were unlikely to appear again (p. 164). The federal structure created a dependency on funding sources at the state or national capital. With the addition of weak local institutions and the intractable problems of increasing poverty and welfare dependency, as well as minority unrest, mayoral hands were tied and their cities became ungovernable.

Adding a major caveat to the work on ungovernable cities, Barbara Ferman's (1985) study sought "to identify the factors that contribute to strong executive leadership at the local level." She defined successful mayors as those who "are able to persuade others, control policy arenas, extend their influence within city government, implement priorities, and mobilize support for electoral and nonelectoral goals" (p. 6). Ferman compared mayoral activity in two nonpartisan cities, San Francisco and Boston, which, to a certain extent, are also similar in size and demography. In addition, both had made the transition to service-based economies. San Francisco and Boston each had roots in machine politics. Boss Abraham Reuf and James Michael Curley played prominent roles in the machine past of their respective cities. However, Boston's Curley outlasted the San Francisco machine; his last hurrah occurred in 1949.

In Boston in a more recent era, governmental structure and particularly municipal culture allowed Mayor Kevin White to govern more successfully than his San Francisco counterparts did. White was able to use material incentives "to achieve centralized control" (Ferman 1985, 199). Because Boston was less fragmented than San Francisco, White also could use formal mechanisms to advance his agenda.

Ferman's case studies of Kevin White and San Francisco's mayor, Joseph Alioto, are a valuable counterthrust to the concept of the ungovernable metropolis. Her depiction of the role of institutions and political culture in municipal governance demonstrates that some cities are more governable than others. This work also shows that some mayors make better use of the tools available to them. Ferman's work illustrates the variations among even seemingly similar cities and makes clear that the idea of an ungovernable city is premature at best.

The concept that local bureaucracies are impregnable to mayoral control also came under attack. Although some scholars found evidence of bureaucratic rules dominating program implementation—even in Richard J. Daley's Chicago (Mladenka 1981, 693–714; Mladenka 1980, 991–998)—Bryan D. Jones (1985) showed that politics still mattered in that city's Buildings Department; a committeeman could assist with variances. Stein's (1991) case study of St. Louis questioned whether the new bureaucratic machines had the same power in every institutional setting. In St. Louis, only the protective services—police and fire—stood their ground when the mayor used the power of his personality to assert authority in a machine-politics setting. There were no "new machines" in St. Louis, and Stein doubted whether they would be present in a very politicized environment with numerous elected officials and active ward and neighborhood organizations.

Ferman and Stein successfully questioned the hypothesis of municipal ungovernability. They found that institutions, political culture, and leadership ability affected whether a mayor could grasp the governmental reins and make an imprint. However, another major sector of urban scholarship had joined Sayre, Kaufman, Lowi, and Yates in downplaying the mayoral role in urban development. Urban political economists, like other social scientists, emphasized economic and social forces rather than actions of political actors. According to these scholars, the commonalities in municipal development were due to those forces.

Urban Political Economy and the Mayor

The influence of private power in cities has been the subject of sometimes bitter debate. Robert A. Dahl's *Who Governs?* (1961) maintained that the local business elite was only one sector that helped determine public policy in New Haven. He posited that different sets of actors dominated different policy areas and felt it was reasonable that the city's leading businesses had taken an interest in land use, particularly in the central business district. Dahl portrayed New Haven's mayor, Richard Lee, as having spearheaded the city's urban renewal. Some scholars disagreed with Dahl's concept of the mayor as the catalyst for substantial redevelopment. Dahl's concept of pluralism, with different segments of society dominating the different sectors, sparked a strong counteraction. In a rebuttal to Dahl, G. William Domhoff (1978) maintained that the private sector shaped the federal urban renewal program to its own liking, pushed minorities away from the periphery of the central business district, built freeways through the heart of the central city, and converted renewal land to serve private interests at public expense. Mayors and other public officials carried out businesses' bidding.

Chambers of Commerce and organizations of realtors certainly supported Title I of the U.S. Housing Act of 1949 because it could be used to benefit business interests. They continued to dislike plans for additional public housing. In almost every major American city, urban renewal became a tool for reviving a decaying central core. Organizations composed of business leaders dedicated to municipal improvement were formed in many cities. The first such entity, Pittsburgh's Allegheny Conference, actually predated the Housing Act of 1949 and federally funded urban renewal. Whether mayors played the pivotal role in mobilizing such organizations and their support for

urban renewal varied from city to city. Schwartz (1993) found that support for renewal programs was quite widespread. Many across the ideological spectrum grasped
at the same solutions to the problems of decaying downtowns and increasing flight to
the suburbs.

All levels of government in the United States historically have been deferential to
the private sector. Private activity has always been seen as preferable to public activity. At the local level, control of land use is a critical function. When city governments
became interested in the built environment after World War II and what they considered decay at the core, it was natural that there be a strong private component, and indeed there was.

The publication of Paul Peterson's *City Limits* (1981) was a clarion call to urban
political economists. They reacted strongly against Peterson's notion that economic
development had to be a city's principal occupation because of its dependency on its
own resources. Aid to the disadvantaged—redistribution—had to be a federal matter,
according to Peterson, because of limited municipal fiscal capacity. Those who rejected Peterson's reasoning attempted to show the guiding hand of capital in the design and execution of urban renewal projects—projects that, in their view, worsened
the plight of the poor and members of minority groups. Those without means did not
benefit from the convention centers, retail complexes, office towers, or luxury housing that replaced supposedly outmoded buildings and decaying neighborhoods. This
type of redevelopment occurred in almost every city, no matter who was serving as
mayor. And in every city African Americans living close to downtown were moved
out. Political economists demonstrated their belief that economic forces governed urban development through the actions of the business elite and transformations in the
national and then the global economy.

This motif is well illustrated in several works. For example, five case studies form
the core of *Restructuring the City* (Fainstein, Fainstein, Hill, Judd, and Smith 1986).
The authors, including political scientists and sociologists, provided excellent data on
the demographic and economic trends that shaped New Haven, Detroit, New Orleans, Denver, and San Francisco. The case studies, by and large, did not omit the role
of the cities' mayors, but the authors did not regard the mayoral role as primary to the
developmental process. Fainstein and Fainstein, for example, acknowledged the impact of New Haven's Richard Lee on renewal in that city, stating that he "handled the
politics of the [renewal] coalition and played a critical role in the Washington connection" (p. 38). However, the Fainsteins also mentioned the limits to the mayor's direct
authority and noted that redevelopment plans actually were all ready to go when Lee
took office (pp. 36–37). He did not formulate them. Although Mayor Lee and his development director, Edward Logue, put together an apparatus that aided city rebuild-
ing in New Haven, the Fainsteins stressed that national and international economic

forces had a critical impact on cities, regardless of their individual nuances or their leadership (Fainstein et al. 1986, 4–6).

The emphasis on economic forces echoes in the other case studies in *Restructuring the City*. Jerome P. Cavanaugh, Detroit's mayor for much of the 1960s, used urban renewal to enhance his control over city agencies, according to Richard Child Hill (p. 95). Detroit elected Coleman Young as its first African American mayor in 1973. Young used a new city charter to establish his imprint throughout city government. A larger-than-life figure in the Motor City, his strong rhetoric inspired his core constituency of lower-income blacks, Young served five terms as mayor. Nonetheless, Hill noted that "Young's political future remained inextricably tied to the investment agenda set by the corporate business community" (p. 108). Given Detroit's dependence on the automobile industry, and the cataclysmic changes that industry experienced during Young's tenure, Hill's statement is understandable. Yet Hill and his fellow political economists failed to allow for the possibility that Cavanaugh or Young or other mayors might have had an independent role in urban development. Their concentration, like that of earlier urban renewal, was on the cities' central business districts. Mayors' powers varied among cities, and different styles of leadership were evident. The Fainsteins and Hill recognized this, but they viewed cities as dependent economically and politically, so that economic actors really called the shots that counted.

Logan and Molotch's (1987) depiction of the urban growth machine included a wide array of actors who sustain programs facilitating capital accumulation. Political actors appeared as enablers of growth for their own gain, cogs in the growth machine instead of drivers. Logan and Molotch noted that "the growth machine will sustain only certain persons as politicians, only those who participate" in the growth process (p. 66). They maintain that large campaign contributors keep elected officials within the confines of the growth machine. This focus takes into account only one dimension of governance and only one political motivator for mayors.

Boston and San Francisco are the primary focus of John H. Mollenkopf's (1983) study of renewal and redevelopment, *The Contested City*, although he also provided an in-depth account of urban policymaking in the nation's capital. Mollenkopf chronicled the activities of various mayors regarding growth, social services, and neighborhood needs. However, he, too, placed economic forces above all others. "The conflicts of the 1960s and 1970s produced new political actors, and the Great Society and its successor programs gave big-city mayors like Kevin White, George Moscone, and Dianne Feinstein both the imperative and the means to incorporate them into the dominant coalition, albeit in a secondary and dependent position" (pp. 271–272). That dominant coalition, of course, was the growth coalition.

Todd Swanstrom's (1985) study of the brief mayoralty of Cleveland's Dennis Kucinich depicted a political figure who challenged economic power. However,

Kucinich was immediately punished for his temerity and vanished from the political scene for two decades. Cleveland's growth alliance of banks, newspapers, and businesses would not allow the young populist mayor to question their wisdom. Kucinich refused to sell the municipal electric utility to private hands, whereupon Cleveland's banks foreclosed on the city.

In the 1980s, one work successfully challenged the primacy of social and economic forces in municipal life, at least in one area. Martin Shefter (1987) demonstrated that municipal bankruptcy in New York City could not be attributed only to loss of population, industry, and revenue. Mayors Robert Wagner, John Lindsay, and Abraham Beame had used short-term debt as a means of funding projects benefiting their constituencies. Their spending on services and construction exceeded the sizable federal grants the city received. In New York City, mayors and political actors controlled at least part of its fiscal destiny. With short-term debt becoming a means to finance previous short-term debt, the banks acted. They finally refused to roll over New York's debt.

Ester Fuchs (1992) later demonstrated that the states of Illinois and New York differed considerably in their approach to municipal finance. Illinois allowed Chicago to create special taxing districts that could ease the burdens on the city's operating budget. New York did not give such power to its cities. In Fuchs's analysis, institutional mechanisms affected mayoral behavior in both Chicago and New York and prevented Richard J. Daley or any other Chicago mayor from experiencing a fiscal crisis like New York City's. Shefter and Fuchs each showed the impact of mayoral actions and municipal institutions, apart from ubiquitous social and economic forces.

Regime Theory

Some political economists added a new dimension to the relationship between political actors and a city's business elite. Clarence N. Stone's (1988) study of Atlanta provoked considerable discussion and some imitation. Stone delved into Atlanta's municipal politics in the years following World War II. Atlanta's business community, led by Coca-Cola's Robert Woodruff, worked closely with four mayors. The relationships were intimate and the contact was frequent. In Stone's view, some manifestation of this relationship characterized governance in many cities. "Because localities have only weak formal means through which coordination can be achieved, informal arrangements to promote cooperation are especially useful" (p. 5). These arrangements constituted a regime. The complexity of a regime could differ from city to city, but the need for cooperation from outside the government to achieve goals remained a constant.

Stone's work is important to those interested in studying mayors. He painted clear portraits of William Hartsfield, Ivan Allen, Maynard Jackson, and Andrew Young.

Hartsfield and Allen made possible an Atlanta that was "too busy to hate." Their terms in office were marked by racial accommodation and large-scale urban renewal.

Business in particular had to adjust to Maynard Jackson, Atlanta's first African American mayor, who had a strong style and stressed minority empowerment. Jackson was particularly interested in black economic advancement in employment and contracting. His concern for employment did not end with municipal hiring; he wanted corporations to make greater efforts at achieving diverse work forces and made those wishes clear. In turn, Jackson had to learn the importance of business cooperation in reaching some of his goals. There were new trade-offs within the regime. Redevelopment goals of downtown businesses remained central to Atlanta's agenda, but Jackson ensured African American participation in building and operating Hartsfield Airport and in hiring on many other projects. Stone contrasted Jackson with Andrew Young, his successor as mayor. Young, who was a national figure and a civil rights veteran when he assumed office, worked well with the Atlanta business community. He acquiesced in their plans without asking for the quid pro quos Jackson had demanded. Young was a compliant mayor who bought into the business agenda for development, disappointing preservationists and some progressives.

Stone's work delineated a regime whose emphases changed over time. It changed at least in part because of who was sitting at the mayor's desk. A mayor's individual traits, capabilities, and interests affected the regime's agenda. Even in the face of a strong and united business sector, Atlanta's mayors played a part in shaping redevelopment in some fashion, and each played the role differently.

Inadequate power at the local level made coalitions or regimes necessary. For Stone, regime theory is a paradigm that "shows how power can be concentrated" and how it can be used for good or ill (p. 145). It also sees "urban leadership in broader terms than the skills and abilities of individuals who occupy the office of mayor" (p. 135). But the actors in each city construct their own unique regime.

One of the more interesting studies of urban regimes is Richard DeLeon's *Left Coast City* (1992). San Francisco is unusual among large U.S. cities. It has been home to a variety of radical political groups as well as to a sizable gay and lesbian community. If any American city were to have an antiregime arise, it would be this left-coast metropolis. For a brief period, an antiregime actually did assume power, but its leader, Mayor Art Agnos, made some compromises that undermined progressive confidence in him and cost him reelection. A conservative, Frank Jordan, succeeded Agnos. The nature and abilities of San Francisco's various mayors, as well as their impact on the city, became clear in DeLeon's study. He also recognized that San Francisco's culture and institutions helped to affect outcomes because of the city's weak-mayor system.

New York City politics and the career of Mayor Edward Koch are the focus of John Mollenkopf's (1992) study, which sheds additional light on regimes. The author readily acknowledged that he could find no semblance of an Atlanta-style regime in New York City, which he maintained was a far more political town than Atlanta (p. 201). In New York, the largest American city, business interests were but one constituency in building a political coalition. The paths toward implementation of development were more complex on a number of levels. Its business community, even just the financial and real estate sections, were more extensive than those in any other city and not as cohesive as Atlanta's.

In terms of the study of mayors, Mollenkopf's work has special importance. New York's three-term mayor, Edward Koch, came alive on the pages of this study. Koch was able to make a significant number of decisions. He was very good to prospective business in New York; he certainly gave away more tax breaks to realtors and developers than necessary to ensure the realization of projects, primarily office towers. Koch's personality, with its mixture of flamboyance and nonstop elocution, also affected race relations in New York City and eventually cost him his office.

Although Stone, DeLeon, and Mollenkopf certainly acknowledged the substantial influence of economic interests in cities, they have shown that individual mayors can also impact policy outcomes. Because of the variation among cities and the individual differences of mayors, it is not always easy to monitor the effects of mayoral action. But such action does not constitute a null set, and some mayors clearly do govern. In the several types of literature examined thus far, a kind of dichotomy emerges. Scholars recognize that forces external to the city affect its well-being and the development it chooses to undertake. However, even though the exercise of mayoral politics is difficult to measure, some writers challenge the dominant paradigm, asserting that mayors influence events and different mayors influence them differently. This leaves a complicated variable mix, but one in which the mayor is not a negligible factor.

Dealing with Diversity

The election of African Americans and Hispanics to the mayor's office is addressed in a growing body of literature. To a considerable extent, scholars have concentrated on the elections rather than on the governing that comes after success at the polls. The election night triumph of an African American mayoral candidate becomes the focus and, by dwelling on this symbolic victory, the writer can brush aside the minuses and pluses of tenure in office. When the election battle is particularly hard fought, with notable racial cleavage in the campaign and at the polls, this is more likely to be the case.

Nelson and Meranto (1977) chronicled the election of the first black mayors in major American cities: Carl Stokes in Cleveland and Richard Hatcher in Gary, Indiana. The election stories were exciting, occurring in at least partially polarized communities. In looking at Stokes's and Hatcher's stays in office, Nelson and Meranto fell back on the concept of the ungovernable city. "Limits on black mayoral power will exist irrespective of the quality of leadership exhibited by the individual mayor. Social, economic, and political constraints that limit his ability to distribute meaningful benefits are rooted in the environment in which he operates. These constraints inevitably produce for the black mayor dilemmas of power that place the goal of thoroughgoing urban reform far beyond the competence of his administration" (p. 336).

Nelson and Meranto agreed with other scholars on the policymaking limitations that any American mayor experiences. But, for African Americans, race is an additional variable that makes their tenure even more difficult. Nelson and Meranto noted that many of the cities likely to elect black mayors were dying cities, with declining population and diminishing resources. The state and federal levels might be unsympathetic to the black mayor's plight. Moreover, the potential existed for opposition from whites in the power structure and resistance from professionals in the city's bureaucracies (pp. 336–339). In addition, the first black mayor might have greater difficulty in finding a trustworthy staff. He or she might also be unfamiliar with the city's business elite and other white community leaders. These factors would diminish the role of a minority mayor, but they do not deny the possibility of some impact on city governance.

Whether "thoroughgoing reform" would be a goal of every nonwhite mayor also is open to question. Mayors of color may be markedly different in their approach to administrative practice or policy direction. Homogeneity for either black or white officeholders is not a tenable assumption. The political culture of a city and its governing institutions help to create the parameters for possible action, regardless of who the mayor is. Depending on their background, African American or Hispanic mayors will be affected by those parameters to some extent.

Nelson and Meranto seemed to join Yates in regarding the mayoralty as a hollow crown. Despite the insufficiency of resources, however, minority mayors can maneuver, using the allocative functions of the office to serve their core constituency. Over and over, in cities that elect minority mayors, there is an increase in minority hiring for municipal jobs and in the selection of minority contractors. This form of targeting, of course, is not sufficient to address the concentration of joblessness in a city's core. However, it makes a symbolic statement: Citizens begin to see people in government who look like them.

Two edited volumes contain case studies dealing with the election of minority mayors in a number of American cities. Preston, Henderson, and Puryear's *The New Black Politics* (1987) and Browning, Marshall, and Tabb's *Racial Politics in American Cities* (1997) provide insight about the politics of race and the nature of the coalitions that elect minority mayors. In many cities, minority candidates have received between

8 and 30 percent of the white vote. However, Sonenshein (1993, 5) succinctly noted that cities with small black populations located in the western and northwestern regions of the United States have less difficulty than other parts of the country in electing an African American mayor. Such cities often have a reformed governmental structure. The elections of Tom Bradley in Los Angeles, Wellington Webb in Denver, Norman Rice in Seattle, and Willie Brown in San Francisco help to prove Sonenshein's point. In these cities, genuine multiracial coalitions supported the winning African American candidate, and rancor was quite limited.

In contrast, cities in the East and Middle West with a history of machine politics and large black and white ethnic populations often experience more discordant campaigns. A smaller portion of the white electorate will vote for the nonwhite. According to Sonenshein (pp. 5–6), personal rewards such as jobs are more likely to be at stake in generally unreformed systems. It is clear from this brief comparison that electing a city's first black mayor may be more consensual in certain locations than in others. In cities with fewer blacks, election of a black mayor does not appear to be as threatening to white residents. It is also probable that the first black mayor would face a different reception from the power structure and the bureaucrats in a city like Denver than he or she would in a midwestern industrial town such as Detroit or Chicago. Demographics, economics, and institutional structure set the table for an incoming mayor. But he or she will have some ability to maneuver after arrival.

Of all African American mayors elected in the late twentieth century, none has garnered more scholarly attention than Chicago's Harold Washington. His election in 1983 was marked by some of the worst manifestations of racism ever displayed in a mayoral contest (see Kleppner 1985). Chicago's legendary political machine had helped to maintain blacks in a decidedly secondary political status for decades. Grimshaw (1992) described how black wards frequently were plantation wards, in that they continued to be represented by white committeemen and aldermen, who were allies of Mayor Richard J. Daley, long after a significant shift in population had taken place. Daley also kept Chicago's black boss, William Dawson, in line for many years and then set him adrift when Daley's coalition needs changed.

Opposition within the power structure certainly confronted Harold Washington when he assumed office. The portents were there: Many white elected officials had supported Washington's Republican opponent, Bernard Epton, in the general election after Washington defeated Jane Byrne and Richard M. Daley in the Democratic primary. Washington's first term was marked by unrelenting opposition from white machine stalwarts on the city council. These infamous "council wars" prevented much new direction from the mayor's office. After his reelection, Washington at last achieved a majority on the council, but his death a few months later gave him only a brief time to enjoy that status.

Chicago's racial schism and Washington's untimely death made him a heroic figure to many. Originally a product of the Chicago machine, Washington used material
incentives to shore up his own political base. Federal community development funds
found their way to nonprofit organizations based in south- or west-side black neighborhoods (Freedman 1988, 847–858). This strategy was similar to Mayor John Lindsay's in New York. Lindsay funded community organizations to deter the violence
endemic to ghetto areas in the 1960s (Shefter 1987). Barred by a court decree and his
own frequently voiced opposition to patronage during his first mayoral campaign,
Washington had to use service contracts instead of jobs to reward core constituents.
Whether Harold Washington could have realized his aim of reorienting economic development policy to favor neighborhoods over downtown will never be known.

Among the other studies of African American mayors is Wilbur C. Rich's (1989)
laudatory biography of Detroit's Coleman Young, written while Young was still in office. Rich showed how Young's personal history shaped the positions he took as
mayor. Despite formidable economic problems caused by global restructuring, Young
kept his city solvent. The developments he spearheaded—the Renaissance Center and
the new General Motors plant in Poletown—were not universally applauded, but
Young brought them to fruition.

Rich makes clear the extent of Young's appeal to Detroit's African American population. The mayor's words resounded in the inner city while at the same time turning off some suburban officials and residents. He was a proud man who was unable
to tolerate any condescension. As mayor for twenty years, he governed during a very
difficult period economically, but his good relationships with Henry Ford II and a Republican governor, William Milliken, softened some blows to the city.

Raphael J. Sonenshein's (1993) apt contrast of city types mentioned earlier is a very
small part of his study of multiracial coalitions in Los Angeles and of Tom Bradley,
the city's first African American mayor. Like Young in Detroit, Bradley was elected
mayor five times and served for twenty years. Sonenshein chronicled Bradley's changing electoral coalition during those years and also detailed his development policies,
which suited the economic power structure. Bradley and Young were opposites in de-
meanor and speech, but they both favored downtown development, with Los Angeles, of course, being more attractive to growth-oriented entrepreneurs. Bradley also
had the good fortune to be mayor of a city with a much healthier economy than Detroit's. The black share of the population in Los Angeles was less than 20 percent when
Bradley was elected. When Young left office in Detroit, the black population stood at
80 percent.

Comparative studies of minority officeholders and the special problems they en-
counter as mayors are yet to be written. The case studies cited here provide good initial material, however. Some recent work has concentrated on African American

mayors and their cities' public school systems. Numerous mayors—black and white—have begun to turn their attention to their struggling schools, whether or not their formal powers encompass public education. It is an area where success is uncertain, and there are no clear guidelines on how to enhance human capital. But inaction can be problematic; poor schools drive middle-income families from central cities.

Rich (1996) analyzed school reform in three cities with large black populations — Detroit, Newark, and Gary—each of which has an African American mayor. These cities experienced extensive commercial and industrial disinvestment and high unemployment. Rich found that all three cities have remained trapped in the "status quo" regarding their school systems. Their black mayors proved unable to resist the efforts of a black "public school cartel" seeking to continue domination of the schools. The cartel was more concerned with its perquisites and status than with genuine reform. Rich illustrated the conflicts a minority mayor could face with a minority-based interest group such as this type of cartel. In the case of the schools, the need for policy reform clashed with the need for political support.

Similar themes are discussed in *The Color of School Reform*, by Jeffrey Henig, Richard Hula, Marion Orr, and Desiree Pedescleaux (1999), who examined public schools in Washington, D.C.; Detroit; Baltimore; and Atlanta. Their work has brought back the notion of the intractability of urban problems and the ungovernable city. But here race is at the forefront of the dilemma, compounding both problem definition and coalition building. Orr's (1999) extensive study of Baltimore reinforces the difficulty an African American mayor (Kurt Schmoke) faced when he tried to reform an African American–dominated institution.

Leadership in the City

On the whole, political scientists appear to weigh guardedly the role of a mayor in setting and implementing urban policy. The discipline's traditional behavioral emphasis has limited studies of an individual mayor, while the prevailing emphasis in urban study has continued to be the role of economic and social forces in determining behavior. Scholars such as Sayre and Kaufman, as well as political economists, have stressed the limitations of any mayor to effect change. Insufficient attention has been devoted to discerning the powers possibly available to a mayor and how to utilize them.

It has fallen principally to historians and journalists to demarcate the potential of a city's highest officeholder and the actual pitfalls that have confronted various mayors. These chroniclers of urban politics employ the case study and often do not look at commonalities or dissimilarities with mayors in other jurisdictions. Nonetheless, their work helps to highlight what Holli (1999, 133–135) calls "contingency leadership." He sees the mayor as a leader either through the tasks he carries out or because of his temperament. Holli, who is a historian, called upon experts to rank the ten best and ten worst American mayors, and he cites the results in his book. the criteria are nebulous, many might dispute the selection. However, Holli clearly believes that mayors who are leaders can make a difference in their cities, regardless of the internal and external problems they face. Holli's work encourages the need for further study of the mayoral role, particularly in a comparative mode.

Addressing the need for examinations of mayoral leadership, Bowers and Rich (2000) chose cities that rarely make headlines nationally. However, these cities have significant economic problems, need redevelopment and improved race relations and better services for their citizens. From Jackson, Mississippi, to Providence, Rhode Island, there are mayors making a difference. The external forces that inhibit action in each city are delineated, but each of the mayors featured in this book is able to break the mold and innovate in some fashion. Yet the difficulties in comparing cities remain; mayors addressed different types of policy or service in each city. For a good comparison, it is necessary to compare a similar action, or lack of action, in a comparable arena. Such a study of minority mayors would also shed greater light on the special constraints these officeholders face and how they must relate to their environment in order to advance their agenda. In either case, the scholar can look at the individual and the regime.

Alan DiGaetano and John S. Klemanski (1999) initiated this type of dialogue in their recent book, which compares four cities, two American and two British. Their serious examination of development policy in these cities led them to advocate a tripartite means of studying cities and discerning the reasons for their policy successes and failures. Three theoretical domains were deemed necessary for inclusion: political economy, institutions, and leadership (p. 251). Emphasizing the salient factors and allowing for individual or coalition leadership, their approach appears worthy of repetition.

While we await further studies of mayoral power by social scientists, the work of some journalists and historians has provided us with full-scale windows on the mayor's office, portraying its various occupants as leaders or, conversely, as people who could not overcome their surroundings and their own history.

Several works rank among the best in this genre. In *Fire in the Prairie,* journalist Gary Rivlin (1992) presented an unvarnished portrait of Harold Washington quite different from those given by political scientists. Rivlin illustrated Washington's style of governing, his relations with staff and other elected officials, and the nature of his opposition. Considerable detail was presented about the events leading to Washington's candidacy and how black leaders unified around the man they considered the best person to challenge Chicago's machine. Rivlin's work is not a hagiography. In fact, he raised some doubts about aspects of Washington's behavior that political scientists have not considered. His book is a veritable source of questions about governance that researchers still need to address in a comprehensive manner.

America's most powerful twentieth-century mayor and the last great machine boss, Richard J. Daley, is the subject of Adam Cohen and Elizabeth Taylor's (2000) book *American Pharaoh*. A significant addition to the extensive literature on Daley, the book delineated Daley's constituencies, his strategies, vision, and pettiness. The work also fleshed out the importance of the local context on the man and on his colleagues. Daley never ranged very far from the values of his working-class neighborhood, Bridgeport, located close to the Chicago stockyards. His dealings with Martin Luther King Jr. and with antiwar demonstrators reflect Bridgeport, the small community where he lived his entire life.

Because Daley was mayor and party leader and relied on an army of patronage workers, he was able to govern without much question. Newspaper and business opposition failed to occur because he fostered downtown redevelopment, which was very amenable to the corporate leaders. Even after the brutal scenes in Chicago's streets during the 1968 Democratic convention, the mayor's popularity remained solid in his city. Daley's story cannot be viewed as exemplifying the limitations or successes of other big-city mayors. No other major city experienced the concentrated machine power present in Daley's Chicago. Nonetheless, Cohen and Taylor's biography sheds considerable light on promises and challenges in Chicago and on its mayor for twenty-one years.

Another journalist, Buzz Bissinger (1997), has produced perhaps the most detailed study of any mayoral term of office. He captured Philadelphia's Ed Rendell in the throes of decision making and in the art of coalition building. Rendell allowed him considerable access during his first term, and Bissinger made the most of this opportunity. His portrait of Rendell shows how a mayor of an old industrial city has to be a cheerleader for that city, selling it both within and outside its borders. However, very mindful of economic and social forces affecting American cities, Bissinger frequently questioned whether the marathon efforts of Rendell and his staff would be sufficient to transform a city plagued by inadequate resources and severe socioeconomic problems. The demise of Philadelphia's Navy Yard is emblematic of urban decline. It shows the growing obsolescence of blue-collar labor and the inability of state and city to work coherently to save jobs in Pennsylvania's largest city.

Bissinger's work returns us to the conundrum in the political science literature. Various scholars have pointed out limits on the ability of mayors to make a difference. For some, mayors are the less important part of a regime focused principally on downtown redevelopment. From this perspective, it seems as if mayors are interchangeable, performing the role of aide-de-camp to the forces of capital. The globalization occurring in the economy, particularly in communications, accentuates the notion of the dependent municipal official. Yet Bissinger's study of Rendell makes it clear that mayors can occasionally take actions that differ from the norm and change a city's lot. When Rendell took office in Philadelphia, the city's fiscal situation was as dour as possible. The city could not borrow; its bonds were rated at the junk level. Through coalition building and extensive bargaining, Rendell restored order to the fiscal arena, especially by getting municipal unions to give back extensive benefits. This was a path no U.S. mayor had successfully trod before.

Conclusion

Studying mayors is not a simple proposition. Studying them in a comparative context is also difficult. Cities vary in their form of government. Some differences are clearly discernible; others are much more subtle. In addition, states do not provide their cities with comparable support or legal powers. Cities also differ in terms of their economies and demographics. However, even given this level of complexity, it is still possible to study cities in the aggregate, specifying variables for the differences mentioned here. However, when one turns to the mayors of these cities, a further problem arises. It is more difficult to explicate the various traits of officeholders in a manner that allows study of large numbers of cities. If certain scholars can be convinced of a mayor's ability to chart a course or affect outcomes, how can this be measured? It means a new appreciation of the personality in history. Federalism and economic and social forces circumscribe municipal freedom, but different mayors respond differently to the hands they have been dealt. For a discipline focused for decades on behavior in the aggregate, approaching behavior in the particular presents a challenge.

The frequently denigrated case study is a necessary work tool to study the particular. Especially useful for theorists is the comparative case study, where roughly similar cities and their mayors can be examined along various dimensions. Both Ferman and Mollenkopf have used this technique successfully, and it is being adopted by some of the students of African American–led cities.

The debate over pluralism forty years ago led many to overlook the importance of a mayor—an individual—in running a city. The concept of the ungovernable city, popularized by Yates and found frequently in the urban literature, also reduced mayors to less important objects of study. The students of New York City—Sayre and Kaufman and then Lowi—said that mayors could not control their own bureaus. Political economists depicted the city as an economic playground manipulated by powerful capitalists. Although other scholars attempted to refute the inevitability arising from these concepts, the idea of a dependent city and a hapless mayor seeped into the collective consciousness. When the concept of a subordinate mayoral role was combined with the difficulty involved in studying mayors in the aggregate, the result was an understudied area.

Historians and journalists have taken up some of the slack. Now it appears that social scientists are beginning to deal with individual mayors as agents of change. But a lot of work remains to be done in the area of municipal leadership, and it needs to be both comprehensive and comparative. Without relegating economics, demographics, or institutions to the background, scholars must find the areas in which mayors can effect change and how it can be done. With many major American cities electing African American and other minority mayors, the need for this research is greater. Are the politics of coalition building different? How are regimes affected? Why are some minority mayors more successful than others? Leadership in cities needs to be a part of that social science analysis.

Suggested Readings

Cohen, Adam, and Elizabeth Taylor. 2000. *American Pharaoh: Mayor Richard J. Daley, His Battle for Chicago and the Nation.* Boston: Little, Brown. A biography by two journalists that helps us understand the Chicago machine as well as Daley himself.

Ferman, Barbara. 1985. *Governing the Ungovernable City: Political Skill, Leadership, and the Modern Mayor.* Philadelphia: Temple University Press. Demonstrating how structure affects leadership, the author compares the mayoralties of Kevin White of Boston and Joseph Alioto of San Francisco.

Lowi, Theodore J. 1964. *At the Pleasure of the Mayor.* New York: Free Press of Glencoe. This classic study argues that powerful bureaucracies dwarf mayoral leadership.

Mollenkopf, John Hull. 1992. *A Phoenix in the Ashes: The Rise and Fall of the Koch Coalition in the Black Community.* Princeton: Princeton University Press. An examination of New York City coalition politics, the election of a black mayor, and the role of interest groups in municipal elections

Stein, Lana. 1991. *Holding Bureaucrats Accountable: Politicians and Professionals in St. Louis.* Tuscaloosa: University of Alabama Press. Elected officials in St. Louis hold sway over a great deal of administrative activity, but the police and fire departments are both impervious to mayoral control.

Stone, Clarence N. 1988. *Regime Politics: Governing Atlanta, 1946–1988.* Lawrence: University Press of Kansas. The author presents an important paradigm—the relationship between business leaders and mayors that is necessary to develop and redevelop the modern American city.

References

Banfield, Edward C. 1963. *Big City Politics.* New York: Random House.
Banfield, Edward C., and James Q. Wilson. 1963. *City Politics.* New York: Vintage Books.
Bissinger, Buzz. 1997. *A Prayer for the City.* New York: Random House.
Bowers, James R., and Wilbur C. Rich, eds. 2000. *Governing Middle-Sized Cities: Studies in Mayoral Leadership.* Boulder: Lynne Rienner.
Browning, Rufus P., Dale Rogers Marshall, and David A. Tabb, eds. 1997. *Racial Politics in American Cities.* 2d ed. New York: Longman.
Cohen, Adam, and Elizabeth Taylor. 2000. *American Pharaoh: Mayor Richard J. Daley, His Battle for Chicago and the Nation.* Boston: Little, Brown.

Craig, Gordon A. 1978. *Germany 1866–1945.* New York: Oxford University Press.

Dahl, Robert A. 1961. *Who Governs? Democracy and Power in an American City.* New Haven: Yale University Press.

DeLeon, Richard Edward. 1992. *Left Coast City: Progressive Politics in San Francisco.* Lawrence: University Press of Kansas.

DiGaetano, Alan, and John S. Klemanski. 1999. *Power and City Governance: Comparative Perspectives on Urban Development.* Minneapolis: University of Minnesota Press.

Domhoff, G. William. 1978. *Who Really Rules? New Haven and Community Powers Reexamined.* New Brunswick, N.J.: Transaction Books.

Fainstein, Norman I., and Susan S. Fainstein. 1986. "New Haven: The Limits of the Local State." In *Restructuring the City: The Political Economy of Urban Redevelopment.* Norman I. Fainstein and Susan S. Fainstein. New York: Longman.

Fainstein, Susan S., Norman I. Fainstein, Richard Child Hill, Dennis Judd, and Michael Peter Smith. 1986. *Restructuring the City: The Political Economy of Urban Redevelopment.* New York: Longman, 27–79.

Ferman, Barbara. 1985. *Governing the Ungovernable City: Political Skill, Leadership, and the Modern Mayor.* Philadelphia: Temple University Press.

Freedman, Anne. 1988. "Doing Battles with the Patronage Army: Politics, Courts, and Personnel Administration in Chicago." *Public Administration Review* 48 (September–October 1998): 847–858.

Fuchs, Ester R. 1992. *Mayors and Money: Fiscal Policy in New York and Chicago.* Chicago: University of Chicago Press.

Grimshaw, William J. 1992. *Bitter Fruit: Black Politics and the Chicago Machine 1931–1991.* Chicago: University of Chicago Press.

Henig, Jeffrey R., Richard C. Hula, Marion Orr, and Desiree S. Pedescleaux. 1999. *The Color of School Reform: Race, Politics, and the Challenge of Urban Education.* Princeton: Princeton University Press.

Hill, Richard Child. 1986. "Crisis in the Motor City: The Politics of Economic Development in Detroit." In *Restructuring the City: The Political Economy of Urban Redevelopment.* Norman I. Fainstein and Susan S. Fainstein. New York: Longman, 80–125.

Holli, Melvin G. 1999. *The American Mayor: The Best and Worst Big-City Leaders.* University Park: Pennsylvania State University Press.

Jones, Bryan D. 1985. *Governing Buildings and Building Government: A New Perspective on the Old Party.* University, Ala.: University of Alabama Press.

Judd, Dennis. 2000. "Strong Leadership," *Urban Studies* 37: 951–961.

Kleppner, Paul. 1985. *Chicago Divided: The Making of a Black Mayor.* DeKalb: Northern Illinois University Press.

Logan, John R., and Harvey L. Molotch. 1987. *Urban Fortunes: The Political Economy of Place.* Berkeley: University of California Press.

Lowi, Theodore J. 1964. *At the Pleasure of the Mayor.* New York: Free Press of Glencoe.

———— 1967. "Machine Politics—Old and New." *Public Interest* (fall): 83–92

Mladenka, Kenneth R. 1981. "Citizen Demands and Human Services: The Distribution of Bureaucratic Response in Chicago and Houston." *American Journal of Political Science* 25 (November 1981): 693–714.

———— 1980. "The Urban Bureaucracy and the Chicago Political Machine: Who Gets What and the Limits to Political Control." *American Political Science Review* 74 (December): 991–998.

Mollenkopf, John H. 1983. *The Contested City.* Princeton: Princeton University Press.

Mollenkopf, John Hull. 1992. *A Phoenix in the Ashes: The Rise and Fall of the Koch Coalition in the Black Community.* Princeton: Princeton University Press.

Nelson, William E. Jr., and Phillip Meranto. 1977. *Electing Black Mayors: Political Action in the Black Community.* Columbus: Ohio State University Press.

Orr, Marion. 1999. *Black Social Capital: The Politics of School Reform in Baltimore, 1986–1988.* Lawrence: University Press of Kansas.

Peterson, Paul. 1981. *City Limits.* Chicago: University of Chicago Press.

Preston, Michael B., Lenneal J. Henderson Jr., and Paul E. Puryear, eds. 1987. *The New Black Politics.* 2d ed. New York: Longman.

Rich, Wilbur C. 1996. *Black Mayors and School Politics: The Failure of Reform in Detroit, Gary, and Newark.* New York: Garland.

———1989. *Coleman Young and Detroit Politics: From Social Activist to Power Broker.* Detroit: Wayne State University Press.

Rivlin, Gary. 1992. *Fire on the Prairie: Chicago's Harold Washington and the Politics of Race.* New York: Holt.

Sayre, Wallace S., and Herbert Kaufman. 1960. *Governing New York City.* New York: Russell Sage Foundation.

Schwartz, Joel. 1993. *The New York Approach: Robert Moses, Urban Liberals, and Redevelopment of the Inner City.* Columbus: Ohio State University Press.

Shefter, Martin. 1987. *Political Crisis/Fiscal Crisis: The Collapse and Revival of New York City.* New York: Basic Books.

Sonenshein, Raphael J. 1993. *Politics in Black and White: Race and Power in Los Angeles.* Princeton: Princeton University Press.

Stein, Lana. 1991. *Holding Bureaucrats Accountable: Politicians and Professionals in St. Louis.* Tuscaloosa: University of Alabama Press.

Stone, Clarence N. 1988. *Regime Politics: Governing Atlanta, 1946–1988.* Lawrence: University Press of Kansas.

———1989. "Paradigms, Power, and Urban Leadership." In *Leadership and Politics,* ed. Bryan D. Jones. Lawrence: University Press of Kansas, 135–165.

Svara, James H. 1990. *Official Leadership in the City: Patterns of Conflict and Competition.* New York: Oxford University Press.

Swanstrom, Todd. 1985. *The Crisis of Growth Politics: Cleveland, Kucinich, and Challenge of Urban Populism.* Philadelphia: Temple University Press.

Yates, Douglas. 1977. *The Ungovernable City: The Politics of Urban Problems and Policy Making.* Cambridge: MIT Press.

7 City Councils

Timothy B. Krebs and John P. Pelissero

A city council is the legislative branch of city government. In some cities, the city council is referred to as the board of trustees, village board, or board of selectmen. Regardless of the official name, the responsibilities of city councils are similar in all cities. The roles and powers of American city councils will vary with the type of government structure that is in place in a community. In the systems model, city councils are part of the political process in which institutions and actors respond to the demands and supports in the political environment. In many cases, the city council will be the first institution to act on the demands and supporting conditions that are associated with major city issues. Indeed, as in other governments, the legislative branch of city governments is specifically charged with formulating and adopting local policies. This chapter explores the legislative organization, the nature of elections, the styles of representation, legislative work, and policymaking in city councils.

The Legislative Branch of City Governments

The legal purpose of city councils is to formulate and adopt local public policy as the legislative arm of city governments. Legislative work in cities is similar to that performed by the Congress at the national level and legislatures in state capitals. But the similarity is limited largely to the broad aspects of legislative activity. City councils are much less powerful than these other legislatures. In most cities, they are constrained by structural and environmental factors.

City councils range in size from those with just two members to large bodies composed of as many as fifty-one members. According to the most recent survey by the International City/County Management Association (ICMA 1998), the average size of a city council is six members. New York and Chicago have the largest councils in the United States, with fifty-one and fifty members, respectively. Larger cities typically have more council members, but Los Angeles, the second-largest city in the country, has just fifteen council members. Pelissero and Krebs (1997) showed that the most common size of city councils in large cities is seven members.

City councils in all but the largest cities are part-time bodies. In general, city council members have full-time jobs that occupy most of their time. A study of cities with populations between 250,000 and 500,000 indicated that two-thirds of these cities had full-time, paid city councils (Haas 1995). With the exception of large cities, council members tend to be political amateurs who help to conduct city business in their spare time. Most full-time councils are mayor-council cities; only about 10 percent of council-manager governments have full-time councils. As a consequence, council members in mayor-council governments receive higher average salaries for their service, about $30,000 a year (Haas 1995, 260). However, most council members are paid less than $5,000 a year.

Regular meetings of city councils are held twice a month in about two-thirds of cities, with weekly meetings being held in fewer than 10 percent of cities (Renner and DeSantis 1998). City councils that meet more often usually do so because they are in a large city whose community needs demand more attention to city issues. The Los Angeles council meets in regular session three times each week (Reardon 1997). Regardless of the frequency of meetings, council members report that they spend considerable time on this "volunteer" duty. Research by Svara (1991) showed that council members spend an average of twenty-seven hours per week on council-related matters. As Svara has noted, "The job of a council member is a time-consuming one" (p. 21).

Most council members are elected to serve a two-year or four-year term. And although most cities permit their council members to run for reelection, the national interest in term limits has caught on in some cities. Renner and DeSantis (1998) note that whereas term limits are still used sparingly in cities, over 55 percent of cities with populations of more than 500,000 have adopted them. This electoral restriction has been more popular among cities in the Mountain states and the Southwest.

City Council Elections

Elections are a supporting input that directly shapes the process of authoritative decision making in the city political environment. Voters—demand makers in the system—select the individuals who will represent them and their interests in city policymaking. Depending on a city's charter, members of the city council may be selected all at once or in a staggered format. In the staggered format, only a portion of the council stands for election at any given time. In more than 60 percent of cities, council elections are held separately from state and national elections, typically in odd-numbered years. Although this enables voters to focus solely on local candidates and issues, it also reduces the level of voter turnout in city elections (Karnig and Walter 1983).

Nonpartisan Ballots

Unlike state and national elections, most city council elections are nonpartisan, and the candidate's party affiliation is not listed on the ballot. Political reformers in the early part of the twentieth century promoted the adoption of nonpartisan ballots in an attempt to end party-machine dominance of local politics and to depoliticize local government. They argued that the basic delivery of city services (the primary job of local government) was not subject to partisan considerations. Their efforts in promoting nonpartisanship were highly successful: nearly 100 years after the pinnacle of the reform movement, close to 75 percent of all cities use nonpartisan ballots to elect council members (Renner and DeSantis 1998).

It would not be an overstatement to say that nonpartisan elections transformed urban politics. Initial studies of the effects of nonpartisan ballots on local elections revealed a strong Republican bias (Hawley 1973; Lee 1960, 56–57; Rogers and Arman 1971, 943; Williams and Adrian 1959; but see Gilbert 1962, 355). In other words, city elections conducted under nonpartisan ballots tended to produce more Republican officeholders than was typical for the area in state or national elections conducted under partisan ballots. The explanation for this pattern centered on the political behavior of Republican and Democratic voters. Because Republican voters relied less on partisan cues when voting, voted more regularly, and were generally more active in the kinds of civic organizations that foster political interest and activity, they enjoyed a distinct advantage over Democrats. Given their level of involvement in local affairs, and the Democrats' relative disorganization in the absence of party labels, Republican interests could easily capture local offices.

Times have changed, however. Today the almost inherent Republican advantage in nonpartisan cities is evident only under certain conditions (see Welch and Bledsoe 1988, 51). Three factors account for the change: (1) African American voters at the local level were heavily mobilized to participate during the civil rights era (Browning, Marshall, and Tabb 1984, 34–35), a pattern that heavily favored Democratic candidates; (2) growth in neighborhood organizations helped Democratic-leaning interests wrest political control from downtown corporate, or Republican-leaning interests; and (3) the shift in many places toward district election schemes favored geographically concentrated groups such as minorities, altering the political composition of many nonpartisan city councils. These changes combined to offset the Republican advantage in nonpartisan cities (Welch and Bledsoe 1988, 52). Most observers have come to realize that trying to remove partisanship from politics is like nailing Jell-O to a wall—an impossible task.

One thing is certain, however. Nonpartisanship has severely weakened local political parties (Bledsoe and Welch 1987). In the absence of overt partisan competition, it is extremely difficult to maintain political organizations and rally committed volunteers to party causes. Groups, however, are not completely absent in city council elections. In nonpartisan cities, group involvement tends to be dominated by middle- and upper-class interests with ties to the business community, good government groups, and homeowners' organizations (Dutton and Northrop 1978; Williams and Adrian 1963). Not surprisingly, studies of nonpartisan cities indicate that candidates endorsed by these groups are highly successful (Bridges 1977; Davidson and Fraga 1988, 387; Fraga 1988; Prewitt 1970). Nonpartisan elections have also tended to favor upper-status candidates or those with high incomes and professional occupations (Adrian 1952, 771; Cassel 1985; Rogers and Arman 1971; Welch and Bledsoe 1988, 50).

Representation Systems

The city council is chosen by city voters to represent community residents in municipal government affairs. How citizens and their demands are represented is determined by the method of representation established in the municipal charter. As we will see, the method of representation has been highly controversial. Progressive reformers in the early part of the 1900s wanted council representation to be at-large (in addition to nonpartisan), a reform that faced great opposition from minority groups in the middle of the century.

Historically, city council members were chosen to represent a particular area of the community, called a district or ward. The number of wards usually equaled the number of council members. Thus a city with ten wards would have a ten-member council. Today, however, less than 20 percent of cities use districts exclusively, but the number has been increasing since 1990 (Renner and DeSantis 1998, 38).

A second method of representation is election at large. In this system, council members are elected citywide, rather than from a specific geographic area within the city, and are expected to represent the needs of city residents more generally. Reformers argued that district systems distorted local representation by producing councils composed of individuals concerned only about the particular needs of their constituents. They argued that cities should replace district or ward systems with at-large systems to reorient councillors' attention on citywide issues and problems. In order to be elected, candidates would have to compete citywide and mobilize a wide range of interests and voters to their cause. Reformers sought this change as a means to improve local government and move it away from the ward-based factionalism common in many older cities of the Northeast and Midwest. Today this remains the most popular method of representation for city councils, with more than 60 percent of cities having at-large systems (Renner and DeSantis 1998, 38).

The third method of representation is a mixed system. In this system, some council members are elected at large and others are elected from districts. The advantage of the mixed system is that city councils include members who will look out for the general interest of the city as well as those who will represent the particular needs of their districts. Through the 1980s, this combination system was the most popular choice for cities changing their methods of representation, with nearly 30 percent of them adopting its use (MacManus 1985). However, the recent trend has been away from the mixed method of representation, with only 22 percent employing it (Renner and DeSantis 1998, 38).

Black Representation. Election systems are not politically neutral. Whether a district or an at-large system is used, there are consequences in terms of who holds power in city government. Often called descriptive representation (Pitken 1967), a term that denotes the degree to which the composition of the city council reflects the diversity of the local population, this form of representation has received a significant amount of attention from urban scholars.

The most profound effect of at-large elections has been to retard the efforts of racial and ethnic groups to achieve fair representation on city councils. The negative effects of at-large systems have been particularly pronounced for blacks, a topic studied by many scholars (Banfield and Wilson 1963; Bullock 1975; Davidson and Korbel 1981; Engstrom and McDonald 1981, 1982; Heilig and Mundt 1982; Jones 1976; Karnig 1976; Karnig and Welch 1982; Latimer 1979; Robinson and Dye 1978, 139; Taebel 1978; Welch 1990; Zax 1990; but see Cole 1974; MacManus 1978). The political disadvantage stems from the fact that African Americans tend to be concentrated geographically, a residential pattern that inhibits their ability to compete on a city-wide basis. For example, if African Americans make up 30 percent of a city's population, one might argue that they should have a fair chance of securing about 30 percent of the seats on the council. But in at-large systems, because nonwhites make up 70 percent of the population, they can easily out vote the African American community and control 100 percent of the local offices. Because at-large systems, in combination with racial bloc voting, may be unfair to minority groups, courts have ruled that this system denies to them their voting rights under the Constitution.

Although black residents and politicians tend to achieve fairer representation in district and mixed systems (Karnig 1976, 230; Taebel 1978, 147; Robinson and Dye 1978, 137; but see MacManus 1978; Karnig and Welch 1982; Zax 1990), the negative effects of at-large systems for African Americans have diminished over time. The Voting Rights Act of 1965, minority group activism, the threat of legal disputes, and growth in the political acceptance of blacks have made it easier for blacks to achieve representation under at-large conditions (Welch 1990, 1072). For example, in Hartford, Connecticut, the political parties have tried to ensure that the council membership reflects the racial and ethnic diversity of the community. In 2000 the six Democrats on the council included two whites, two blacks, and two Hispanic members—roughly proportional to the makeup of the city's racial and ethnic population (Gurwitt 2000).

That scholars have focused so much attention on this issue stems from the belief that electoral institutions matter. Indeed, greater minority representation can be achieved rather quickly by simply changing the election system. Other factors that have helped to elect minorities are the presence of a large minority population (Cole 1974; Bullock 1975; Taebel 1978, 149; Robinson and Dye 1978); minority group mobilization (Campbell and Feagin 1975; Karnig 1979; Karnig and Welch 1979); and a minority population with higher education and income (Cole 1974, 37; Karnig 1976; 1979; Karnig and Welch 1979, 475; MacManus 1978, 160; Robinson and Dye 1978; Zax 1990). The size of the city council also affects minority representation, but the effects are clearer when representation is measured as "presence" on the council (Taebel 1978, 151; Alozie and Manganaro 1993, 281) rather than "parity" on the council (Bullock and MacManus 1987, 549; Bullock and MacManus 1990; Welch 1990; but see Jones 1976; Karnig and Welch 1979; Latimer 1979).[1]

Latino Representation. Latinos will usually do better under district systems. The case study experience in many large cities with sizable Latino populations supports this view. In Miami, Latino representational gains were also associated with the creation of more Latino-majority council districts (Warren 1997). Chicago witnessed a dramatic increase in Latino city council members, from one member in 1983 to seven in 1995, all elected from Latino-majority districts. Intergroup coalition building and a change to district elections increased Latino representation on the Sacramento city council (Browning, Marshall, and Tabb 1984).

The relationship between electoral structure and representation, however, is not as clear for Latinos as it is for African Americans. Due to their lower levels of residential concentration, Latinos may experience only weak gains under district formats, and some suggest that Latino candidates will do somewhat better in mixed and at-large systems. Cross-sectional and case study research has shown this to be more or less correct (Welch 1990). For instance, research on Denver and Pueblo, Colorado, has demonstrated that Latinos fare better under mixed systems, with minorities being elected more commonly from districts, not the at-large seats in those cities (Hero 1997). In cities like Los Angeles, Latino candidates face another hurdle, even under district elections. Latinos may constitute a majority, or even supermajority, of a district's population, but the presence of large numbers of noncitizens who are ineligible to vote depresses the likely vote for Latino candidates. Under such circumstances, successful Latino candidates must pursue a wide appeal across racial and ethnic groups, or what is known as a "deracialized strategy" (Underwood 1997), in order to win office. The risk in this strategy, however, is that Latino candidates may be criticized for "selling out" to non-Latino (in most cases, white) interests. In general, electoral structure may not affect Latino representation as dramatically as it has affected black representation (Taebel 1978; MacManus 1978; Karnig and Welch 1979; Welch 1990, 1067; Zax 1990). The apparent reasons for this include factors that diminish the electoral power of single-member districts: less residential concentration, large numbers of noncitizens, and lower voter participation rates.

Female Representation. Electoral structure has not hurt the ability of women to get elected to city councils (Alozie and Manganaro 1993). Although some have suggested that female candidates are more common in nonpartisan settings (Welch and Karnig 1979), the success of female candidates is actually more likely in partisan systems (Karnig and Walter 1976). Whereas women are typically underrepresented on city councils (Karnig and Welch 1979), some studies suggested that females were overrepresented in cities with at-large systems, contrary to what we know of other groups historically subject to discrimination (Bullock and MacManus 1991; MacManus and Bullock 1993; Welch and Karnig 1979). There is also a regional dimension to female representation; they are more consistently underrepresented in the Northeast and South (Bullock and MacManus 1991, 85), but more fairly represented in the West (Alozie and Manganaro 1993, 291). Finally, both environmental and structural factors are important; women tend to be elected more frequently in larger cities (Bullock and MacManus 1991, 185) and in cities with larger councils (Alozie and Manganaro 1993, 395).

City Council Candidates

Whereas structural aspects of local political systems, such as nonpartisan ballots and district, at-large, and mixed election systems, shape election outcomes in the aggregate, there are often subtle processes at work that shape not only the decision to run for city council but also the type of individual who seeks local office. Here we focus on the backgrounds of city councillors and some of the dynamics associated with their emergence as candidates. It is important to point out that not all cities are alike and that different patterns will be seen, depending on the places being examined.

More city council members come from the business community than from any other occupational category, including the legal profession (Bledsoe 1993, 54). This is not surprising, given the prominence of economic development matters and concerns of local business leaders on city government agendas (Peterson 1981). But it does stand in contrast to the backgrounds of those serving in state legislatures and Congress, most of whose members come from the legal profession. Variation exists across cities, however. More prestigious councils—those in large cities that require full-time service and provide high salaries and ample staff support—tend to attract more lawyers and professionals than less prestigious councils do (Bledsoe 1993, 43). It is possible that these individuals are intent on building political careers on the council or that they plan to use the council as a steppingstone to higher office.

Prior government or political service is not generally an important characteristic of those desiring a spot on the city council. Approximately two-thirds of council members do not serve in any governmental or community leadership capacity prior to joining the council, but of those who do, the typical experience is a seat on a school board, a position on a city commission, or a leadership role in a local community organization. In the most competitive cities, however, prior civic or political involvement is important to political success (Bledsoe 1993, 58–60; see also Engstrom and Pezant 1975; Feld and Lutz 1972; Krebs 1998, 2001; Prewitt 1970).

Education and income levels of city councillors are generally higher in cities with reformed institutions—council-manager government, nonpartisan ballots, and at-large elections—than in cities with unreformed institutions. Blacks are elected in greatest number in large southern cities with partisan ballots. In general, southern council members tend to be older and wealthier than those in other regions of the country. Younger council members serve most frequently in unreformed cities of the Northeast, which also has the largest number of partisan Democrats. In contrast, councillors in the western United States are more strongly Republican than those in other regions (Bledsoe 1993, chap. 2).

Candidate Recruitment

A separate question centers on the political processes that guide candidate emergence. A major study of city councils in the San Francisco Bay Area uncovered a relatively closed process of candidate recruitment. Incumbent officeholders and local business and civic groups dominated candidate recruitment in order to ensure that the "best" individuals were elevated to local office (Prewitt 1970). Councillors had been groomed for the office, initially as members of the local business community and subsequently as appointed members of a city advisory body (Prewitt 1970, 121). A more recent, national sample of councillors, however, revealed that they are generally self-starters, not recruited by any organized group or informal socialization process (Bledsoe 1993, 66).

Scholars have uncovered gender differences in candidate recruitment at the city council level. Male candidates tend to be drawn from the ranks of high-status occupations and move somewhat laterally into local office, whereas females work their way up through the ranks of nonpartisan civic and volunteer organizations (Merritt 1977; Miller 1986). Others have argued that aspects of the immediate political environment, such as the costs and benefits of gaining and holding local office (Black 1972) and the likelihood of success (Krebs 1999), shape decisions to run. Age may also be a factor. A recent study of Florida city council members indicated that younger people tend to be less interested in local politics and more easily dissuaded than older people by the time commitments, public pressure, and media scrutiny of local officeholding. Younger people may also be more cynical about serving in local government (Mac-Manus 1998).

City Council Campaigns and Elections

Once the decision has been made to enter a city council race, the campaign begins in earnest. Important considerations at this stage include the type of constituency, whether citywide or district, heterogeneous or homogeneous in composition, and the nature of the ballot, whether partisan or nonpartisan. These aspects of the local political environment will shape the broad outlines of the campaign. Three candidate-specific factors, however, will ultimately determine the campaign's success: personal contact with voters, endorsements, and fund raising (Fleischmann and Stein 1998; Fraga 1988; Heilig and Mundt 1984, 70–76; Howell and Oiler 1981; Krebs 2001; Lieske 1989; Raymond 1992). Personal contact with voters amplifies a candidate's virtues, such as his or her qualifications, experience, and concern for the community (Raymond 1992), while endorsements lend credibility to a campaign (Lieske 1989). Fund raising enables candidates to buy advertising and to communicate their backgrounds, endorsements, and policy views to the public. Endorsed candidates with impressive backgrounds, especially in politics, also have an easier time raising money (Krebs 2001). All three factors have been shown to affect election outcomes (Krebs 1998; Lieske 1989).

The chief strategic concern of campaigns is how best to communicate with the voting public. This concern is especially acute in nonpartisan cities where voters are at least officially denied knowledge of candidates' partisan leanings (Schaffner, Streb, and Wright 2001). What has not been stated explicitly, however, is that incumbents have typically cornered the market on the most important means of communication: personal contact, endorsements, and fund raising. Thus, despite the effort that goes into campaigning, the dominant element in city council elections is incumbency (Hagensick 1964; Howell and Oiler 1981, 155; Jamieson 1971; Kirlin 1975; Krebs 1998; Lieske 1989; Pohlmann 1978).

Incumbents have numerous advantages when it comes to winning reelection. First, they are better known than any of their challengers. Second, because they have had time in office to do favors for constituents and prominent groups, they are far more likely to receive official endorsement from such groups. Furthermore, because incumbents are very likely to be returned to office, and because contributors typically support likely winners, incumbents have a much easier time raising money to ward off strong challengers and to compete with them effectively.[2] Incumbents, however, are not invulnerable to defeat; their electoral security may be threatened by well-financed, politically experienced challengers (Krebs 1998, 930), or when demographic shifts alter the successful voting coalitions they have built (Vanderleeuw 1991). That the percentage of communities employing term limits (9 percent) as a means to ensure council turnover nearly doubled during the early 1990s is one indication that voters see the incumbency advantage as a threat to local democracy (Renner and DeSantis 1998, 38).

In summary, a cluster of factors shapes city council campaigns and elections. Incumbency is the 800-pound gorilla in city council elections, as it is in state and national elections. Besides incumbency, candidates' background characteristics, contact with voters, endorsements, and spending help determine election outcomes. It is important to keep in mind, too, that this discussion has been about individual-level factors that affect campaigns and elections, as opposed to things like electoral institutions that affect election outcomes in the aggregate.

Substantive Representation

Once elected, a member's attention turns to the job of representing constituents and making laws. Earlier we explained descriptive representation, which is essentially the degree to which the demographic profile of the council matches that of the local population. Here we explore substantive representation, which deals more directly with the act of representation. Two questions are central: First, who is being represented? Second, how is representation provided? How representation is provided has a lot to do with the personal motivations people have when they first seek office and also with the local political culture. Who is represented is a question of demand makers and influence, whereas how political culture affects roles is a supporting input to the actors in the system.

Role Orientations

In thinking about their role on the city council, elected officials will start with the nature of their constituency, whether they represent a district or the city as a whole as an at-large member. Council members who represent districts tend to focus more on the neighborhood or area from which they are elected, whereas at-large representatives regard the entire city as their primary constituency (Welch and Bledsoe 1988, 77). District representatives are more likely to favor government programs targeted to particular groups or constituencies than other councillors do, in part because of their desire to provide constituents with tangible benefits (Clingermayer and Feiock 1995). This, of course, does not mean that at-large members will never think about the needs of specific areas or that district representatives will never consider the needs of the entire community, but, in both cases, council members will look after their core constituency. Political rationality is why elected officials concentrate on those who elected them: to maintain their positions, they must please their constituents.

A member's attitude about council service also affects his or her view of representation. Scholars have classified elected officials as delegates, trustees, or politicos. Delegates view their role as simply being a mouthpiece for constituent preferences. Trustees tend to view the job more in terms of exercising independent judgment and doing what is in the best interest of city residents, however they define that interest. Politicos fall in between these two categories; on some issues, members will behave like delegates, on others like trustees.

A councillor's motivation for seeking local public office will also affect that person's view of representation. Prewitt (1970) has demonstrated that council members tended to view their public service as a form of civic duty or obligation, not dissimilar to leadership in a civic organization. This viewpoint often led to an attitude of "volunteerism," in which council members' behavior was less responsive to public sentiment or electoral accountability than might have been expected. For example, Prewitt found that council members were more likely to vote against perceived public opinion on issues, less sensitive to public pressures, unlikely to be concerned with future elections when making decisions, less likely to want constituents or groups involved in policymaking, and less interested in providing constituent services (p. 11). He attributed much of this behavior to the lack of political ambition among these council members, many of whom first came to the office not by winning an election but by being appointed to fill a vacancy. This produces greater trustee behavior when deciding what is good for the community (see also Feld and Lutz 1972).

Although this rather narrow view of representation may still exist in smaller, reformed cities, it is unclear if this was ever the case in larger, more politicized communities where the desire for political advancement was the primary motivation of those seeking local office (Engstrom and Pezant 1975). If political advancement is a key motivating force, the behavior of council members is likely to be especially attuned to the needs of constituents. City council members who view their position as a stepping-stone to higher office tend to be more attentive to citizens and pursue the role of being a delegate and ombudsman for their constituents. This practice is generally well received by citizens, who may then vote for the councillor who pursues another elected position. In contrast, the councillor with a volunteeristic view of public service may eschew acting on constituent demands or public opinion in order to pursue broader civic objectives.

Scholars have identified other motivations besides the civic volunteer and professional politician. Bledsoe (1993) identified four primary motivations underlying decisions to seek city office: (1) a desire to advance a cause or issue, which he labeled "particularism"; (2) a desire to help people, either specific individuals or a political party, which he labeled "localism"; (3) a desire to advance self-interest, which he labeled "self-regarding"; and (4) a desire to be involved in politics for the sheer enjoyment of it, which he labeled "politico." Bledsoe reached his conclusions after collecting data on council members from all parts of the country, a process that enables one to appreciate the full range of explanations for why a person seeks a city council seat. Different motivations will directly affect how one approaches the representational role.

Local political culture is also important to understanding the way councillors go about representing constituents. This, too, is subject to change. In Concord, California, one of the cities studied by Prewitt, the emphasis on amateurism and volunteer service by citizen-legislators gave way in the 1980s to professional, that is, full-time, leadership by political operatives intent on advancing strongly ideological solutions to local issues (Ehrenhalt 1992, 42–64). This is quite the opposite of the amateur councillors of old, motivated almost solely by their sense of duty to the community. Suburbia, once the home of status quo–oriented, caretaker government, has seen its share of entrepreneurial leaders who have emerged in response to controversies over the pace of growth in their communities (Schneider, Teske, and Mintrom 1995).

Constituent Service

The role city councillors play in responding to inputs such as public demands for constituent service, or what is sometimes referred to as casework, is another aspect of council representation. The amount of casework or service in which city council members engage is a reflection of personal preferences (some may simply enjoy it more than others) and demand from constituents. Although we have little information about how much council members enjoy casework, we know slightly more about the demand for casework. A recent survey by Clingermayer and Feiock (1994) reached several conclusions: (1) district members, by virtue of the fact that they represent particular geographic areas, usually receive more requests than at-large councillors do; (2) devotion to council work stimulates requests for service; (3) among district members, those with a diverse network of campaign supporters receive more calls for assistance than do district members with homogeneous bases of political support; and (4) demand for constituent service increases in response to greater media coverage.

Which council members are most likely to act on behalf of constituents? Again, the nature of the election system influences behavior. District members tend to devote more time and energy to constituent service than do members elected at large, whose connections to particular constituents and willingness to work on specific problems are weak in comparison (Clingermayer and Feiock 1993; Heilig and Mundt 1984, 96; Welch and Bledsoe 1988, 73–75). There is some variation among district members, however. Electoral considerations are important; district members with diverse and fractious constituencies use casework as a means of responding to competing group needs. More senior council members also are more likely to respond to inquiries than newly elected members are (Clingermayer and Feiock 1993). Perhaps because of their experience, they are more likely to know how to get things done and to be able to resolve problems effectively.

How councillors relate to their constituencies is influenced by the structure of the election system, attitudes toward the legislator's role, and motivations for seeking office. There is also evidence indicating that one's orientation to the job is influenced by age, political considerations, and constituency pressure. Another important aspect of substantive representation is policymaking. We now turn our attention to that topic and the kinds of things that might influence policymaking on city councils.

Legislative Structure

In addition to representation and serving constituents through service and casework, city councils are charged with responding to community concerns by means of lawmaking. Like other aspects of city councils discussed in this chapter, the council's role in legislative policymaking reflects the institutional setting of local government. Some of the internal features of council operations will be discussed before proceeding to an exploration of how structure affects council policymaking more generally. Here we will see how these institutions and actors of the legislative branch organize and carry out their lawmaking role in response to inputs from the political environment.

Leadership Roles

In order to help produce collective action, legislative bodies require leaders. Leaders guide the council through the legislative process, manage relations with the public and other political institutions, and generally help coordinate the council's policy agenda. Leaders are expected to stimulate discussion about public issues and to offer solutions to deal with them.

The structure of city government may establish that the elected mayor will serve as the presiding officer of the council. This would be most common in a council-manager or weak mayor-council setting. But often the council is able to choose its own leadership from among its members. A council president is often elected and has a powerful role in those cities in which a real system of checks and balances is operating between the legislative and executive branches (a strong mayor, for example). Council presidents may make appointments to council committees, select staff, and organize the council's policy agenda. Many cities also choose a council member to serve as president pro tempore, a post established to ensure that someone is available to lead meetings in the absence of the presiding officer. The other council leadership posts are those associated with committees. Council members who chair legislative committees perform important policy-related leadership roles.

Staff

City council members, particularly in large cities, need support staff to assist with their legislative and representational duties. Larger staff operations are more common in mayor-council cities than in council-manager governments. However, the trend has been toward increasing the level of staff support for the council as a whole, for committees, and for individual members. Council members from districts, who spend considerable time on casework, are likely to have more staff than at-large representatives have (Svara 1991). The use of staff is a response to public demands placed on the city council.

Legislative Committees

The average city council has only five committees, but the number exceeds thirty in some places. The establishment of committees represents a logical response to the complex policy environment within which council members function. Seeking to become better informed about the range of policy issues they must address, council members create committees to, among other things, study legislation, hear testimony, evaluate programs, and craft policy (Pelissero and Krebs 1997).

Given that committees most often arise in response to public demands, it is not surprising that council committees are found most often in the nation's largest cities (DeSantis 1987, 3; Svara 1991, 44). Table 7-1 shows that 70 percent of cities with populations over 100,000 have legislative committees. Nearly all cities with populations over 300,000 use a committee system (Pelissero and Krebs 1997). Council size also is an important predictor of whether a city will employ committees in the legislative process. Smaller city councils are less likely to use committees than larger ones are. Indeed, every city with a council size of twelve or more has a system of legislative committees.

Committee use also is influenced by the governmental and electoral structure of city government. In council-manager cities, councils are smaller and typically part-time, and policymaking is centered in the city manager's office and the professional bureau-

Table 7-1   Legislative Committees in City Councils by Government Structure

Commitees Used		Form of Government		Election Ballot		Representation		
		Mayor-Council	Council-Manager	Partisan	Nonpartisan	District	At Large	Mixed
Yes	70%	84.8%	55.6%	88.6%	65.0%	84.1%	50.0%	74.6%
	(112)							
No	30%	15.2	44.4	11.4	35.0	15.9	50.0	25.4
	(49)							
Total	(161)							

Source: Survey of city clerks in cities with population of 100,000, conducted in 1992–1993 by the authors. See Pelissero and Krebs (1997) for other findings from this survey.

cracy. Thus there are few incentives for council members to undertake costs associated with building and maintaining a strong committee system. The incentives for using committees in mayor-council cities generally work in the opposite direction. As the chief policymaking actor in city government, councils in weak-mayor cities often require more elaborate committee systems. A similar, but not identical, institutional rationale exists in strong-mayor cities, where mayors monopolize information and policy expertise. To maintain a sense of institutional balance and to enhance their capacity to make policy independent of the mayor's office, councils in these cities typically expand their use of committees. The data on committee use in Table 7-1 are generally consistent with these propositions. Mayor-council cities are more likely to use committees (85 percent) than council-manager cities are (56 percent). But even though committees are more frequently used in strong-mayor cities than in weak-mayor cities, the latter tend to have larger committee systems than strong-mayor cities do.[3]

The electoral environment also shapes the use of committees. They are used in most cities with partisan ballot systems. And whereas most cities with district or mixed systems of representation employ committees, only half of cities with at-large representation systems use committees. This is due to the smaller city councils in at-large systems and the greater reliance on city managers to formulate policy in reform-style governments that typically use at-large representation. Both factors lead at-large city councils in many cities to study policy as a council of the whole rather than to rely upon committees. Another factor leading to greater committee use is the full-time council. Cities in which the council meets more frequently typically have greater responsibilities placed on them by the public. And as these full-time councils address a broader range of issues, they rely more on committees to help them manage their workload. Seventy-three percent of councils that meet weekly have committees, compared with 67 percent of councils meeting less often. In general, the likelihood of having committees decreases with the presence of more reformed government features. In fact, 86 to 100 percent of cities with relatively unreformed governments use committees, compared with only 38 percent of those cities that have adopted all elements of municipal reform: council-manager government, at-large representation, and nonpartisan ballots (Pelissero and Krebs 1997).

Policymaking

How do legislative organization, types of electoral systems, council role orientations, and legislative structure affect the policymaking by city councils? The topics discussed in previous sections of the chapter are now used to help us understand the key role that city councils play in policymaking. Here we examine the city council's impact on policy outputs and policy outcomes in the urban political system.

Structure Makes a Difference

Svara (1990) divides the local government process into four parts: mission, policy, administration, and management. Mission is concerned with setting the broad parameters or scope of city government policy, while policy refers to lawmaking pursuant to mission objectives. Administration deals with policy execution or implementation, while management "includes the internal organization and assignment of authority; methods for hiring, developing, motivating and appraising staff; systems for budgeting and fiscal control, procedures for purchasing and contracting," and so forth (p. 17). The role of the city council in these four dimensions is likely to be strongest in mission and policy and weakest in administration and management, which is more the job of city mangers and administrative staff.

Svara applied his model of the local government process to six pairs of cities, including council-manager, weak-mayor, and strong-mayor forms of government: New Haven and Hartford, Connecticut; Knoxville, Tennessee, and Greensboro, North Carolina; Akron and Dayton, Ohio; Minneapolis, Minnesota, and Kansas City, Missouri; Memphis, Tennessee, and Charlotte, North Carolina; and Lincoln, Nebraska, and Charlotte, North Carolina. He concluded that councillors, regardless of the formal governing arrangements, are generally weak in their roles as policymakers and governors, but they are far better at and more concerned about representing constituent interests, especially those dealing with city services and how the government treats citizens (p. 160). Councils in strong-mayor cities struggle with executive mayors for control and influence over policy and thus serve more as a counterweight to mayoral initiatives in all four parts of the process. Councils in council-manager cities have more power to exercise influence in all four areas of governance but may come under the sway of the manager's formidable organizational and informational advantages. Weak-mayor councils may also play an important role in all four dimensions of governing, but power in this form is highly fragmented and subject to the personal political skills of elected mayors (chap. 5).

Councillors in council-manager cities are more likely to say that they understand their role in administration than is the case with councillors in strong- mayor cities. They are also less likely than are councillors in strong-mayor cities to agree with the statement that they exist simply to approve or veto policy decisions made by chief executives. A large percentage of councillors in both forms of government agree that the council deals with administrative matters more than with policy formation and that councils do not have time to deal adequately with their city's major policy concerns (Svara 1990, 160). The portrait of city councils' role in governance painted by Svara shows a weak role in governance but a very strong role in linking city residents with city government through advocacy.

One might advance a rational explanation for this. Representing constituents through stands on public issues and service is somewhat easier than delving into the nitty-gritty of policy formation. More importantly perhaps, the political reward for effective constituent representation is far greater, because council members can claim individual credit for it. Policy formation is a collective enterprise, usually requiring council members to share the credit. Given this, it is no wonder that council members tend more toward constituent advocacy than policy creation.

As previously discussed with respect to council committees, the extent to which councils can be strong policy actors depends, in part, on the city's form of government. City councils are also typically, although not necessarily, weak in relation to other institutional actors. This is especially problematic in council-manager and strong mayor-council cities. In these cities, other political institutions besides the council monopolize executive expertise and information (the city managers and staff in council-manager cities, and the mayors and department heads in strong mayor-council cities). As a consequence, councils are often at a disadvantage in terms of information and policy advice, and thus they struggle to create viable policy solutions and to act independent of strong executives.

An exception to this rule might be the councils in weak-mayor governments. Given their legislative and executive duties, these councils can be powerful. This can lead to efforts to change municipal institutions in order to increase the executive's power at the expense of the council, as seen in the recent charter reform designed to weaken the council in Los Angeles (Fulton and Shigley 2000). City councils in council-manager cities are not weak by design, but given the amateur and part-time nature of council service on these bodies, it is most often the case that such councils react to policy initiatives generated elsewhere. Politically, it is often more beneficial for council members to criticize these initiatives than to create and propose their own solutions, which might entail political risk.

Electoral Systems and Policy Conflict

The electoral process and policymaking are intimately connected. One important connection is how ballot structures and systems of representation shape the council's policymaking process. Welch and Bledsoe (1988, 80–103) asked a nationwide sample of city council members a series of questions about the level (or amount) and nature (the form) of policy conflict or disagreement within their council. Their responses reflected the connections between election systems and the policy process. For example, district members reported higher levels of policy conflict than at-large members did. Districts tend to create turf battles, as each member acts to protect his or her constituents in the struggle for more and better city services, public improvements, economic development, police protection, and so forth. Welch and Bledsoe's results also indicated that the nature of conflict in partisan cities reflects Republican and Democratic policy priorities. The election system seems to have important effects on council policymaking, although the differences should not be overstated.

Policy Views

Does the structure of city government produce council members with significantly different policy views? Although early research suggested that reformed governments tended to produce more conservative officeholders, more recent research casts doubt on those findings. Examining a range of hypothetical policy topics, including taxes, federal aid to cities, economic development, unionization of city employment, and resource distribution, Welch and Bledsoe (p. 91) found few significant policy differences between members elected under unreformed electoral institutions and those elected under reformed electoral institutions. In their assessment of councillor views, the major source of difference was ideology, whether one was liberal or conservative, not whether one was elected at large or through a nonpartisan ballot. A more recent set of findings attributes policy differences to age. MacManus (1998, 629) found that older council members in the state of Florida perceived greater generational conflict within their constituencies on crime, police, welfare, moral issues, and transportation.

Council Composition and Municipal Hiring Policy

One way that system inputs affect system outputs is seen in municipal hiring policies. For example, one would expect that greater minority representation on city councils would translate into more black and Latino job applicants being hired for city jobs, as they use their power to alter the composition of the city workforce. Examining numerous categories of municipal employment, scholars have generally concluded that black and Latino representation on city councils leads to greater diversity in city hiring (Browning, Marshall, and Tabb 1997; Dye and Renick 1981, 481; Kerr and Mladenka 1994; Mladenka 1989a, 1989b, 1991; but see Alozie and Ramirez 1999; Eisinger 1982). Studies of the impact of female council members on female employment are more mixed. Early work showed gains in female employment as a result of female officeholding (Dye and Renick 1981; Warner, Steel, and Lovrich 1989). More comprehensive studies, however, have indicated little impact from female council representation, although female mayors appear to increase the presence of women as officials and administrators of city governments (Kerr, Miller, and Reid 1998, 572). At best, we may say that minority and female officeholders try to use their institutional power to shape city policy in ways favorable to their key constituency groups.

Roll Call Analysis

Others have explored council policymaking by analyzing the voting patterns of city councils, or roll call votes. Heilig and Mundt (1984) used roll call votes to study the effects of district systems of representation on council decision making in eleven U.S. cities. All eleven cities had changed from at-large to district election systems. They discovered that district election systems altered council voting blocs in ways that reflected political changes produced by the new electoral arrangements. Districts, because they resulted in the election of a larger number of minority group members, altered the nature of voting blocs on the city council (Heilig and Mundt 1984, 128–129). The adoption of districts, however, did not affect the level of conflict on the council as measured by roll call votes (Heilig and Mundt 1984, 113).

Simpson (2001, 298) examined a sample of nonunanimous roll call votes taken in the Chicago city council between 1863 and 1994, a process that yielded 1,500 divided roll call votes and over 75,000 votes cast by individual council members. His statistical analysis uncovered three distinct patterns of behavior in the many city councils that served Chicago during that period, which he labeled: Fragmented, Rubber Stamp, and Council Wars (p. 300). In Fragmented Councils, the mayor is a relatively weak policy actor, and the council is generally uncoordinated, resulting in each member pursuing his or her self-interest and very little substantive legislative output. Rubber Stamp Councils are characterized by the unwillingness of council members to buck powerful mayors supported by a strong party organization. The best example here is of city councils in place during the Richard J. Daley years (1955–1976), when the council essentially acquiesced to mayoral demands. Council Wars is a way to describe highly polarized council voting patterns. During the mid-1980s, following the election of Harold Washington, Chicago's first African American mayor, voting patterns on the council were highly polarized along racial lines, as white councillors attempted to thwart the initiatives of Washington and his minority allies on the council.

A third study of council roll call votes investigated the relationship between descriptive and substantive representation. Some have argued that greater descriptive representation for minority groups may not translate into higher levels of substantive representation if minority legislators are simply outvoted on legislation. In other words, minority gains in the electoral arena may be meaningless if whites on city councils engage in bloc voting to deny minority legislative priorities. Evidence on this question at the city council level suggests that this pattern of behavior is not occurring generally but does show up on specific issues such as housing and police-community relations (Austin 2002).

Conclusion

Our review of research and practice on America's city councils has indicated that these bodies are complex, diverse, and important to the political process of city governments. Comparative research and case studies reveal a significant degree of variation across cities in the organization, elections, legislative roles, and policymaking impact of city councils. Much of the variation was shown to be related to structural differences in the form of government used. In particular, many characteristics of city councils differ when examining a mayor-council government and comparing it to a council-manager system. Table 7-2 shows the most common differences in the characteristics of city councils under these two governing arrangements.

Although form of government is not the only determinant of the features of a city council, we can summarize what is most common for each government organization. As shown in Table 7-2, city councils in mayor-council governments are typically larger, engaged in full-time work at frequent meetings for which they are well compensated. Whereas most council elections are nonpartisan, the remnants of partisan municipal elections are greater in mayor-council governments, which also more frequently use the district method of representation. These councils also have a more developed legislative committee structure and larger staff. The elected council members tend to be from more diverse racial, ethnic, income, and occupational backgrounds. And perhaps because of the greater diversity, such councils tend to have a higher level

Table 7-2   Common Characteristics of City Councils under Two Forms of Government

Characteristics	*Mayor-Council Governments*	*Council-Manager Governments*
Size of council	Larger	Smaller
Nature of work	Full time	Part time
Compensation	Higher pay	Lower or no pay
Meetings	More frequent	Less frequent
Party roles	Partisan and nonpartisan	Nonpartisan
Representational method	District	At large
Committees	More	Fewer
Staff	More	Smaller
Diversity	More	Less
Representational style	Delegates	Trustees
Constituency service	More casework	Less casework
Policymaking roles	Advocates–adopters	Respondents–adopters
Conflict	Higher	Lower

Source: Compiled by the authors.

of conflict in their legislative environments. The representational style of these councillors is closer to that of an instructed delegate who performs a significant amount of
casework. Their policy orientations are best described as advocates for their constituents as they perform their legal function of policy adoption.

In contrast, the councils in manager-led governments are smaller and spend less
time on council duties. They are working in less partisan environments. Their at-large
constituency base leads to less individual casework and a style of representation that
is closer to that of a trustee. Because of the executive-dominated governing structure,
they have less involvement in policy activity and a lower need for legislative committees and staff. Indeed, as policy adopters, they are best described as respondents to the
policy initiatives of the city manager. Greater homogeneity among the council members is reflected in lower levels of conflict.

These are the most common features of councils in the council-manager system,
but they should not be interpreted as characteristics of all such councils. If we have
been able to learn one thing from our review, it is that city councils in the United
States are not all alike.

The research on city councils has yielded many important insights. For example,
we know with great specificity the degree to which electoral arrangements have influenced the descriptive representation of minority groups. We also know a great deal
about how the composition of councils influences city employment patterns. Both of
these areas address different aspects of the political system; on the one hand, the nature of the electoral environment (a system input) creates opportunity for particular
groups and helps shape the composition of city councils, an important institutional
actor in city politics. The composition of the city council, in turn, shapes city employment decisions (a system output).

We also know a great deal about how electoral arrangements influence the representational roles of council members, and about the personal motivations of individuals who want to help govern their communities as city council members. Finally,
Svara's research has taken us inside the "black box" of systems analysis to uncover
both the constraints and the opportunities for council governance within different
governmental arrangements. As Susan MacManus (1999) has suggested, today's city
councils are enjoying a resurgence of influence in city politics.

In general, however, our knowledge is less impressive when it comes to the internal workings of city councils. The research that has been done has looked at only a few
cities. We know little about the inner workings of committees, the power of council
leaders, and the role of personal staff. Congressional and state legislative scholars have
spent a great deal of time studying the relationship between committees and the legislative bodies that create and employ them. Urban scholars should be addressing
similar questions to those that have been the subject of research on other levels of gov-

ernment. For example, to what degree do the agendas of committee members diverge from the preferences of council majorities? Do committee preferences reflect the wishes of council leaders, or are committees simply tools for strong mayors? What kinds of tools do council leaders use to persuade rank-and-file council members to support their agenda? What is the role of council staff? What power do they have? Why are they powerful? Many of these questions will be directed at councils in the nation's largest cities that utilize these kinds of internal mechanisms and resources.

We also know little about the interaction between mayors and councils. To what extent is there conflict between chief executives and legislatures? This may be a particularly interesting time to study this question in light of the election of generally more conservative mayors in big cities previously controlled by liberal Democrats. How do public opinion and sources of campaign funds affect council agendas and decision making? The electoral dimension of council behavior needs to be explored more carefully and explicitly.

Insights from congressional and state legislative scholars may be borrowed to help illuminate the workings of councils, especially in the area of policy formation. But they may also be used to help us more fully understand campaigns and elections at the individual, as opposed to the aggregate, level. Although much research has been done, the literature on city councils is far from fully developed.

Suggested Readings

Bledsoe, Timothy. 1993. *Careers in City Politics: The Case for Urban Democracy.* Pittsburgh: University of Pittsburgh Press. An empirical assessment of the career motivations of city councillors, both before and during their careers on the council.

Heilig, Peggy, and Robert J. Mundt. 1984. *Your Voice at City Hall.* Albany: State University of New York Press. An interesting comparative case study that shows the impact of city council representation methods on politics, decision making, and policy outcomes.

MacManus, Susan A. 1999. "The Resurgent City Councils." In *American State and Local Politics: Directions for the 21st Century,* ed. Ronald E. Weber and Paul Brace, 167–193. New York: Chatham House. An overview of the renewed importance of city councils in American cities.

Prewitt, Kenneth. 1970. *The Recruitment of Political Leaders: A Study of Citizen-Politicians.* New York: Bobbs-Merrill. A classic work that highlights the political culture and attitudes of municipal officials and the impact of "volunteerism" on local government.

Simpson, Dick. 2001. *Rogues, Rebels, and Rubber Stamps: The Politics of the Chicago City Council from 1863 to the Present.* Boulder: Westview Press. A political history of Chicago's councils and mayors that demonstrates the divergent patterns of city council-mayor relations through analysis of elections and roll call voting data.

Welch, Susan, and Timothy Bledsoe. 1988. *Urban Reform and Its Consequences.* Chicago: University of Chicago Press. One of the best survey research studies of the political and policy consequences of urban reform in American cities and its impact on city council representation, roles, and decision making.

References

Adrian, Charles. 1952. "Some General Characteristics of Nonpartisan Elections." *American Political Science Review* 46 (September): 766–776.

Alozie, Nicholas O., and Lynne L. Manganaro. 1993. "Black and Hispanic Council Representation: Does Council Size Matter?" *Urban Affairs Quarterly* 29 (December): 276–298.

Alozie, Nicholas O., and Enrique J. Ramirez. 1999. "A Piece of the Pie and More: Competition and Hispanic Employment on Urban Police Forces." *Urban Affairs Review* 34 (January): 456–475.

Austin, Rory. 2002. "Seats That May Not Matter: Testing for Racial Polarization in American City Councils." *Legislative Studies Quarterly.*

Banfield, Edward, and James Q. Wilson. 1963. *City Politics.* New York: Random House.

Black, Gordon S. 1972. "A Theory of Political Ambition: Career Choices and the Role of Structural Incentives." *American Political Science Review* 66 (March):144–159.

Bledsoe, Timothy. 1993. *Careers in City Politics: The Case for Urban Democracy.* Pittsburgh: University of Pittsburgh Press.

Bledsoe, Timothy, and Susan Welch. 1987. "Patterns of Political Party Activity among U.S. Cities." *Urban Affairs Quarterly* 23 (December): 249–269.

Bridges, Amy. 1997. "Textbook Municipal Reform." *Urban Affairs Review* 33 (September): 97–119.

Browning, Rufus P., Dale Rogers Marshall, and David H. Tabb. 1984. *Protest Is Not Enough.* Berkeley: University of California Press.

———— 1997. *Racial Politics in American Cities.* 2d ed. New York: Longman.

Bullock, Charles. 1975. "The Election of Blacks in the South." *American Journal of Political Science* 19 (November): 727–739.

———— 1987. "Staggered Terms and Black Representation." *Journal of Politics* 49 (May): 543–552.

———— 1990. "Structural Features of Municipalities and the Incidence of Hispanic Councilmembers." *Social Science Quarterly* 71 (December): 665–681.

———— 1991. "Municipal Electoral Structure and the Election of Councilwomen." *Journal of Politics* 53 (February): 75–89.

Campbell, D., and Joe Feagin. 1975. "Black Politics in the South: A Descriptive Analysis." *Journal of Politics* 37 (February):12–59.

Cassel, Carol A. 1985. "Social Background Characteristics of Nonpartisan City Council Members: A Research Note." *Western Political Quarterly* (September): 495–501.

Clingermayer, James C., and Richard C. Feiock. 1995. "Council Views toward Targeting of Development Policy Benefits." *Journal of Politics* 57 (May): 508–520.

———— "Campaigns, Careerism, and Constituencies: Contacting Council Members About Economic Development Policy." *American Politics Quarterly* 4 (October): 453–468.

———— 1993. "Constituencies, Campaign Support, and Council Member Intervention in City Development Policy." *Social Science Quarterly* 74 (March): 199–215.

Cole, Leonard A. 1974. "Electing Blacks to Municipal Office: Structural and Social Determinants." *Urban Affairs Quarterly* 10 (September): 17–39.

Davidson, Chandler, and Luis Ricardo Fraga. 1988. "Slating Groups as Parties in a 'Nonpartisan' Setting." *Western Political Quarterly* 41 (June): 373–391.

Davidson, Chandler, and George Korbel. 1981. "At-Large Elections and Minority Group Representation: A Re-Examination of Historical and Contemporary Evidence." *Journal of Politics* 43 (November): 982–1005.

DeSantis, Victor S. 1987. "Council Committees." *Baseline Data Report*. Washington, D.C.: International City/County Management Association.

DeSantis, Victor S., and Tari Renner. 1994. "Term Limits and Turnover among Local Officials." In *The Municipal Year Book 1994*, 36–42. Washington, D.C.: International City/County Management Association.

Dutton, William H., and Alana Northrop. 1978. "Municipal Reform and the Changing Pattern of Urban Party Politics." *American Politics Quarterly* 6 (October): 429–451.

Dye, Thomas R., and James Renick. 1981. "Political Power and City Jobs: Determinants of Minority Employment." *Social Science Quarterly* 62 (September): 475–486.

Ehrenhalt, Alan. 1992. *United States of Ambition: Politicians, Power, and the Pursuit of Office*. New York: Times Books.

Eisinger, Peter K. 1982. "Black Employment in Municipal Jobs: The Impact of Black Political Power." *American Political Science Review* 76 (June): 380–392.

Engstrom, Richard, and Michael McDonald. 1982. "The Underrepresentation of Blacks on City Councils: Comparing the Structural and Socioeconomic Explanations for South/Non-South Differences." *Journal of Politics* 44 (November): 1088–1099.

———— 1981. "The Election of Blacks to City Councils: Clarifying the Impact of Electoral Arrangements on the Seats/Population Relationship." *American Political Science Review* 75 (May): 344–354.

Engstrom, Richard L., and James N. Pezant. 1975. "Candidate Attraction to Politicized Council Office: New Orleans." *Social Science Quarterly* 56 (March): 975–982.

Feld, Richard D., and Donald S. Lutz. 1972. "Recruitment to the Houston City Council." *Journal of Politics* 34 (August): 924–933.

Fleischmann, Arnold, and Lana Stein. 1998. "Campaign Contributions in Local Elections." *Political Research Quarterly* 51 (September): 673–689.

Fraga, Luis Ricardo. 1988. "Domination through Democratic Means: Nonpartisan Slating Groups in City Electoral Politics." *Urban Affairs Quarterly* 23 (June): 528–555.

Fulton, William, and Paul Shigley. 2000. "Putting Los Angeles Together." *Governing* 13 (June): 20–26.

Gilbert, Charles. 1962. "Some Aspects of Nonpartisan Elections in Large Cities." *Midwest Journal of Political Science* 6 (November): 345–362.

Gurwitt, Rob. 2000. "Rudderless in Hartford." *Governing* 13 (September): 75–78.

Haas, Peter J. 1995. "An Exploratory Analysis of American City Council Salaries." *Urban Affairs Review* 31 (November): 255–265.

Hagensick, A. Clarke. 1964. "Influences of Partisanship and Incumbency on a Nonpartisan Election." *Western Political Quarterly* 17 (March): 117–124.

Hawley, Willis D. 1973. *Nonpartisan Elections and the Case for Party Politics*. New York: Wiley.

Heilig, Peggy, and Robert J. Mundt. 1982. "Districts and City Council Decision-Making." *Urban Affairs Quarterly* 17 (March): 371–377.

———— 1984. *Your Voice at City Hall*. Albany: State University of New York Press.

Hero, Rodney E. 1997. "Latinos and Politicos in Denver and Pueblo, Colorado: Differences, Explanations, and The 'Steady-State' of the Struggle for Equality." In *Racial Politics in American Cities*, 2d ed., ed. Rufus P. Browning, Dale Rogers Marshall, and David H. Tabb, 247–258. New York: Longman.

Howell, Susan, and William Oiler. 1981. "Campaign Activities and Local Election Outcomes." *Social Science Quarterly* 62 (March): 152–160.

International City/County Management Association. 1998. *The Municipal Year Book, 1998*. Washington, D.C.: ICMA.

Jamieson, James B. 1971. "Some Social and Political Correlates of Incumbency in Municipal Elections." *Social Science Quarterly* 52 (March): 946–952.

Jones, Clinton. 1976. "The Impact of Local Election Systems on Black Political Representation." *Urban Affairs Quarterly* 11 (March): 345–354.

Karnig, Albert K. 1979. "Black Resources and City Council Representation." *Journal of Politics* 41 (February): 134–149.

———. 1976. "Black Representation on City Councils: The Impact of District Elections and Socioeconomic Factors." *Urban Affairs Quarterly* 12 (December): 223–242.

Karnig, Albert K., and Oliver Walter. 1976. "Election of Women to City Councils." *Social Science Quarterly* 57 (March): 605–613.

Karnig, Albert K., and Oliver Walter. 1983. "Decline in Municipal Voter Turnout." *American Politics Quarterly* 11 (October): 491–506.

Karnig, Albert K., and Susan Welch. 1982. "Electoral Structure and Black Representation on City Councils." *Social Science Quarterly* 63 (March): 99–114.

———. 1979. "Sex and Ethnic Differences in Municipal Elections." *Social Science Quarterly* 60 (December): 465–481.

Kerr, Brinck, and Kenneth R. Mladenka. 1994. "Does Politics Matter? A Time-Series Analysis of Minority Employment Patterns." *American Journal of Political Science* 38 (March): 918–943.

Kerr, Brinck, Will Miller, and Margaret Reid. 1998. "Determinants of Female Employment Patterns in U.S. Cities: A Time-Series Analysis." *Urban Affairs Review* 33 (March): 559–578.

Kirlin, John P. 1975. "Electoral Conflict and Democracy in Cities." *Journal of Politics* 37 (February): 262–269.

Krebs, Timothy B. 2001. "Political Experience and Fundraising in City Council Elections." *Social Science Quarterly* 82 (September): 536–551.

———. 1999. "The Political and Demographic Predictors of Candidate Emergence in City Council Elections." *Urban Affairs Review* 35 (November): 279–300.

———. 1998. "The Determinants of Candidates' Vote Share and the Advantages of Incumbency in City Council Elections." *American Journal of Political Science* 42 (July): 921–935.

Latimer, Margaret. 1979. "Black Political Representation in Southern Cities." *Urban Affairs Quarterly* 10 (September): 65–86.

Lee, Eugene. 1960. *The Politics of Nonpartisanship.* Berkeley: University of California Press.

Lieske, Joel. 1989. "The Political Dynamics of Urban Voting Behavior." *American Journal of Political Science* 33 (February): 150–174.

MacManus, Susan A. 1978. "City Council Election Procedures and Minority Representation: Are They Related?" *Social Science Quarterly* 59 (June): 153–161.

———. 1999. "The Resurgent City Councils." In *American State and Local Politics: Directions for the 21st Century,* ed. Ronald E. Weber and Paul Brace, 167–193. New York: Chatham House.

———. 1998. "Seniors in City Hall: Causes and Consequences of the Graying of City Councils." *Social Science Quarterly* 79 (September): 620–633.

———. 1985. "Mixed Electoral Systems: The Newest Reform Structure." *National Civic Review* 74 (November): 490.

MacManus, Susan A., and Charles S. Bullock III. 1993. "Women and Racial/Ethnic Minorities in Mayoral and Council Positions." In *The Municipal Year Book 1993,* 70–84. Washington, D.C.: International City/County Management Association.

Merritt, Sharyne. 1977. "Winners and Losers: Sex Differences in Municipal Elections." *American Journal of Political Science* 21 (November): 731–743.

Miller, Lawrence W. 1986. "Political Recruitment and Electoral Success: A Look at Sex Differences in Municipal Elections." *Social Science Journal* 23 (January): 75–90.

Mladenka, Kenneth R. 1989a. "Blacks and Hispanics in Urban Politics." *American Political Science Review* 83 (March): 165–191.

———— 1989b. "Barriers to Hispanic Employment Success in 1,200 Cities." *Social Science Quarterly* 70 (June): 391–408.

———— 1991. "Public Employee Unions, Reformism, and Black Employment in 1,200 American Cities." *Urban Affairs Quarterly* 26 (June): 532–549.

Pelissero, John P., and Timothy B. Krebs. 1997. "City Council Legislative Committees and Policy-Making in Large United States Cities." *American Journal of Political Science* 41 (April): 499–518.

Peterson, Paul E. 1981. *City Limits*. Chicago: University of Chicago Press.

Pitkin, Hanna Fenichel. 1967. *The Concept of Representation*. Berkeley: University of California Press.

Pohlmann, Marcus D. 1978. "The Electoral Impact of Partisanship and Incumbency Reconsidered: An Extension to Low Salience Elections." *Urban Affairs Quarterly* 13 (June): 495–503.

Prewitt, Kenneth. 1970. *The Recruitment of Political Leaders: A Study of Citizen-Politicians*. New York: Bobbs-Merrill.

Raymond, Paul. 1992. "The American Voter in a Nonpartisan Urban Election." *American Politics Quarterly* 20 (April): 247–260.

Reardon, Patrick T. 1997. "L.A. Council, not Mayor, lays Down Law." *Chicago Tribune*, October 24.

Renner, Tari, and Victor DeSantis. 1998. "Municipal Forms of Government: Issues and Trends." *The Municipal Year Book 1998*, 30–41. Washington, D.C.: International City/County Management Association.

Robinson, Theodore, and Thomas Dye. 1978. "Reformism and Black Representation on City Councils." *Social Science Quarterly* 59 (June): 133–141.

Rogers, Chester B., and Harold D. Arman. 1971. "Nonpartisanship and Election to City Office." *Social Science Quarterly* 52 (March): 941–945.

Schaffner, Brian F., Gerald Wright, and Matthew Streb. 2001. "Teams without Uniforms: The Nonpartisan Ballot in State and Local Elections." *Political Research Quarterly* 54 (March): 7–30.

Schneider, Mark, Paul Teske, with Michael Mintrom. 1995. *Public Entrepreneurs: Agents for Change in American Government*. Princeton: Princeton University Press.

Simpson, Dick. 2001. *Rogues, Rebels, and Rubber Stamps: The Politics of the Chicago City Council from 1863 to the Present*. Boulder: Westview Press.

Svara, James H. 1990. *Official Leadership in the City: Patterns of Conflict and Cooperation*. New York: Oxford University Press.

———— 1991. *A Survey of America's City Councils*. Washington, D.C.: National League of Cities.

Taebel, Delbert. 1978. "Minority Representation on City Councils: The Impact of Structure on Blacks and Hispanics." *Social Science Quarterly* 59 (June): 142–152.

Underwood, Katherine. 1997. "Ethnicity Is Not Enough: Latino-Led Multiracial Coalitions in Los Angeles." *Urban Affairs Review* 33 (September): 3–27.

Vanderleeuw, James. 1991. "The Influence of Racial Transition on Incumbency Advantage in Local Elections." *Urban Affairs Quarterly* 27 (September): 36–50.

Warner, Rebecca L., Brent S. Steel, and Nicholas P. Lovrich. 1989. "Conditions Associated with the Advent of Representative Bureaucracy: The Case of Women in Policing." *Social Science Quarterly* 70 (September): 562–578.

Warren, Christopher L. 1997. "Hispanic Incorporation and Structural Reform in Miami." In *Racial Politics in American Cities*, 2d ed., ed. Rufus P. Browning, Dale Rogers Marshall, and David H. Tabb, 223–246. New York: Longman.

Welch, Susan. 1990. "The Impact of At-Large Elections on the Representation of Blacks and Hispanics." *Journal of Politics* 52 (November): 1050–1076.

Welch, Susan, and Timothy Bledsoe. 1988. *Urban Reform and Its Consequences.* Chicago: University of Chicago Press.

Welch, Susan, and Albert A. Karnig. 1979. "Correlates of Female Office-Holding in City Politics." *Journal of Politics* 41 (May): 478–491.

Williams, Oliver, and Charles Adrian. 1959. "The Insulation of Local Politics under the Nonpartisan Ballot." *American Political Science Review* 53 (December): 1052–1063.

Williams, Oliver P., and Charles R. Adrian. 1963. *Four Cities: A Study in Comparative Policy Making.* Philadelphia: University of Pennsylvania Press.

Zax, Jeffrey S. 1990. "Election Methods and Black and Hispanic City Council Membership. *Social Science Quarterly* 71 (June): 338–355.

Notes

1. Presence on the council simply indicates whether or not a minority group member serves on the council, whereas parity indicates a roughly equal relationship between the percentage of the minority in the local population and its percentage on the city council.

2. A survey in the mid-1990s indicated that incumbents were returned to office 84 percent of the time they sought reelection (DeSantis and Renner 1994, 41). One study of Chicago elections showed that incumbents enjoy an advantage of between 20 and 30 percentage points over their challengers (Krebs 1998, 927).

3. Pelissero and Krebs (1997) showed that 90 percent of strong-mayor cities use committees, compared with only 72 percent of weak-mayor cities.

8 City Managers and the Urban Bureaucracy

Robert E. England

City managers and local bureaucrats are prominent participants in the urban policymaking process. Along with city council members, at least in a council-manager form of government, the city manager and the bureaucracy (the city staff and operating departments) are the political elites who make and implement urban policy. Responding to various environmental inputs, these policymakers convert real and perceived needs, wants, and demands into local policies. Converting human and fiscal resources into goods and services to be consumed by the citizenry is the quintessential job of policymakers in the urban political system.

Who are city managers and these local administrative officials who affect citizens so much on a daily basis? What do they do and how do they do it? The purpose of this chapter is to provide responses to these questions, as well as to discuss emerging issues and theories affecting the city management profession and local bureaucrats. We begin with a discussion of city managers. Next, responses to who, what, how, and why questions about the urban bureaucracy are offered. Third, contemporary issues affecting local policymaking and emerging theories relevant to it are discussed. Finally, an agenda for future research concerning these policymakers is presented.

City Managers

As a group, city managers are a small cadre of professionally trained administrators who serve as the chief executive officers (CEOs) of the cities they serve. This section provides an overview of the city management profession. The contextual analysis includes a discussion of the origins of the city management profession and the demographics of city managers—where they are found and their personal characteristics. The section ends with a discussion of what city managers do as CEOs.

Why the Need for City Managers?

Politics concerns the allocation of values (Easton 1953). First, and foremost, the rise of the city management profession was a political process representing a reallocation of values (Banfield and Wilson 1963; Hofstadter 1955; Judd and Swanstrom 1998). The council-manager form of government was introduced as part of the urban reform movement to address the graft, corruption, and inefficiency associated with local government in the mid- and late nineteenth century. Urban reformers advocated "good government" structures and processes to rid cities of "political machines" and the "bosses" (such as "Boss" Tweed of Tammany Hall in New York City) who controlled them.

The city machine was a political organization concerned with the pursuit of wealth and the control and distribution of the spoils of office, which included city jobs and contracts, favors in the administration of the law, and jobs with the machine. City machines were party based. Since the political machine was not ideologically centered, it did not matter, from a policy perspective, which party controlled the city. In other words, a political party served as a means to an end: control of the spoils of office.

Ethnic immigrants arriving in the United States in massive waves prior to the early 1900s traded their votes to a city machine for city jobs and other favors. This quid pro quo system worked well until one machine lost support among ethnic-based neighborhoods and a new regime took over. Then literally thousands of police officers, gas trust workers, and public works employees would be replaced by the supporters of the new machine. Patronage ruled, and urban service delivery was neither efficient nor equitable. Pragmatism and favoritism dominated the urban policy process. The goal was to keep control of the spoils of office and use politics as a mechanism to acquire wealth and power. Political machines were, however, very responsive to the needs of their supporters; they built the infrastructure of all major northeastern industrial cities, helped assimilate millions of immigrants, and provided a very personal style of government.

The antidote prescribed for the maladies of the political machine was the urban reform movement, which advocated "good government" to bring honesty and efficiency to local government. Good government structures and processes included (Boynton 1976, 67–77; Herson and Bolland 1998, 59–62):

- The council-manager form of government to replace the weak- or strong-mayor system used by political machines. The city would be run like a business by a professionally trained city manager appointed by the city council.
- Civil service systems to recruit and select city employees based on merit (knowledge, skills, and abilities).
- At-large elections to replace ward/district elections. At-large elections would emphasize the general public interest of a community instead of the particularistic, parochial interests of a city ward.
- Nonpartisan elections to bypass political parties that had been used as the means to institutionalize political machines, and direct primaries to bypass party-controlled nominations in smoked-filled back rooms.
- The short ballot to give city managers the ability to appoint well-qualified department heads.

- Small city councils of five to seven members (to lessen debate and conflict), with members serving overlapping terms (to allow for policy continuity and stability) and city elections occurring in off years (to emphasize the importance of local affairs by not being overshadowed by state and national elections).

Since the tenets of urban reform represent political values, these tenets were more acceptable to some citizens than they were to others. Acceptance is often based on a number of factors such as city size, region, city type, and demographic characteristics of the community.

Where Are City Managers Found?

Sumter, South Carolina, was the first city to adopt the council-manager form of government, in 1912. One year later, Dayton, Ohio, was the first large city to adopt the reform system. Since the early 1900s, council-manager government has spread rapidly and is now the most popular and fastest growing system of government for U.S. cities with 2,500 or more residents (Hansell 2000, 17–21).

Currently, about 48 percent of all U.S. cities with populations greater than 2,500 operate under the council-manager form of government (Hansell 2000, 17–21). The comparable percentage for the mayor-council form is about 43 percent. The commission (2 percent), town meeting (5 percent), or representative town meeting (1 percent) forms are used in the remaining cities. Between 1984 and 2000, the percentage of cities preferring the council-manager form increased from 34.7 percent to 48.3 percent. Expressed another way, between 1984 and 2000 an average of sixty-three cities per year adopted the council-manager plan. During this time span, the mayor-council form of government decreased as the system of choice, from 55.8 percent of cities with populations over 2,500 in 1984 to 43.7 percent in 2000.

Unless state constitutional and/or statutory requirements place constraints on choice, citizens in communities throughout the United States are able to select not only the form of government they prefer but also other governmental structures such as ballot type and electoral system. As noted earlier, urban reformers advocated the council-manager plan as a way to promote the general interest of the city over the private, parochial interests of ward-based party politics. The city should be run like a business. These reformers also insisted on other reforms such as merit systems, at-large elections, nonpartisan ballots, and small city councils. As urban reformers had hoped, good government structures tend to be cumulative or additive in nature.[1]

Council-manager cities are much more common in small- to medium-sized communities; large cities (population over 500,000) tend to resist reform structures in general (except for the use of nonpartisan ballots and merit-based personnel systems) (Morgan and England 1999, 61). A few large cities do, however, use the council-manager form of government, such as Dallas, San Diego, San Jose, Oklahoma City, and Phoenix.

Region, type of city (central city, suburb, or independent), and social and economic characteristics are also linked to reformism (Morgan and England 1999, 61). Sun Belt cities of the South and West are more likely to employ the council-manager form of government. Central cities are more likely to operate under the mayor-council form. Communities with more homogeneous populations have a greater tendency to embrace the "good government" principles associated with council-manager government, particularly growing cities with white middle-class populations and cities with mobile populations. In contrast, ethnically diverse and industrial cities still prefer the more traditional mayor-council form of government.

Who Are City Managers?

In 2000, the International City/County Management Association (ICMA) surveyed appointed local government managers in all municipalities and counties with a population of 2,500. Responses are from county executives, town administrators, and chief administrative officers (CAOs) operating in mayor-council cities, as well as from city managers. Although survey results are not exclusively for city managers operating in council-manager cities, the results do represent the general pool of managers who are eligible to serve as a city/county manager or CAO and are reflective of the local government management profession.[2]

Most local managers (48 percent) fall into the 46–55 age bracket. Few of them are less than 41 years old (8 percent) or over 60 years old (6 percent). Ninety-five percent of managers are white. Today 2 percent of managers are African Americans, 2 percent are Hispanics, and 1 percent are Asian American, Native American, or belong to another ethnic group.

In 2000, 88 percent of managers were men. In 1974, only 1 percent of local managers were women. Gender diversification is proceeding, although slowly. Fox and Schuhmann (1999) suggest that this gender diversification may have important policy implications. They report that, compared with men, women city managers are more likely to incorporate citizen input in their decisions, are more likely to emphasize the importance of communication with citizens and with elected and appointed government officials in carrying out their duties, and are less likely to see themselves as policy entrepreneurs and more likely to see their role as that of manager and facilitator (Fox and Schuhmann 1999, 231–242). In sum, "Women in this study were more likely to value citizen input and would prefer to be in the middle of a 'web' of interactions rather than to be on top of the hierarchy" (p. 240).

Education levels of all local managers are extremely high, with 89 percent of them holding a bachelor's degree, 60 percent a master's degree, 2 percent a law degree, and 1 percent a doctorate. Managers in larger cities have the highest education levels.

The tenure of the average local manager has increased from 5.4 years in 1989 to 6.9 years in 2000. The average length of service has increased from 10.1 years in the 1989 survey to 17.4 years in 2000. These data show that the average city manager is remaining in his or her job 28 percent longer than was the case a decade ago and that average tenure in the profession has increased by 72 percent over the past decade. This growing job security and longevity may be just what is needed to provide an additional incentive to young people to enter what has traditionally been viewed as a "serve and move" profession.

In general, local managers seem to be a satisfied group, with 66 percent being moderately to highly satisfied with their positions.

What Do City Managers Do and How Do They Do It?

Beginning in the late 1880s, academicians created and fostered the concept—some say "myth" (Svara 2001)—of a "politics-administration dichotomy" to guide the development of the city management profession (as well as the larger field of public administration). According to this normative theory, the job of city council members is to formulate policy. The job of city managers and local bureaucrats, acting "above politics," is to execute or implement council policies in an apolitical, neutral fashion. The politics-administration dichotomy was a very important myth, as it allowed the fledgling discipline of public administration to distance itself from the fraud, corruption, and inefficiency associated with party politics and political machines at the turn of the nineteenth century.

In later years, a number of scholars questioned the validity of the politics-administration dichotomy, both on empirical and normative grounds. Numerous books and articles written in the past several decades have shown the extent to which city managers and local bureaucrats are involved in local politics and policymaking.[3] As Nalbandian (2000, 7) reminds us: "It has been acknowledged for a long time that city and county managers play a prominent role in policymaking. It can be no other way."

Svara (1998, 51–58) suggests that the politics-administration dichotomy model be viewed as an aberration. He asserts that the framers of the council-manager form of government called for a model of complementarity of politics and administration rather than a dichotomy of politics and administration. This interdependent model of shared policymaking responsibility between elected officials (mayors and city council members) and administrators (city managers and local bureaucrats) complements and, in fact, essentially defines the systems model of urban policymaking.

According to this model, urban policymakers working together respond to the wants, demands, and preferences of citizens and local groups. Environmental opportunities (for example, federal grants-in-aid and economic development initiatives) and constraints (such as taxing and spending limits and the city's economic base) help define the nature of local policies. Policies are made and shipped off to the citizenry for consumption, review, and comment. Citizens, in turn, respond with new wants, demands, and policy preferences, and the cycle continues. Or perhaps local policy-makers decide not to decide and offer no policy at all. Sometimes local decisions are better not made or delayed.

In essence, then, this is what city managers do now and have been doing since the inception of the council-manager form of government. They work with other policy-makers to develop policies and procedures that manage local conflict and deliver services to the citizenry.

From a more pragmatic, day-to-day operational point of view, according to the ICMA, city managers have four primary responsibilities (Morgan and England 1999, 99). First, they formulate policy on overall problems. Second, they prepare the local budget, present it to the council, and administer it after it has been approved by the council. Third, they appoint and remove department heads, such as the police chief and parks and recreation director. Finally, they form extensive external relationships to help resolve local issues and problems.

In a classic study of city managers, Deil Wright (1969, 218) suggests that city managers' duties can be grouped in three categories—managerial, policy related, and political. Managerial tasks include daily execution of city policies and the budget. In addition, the effective manager must provide guidance, develop, and support members of the various operating departments—the local bureaucracy. The policy-related role concerns the city manager's relationships with city council members and the mayor. These relationships are important not only for the development of sound public policy but also for the manager's tenure: a city manager serves at the pleasure of a majority of the council. Finally, in the political role the city manager must interact, bargain, negotiate, and probably compromise with numerous other individuals and groups. Sometimes these individuals represent other governmental units—county, school district, state, and federal officials. Sometimes they are individuals and groups within the city, such as neighborhood associations, interest groups, local unions, and representatives of various social, fraternal, and business organizations.

How much time is devoted to each of these three basic categories of tasks? In a study of city executives, Newell and Ammons (1987, 250) note that city managers spend about 50 percent of their time performing managerial duties, about 32 percent in policy-related activities, and about 17 percent in political activities. Interestingly, this equates with the amount of time that city managers in the survey indicated they wanted to spend on each of the tasks. Building upon a rich tradition of empirical studies (Morgan and England 1999, 101–102), recent research continues to elucidate the policy-related role city managers must maintain with city councils and mayors.

Council-Manager Relations. In the 2000 ICMA survey discussed above, almost one-half (47 percent) of the city managers ranked their council as highly supportive (Renner 2001, 41–43). Another 15 percent said council support was moderate to high. About one-third of the city managers felt the relationship with their councils had improved, with most reporting no change, and 8 percent said the relationship had worsened. How effective are the councils in the eyes of the city executives? About 84 percent of them believe that their council performs its duties very effectively.

Svara (1999) examines city council and city manager roles and relationships in cities with populations over 200,000. He finds that traditional boundaries between elected council members and city managers are blurred and shifting in large council-manager cities. City council members are increasingly becoming more involved in administration and management, whereas the city manager and staff are more involved in setting the mission of the city and long-range plans. Svara labels this city council–city manager pattern of interactions "activist-initiator," with council members active proponents of policies to solve problems and city managers involved in initiating broad-range, long-term as well as middle-range polices. "It appears that council members want to maintain greater control by being involved in determining the details of policy and implementation . . . they are concerned about the 'devil in the details'" (p. 50).

Does this apparent role reversal, with administrators making policy and elected officials implementing policy, threaten democracy? After all, city managers are not elected and cannot be held directly accountable for their actions at the ballot box. Svara suggests not: "The interaction between city managers and elected officials is so extensive and the interface is so close that the behavior of city managers necessarily affects the democratic process"(p. 51).

Research by Selden, Brewer, and Brudney (1999) supports Svara's "complementarity model of politics and administration." Based on a survey of about 1,000 city managers, they suggest that although city council members posses the means to control city managers (evaluations and oversight, for example), most councils opt "for less complex solutions involving trust and role sharing" (p. 124). The authors offer a typology of city manager roles based on their involvement in the policy process and the extent of autonomy exercised. Not surprisingly, most of the city managers in the sample are classified as "active managers" (70 percent); they have high degrees of autonomy and are extensively involved in policy initiation and development. "Based on Svara's historical account of the council-manager form of government, this 'active' city manager comports with the intent of the original framers of the council-manager form of government" (Selden, Brewer, and Brudney 1999, 142).

Manager-Mayor Relations. Theoretically, mayors in a council-manager form of government are "weak." Many are not even chosen directly by the people; they are selected by their peers, other council members. They do not formulate or implement the budget, which is viewed as the official statement of the allocation of values. Nor does the mayor run the city on a day-to-day basis. This is what the council hired the city manager to do. Nonetheless, research suggests that the role of the mayor in the council-manager city is important. He or she can serve as the "stabilizer" that allows the system to operate efficiently and effectively (Svara 1994, 224).

Drawing on national survey data, Morgan and Watson (1992) analyze mayor-manager relations. In large cities, they find, managers and mayors often form teams. In smaller communities the city manager is more likely than the mayor to be the dominant leader, or the two officials act as a team. In about one-third of the cities, a "caretaker" management philosophy results in the lack of decisive local management leadership.

According to Svara, mayors in council-manager cities must be facilitators. "The facilitative mayor leads by empowering others—in particular, the council and the manager—rather than by seeking power for himself or herself; the mayor accomplishes objectives by enhancing the performance of others" (Svara and associates 1994, 6). Based on the "lessons learned" from case studies, Svara and Associates (pp. 236–237) suggests three characteristics of the mayor as a facilitative leader. The first characteristic is the mayor's attitude toward other officials. He or she must not attempt to control or diminish the contributions made by other officials, must empower others by soliciting their contributions and helping them achieve their goals, and must value and maintain mutual trust and respect. Second, the interactions fostered by the mayor as facilitative leader must promote open and honest communication, seek to manage conflict and resolve differences so that the mutual interests of all officials are advanced, be willing to share leadership and create partnerships, and foster an understanding of distinct roles and coordinate efforts among officials. Finally, in terms of the mayor's approach to goal setting, she or he must foster the creation of a shared vision, which incorporates not only his or her goals but also those of others, and promote a commitment to the shared vision (Svara and Associates 1994, 236–237).

Attention now turns to managerial duties, the work that consumes most of a city manager's time. In order to run the city, he or she must have the support and help of the local bureaucracy.

The Urban Bureaucracy

Bureaucracy is a way to organize and process work. Most large-scale organizations, public or private, use the bureaucratic model to deliver goods and services. Those who deliver goods and services are often called bureaucrats. This section begins with a discussion of the nature or characteristics of bureaucracy and then explains who bureaucrats are, what they do, and how they deliver goods and services.

What Is Bureaucracy?

The rise of modern bureaucracy (Riggs 1997, 347) temporally coincides with the urban reform movement. The urban reform movement was an American phenomenon aimed at making local government more honest and efficient, whereas the rise of modern bureaucracy was a process that literally transformed Western society. In fact, German sociologist Max Weber, regarded by many as the father of modern bureaucracy, "considered bureaucracy to be a major element in the rationalization of the modern world and the most important of all social processes" (Fry 1989, 30).

Writing from the late nineteenth century to the 1920s, Weber claimed that bureaucracy was the most rational and efficient form of organization. It is rational "because it involves control based on knowledge, it has clearly defined spheres of competence, it operates according to intellectually analyzable rules, and it has calculability in operations" (Fry 1989, 32). It is efficient because of its "precision, speed, consistency, availability of records, unity, rigorous coordination, and minimization of interpersonal friction, personnel costs, and material costs" (Fry 1989, 32). Weber provides an "ideal type" of bureaucratic organization. His model of organization is both descriptive (empirical), based in part on his German military service, and prescriptive (normative)—what ought to be. Terms of employment in Weber's ideal type of organization require that

- workers are personally free and work on a contractual basis.
- officials are appointed and not elected in order to limit the number of people to whom they are responsible (each worker should have only one direct supervisor).
- workers are hired for positions based on professional qualifications (knowledge, skills, and abilities).
- workers have a fixed salary and pension rights, which limits arbitrary actions by superiors.
- the position held by the worker is his or her sole occupation, which allows the further development of specialized skills and promotes loyalty to the organization.
- workers are offered a career structure, with promotion based on merit.
- the official is subject to unified control and disciplinary actions, with clearly articulated rules defining both control and disciplinary procedures. (Fry 1989, 3)

The purpose here is not to provide a critique of Weber's model. Suffice it to say that the "ideal" type of organization that he envisioned over a hundred years ago continues to capture many of the complexities and realities of modern-day large-scale organizations. These organizations are defined by hierarchy, specialization of tasks and functions, and are rule bound. For example, the model allows city services such as police, fire fighting, parks and recreation, sanitation, and public works to be organized by function. Brought into these functional departments are employees with specialized knowledge, skills, and abilities (KSAs). Today, regardless of size or location, most cities recruit, promote, and dismiss employees in accordance with civil service rules (Saltzstein 1995, 37–53). In turn, these employees deliver goods and services to the public, following rules, policies, and procedures.

Although Weber's "ideal type" of bureaucratic organization remains relevant to large-scale organizations today, his model is limited in contemporary practice in several ways. First, and perhaps most prominent, is the increased role of government bureaucracies in the modern, positive state. Although Weber acknowledged the power of bureaucracy, he did not have the opportunity to witness the tremendous growth of government in Europe and the United States beginning in the 1930s; he died in 1920 at the age of fifty-six. As discussed below, bureaucracy is now considered a powerful political actor in the managerial state. While bureaucracy remains a mainstay in the modern state, many tenets of the bureaucratic model offered by Weber and others have come under attack. Advocates of the new public management model (discussed later in this chapter) argue, for example, that modern bureaucracy is too hierarchical, too rule bound, and too controlling. The call is to modify twentieth-century bureaucratic structures and processes to make them more applicable to managing public organizations in the twenty-first century.

Who Are Bureaucrats?

As Charles Goodsell (1994) reminds us, government bureaucrats are "ordinary people." Urban bureaucrats include sanitation workers, receptionists at city halls, urban planners, code enforcement officers, and a host of other civil servants providing goods and services to the public. Many of these people interact directly with the public on a day-to-day basis. Michael Lipsky (1980) calls these government workers "street-level bureaucrats." These social workers, teachers, court officers, public health workers, and police, fire, and emergency medical professionals may provide the only interaction that people have with their local government. Relatively speaking, few people vote in local elections or contact local government officials.

Using Phoenix, Arizona, as an example, Figure 8-1 provides a representation of how a typical big city bureaucracy might be organized. Often recognized as one of the "best run" cities in the United States, Phoenix is one of the few cities in the nation with a population in excess of one million residents that has a council-manager form of government.[4] City manager Frank Fairbanks has been with the city in a number of management-related positions since 1972 and has served as the city manager since 1990. In 1994, he was recognized as one of *Governing* magazine's "Public Officials of the Year."

Figure 8–1 Organizational Chart—City of Phoenix, Arizona

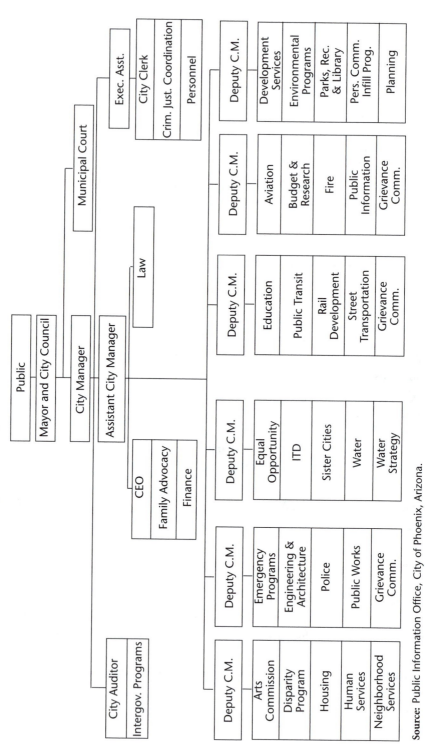

Source: Public Information Office, City of Phoenix, Arizona.

Note the many operating (police and public works, for example) and staff (auditor and personnel, for example) departments in the city. Given the size of Phoenix, the city manager needs many assistants to help him run the city on a day-to-day basis. Each deputy city manager has five department heads who report to him or her. The six deputy city managers report to the assistant city manager, who in turns reports to the city manager. The city manager works at the pleasure of the council. The various public services the city delivers to residents are divided into departments, meeting Weber's bureaucratic requirement of functional responsibility.

If we were to examine the organization of one of the operating departments in Phoenix, a good selection would be the fire department, which is often recognized as one of the best and most innovative in the nation. The fire department has several divisions, each performing a specialized function (among them, emergency medical services, operations, and community affairs). Within each division, personnel are hired on the basis of civil service rules and are considered classified (merit) employees. In performing their jobs, fire fighters follow specific guidelines provided by their training validation professional association (National Fire Protection Association), their organization, and the city. Many fire fighters stay with the city for twenty years and advance in rank (Weber's career system). Their rights and duties of employment are spelled out in the union contract that they negotiate with the city manager or his representative. Although Weber's ideal type of organization called for impersonal relationships between coworkers and with clientele, the informal organization (relationships based on convenience, in-group solidarity, professional ties, and so forth) in fire stations, and in most other city agencies, is strong. In Phoenix, the fire chief, the person at the top of the departmental hierarchy, insists that every citizen be treated in a very personal and professional fashion. From the chief's vantage point, the citizens own the fire department (Brunacini 1996).

What Do Bureaucrats Do and How Do They Do It?

What do bureaucrats do? In the case of a fire department, they put out fires, provide emergency medical services, make sure that public and commercial buildings meet fire codes, and educate children to "drop and roll." In short, bureaucrats deliver goods and services to the people.

But bureaucrats do more, much more. In the modern, positive (versus minimalist) state, bureaucrats make policy. Theodore Lowi, in fact, argues that the new urban machines, local bureaucracies, have replaced the old party-based machines discussed earlier. He asserts, *"The legacy of Reform is the bureaucratic city-state."*[5]

The urban reformers were successful in their efforts to clean up city government and eliminate city bosses. But the urban reform movement did more than this. According to Clarence Stone and his associates, "good government" reform efforts, in tandem with the rise of the modern (bureaucratic) state, resulted in a "clash of values" in urban policymaking—from a traditional to a modern outlook (Stone, Whelan, and Murin 1986, 103–105).

The traditional policymaking model was personal and intuitive. The machine was ward based, and one did what was necessary to take care of family, friends, and the neighborhood. Loyalty to the machine (party) resulted in its providing goods and benefits to individuals and/or neighborhoods. Service delivery patterns were not, however, guided by an overall urban general plan or for the betterment of the entire city per se. Political decisions were more intuitive, sentimental, and pragmatic.

In contrast, as suggested by Weber, modern bureaucracies are more impersonal. Sentiment and loyalty to family, friends, and/or the neighborhood do not drive urban policy decisions. The modern outlook is based on formal knowledge, professionally learned policies and procedures, and a detached, technical, and scientific approach to problem solving. The modern outlook is based on the assumption "that local government is a mechanism through which collective problems can be solved, services provided, and social change directed" (Stone, Whelan, and Murin 1986, 105).

In order to solve modern technical issues and problems, specialized knowledge is required. Urban administrative officials are key policymaking figures because they possess the knowledge to address local issues and problems. They have the ability to make the rules and regulations and develop the policies and procedures needed to implement urban public policies. As discussed earlier, many bureaucrats work at the street level and bring services directly to the people. In the day-to-day implementation of urban policies, these street-level bureaucrats exercise discretion and, in doing so, literally shape the nature and meaning of the policies.

Meier (2000) offers a lucid explanation for the growth of bureaucratic power in the positive state and, in doing so, answers the question, What do bureaucrats do? First, the nature of politics requires the expertise of bureaucracies to solve all kinds of problems—social, economic, cultural, and political. Who gets what, when, where, and how (Lasswell 1936) are political questions being answered by urban bureaucracies. The organization of city governments makes bureaucrats good, stable allies and is another reason for their power. Because agencies deliver goods and services that are consumed by or regulate the various interests, it benefits citizens and interest groups to support and develop relationships in administrative agencies. According to Meier, task demands also serve to enhance bureaucratic power. Current task demands of city governments require expert knowledge, a need fulfilled by bureaucrats. Finally, the bureaucracy gains power because of the nature of the bureaucratic function. Although bureaucracy is involved in all stages of the public policy process, the primary function of administrative agencies is to implement public policy. Since legislation is often vague and general, "The function of bureaucracy is to fill in the gaps of official policy, and filling in the gaps means the exercise of discretion" (Meier 2000, 47). This discretion is exercised in making administrative rules and regulations, in determining the interpretation of standard operating procedures, and in implementing policies at the street level.

In sum, bureaucracy is a policymaking institution. In the modern, positive state, bureaucracy must assume this policymaking role.

Contemporary Issues and Theories Affecting City Management

In the 2000 ICMA "State of the Profession" survey, managers were asked to rate the importance of twenty-five urban policy issues (Renner 2001, 43–45). Providing a quality educational system was the policy area that received the highest percentage of "very important" responses (47 percent). The next four highest-rated "very important" policy areas were finding creative ways to generate new revenues (34 percent), hiring and retaining qualified employees (30 percent), aging/deteriorating infrastructure (28 percent), and growth management (25 percent).

A number of other policy areas cited in the survey certainly seem to be issues and challenges to city managers. These include citizen involvement in local government (40 percent), effective use/management of information technology (39 percent), providing health coverage for employees (38 percent), drug prevention, enforcement, and related programs (38 percent), and air and/or water quality (36 percent).

A number of theories currently affect the city management profession. The promises and limitations of one notable model are discussed in this section. As Robert Behn (1998) notes, what we generically refer to here as the new public management (NPM) model (Hood 1991) is called different things by different people. NPM has been referred to as "civic-regarding entrepreneurship" (Bellone and Goerl 1992), the "post-bureaucratic paradigm" (Barzelay and Aramajani 1992), "managerialism" (Hughes 1998), and "neo-managerialism" (Terry 1998). It was journalist David Osborne and former city manager Ted Gaebler's label "reinventing government" (REGO), however, that popularized NPM and captured the fancy of the popular press and the attention of elected officials at all levels of government.

In their book *Reinventing Government: How the Entrepreneurial Spirit Is Transforming the Public Sector,* Osborne and Gaebler (1992) provide stories of how public officials are using total quality management (TQM) principles and market-based theories to transform the nature and functioning of government. They offer a ten-principle prescription for "reinventing government." Government should be a *catalyst,* directing activities more than running programs; *community owned,* involving and empowering clients and citizens; *competitive,* encouraging and promoting competition in service delivery; *mission driven,* stressing overall goals while minimizing rules and requirements; *results oriented,* concerned more with outcomes and less with inputs or resources used; *customer driven,* treating service recipients as valued customers; *enterprising,* interested in earning as well as spending money; *anticipatory,* preventing problems instead of merely curing them; *decentralized,* flattening the organizational hierarchy to encourage more participation and teamwork among employees; and *market oriented,* leveraging change by using government incentives to affect market behavior.

The NPM model, or paradigm, is based on what Gill and Meier call "neoconservative economics" (Gill and Meier 2001). These market-based theories, in general, assume that a rational person will seek to maximize benefits and minimize costs, thereby enhancing efficient use of scarce resources (Hughes 1998, 10–14). The market-based models do not always hold for bureaucrats (Buchanan and Tullock 1962; Downs 1967; Niskanen 1994). Rather, given the lack of a well-defined tool (that is, profits) to measure success, bureaucrats may maximize their own utility—power, prestige, income, agency budget. Also, the NPM places a heavy emphasis on reducing the size of government through contracting. In short, neoconservative economics is based on the assumption that better public policy outcomes involve "a maximum role for market forces and a minimal role for government" (Hughes 1998, 11).

The serious student of urban politics and management should read and understand the theoretical literature critiquing the NPM model. The stakes—the survival of democracy in the administrative state—are too high not to do so. Kearney and associates offered the following assessment of the debate surrounding the movement (Kearney, Feldman, and Scavo 2000, 546):

The dimensions of reinvention are somewhat vague and changing, and it will be a work in progress rather than a finished product. . . . There are clear limits to the success of reinvention, many of them political. And certainly there are important concerns about the principles of reinvention that dilute accountability and threaten to undermine the public law basis of public administration. . . . Nonetheless, reinvention is an unavoidable issue for many—if not most—local governments in the United States. As the latest wave of administrative reform, it has strong legs that promise to carry it for many years to come.

To what extent have local governments been reinvented? What variables are associated with the propensity to reinvent? How successful have reinventing efforts been? Two recent studies provide responses to these questions.

Ruhil and associates studied reinventing efforts through a survey of about 800 municipal suburban communities in twenty different states (Ruhil, Schneider, Teske, and Ji 1999). Despite media and popular attention, "a substantial number of communities . . . reported zero reforms" (p. 436). The authors created four reform indexes: total reform activity (summarized across the sixteen policy innovations); civil service reforms (ten policy reforms); employee empowerment reforms (two policy reforms); and private-sector reforms (four policy reforms). For all cities, the mean number of reforms implemented is about four out of sixteen. In short, the extent of efforts to reinvent government, at least in suburban communities, according to the authors, is "muted" (pp. 437–438). They also found that

- the city manager is the single most important actor exerting influence on the adoption of reinventing-government policy innovations in his or her city. The presence of a city manager increased the probability of civil service reforms by 11 percent, employee empowerment by 9 percent, private-sector reforms by 11 percent, and overall reform activity by 7 percent.
- local interest groups, public-sector unions, and/or the use of district elections in a community also significantly enhanced the probability of a suburban municipality's adoption of the three types of policy reforms (civil service, employee empowerment, or private sector) or the total number of policy reforms adopted.

Richard Kearney and associates offer the second systematic study assessing efforts of local governments to implement the reinventing-government reform agenda and to identify the factors explaining the propensity to reinvent (Kearney, Feldman, and Scavo 2000). Their research is based on the reinvention sentiments and actions of about 900 city managers in U.S. cities with 10,000 or more residents. "As a group, managers express high levels of agreement with reinvention principles" (p. 542).

To what extent have city managers recommended that specific reinventing-government actions be included in their budgets? The twelve reinventing-government actions were summed into an additive scale (from none to all twelve actions). About 3 percent of the managers reported recommending all of the actions; about 8 percent recommended eleven or twelve; and 22 percent recommended ten or more actions. Less than 7 percent recommended three or fewer actions. The mean score of recommended actions was 7.4 out of twelve possible innovations. The best predictor is the city manager's attitude on reinventing government. Second, the longer a city manager has been in government service, the more likely it is that he or she will recommend reinventing-government actions in the municipal budget. City managers located in Sun Belt (southern and western) cities are more likely to make such recommendations. Cities with more full-time employees adopted more reforms.

Conclusion

This chapter has attempted to answer who, what, when, how, and why questions about city managers and local bureaucracies. The literature provides responses to these questions, using a rich variety of theories, contexts, and methods. Some responses are based on normative theory, and others are empirically defined. Case studies and the cross-sectional analysis of survey data seem to be the most prevalent methods used to study the nature and functioning of city managers and local bureaucracies. The responses offered are instructive but not definitive. Theories are tested, refined, and reformulated within the context of a body of knowledge. The body of knowledge about urban politics and management remains incomplete. But, as in previous chapters, the call to action here is limited to suggesting future research needs not for the general field of urban politics and management but for a slice of the area of inquiry—city managers and bureaucracies. The agenda for future research includes three items.

First, and foremost, we need to build on the research offered by Kearney and associates (2000) and Ruhil and associates (1999). These scholars have moved the debate about reinventing government from rhetoric to analysis. They offer models, variables, and methods that can be used to test empirically the assumptions of the new public management model. Much of the evidence about reinventing government is anecdotal and impressionistic. Much of the debate about the new public management model is normative. There is, and must be, room in the literature for the stories and the discourse, but we also must begin the process of modeling, explaining, and predicting the consequences of reinventing government.

The new public management model can serve as a mechanism to examine a number of topics of historical interest to urban scholars, such as diffusion of policy innovations; the impact of structural, economic, and demographic variables on urban policy development and implementation; and executive-bureaucratic relations, as city managers perform the task of directing bureaucratic activities. In other words, old as well as new issues can be tested using the NPM/REGO paradigm.

A second area for future research concerns the need for studies that offer more contextual findings. Organization theory and behavior scholars often remind us that much about management is situational or contingent (Gortner, Mahler, and Nicholson 1997). For example, organizational form follows function. Organizational structures and processes required for integration and coordination are dependent upon organizational differentiation and specialization. Those looking for the "one best" management model or practice will surely be disappointed by the realities of the real world, as will those looking to read a study and assume that the findings apply to all city managers in all cities at all points in time. A recent study illustrates the type of contextual research alluded to here.

Based on survey data and using multiple regression analysis, research by Crewson and Fisher (1997) indicates how the skill and knowledge needs of city administrators evolve as they gain experience, migrate from smaller to larger jurisdictions, and interact with differing political environments. Crewson and Fisher create an "art-science" knowledge preference variable, using several questions for each type of knowledge. The "art" designation, not surprisingly, is for knowledge and skills of a less scientific nature such as politics, human relations, community building, and negotiating/bargaining. The "science" designation is for more administrative applications such as financial analysis and statistics. Findings show that administrators in council-manager governments and managers with graduate degrees prefer skills in the art rather than the science of public administration, whereas managers from smaller jurisdictions or those with less experience rate the importance of science skills as more important than the art of public administration. Early- and mid-career managers are more likely to need skills rather than art knowledge, regardless of a city's form of government or the individual's years of experience. The opposite is generally true for managers working in large cities.

The final agenda item for future research on city managers and the urban bureaucracy is the call to replicate previous research. We should not be afraid to ask or study the same questions again. This is exactly what Nalbandian (1999) did in a recent study. In the early 1990s, he interviewed a number of city and county managers to determine the nature of the profession. Based on these interviews, he concluded that the city management profession by the early 1990s had transformed itself over the previous several decades in three important ways. The profession had

moved from an orthodox view of a dichotomy between politics and administration to the sharing of functions between elected and appointed officials; from political neutrality and formal accountability to political sensitivity and responsiveness to community values themselves; and from efficiency as the core value to efficiency, representation, individual rights, and social equity as a complex array of values anchoring professionalism (Nalbandian 1999, 188).

In the late 1990s, Nalbandian interviewed many of the old as well as new city and county managers to determine contemporary roles, responsibilities, and values of the profession. He concludes that much has changed over the ten years. The now-and-then analysis reveals the following changes: Community building has become part of the city management professional's responsibility; managers are expected to facilitate participation and representation and to develop partnerships; there is less adherence to council-manager government as the "one best form" of government; and the manager's internal administrative role has become more process oriented.

As students of urban politics and management, we have the responsibility to ask questions. They can be old questions studied again or old questions asked again in a new way. Or the questions may be new, as we frame the issues that will define the discipline at the dawn of the twenty-first century.

Suggested Readings

Ammons, David N. 2002. *Tools for Decision Making: A Practical Guide for Local Government.* Washington, D.C.: CQ Press. An indispensable guide to practical techniques of analysis that can be used by city practitioners to address everyday problems encountered in managing local governments.

Goodsell, Charles T. 1994. *The Case for Bureaucracy.* 3d ed. New York: Chatham House. A much needed antidote to the "bureaucratic bashing" literature.

Kaufman, Herbert. 2001. "Major Players: Bureaucracies in American Government." *Public Administration Review* 61 (January–February): 18–42. This article, written by one of America's most influential scholars of public administration, offers a succinct and precise statement on the nature and functioning of American bureaucracy.

Meier, Kenneth J. 2000. *Politics and the Bureaucracy: Policymaking in the Fourth Branch of Government.* 4th ed. New York: Harcourt, Brace. Required reading for those who wish to understand the politics of bureaucracy.

Morgan, David R., and Robert E. England. 1999. *Managing Urban America.* 5th ed. New York: Chatham House. This textbook provides an overview of the issues, politics, and processes associated with managing American cities and towns.

Schachter, Hindy Lauer. 1997. *Reinventing Government or Reinventing Ourselves.* Albany: SUNY Press. The author reminds us that democracy requires an active, participatory citizenry.

References

Ammons, David N., and Charldean Newell. 1989. *City Executives.* Albany: State University of New York.

Banfield, Edward C., and James Q. Wilson. 1963. *City Politics.* New York: Knopf.

Barzelay, Michael, and Babak Aramajani. 1992. *Breaking through Bureaucracy: A New Vision for Managing Government.* Berkeley: University of California Press.

Behn, Robert D. 1998. "What Right Do Public Managers Have to Lead?" *Public Administration Review* 58 (May–June): 209–224.

Bellone, Carl J., and George Frederick Goerl. 1992. "Reconciling Entrepreneurship and Democracy." *Public Administration Review* 52 (March–April): 130–134.

Boynton, Robert P. 1976. "City Councils: Their Role in the Legislative System." In *The Municipal Year Book 1976.* Washington, D.C.: ICMA, 67–77.

Brunacini, Alan V. 1996. "Essentials of Fire Department Customer Service." Stillwater, Okla.: Fire Protection Publications.

Buchanan, James A., and Gordon Tullock. 1962. *The Calculus of Consent: The Logical Foundations of Constitutional Democracy.* Ann Arbor: University of Michigan.

Crewson, Philip E., and Bonnie S. Fisher. 1997. "Growing Older and Wiser: The Changing Skill Requirements of City Administrators." *Public Administration Review* 57 (September–October): 380–386.

Downs, Anthony. 1967. *Inside Bureaucracy.* Boston: Little, Brown.

Easton, David. 1953. *The Political System.* New York: Knopf.

Fox, Richard L., and Robert A. Schuhmann. 1999. "Gender and Local Government: A Comparison of Women and Men City Managers." *Public Administration Review* 59 (May–June): 231–242.

Fry, Brian R. 1989. *Mastering Public Administration.* Chatham, N.J.: Chatham House.

Gill, Jeff., and Kenneth J. Meier. 2001. "Ralph's Pretty-Good Grocery versus Ralph's Super Market: Separating Excellent Agencies from the Good Ones." *Public Administration Review* 61 (January–February): 9–17.

Goodsell, Charles T. 1994. *The Case for Bureaucracy.* 3d ed. Chatham, N.J.: Chatham House.

Gortner, Harold F., Julianne Mahler, and Jeanne Bell Nicholson. 1997. *Organization Theory: A Public Perspective* 2d ed. New York: Harcourt, Brace.

Hansell Jr., William H. "Council-Manager Government: A Form Whose Time Has Come . . . Again." http://icma.org/download/cat15/grp120/sgp186/114565.htm

——— 2000. "Evolution and Change Characterize Council-Manager Government." *Public Management* 82 (August): 17–21.

Herson, Lawrence J. R., and John M. Bolland. 1998. *The Urban Web: Politics, Policy, and Theory.* 2d ed. Chicago: Nelson-Hall.

Hofstadter, Richard. 1955. *The Age of Reform.* New York: Knopf.

Hood, Christopher. 1991. "A Public Management for All Seasons." *Public Administration* 69 (spring): 3–19.

Hughes, Owen E. 1998. *Public Management and Administration: An Introduction.* 2d ed. New York: St. Martin's Press.

Judd, Dennis R., and Todd Swanstrom. 1998. *City Politics: Private Power and Public Policy,* 2d ed. New York: Longman.

Kaufman, Herbert. 2001. "Major Players: Bureaucracies in American Government." *Public Administration Review* 61(January–February): 18–42.

Kearney, Richard C., Barry M. Feldman, and Carmine P. F. Scavo. 1999. "Reinventing Government: City Manager Attitudes and Actions." *Public Administration Review* 60 (November–December): 535–547.

Lasswell, Harold. 1936. *Politics: Who Gets What, When, and How.* New York: McGraw-Hill.

Lineberry, Robert, and Edmund Fowler. 1967. "Reformism and Public Policies in American Cities." *American Political Science Review* 61 (September): 701–716.

Lipsky, Michael. 1980. *Street-Level Bureaucracy: Dilemmas of the Individual in Public Services.* New York: Russell Sage.

Lowi, Theodore J. 1984. "Machine Politics—Old and New." In *Readings in Urban Politics.* 2d ed. Ed. Harlan Hahn and Charles H. Levine, 98–105. New York: Longman.

Meier, Kenneth J. 2000. *Politics and the Bureaucracy: Policymaking in the Fourth Branch of Government.* 4th ed. New York: Harcourt.

Morgan, David, and John Pelissero. 1980. "Urban Policy: Does Political Structure Matter?" *American Political Science Review* 74 (December): 999–1006.

Morgan, David R., and Sheilah S. Watson. 1992. "Policy Leadership in Council-Manager Cities: Comparing Mayor and Manager." *Public Administration Review* 52 (September–October): 438–445.

Morgan, David R., and Robert E. England. 1999. *Managing Urban America.* 5th ed. New York: Chatham House.

Nalbandian, John. 1999. "Facilitating Community, Enabling Democracy: New Roles for Local Government Managers." *Public Administration Review* 59 (May–June): 187–197.

——— 2000. "The Manager as Political Leader: A Challenge to Professionalism?" *Public Management* 82 (March): 7–12.

Newell, Charldean, and David N. Ammons. 1987. "Role Emphases of City Managers and Other Municipal Executives." *Public Administration Review* 47 (May–June): 246–253.

Niskanen, William A. 1994. *Bureaucracy and Public Economics.* Aldershot, England: Edward Elgar.

Osborne, David, and Ted Gaebler. 1992. *Reinventing Government: How the Entrepreneurial Spirit Is Transforming the Public Sector.* Reading, Mass: Addison-Wesley.

Renner, Tari. 2001. "The Local Government Management Profession at Century's End." In *The Municipal Year Book 2001.* Washington, D.C.: ICMA, 35–46.

Riggs, Fred W. 1997. "Modernity and Bureaucracy." *Public Administration Review* 57 (July–August): 347–353.

Ruhil, Anirudh V. S., Mark Schneider, Paul Teske, and Byung-Moon Ji. 1999. "Institutions and Reform: Reinventing Local Government." *Urban Affairs Review* 34 (January): 433–455.

Saltzstein, Alan. 1995. "Personnel Management in the Local Government Setting." In *Public Personnel Administration: Problems and Prospects*, 3d ed., ed. Steven W. Hays and Richard C. Kearney, 37–53. Englewood Cliffs, N.J.: Prentice Hall.

Selden, Sally Coleman, Gene A. Brewer, and Jeffrey L. Brudney. 1999. "The Role of City Managers: Are They Principals, Agents, or Both?" *American Review of Public Administration* 29 (June): 124–148.

Stone, Clarence N., Robert K. Whelan, and William J. Murin. 1986. *Urban Policy and Politics in a Bureaucratic Age.* 2d ed. Englewood Cliffs, N.J.: Prentice Hall.

Svara, James H. 1987. "Mayoral Leadership in Council-Manager Cities: Preconditions versus Preconceptions." *Journal of Politics* 49 (February): 207–227.

———— 1998. "The Politics-Administration Dichotomy Model as Aberration." *Public Administration Review* 58 (January–February): 51–58.

———— 1999. "The Shifting Boundary between Elected Officials and City Managers in Large Council-Manager Cities." *Public Administration Review* 59 (January–February): 44–53.

———— 2001. "The Myth of the Dichotomy: Complementarity of Politics and Administration in the Past and Future of Public Administration." *Public Administration Review* 61 (March–April): 176–183.

Svara, James H., and Associates. 1994. *Facilitative Leadership in Local Government: Lessons From Successful Mayors and Chairpersons.* San Francisco: Jossey-Bass.

Terry, D. Larry. 1998. "Administrative Leadership, Neo-Manageralism, and the Public Management Movement." *Public Administration Review* 58 (May–June): 194–200.

Wright, Deil S. 1969. "The City Manager as a Development Administrator." In *Comparative Urban Research: The Administration and Politics of Cities*, ed. Robert T. Daland. Beverly Hills, Calif.: Sage, 208–248.

Notes

1. Several classic studies, for example, add reform features (for example, a council-manager form of government, at-large elections, a small city council) to create a reformism measure. See Robert Lineberry and Edmund Fowler, "Reformism and Public Policies in American Cities," *American Political Science Review* 61 (September 1967): 701–716; and David Morgan and John Pelissero, "Urban Policy: Does Political Structure Matter?" *American Political Science Review* 74 (December 1980): 999–1006.

2. Unless otherwise noted, all data in this section about city managers comes from Tari Renner, "The Local Government Management Profession at Century's End," *The Municipal Year Book 2001* (Washington, D.C.: ICMA, 2001), 35–46.

3. For a concise review of the historical development of the politics-administration dichotomy debate and a review of early research addressing the dichotomy, see David N. Ammons and Charldean Newell, *City Executives* (Albany: State University of New York, 1989), 41–52. For a more recent study addressing the involvement of city managers in politics, see Sally Coleman Selden, Gene A. Brewer, and Jeffery L. Brudney, "The Role of City Managers: Are They Principals, Agents, or Both?" *American Review of Public Administration* 29 (June 1999): 124–148.

4. Much of the information about Phoenix, Arizona, is derived from the city's Web site and personal contacts with city officials. The Web site is http://www.ci.phoenix.az.us.

5. Theodore J. Lowi, "Machine Politics—Old and New," in *Readings in Urban Politics*, 2d ed., ed. Harlan Hahn and Charles H. Levine (New York: Longman, 1984), 98–105. Emphasis in the original.

9   The Politics of Revenue and Spending Policies

Robert M. Stein

The governance of cities was an afterthought in the writing of the U.S. Constitution. The Constitution makes no mention of cities, towns, villages, or any other type of local government. The federal and state governments were preeminently on the minds of those who wrote, debated, and ratified the document that governs our nation. Local government was left to the states to create, regulate, and, when necessary, eliminate.[1] Consequently, it should come as no surprise that those who study the politics of local taxing and spending focus on the subsidiary role of cities in the American federal system. Students of urban governance have long debated whether the taxing and spending decisions of cities are significantly constrained by their subordinate position. Some argue that politics has a negligible role in the formulation of urban taxing and spending decisions and that cities are in every sense creations of higher-level government. States heavily regulate the scope, content, and means by which cities fulfill the policy demands of their citizens.[2] As a consequence, local politics (that is, the representation of local demands) has a very muted effect on the taxing and spending decisions of local governments.

This chapter reviews the literature on the politics of urban taxing and spending decisions. It centers on the debate over whether and how politics shapes the scope and content of these policies. For the purposes of this essay, politics is defined as the process by which individual and/or group preferences shape the government's authoritative allocation of scarce resources (taxing and spending decisions), perhaps the most important policy outputs of the urban political system (see Lasswell 1936).

Local governments have the legal authority to tax their residents and to make decisions that are legally binding on them. There is a limit, however, to the amount of revenue cities can raise through taxation, because everyone prefers to be taxed less rather than more. In addition, local residents preferences for taxing and spending are both diverse and subject to change. Consequently, decisions on these matters are the subject of considerable debate and sometimes bitter contention. Without the local government's legal authority to make binding policy decisions, competing interests would subject cities to political instability.

The first section of this chapter reviews the basic features of urban public finance, identifying the principal sources of municipal revenues and the functions that cities finance. The second section reviews the major theories of urban public finance and supporting empirical evidence for these theories. This section concludes with a discussion of the paradox present in many municipalities: despite theoretically sound advice and supporting evidence, they pursue popular policies that seem to undermine the community's economic and social well-being. How is this possible? The third section offers an answer to this paradox and an alternative explanation of how cities cope with it.

Basic Features of Municipal Revenue and Spending Policies

With some notable exceptions, the basic features of municipal revenue and spending policies have remained largely unchanged over the past fifty years. Moreover, municipal governments draw from a variety of revenue sources but spend their revenues on a relatively narrow range of goods and services.

Revenue Sources

Municipal governments draw upon several sources to finance their public policy outputs. In addition to state and federal aid, these include a variety of taxes, including taxes on property (mainly residential and commercial) and on income (both personal and business), the sale of goods and services, fees and charges for the use of specific goods and services, and bonded indebtedness. State law often governs the specific mix of these revenue sources available to local governments. It is important to distinguish between the sources of municipal revenues. Individuals and businesses residing, working, or partaking in recreation in the community provide revenues such as property taxes and fees. Other revenues, such as federal and state aid, originate outside the community and are paid in part by entities other than residents of the community. Figure 9-1 shows the percentage of total municipal revenues from selected tax and user-fee sources.

The largest single own source of revenues for all municipal governments is a tax on residential and personal property (for example, home furnishings). City governments have traditionally preferred levying taxes on property, because, unlike personal income, it is not mobile and its value can be more readily assessed. Historically the property tax has been the workhorse of municipal governments, though its dominance has waned considerably over the past forty years. In 1962 the property tax accounted for half of all revenues and nearly all tax revenues raised by municipal governments in the United States. In 1998, however, the percentage of own-source revenues and tax revenues raised through property declined to below 40 percent.

The second largest reserve of own-source revenues is fees and charges. These include water, garbage, and sewerage services and charges for the use of parks and other

Figure 9-1   Own Source Local Government Revenues, 1998–1999

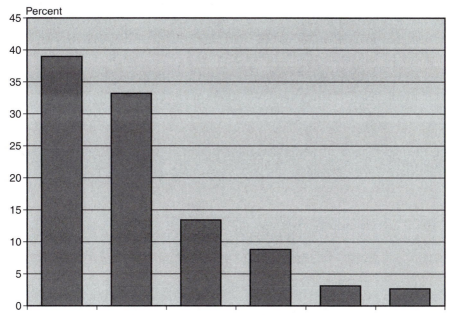

Source: U.S. Bureau of the Census, *Government Finances, 1998–1999* (Washington, D.C.: U.S. Government Printing Office), 1999. Available at http://www.census.gov/govs/estimate/ 99allpub.pdf.

facilities such as golf courses and municipal swimming pools. Sales tax and other taxes, including personal income and corporate income taxes, constitute a smaller portion of the own-source municipal revenues.

An external source of funding is federal and state aid, which comes in a variety of forms, often with mandates and conditions that require the recipient government to perform certain functions. Historically, federal assistance to cities has focused on social services (health, education, and welfare) that redress the fiscal disparities between center city residents and their suburban neighbors. Federal assistance to cities reached its highest point during President Lyndon B. Johnson's Great Society and War on Poverty initiatives during the 1960s. Since 1964, federal assistance to cities has declined steadily. Now a large portion of federal assistance to cities is transferred directly to state governments, which disburse these moneys to cities and other localities. State aid to municipal governments generally comes from funds raised by states on their own taxing authority. States generally levy a tax on the sale of goods and services. These taxes are collected by local merchants and businesses and remitted to the state government. In turn, the state governments return a portion of sales tax receipts to the jurisdictions where the sales were made. Another significant purpose of state aid is to fund local primary and secondary education, highway construction and maintenance, and public assistance.

In addition to tax revenues and user fees, municipal governments have variable authority to borrow money. The ability of local governments to incur debt is generally regulated by state law. Cities incur debt by means of general obligation bonds and revenue bonds. A general obligation bond allows municipalities to borrow in the commercial credit market. The amount lent (the principal) and the interest paid to the lender are repaid by the city's authority to tax its residents. This is sometimes known as the *full faith and credit* of the city. This type of borrowing mechanism is attractive to lenders, because they enjoy certain tax advantages (for example, income from a general obligation bond is free from federal income taxes), and the income from the interest and repayment of the principal are generally assured, providing a high degree of safety for the lender. General obligations bonds enable cities to borrow funds in the commercial credit market, but under restrictions imposed by the state.

One significant restriction on the use of general obligation bonds is the need for voter approval through a public referendum. These referenda set limits on the amount of money that can be borrowed and the functions for which it can be used. These restrictions are sufficiently onerous to make many cities seek other means of borrowing money that are not restricted by voter approval and state-imposed requirements. An increasingly popular alternative is the revenue bond, which generally does not require voter approval. Revenue bonds raise money for specific projects and are often issued to pay for capital projects such as the construction of roads, buildings, and other large structures. The repayment of these bonds is made from the revenues generated by the newly constructed facility. Construction of many municipal stadiums, parking garages, and roads is funded from moneys generated by use of the constructed facility (for example, tolls on new roadways).

As previously noted, the relative importance of these revenue sources has changed over time. An overwhelming majority of local revenues traditionally came from property taxes. Today, however, revenue generated from user fees and bonds is often greater than that obtained from the property tax. There are several reasons why U.S. cities have reduced their reliance on the property tax. First, it is a regressive tax. This means that the poor and the middle class often pay a much higher percentage of their personal income on personal and residential property taxes than the wealthiest citizens do. As a result, the property tax is one of the most unpopular forms of taxation levied by any level of government (Conlan 1998).

The regressive nature of the property tax is particularly troublesome for low-income and property-poor communities. Communities, like individuals, can be described in terms of the value of their personal property. A community's tax base is the sum of all property values to be taxed in that locality. Two communities of equal size but with very different tax bases present a picture of disparity and unequal access to basic goods and services. Consider two hypothetical cities, Dorchester and Exeter, each composed of 50,000 households. The tax base of Exeter is $1.5 billion, but that of Dorchester is only $1 billion. Assuming both communities provide the same functions and services for their citizens, the per capita cost to Dorchester's residents will be 33 percent higher than it is for the people in Exeter. If Dorchester prefers to maintain a lower tax per household, the city can, of course, choose not to provide its residents with certain services, but this choice would deprive the community of some services. Efforts to reduce and eliminate the regressiveness of the property tax by providing exemptions for the poor and the elderly have succeeded in equalizing the percentage of personal income paid in property taxes across households with different incomes.[3]

Second, the property tax is an inefficient form of taxation. The assignment of property values is a complicated, contentious, and expensive activity that is essential to the levying and raising of these taxes. In some cases, citizens in many communities have protested what they see as arbitrary and unfair tax assessments. This has resulted in the establishment of assessment boards to oversee the process and appeal procedures to ensure that citizens' complaints are heard. One consequence of these safety nets is the increased cost of levying the property tax.

Accompanying the decline in municipal governments' reliance on the property tax is the rise of user fees, bond indebtedness, especially revenue bonds, and taxes on income, both personal and business. Bond indebtedness refers to the amount of principal and interest that cities owe to lenders. This indebtedness is repaid over a fixed period of time (for example, fifteen years) from taxes and other revenues raised by the city. User fees and bonded indebtedness, however, have significant administrative and political advantages over the traditional property tax. Indebtedness of any sort allows the municipal borrower to obtain immediate benefits (and political gratification) without an immediate expenditure by taxpayers. Like any private consumer, cities like to "buy now and pay later." Bonds enable cities to pay at a later time for what the city and its residents can receive immediately. An electorate grateful for benefits they do not immediately have to pay for in full is likely to show its gratitude by reelecting incumbent officeholders. Bonds, especially revenue bonds, are paid for with future revenues and by future taxpayers and voters. This practice allows politicians to shift forward the cost of benefits they bestow on the citizenry.

Functional Spending

Figure 9-2 reports the mean percentage of total municipal expenditures by selected functions. Two important observations can be made about the scope and content of

Figure 9-2   Total Expenditures for Selected Services: Cities over 25,000 in Population, 1990

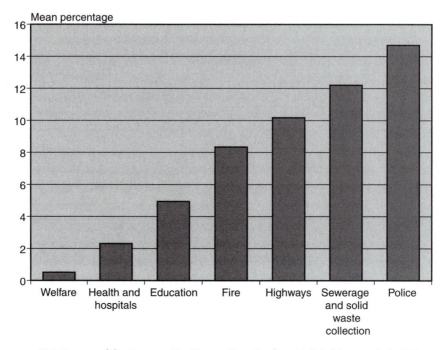

Source: U.S. Bureau of the Census, *City/County Data Book*, 1994 (Washington, D.C.: U.S. Government Printing Office). 1994.

municipal functional responsibility. First, cities are largely responsible for a narrow range of functions. These are confined to basic, or "housekeeping" activities and services essential to the operation of any municipality. Public safety (police and fire) and roads and utilities (water, solid waste collection, and sewerage) dominate the spending of municipal governments. These are services that individual citizens cannot readily purchase and consume privately, making some form of collective action necessary.

Also indicated in Figure 9-2 is the limited scope of municipal responsibility and level of spending for many social services, including public health programs, hospitals, and general welfare. Several of the theories of municipal taxing and spending policy discussed in this chapter explain the paucity of municipal spending on social services as being both desirable and a product of the constraints placed on cities by their state governments and their unique position in the American federal system. Other explanations of municipal taxing and spending policy, however, argue that the limited spending for social services is neither desirable nor inevitable and can be reversed.

Although the property tax remains the main source of revenues for municipal governments, its dominance has declined over the past several decades. User fees, bond indebtedness, and intergovernmental aid transfers have increased in size and importance for municipal governments. Their spending has been constrained to a narrow range of basic goods and services. Cities have some responsibility, albeit limited, for social services.

Theories of Municipal Fiscal Policies

Several prominent theories and explanations of the politics of urban revenue and expenditure policies can be identified in the literature. Central to each of these theories is a single question: who has the power to makes decisions in the city? The first two, the elitist and the pluralist theories, are competing explanations. A third, market theory, comes from the field of economics and explains urban public policies in those terms. The remaining literature reviewed examines institutional explanations of the politics of taxing and spending policies in U.S. cities.

Elitist Theory

Sociologists were among the early students of local government who asked, Who has the power to make decisions? Helen and Robert Lynd provided an answer to this question in their comprehensive study of local decision making in Muncie, Indiana. With the publication of *Middletown* (1929), the Lynds put forth an explanation of local decision making that emphasized the importance of individuals—specifically elites—whose powerful positions in the community enabled them to influence, if not determine, policy decisions. In the case of Muncie, the Lynds identified a local business family whose financial interests in the community were so dominant that their preferences on various public policies strongly influenced the decisions of local elected officials. The Lynds' analysis focused on economic elites, reasoning that those who control capital and the hiring of labor are instrumental, if not dominant, in the public sector. Subsequent work by Floyd Hunter on Atlanta (1953; 1963; 1980) and national studies by C. Wright Mills (1956) and G. William Domhoff (1967) established the power-elite thesis of government decision making. Extending the Lynds' work, these scholars identified the power elite as

composed of men whose positions enable them to transcend the ordinary environments of ordinary men and women; they are in positions to make decisions having major consequences. . . . [E]lites are among the wealthiest, most celebrated people. . . . [A] power elite "creates" demands and causes others to meet them. (Mills 1956)

Hunter provided an important addition to elite theory by devising a standard methodology for identifying the power elite. He asked individuals from four groups—business, government, civic associations, and "society"—who, in their opinion, were members of the community's power elite. The reputational technique provided researchers with a low-cost method for identifying community elites. This methodology solidified the prominence of an elite explanation of local decision making during the 1960s and 1970s. It allowed for an empirical test of elite theory by examining the congruence between the taxing and spending decisions of local governments and the preferences of those identified as the power elite. When researchers could not establish this relationship, they would conveniently explain the nonfindings in terms of their failure to properly identify elites in the community.

Elite theory also provided a convenient explanation for the significant social disparity that existed and continues to pervade American society. Disparities in the distribution of wealth and public services, particularly between Anglo and non-Anglo populations, have conveniently been explained in terms of a self-interested power elite. Moreover, this continuing and widening social inequality is often cited as further evidence of the existence and influence of power elites.

Elite-influenced taxing and spending decisions are expected to produce policies favorable to the wealthy and propertied interests. Elite theorists found a strong bias against spending for redistributive social services that help the poor (welfare, housing, and health services) and an equally strong preference for spending on capital-intensive infrastructure that ultimately helps the wealthy (such as roads and water and sewer systems) and subsidies for new businesses and industry. Curiously, this empirical finding is not unique to elite theory. Advocates of several other explanations of municipal taxing and spending policies have found that in central cities and surrounding suburbs these policies significantly favor business and commercial interests (Peterson 1981).

There are several problems with elite theory. Scholars such as (Polsby 1963) have noted that it is nonfalsifiable. Elites are assumed to exist, and failure to identify them and their influence on policy is merely a methodological problem, not one of theory. Critics of elite theory further suggest that even among the power elite there is considerable variation, even disagreement, on the proper role of local government. Furthermore, the existence of a power elite does not provide a compelling reason to believe these individuals have unitary interests when it comes to the government's taxing and spending decisions. Elite theory and its critics have had an important influence on American politics, particularly on urban politics. In the 1960s many governments implemented programs to ensure that local governments would be more accessible to groups and individuals who were traditionally excluded from government decision-making processes. Federal and municipal requirements for greater direct citizen participation resulted in the creation of a host of new government institutions and structures, including civilian police review boards and community action councils that empowered citizens with policymaking authority.

Increased citizen participation, however, was often difficult to sustain and did not always accomplish its intended goals. For example, New York City decentralized its school board in 1968, creating thirty-two district boards. Representation on these boards better approximated the composition of local school districts and brought many more racial and ethnic minorities into the governance of the city's public schools. Nearly thirty-three years later this experiment in greater citizen participation was reversed. In June 2002 the New York State legislature passed an act that returned control of the city's school system to the mayor and abolished the thirty-two district boards. Dissatisfaction with school performance under the system of district boards provided the impetus for this change. One policy analyst explained, "We are now putting authority for the schools in the hands of experts, not in the hands of all kinds of amateurs."[4]

In the 1970s Atlanta experienced a significant renaissance of organized citizen involvement in community planning. Stone (1989) reports that a substantial number of neighborhood organizations were brought into the city's decision-making process for the first time. He notes, however, that greater citizen participation did not always result in policies congruent with the newly empowered citizen groups, nor were these groups able to sustain political power indefinitely.

Pluralist Theory

In response to the deficiencies of elite theory, some scholars argued that considerably more interests are involved in local decision making than a small homogeneous group of high-status persons. Pluralists believe that decision making in communities resides in a larger and more diverse cross section of the community. Furthermore, pluralists replaced a reputational methodology for testing theories of decision making with one based on observable behavior, documenting who actually makes policy decisions.

In *Who Governs? Democracy and Power in an American City,* Robert Dahl (1961) set out the arguments for a pluralist theory of community decision making. Dahl and others (Wolfinger 1974; Polsby 1963) did not dispute the existence of unequally distributed wealth, political resources, and government services. Instead they contested the positive relationship between the distribution of political resources and the distribution of community influence. They argued that numerous types of political resources are not evenly distributed among the residents of a community. Different groups and individuals control different resources that may be used to influence different types of public policies. Dahl found that prior to 1900 economic elites did, in fact, have a disproportionate amount of influence on the policy outputs of municipal governments. However, with industrialization and the accompanying increase in immigration to the United States, the sheer number of new voters, entrepreneurs, and diverse social and economic interests supplanted the power of preindustrial elites.

Pluralist theory readily accommodates the possibility that elites influence public policy, but not to the exclusion of other groups or organized interests. Dahl found that decision-making power is not concentrated in any one group but rather is distributed to a wide range of individuals and groups across several different policy areas.

Pluralists did, however, find that these municipal policies could not be linked with the actions of a homogeneous group of economic interests. On the contrary, pluralist researchers found that whatever the content of urban public policy, its origins emanated from a diverse group of individuals and interests. Consequently, the diversity of preferences that shaped urban taxing and spending policies could not be consistently linked with either a pro-business or other distinctive interest group.

Pluralists assumed that the preferences of those who had power would, under the proper conditions, mirror the policy preferences of the public. This is true, of course, only if those who have power are representative of the public's preferences. Otherwise, those who make decisions must be willing or be induced to represent the public interest rather than a minority policy choice. Pluralists left unanswered an important question: what is the link between urban policy and the preferences of urban residents, and what facilitates (or impedes) this relationship?

For example, several researchers (Welch 1975; Peterson 1981) have demonstrated that the greater representation of African Americans and other historically underrepresented minorities has not always produced policies that reflect the needs and demands of these constituencies. Pluralism has fallen short of explaining why the greater representation of these constituencies has not produced taxing and spending policies that approximate the preferences of these newly empowered groups.

Market Theory

As a means of explaining local taxing and spending decisions, the debate between elite and pluralist theory focuses on who has power and who exercises it in a community. These explanations of local governance argue that the resolution of competing preferences is the essential process by which taxing and spending decisions are formulated. Market theorists ask a different question: what do governments do and why? In contrast to elite and pluralist theorists, market theorists expanded their explanation of municipal taxing and spending decisions to include forces both inside and outside the city. At the national level the answer to this question is straightforward: government's role is limited to those activities and responsibilities for which the private market is ill suited. The scope of government's functional responsibilities is identified by those goods and services that private-sector vendors are unable to produce due to significant inefficiencies and external factors. For example, the inability to exclude individuals from obtaining certain goods and services (such as clean air and national defense) limits the role of private markets in providing these goods and services. Consequently, the national government assumes a large, if not exclusive, responsibility for supplying them.

Tiebout's (1956) model of local public expenditures has provided the theoretical foundation for most of the empirical research on the market determinants of urban and metropolitan area public policies. Tiebout maintains that individuals select communities in accordance with their preferences for publicly provided goods and services, that is, they "vote with their feet." The content and level of municipal service packages are defined by the preferences of the average voter in each community. For Tiebout, an efficient market mechanism for the production of goods and services exists by virtue of (1) the number and diversity of states and communities, and (2) the mobility of voters to choose from among these communities the one that best approximates their preferences for goods and services. From these assumptions, a number of testable propositions have been derived (Dowding, John, and Biggs 1994, 768):

- The larger the number of competing jurisdictions, the greater the satisfaction level of consumer voters.
- The larger the number of jurisdictions in the same metropolitan area, the greater the competition between them for consumer voters.
- The larger the number of competing jurisdictions, the more homogeneous each jurisdiction will be.
- Taxes as well as services influence residential mobility.
- The higher the quality of the services (tax levels), the higher (or lower) the property values in the jurisdiction.

Tiebout's model of local expenditures is neutral regarding the content of governmental functional responsibility and the functions that state and national governments should assume. For example, Tiebout does not identify a set of services like public safety, utilities, and roads as being essential to the operation of municipal government. Instead, he argues that the content of functional responsibilities is limited only by the median voter's preferences. Tiebout provides an engine, namely, the market, for assigning service responsibilities. Others have used this market engine to deduce a set of hypotheses for assigning functional responsibilities across different levels of government, thereby defining the taxing and spending decisions of municipal governments.

Buchanan (1971), Peterson (1981), and Miller (1981) introduce an important qualification to Tiebout's theory of local expenditures that significantly informed the debate on the scope and content of municipal public policy. Each author notes that the mobility of residents in a metropolitan area produces a significant bias for the retention of wealthier residents. Buchanan demonstrates that municipal governance under majority rule will advantage low-income citizens at the expense of high-income residents. The result is income redistribution, a cost for middle- and high-income persons that can be avoided if they migrate to another locale. Peterson further explores this bias toward the retention of wealthy residents. His thesis is that "local politics is not like national politics"; consequently, "there are crucial kinds of public policies that local governments simply cannot execute" (Peterson 1981, 4). By inference, he claims there are policies that only the national government can efficiently perform.

Peterson maintains that the scope and level of a community's functional responsibilities are constrained by the inability of cities, and to a lesser extent states, to control the mobility of capital and labor across their respective borders. Though national governments can control the flow of money and people across their borders, states and cities are less effective at preventing their citizens, businesses, and capital base from migrating to other locales where tax-to-benefit ratios are superior. Consequently, local governments seek to maximize their economic well-being by pursuing policies that enhance the community's economic base while avoiding those policies and activities that threaten the community with the loss of productive capital and labor. This means that cities, states, and other subnational units of government pursue developmental policies (roads and highways) that generate economic resources (tax base) that can in turn be used for the community's collective welfare. At the same time, city governments are expected to avoid redistributive public policies that benefit dependent and nonproductive persons (for example, welfare, housing, and health care), because these policies draw resources away from productive citizens without providing them with commensurate benefits. Again, by implication, the responsibility for redistributive policies is less harmful to states and national governments than it is to local governments because of the significant transaction costs associated with migration between states and nations.

For Buchanan, Miller, and Peterson, the hypotheses derived from Tiebout's work provide the theoretical foundation for their own empirical expectations about the assignment of functional responsibility in a federal system. These hypotheses include:

- Expenditures on redistributive services are a function of fiscal capacity (wealth), not demand and public preferences in the community.
- Expenditures on developmental services are a function of demand (population size).
- Tax rates and tax burden (local taxes as a percentage of personal income) will tend toward uniformity among communities competing in the same market for consumer voters (that is, a metropolitan area).

For political scientists, a number of significant implications flow from the theoretical work of Tiebout, Buchanan, and Peterson. First, politics, at least at the subnational level, is marginalized, because demand and public preferences do not drive spending policies for redistributive social services. Spending for redistributive policies at the subnational level is largely a function of wealth. Politics is not important to the formation of most municipal public policies, at least not for those associated with significant redistributive effects. Finally, by implication, subnational units of government are more efficacious when they engage in developmental policies, and less efficacious when pursuing redistributive social policies. The delivery of redistributive social services is more efficiently handled by the national government.

The evidence to support Peterson's empirical hypotheses is mixed. Municipalities spend considerably more on developmental and allocation functions (road, street, water, and other infrastructure) than on redistributive goods and services (health, welfare, and housing). Peterson further shows that demand for social services is unrelated to spending for redistributive social services. If politics mattered in the formation of urban taxing and spending policies, we would expect to observe a positive relationship between indicators of poverty and municipal spending for social services. Peterson (1981), however, reports that municipal spending for an array of social services, including housing, welfare, public hospitals and health services, is unrelated to indicators of poverty, minority population, and other related indices of need and demand.

Stein (1990) reports, however, considerable variation in the range of municipal spending on redistributive social services. Many more communities play an active role in the provision of social policies that are potentially harmful to the interests of the city than Peterson or other market theorists would lead us to believe. Why?

Institutional Determinants

Rules governing how cities make decisions (by plurality, simple majority, or super majority), the method of representation (at-large or single-member districts, and partisan or nonpartisan elections), and the nature of the executive office (elected mayor or city manager) have been found to directly influence the content of urban public policies. Several researchers have found that different rules and procedures favor certain types of spending and taxing policies that impose disproportionate costs and benefits on different segments of a community.

Banfield and Wilson (1963) were the first to argue that certain institutional arrangements promote the interests and preferences of different groups and also translate those preferences into policy outputs. The authors observed that unreformed municipal governments with single-member district representation, partisan elections, and a mayoral form of government tend to produce policies that are more private regarding rather than public regarding. Public-regarding policies focus on the needs and interests of the entire community, whereas the narrower private-regarding policy outputs distribute benefits to specific geographic areas and ethnic and partisan interests, independent of the need for these policies. Governments with reformed structures, including nonpartisan elections, a city manager, and at-large elections are thought to minimize partisan, ethnic/racial, and geographic influences on the formulation of local public policies.

Empirical tests of Banfield and Wilson's thesis have produced mixed and inconclusive findings. Lineberry and Fowler (1967) found significant differences in the taxing and spending decisions of local governments with reformed and unreformed institutional arrangements, confirming Banfield and Wilson's hypotheses. More sophisticated time-series analysis by Morgan and Pelissero (1980), however, failed to produce significant differences in the spending and taxing outputs of reformed and unreformed governments, leading these authors to conclude that "in the long run, government structure may matter very little—at least when it comes to city taxing and spending policies" (p. 105). This conclusion may be premature and overlooks other important rules and procedures governing the urban policymaking process.

A different perspective on the institutional determinants of urban taxing and spending decisions identifies alternative ways for cities to provide various goods and services. Stein (1990, 3) argues that "the way in which governments organize themselves to perform policy functions has a significant effect on the scope and content of municipal policy performance." The conventional view of municipal public policy is that urban governments are solely responsible for all phases of service provision, including the choice of services, the means of funding, and producing and delivering goods and services. This view, however, is both naive and wrong. A wide range of urban public policies are financed, produced, and delivered by a host of alternative methods that involve agencies in the private, nonprofit, and public sector. These alternative arrangements are associated with significant savings in providing certain types of services. The quandary of cities providing redistributive social services is partly answered by the use of alternative institutional arrangements. Stein and several other researchers (see Hodge 2000) have demonstrated that these alternative arrangements produce significant savings to cities that mitigate the potentially harmful consequences associated with the municipal provision of social services.

A Paradox Partially Answered: Municipal Service Arrangement

The paradox in the taxing and spending policies of U.S. municipalities has been a central theme in this chapter. Despite sound theoretical advice, many municipalities pursue service responsibilities that potentially undermine their economic, social, and political well-being. Several theories have been advanced to address this paradox, and each has been found deficient in its explanation and supporting empirical evidence.

How cities pursue spending and taxing policies that are antithetical to their interests can be explained in terms of how they organize for the provision and production of services.

Cities face two choices when arranging to provide a specific service. They can produce the service with their own resources, using their own public employees and equipment to collect the garbage, clean the water supply, trim trees, or perform any other function the city chooses to provide. Alternatively, cities can purchase needed services from other governments (for example, adjacent cities or an overlapping county) or private companies. Governments choose such an alternative either to save on production costs or to obtain access to goods and/or services that might not be within the city's means to provide. For example, many communities are too small to pay for the construction of their own sewage treatment plant or to purchase garbage trucks for the collection of solid waste. For smaller-sized communities, contracting with a larger adjacent community or a private vendor may be the only way to obtain these services for their citizens. For example, Houston, Texas, sells water as well as sewage treatment services to several metropolitan area suburbs. These communities could not raise the tax dollars or borrow the funds needed to construct sewage treatment plants or a water distribution system without imposing higher taxes on their citizens. Larger communities or private vendors who can service large populations experience a lower per unit cost of production for services like sewerage, water, solid waste collection, and other public utilities. This is known as an economy of scale: costs per unit of production decline with an increase in production. A municipal bus system exemplifies an economy of scale. Public buses have relatively fixed costs, such as the purchase of the vehicle, gas, and wages for a driver. If ten people ride the bus each day, the cost per rider is one-tenth of the total cost of operating the bus for one day. However, if 3,000 persons ride the bus in one day, the unit cost of operating the bus plummets, because it is getting revenue from 3,000 rather than ten passengers without significantly increasing its cost of operation.

Even large communities may find it advantageous to use other governmental units or private companies to produce and deliver city services. Cities, for obvious political reasons, rely on union labor, which receives higher wages and more generous health and retirement benefits than nonunion labor does. Private-sector vendors can better resist the political pressures to hire union workers and can therefore reduce their labor costs by employing nonunion workers.

Contracting out for some services can produce significant savings for a city, especially when the largest production cost is human labor. For many social services, including public health programs and hospital and mental health services, labor is the largest expense. For other core city functions, including solid waste collection, water, sewerage, and roads, the principal factor of production is money for the construction of plants and equipment purchases. The labor costs of operating these facilities are a small portion of the total cost of providing these services. For example, many cities use side-loading garbage trucks that enable the driver to use automated equipment to lift garbage cans and deposit their contents in the truck. As a result, only one person is needed to operate the truck, rather than a crew of four (one driver and three loaders).

The savings realized from the use of nonmunicipal employees, as well as the reduced costs associated with the economies of scale that accompany nonmunicipal vendors, might resolve the paradox of municipal service responsibility. The incidence of cities using vendors and employees other than their own to provide redistributive social services may account for how cities are able to offer these potentially problematic services without suffering the economic and political ills predicted by Peterson, Buchanan, and Miller. The savings from using more efficient vendors to provide these services mitigates the income redistribution associated with municipal responsibility for these social services.

Stein reports a 1982 survey of municipal governments indicating that "if alternatives to direct service provision and production are not available, the mean scope of functional responsibility for social services would drop from 43.3 percent to only 24.3 percent for the surveyed cities" (1990, 198).

Table 9-1 reports the findings of a 1997 national survey of 1,200 municipal governments. The study queried municipalities about their responsibility for sixty-four different services and how they arranged to provide them. The first column reports the percentage of cities that reported responsibility for selected services. The second column reports the percentage of cities with responsibility for each function that reported using only municipal employees to provide each service. For all but one social service (programs for the elderly), 75 percent of the cities that reported responsibility for a social service stated that the service was provided by employees from another government and/or private entity. As expected, the most frequent means for providing social services is use of other vendors and their employees.

The tentative conclusion that can be drawn from these findings is that cities seeking savings by outsourcing the provision and production of services are more likely to assume responsibility for social services and functions that are potentially contentious. Moreover, this finding provides a more nuanced explanation of the role that municipal politics plays in shaping the taxing and spending policies of American cities. What governments do and specifically how they perform their functional responsibilities appear to be determined by the policy demands that arise among needier and high-demand constituents: the poor, elderly and, infirm. The effect of these demands on taxing and spending policies is mediated by the choices municipal governments make about the scope and content of functional responsibilities and how they organize for the provision and production of these

Table 9-1 Functional Responsibility and Mode of Service Arrangement for Selected Services, 1997 (in percent)

Function	Cities responsible for services	Cities using only municipal employees
Basic services		
Roads	92.5%	39.3%
Sewerage	69.1	59.3
Solid waste collection	62.5	36.3
Police	96.2	89.1
Average	80.7	56.0
Social services		
Homeless	19.1	1.7
Mental health	27.3	10.4
Hospitals	17.5	5.1
Day care	20.5	16.0
Child welfare	29.9	23.1
Elderly services	59.8	26.1
Average	29.0	13.2

Source: International City/County Management Association. 1998. *Profile in Local Government Service Delivery 1997*, http://icma.org/download/cat15/grp120/sgp224/asd97web.pdf

services. Consequently, politics matters in the making of urban public policy, but not always in a manner that is transparent or direct.

Conclusion

What conclusions can we glean from the literature on the politics of municipal taxing and spending? The politics of municipal taxing and spending is very much a story of constrained behavior. Cities occupy an institutionally and physically weak position in the American federalist system. Unlike nations and states, cities have porous borders. Productive capital and labor are free to choose from among a host of metropolitan area governments without incurring any significant moving costs. Municipal borders matter, because they place metropolitan area communities in competition with one another for the most productive capital and labor in the region. As creations of state government, cities do not have sufficient authority to be completely sovereign over their taxing and spending policies. State home-rule laws and restrictions on municipal taxing and spending policies influence the scope and content of urban public policies.

An enduring debate in the literature concerns the role of politics in shaping local public policy, especially fiscal policies. This question is about whether localities are able to operate independent of their physical and institutional constraints. Market theorists (Peterson, Miller, and Buchanan) downplay the influence of politics—and public preferences—on the formation of urban policies. Elite, pluralist, and regime theorists identify politics as a seminal force in shaping urban public policies. The tension in this debate is between the fulfillment of individual and group preferences and the interests of the city, that is, the attraction and retention of productive capital and labor. The empirical literature suggests that cities do act in a manner that is at variance with market theorists' predictions (prescriptions) to eschew responsibility for taxing and spending policies harmful to the city's interests. Moreover, the incidence of this policy practice parallels public support for these policies. Curiously, however, cities appear to succeed at providing redistributive social services without suffering excessive losses of productive capital and labor and related social and economic problems. Why? One explanation is the way cities organize themselves for the provision of services. Employing alternative modes of service provision can enable cities, through sufficient gains in efficiency, to partially offset the expenses associated with costly social services. But whatever the savings garnered from these alternative modes, they do not provide an absolute defense against the dangers of porous borders.

Suggested Readings

Miller, Gary. 1980. *Cities by Contract: The Politics of Municipal Incorporation.* Cambridge: MIT Press. An insightful analysis of the Los Angeles metropolitan area's love affair with the formation of new governments and how these new governments cope with financing municipal services.

Peterson, Paul. 1981. *City Limits.* Chicago: University of Chicago Press. An important restatement of Tiebout's classic thesis about urban politics and public policy, which argues that cities have a unique "self-interest" focusing on policies that develop their economy, preventing them from pursuing redistributive social services.

Stein, Robert. 1990. *Urban Alternatives: Public and Private Markets in the Provision of Local Services.* Pittsburgh: University of Pittsburgh Press. An alternative explanation of Peterson's *City Limits,* based on the way governments arrange for the provision of different goods and services.

Tiebout, Charles. 1956. "A Pure Theory of Local Expenditures." *Journal of Political Economy* 64 (October): 416–424.

References

Banfield, Edward C., and James Q. Wilson. 1963. *City Politics.* Cambridge: Harvard University Press.

Buchanan, William. 1971. "Principles of Urban Fiscal Strategy." *Public Choice:* 4–16.

Conlan, Timothy. 1998. *From New Federalism to Devolution.* Washington, D.C.: Brookings Institution Press.

Dahl, Robert. 1961. *Who Governs? Democracy and Power in an American City*. New Haven: Yale University Press.

Domhoff, William. 1967. *Who Rules America?* Englewood Cliffs, N.J.: Prentice-Hall.

Dowding, Keith, Peter John, and Stephen Biggs. 1994. "Tiebout: A Survey of the Empirical Literature." *Urban Studies* 31 (March):767–797.

Dowding, Keith, and Peter John. 1996. "Exiting Behavior under Tiebout Conditions: Towards a Predictive Theory." *Public Choice* 88 (December): 393–406.

Dreier, Peter, John Mollenkopf, and Todd Swanstrom. 2001. *Place Matters: Metropolitics for the Twenty-first Century*. Lawrence: University Press of Kansas.

Hill, Richard C. 1974. "Separate and Unequal: Governmental Inequality in the Metropolis." *American Political Science Review* 68 (December): 1557–1568.

Hodge, Graeme A. 2000. *Privatization: An International Review of Performance*. Boulder: Westview Press.

Hunter, Floyd. 1953. *Community Power Structure: A Study of Decision Makers*. Chapel Hill: University of North Carolina Press.

———— 1980. *Community Power Succession: Atlanta's Policy Makers Revisited*. Chapel Hill: University of North Carolina Press.

Lineberry, Robert, and Edmund Fowler. 1967. "Reformism and Public Policies in American Cities." *American Political Science Review* 61 (September): 701–716.

Lynd, Robert S., and Helen M. Lynd. 1929. *Middletown*. New York: Harcourt Brace.

Mayhew, David. 1974. *Congress: The Electoral Connection*. New Haven: Yale University Press.

Miller, Gary. 1981. *Cities by Contract: The Politics of Municipal Incorporation*. Cambridge: MIT Press.

Mills, C. Wright. 1956. *The Power Elite*. New York: Oxford University Press.

Morgan, David, and John Pelissero. 1980. "Urban Policy: Does Political Structure Matter?" *American Political Science Review* 74 (December): 999–1006.

Polsby, Nelson. 1963. *Community Power and Political Theory*. New Haven: Yale University Press.

Peterson, Paul. 1981. *City Limits*. Chicago: University of Chicago Press.

Schneider, Mark. 1980. *Suburban Growth Policy and Process*. Brunswick, Ohio: King's Court Communications.

Stein, Robert. 1990. *Urban Alternatives: Public and Private Markets in the Provision of Local Services*. Pittsburgh: University of Pittsburgh Press.

Stone, Clarence. 1989. *Regime Politics: Governing Atlanta, 1946–1988*. Lawrence: University Press of Kansas.

Tiebout, Charles. 1956. "A Pure Theory of Local Expenditures." *Journal of Political Economy* 64 (October): 416–424.

Welch, Susan. 1975. "The Impact of Urban Riots on Urban Expenditures." *American Journal of Political Science* (November): 741–760.

Wolfinger, Raymond. 1974. *The Politics of Progress*. Englewood Cliffs, N.J.: Prentice-Hall.

Notes

1. For a further discussion of the dissolution of city governments by state authorities, see Mark Gelfand, *A Nation of Cities: The Federal Government and Urban America, 1933–1965* (New York: Oxford University Press, 1975).

2. See Dillion's Rule, *Clinton v. Cedar Rapids and Missouri River R.R. Co.*, 24 Iowa 455 (1868).

3. See Ronald Edelstein, "Appraisal of Residential Property Tax Regressivity," *Journal of Financial and Quantitative Analysis* 14 (1979): 753–768.

4. Mitchel Ross, Rice Professor of Urban Politics and Planning, New York University, quoted in "The Odd Circle of School Control: 'Power to People' in 1960s Is Now Seen as 'Amateur Hour'", *New York Times,* June 16, 2002, 21.

10 Economic Development Policies

Richard D. Bingham

What Is Economic Development?

Some years ago, the American Economic Development Council (AEDC), then the major professional association in the urban economic development field, defined economic development as "the process of creating wealth through the mobilization of human, financial, capital, physical and natural resources to generate marketable goods and services" (AEDC 1984, 18). For the public sector, over the years, this has meant an emphasis on the creation of jobs and wealth. More recently, an added focus has been to create jobs and wealth that benefit the local population. Thus local government's role in economic development is to "facilitate and promote the creation of jobs and wealth by the private sector, *and to ensure that it does so in a way that serves the short- and long-run interests of the broad population*" (Bingham and Mier 1993, vii) [emphasis in original]. The economic development policies of local government are those designed to create private-sector jobs and wealth in the interest of the local population.

The systems approach provides an understandable framework for examining economic development policy. The systems model invites a look at the individual components of an allocative system and emphasizes their interconnections. This analytical approach to imposing order makes systems analysis highly compatible with empirical research. In certain respects it is like building a complex "black box." The box serves the function of converting resources into outputs and eventually into outcomes. Economic development is presumably the system that converts resources like land, labor, and capital into gross state product and/or other outcomes.

Because systems analysis is allocative, it is also political. It requires answers to political questions. For example, how are land, labor, and capital allocated to optimize the growth of gross state product? Penetrating the black box of the relationship between the political process and the process of urban growth is the objective of economic development theories in a wide variety of disciplines.

The Theory Problem

The varied interests of disciplines in economic development and economic development theory are illustrated in a now somewhat dated book, *Theories of Local*

Economic Development: Perspectives from Across the Disciplines (Bingham and Mier, 1993). The book identified more than fifty theories of economic development from the perspectives of various social sciences and professions as represented by the chapter authors. The theories include transportation cost models, agglomeration economies, price equilibrium models, central place theory, product cycle theory, profit cycle theory, Marxian theory, skills mismatch, growth machine theory, and innovation theories, among others. On the one hand, this makes for an extremely rich literature; on the other, it leads to confusion. The theory problem is reminiscent of the children's fable "The Blind Men and the Elephant":

Four blind men found an elephant and did not know what it was.
"It is like a log," said one, who had flung his arms around the elephant's leg.
"No! It is like a rope," said another, who had caught hold of its tail.
"It is more like a fan," said the third. He was feeling the shape of the elephant's ear.
"It is something with no beginning and no end," said the fourth, who was walking round and round the animal, feeling its sides. . . .
"What is it?" they said.

What it is, is defined by one's perspective.

It is obviously beyond the scope of this chapter to cover the range of development theories, but a subsequent discussion will focus on the perspectives of political scientists relative to economic development. This is particularly pertinent with regard to systems theory.

History of Urban Economic Development Efforts

Urban economic development, as we know it today, has been around for a long time, dating back to 1937, when the first industrial development bond was issued in Mississippi. Donald Haider (1989) identified four eras with differing approaches to economic development in the recent past. The first, running from the 1930s to about the early 1960s, made use of incentives like industrial development bonds. In that era, states attempted to attract manufacturing plants from other states to redistribute employment.

In the second era, during the 1950s and into the 1960s, the federal government began taking an active interest in economic development. Its goal was to reduce economic inequities between regions of the country through focused development. For example, in 1961 the Area Redevelopment Administration (later to become the Economic Development Administration) was established in the Department of Commerce to provide technical assistance, grants, and loans to local governments for public projects (for example, infrastructure), particularly those that would attract private businesses.

Federal efforts became more focused during the 1960s and early 1970s. New programs were devised to target economic development in depressed areas and declining city neighborhoods through programs of industrial recruitment and private-sector investments. The key concept of the era was *public–private* partnerships, basing government assistance on substantial participation by the private sector in government-approved projects. Characteristic of this phase of development was the federal Urban Development Action Grant (UDAG).

Haider calls the fourth era—the decade of the 1980s—one of *generative development*. David Birch (1978) suggested that small businesses were the real generators of new jobs in the United States. During this period governments shifted their economic development focus to entrepreneurship and assisting small businesses.

Haider focused on eras of economic development practice, while, in a related article, Mier and Fitzgerald (1991) looked at the scholarly literature on economic development. In this literature they found three phases of development, not entirely divorced from those identified by Haider. The first was a concern with the early practice of "smokestack chasing" by means of tax abatements, land development, and other such efforts designed to attract firms from one location to another.

According to Mier and Fitzgerald, the second phase emerged in the 1960s, with the appearance of a literature concerned with the distributional aspects of economic development practice. This analysis of the political economy of development was largely a critical one, based on a Marxist framework.

The third phase is reflective of public–private partnerships. The emphasis here is on the promotion of development from within—to reduce local dependence on non-local corporations and to emphasize the distribution of economic development's benefits.

The Evolution of Local Economic Development

The previous sections suggest the approaches that this chapter will take. First, economic development can be a difficult subject to understand theoretically, because, as noted, it is of interest to so many disciplines. Here we will examine only two of these disciplinary approaches in an effort to understand their similarities and differences—economic development as it is studied by political scientists and by economists. Economic development policies are the *outputs* of the local political system. Economic development (the creation of jobs and wealth) signifies the *outcomes* (it is hoped) of those policies. Political scientists are most often concerned with the outputs. They want to know how and why policies are adopted (for example, Reese 1997). Economists, however, are most often concerned with the outcomes. They want to know if jobs are actually created or taxes actually increased (for example, Bartik 1991).

Second, we will seek to understand local economic development by looking at the evolution of the modern tools of economic development. These tools are, in effect, economic development policies. The chapter will conclude with a short critique of the approaches and policies and will suggest areas of future research.

The Political Science Approach—Concern with Outputs

Harold Wolman (with David Spitzley) published an excellent review of the literature on the politics of urban economic development (1996). The review is particularly useful because it outlines the basic concerns of political scientists conducting research in the economic development arena and also critiques much of this research. But even more useful, for us, is the insight it provides into the way political scientists think about issues.

Wolman places the literature in the following categories:

- The forces behind local economic development activity.
- The outcomes sought by local economic development activity.
- What accounts for variation in local economic development activity?

What is so interesting about these categories? It is the fact that they mirror urban political science's wholehearted adoption of the systems approach. All of them presume to answer questions about the black box—inputs to it, outputs from it, and its inner workings.

The Forces behind Local Economic Development Activity. Wolman first asks: "What are the factors that impel local governments to engage in economic development activity, and why has local economic development activity increased so substantially in recent years?" (p. 119). This question is about the inputs to the economic development black box and has a range of potential answers. Some scholars have argued that cities have an overriding interest in their economies and in attracting new economic activity (Peterson 1981), especially to increase the tax base (Pagano and Bowman 1995; Swanstrom 1985). One growth machine argument (Molotch 1976; Logan and Molotch 1987) states that cities pursue growth policies to drive up land use (and thus land values and rents) for the benefit of the members of the growth machine. Stone (1989) holds that there are development-oriented urban regimes that pursue development policies in order to serve public needs or achieve policy objectives.

This input to the economic development black box might come from any of three directions: urban officials responding to fiscal stress by seeking ways to expand the tax base, a business elite seeking to enhance its own private interests, or an urban regime seeking to enhance the public enterprise.

The Outcomes Sought by Local Development Activity. When city officials are asked what goals they are pursuing when they engage in economic development activities, they are essentially being asked, What are the hoped-for outcomes of the economic development outputs (policies)? What does the arrow out of the black box produce? There are usually a variety of answers (Bowman 1987a), but two things are always at the top of the list: to increase local revenues or taxes (Jones and Bachelor 1993; Pagano and Bowman 1995) and to create jobs and employment in the community (Blair, Fictenbaum, and Swaney 1984; Furdell 1994). Of course these objectives are not necessarily mutually exclusive, and most urban officials see them both as important reasons to pursue economic development activities.

What Accounts for Variation in Local Economic Development Activity? Why do local governments engage in different levels and kinds of economic development activities? Why are the outcomes from the black box so different from one community to another? This is probably the question that political scientists have most frequently sought to answer. Is the specific package of activities that a local government elects to use a function of the characteristics of the community (for example, poverty), the structure of the governmental entity, the leadership of the body politic, or a decision made by economic development officials? A wide variety of hypotheses are offered in the literature to explain economic development policies, and a substantial literature exists to test these hypotheses.

Wolman looked at sixteen different studies that attempt to explain variations in the extent of local economic development activity. He found that the most frequently included conceptual variables in explanatory models were local government institutional structure (nine times), fiscal stress (nine times), need or deprivation (five times), economic distress (five times, although this might overlap the need variable, depending on operationalization), openness or citizen access (four times), and city size (three times).

Wolman, however, is justifiably critical of most of these studies, as he makes clear in the following insightful comments:

The first problem is the dependent variable itself. Few of the studies make any effort to present a conceptual definition, but clearly most, in one way or another, are concerned with the extent of local economic development activity by local government. This is usually operationalized in one of two ways. In the first method, the dependent variable is dichotomous: the adoption or nonadoption (or use or nonuse) of a specific local economic development tool, technique, or strategy. In most cases, several such tools are examined separately. . . . The second method of operationalization involves a simple count of the different kinds of economic development tools used. Typically, this involves a survey instrument, sent to local authorities, asking the respondent to put a check next to each of a list of economic development tools, techniques, policies, or strategies used over some period. . . . There is no other way to say it: Both of these measures are very poor operationalizations of the concept of extent of economic development activity. The dichotomous variable simply gives an indication of whether a technique has been employed but says nothing about the extent to which it has been employed. The count of techniques used suffers in a similar fashion: It perhaps provides a measure of diversity of tools or complexity of approach—or, more broadly, the administrative and policy development capability of local governments with respect to economic development—but it is an inadequate measure of the extent of economic development activity. (Wolman with Spitzley 1996, 124)

From a policy perspective, what can we say about this rather extensive body of literature? We hate to use the old cliché, but it is appropriate here: the field is about a mile wide and an inch deep.

The Economics Approach—Concern with Outcomes

As previously stated, political scientists are concerned with *outputs,* or the development of economic development policies. Economists, however, are concerned with *outcomes,* or the impact of policies. When referring to economists, one thinks of a significant number of researchers using econometric techniques and models to determine if urban economic development programs work, that is, actually do create jobs and wealth. Unfortunately, no such volume of research activity has ever happened. In recent years, only a handful of economists have been interested in economic development, with the best work sponsored by the W. E. Upjohn Institute for Employment Research. However, these works contrast effectively with the political science approaches.

The Impact of Incentives on Local Growth.   The earliest of the Upjohn–sponsored research projects was by Timothy Bartik (1991). Although his research is helpful, Bartik's concern with a combination of state and local economic development policy makes it impossible to separate the impact of local policy from that of state policy. Bartik confronts the *zero-sum game* issue: "The zero-sum game argument against economic development is that development policies only redistribute jobs among state or local areas. The number of jobs in the nation is unchanged, and the efficiency of the national economy is unaffected. The gains of the unemployed in one local area are offset by the losses of the unemployed in other local areas" (p. 187). Bartik does not examine this question empirically but argues that so long as jobs increase in an area of significant unemployment, the outcome is not zero sum. Furthermore, he notes that the literature generally suggests that it is the neediest places that are most likely to play the economic development game (Bowman 1987b; Rubin and Rubin 1987).

Bartik is not directly concerned with the primary outcomes of economic development policy but rather with the secondary outcomes. From the literature he assumes a primary outcome: "The review of previous research suggests that state and local policies can have a significant effect on local growth. A state and local business tax reduction of 10 percent, without reducing public services to business, probably increases business activity in a state or metropolitan area in the long run by 2.5 percent" (p. 205). Empirically Bartik finds that an increase in local employment reduces local unemployment, increases labor force participation, and increases average annual earnings. Furthermore, faster local growth has a strong impact on African American employment and on less-educated individuals.

The Impact of Incentives on Firms. Peter Fisher and Alan Peters (1998) were interested in determining the impact of typical economic development incentives (like tax abatement) on business firms—their bottom line. Using hypothetical firms typical of manufacturing plants, they measured the value of competitive incentives. The implementation of this method resulted in what they called the tax and incentive model (TAIM). The model began with the construction of financial statements for firms representative of various industries and sizes. TAIM then measured the net returns to each firm, after state, local, and federal taxes, on a new plant investment. Thus the value to the firm of a locality's incentive package is the amount the package adds to the profitability of a new investment in that locality.

Fisher and Peters then used the TAIM to compute the value of the incentives for each of the firms, small and large, in the eight industries they analyzed in 112 selected city locations. They converted the "savings" to the company in terms of the hourly wage per employee, assuming a forty-hour work week over a fifty-week year for the twenty-year life span of the plant. For each industry (both large and small plants), they computed an hourly wage rate equivalent to the range from the location with the lowest value incentives to the location with the highest value incentives. For a large auto manufacturing plant, for example, the range was 81 cents, meaning that the incentive package in the best location (from the firm's position) was worth 81 cents more per employee per hour than the incentives at the worst location—for a period of twenty years. This is obviously a huge difference. For an auto plant at the worst location to be competitive, it would need to pay its employees 81 cents per hour less than the plant at the best location—just to make up the value of the incentives. The smallest range was for large furniture and fixture manufacturers—48 cents. The largest range was for large drug manufacturing firms—$1.82.

For Fisher and Peters, incentives in some places probably make a difference:

Since the severity of local tax and incentive regimes does not appear to be inversely related to factor costs, tax and incentive differentials between top- and bottom-ranked locations could reasonably be expected to influence plant location decisions in some locations. Obviously, most cities are not at the very top or the very bottom of the range, but in the broad middle, where not much separates most locations' tax and incentive regimes. In these cases, tax and incentive differentials may or may not have a decisive impact on plant location decisions; it will all depend on the other factor costs at the various sites competing for the investment. More generally, we are inclined to believe that, unless they have some special factor cost advantage, cities and states with severe tax and incentive regimes will tend to be eliminated from location searches. In other words, the greatest impact of tax and incentive regimes may be to exclude at the outset some cities and states from the game—from competing for a new investment opportunity. (pp. 207–208)

The Impact of Incentives on Communities. John Anderson and Robert Wassmer (2000) were concerned about the impact of development incentives on local communities. They studied incentive use in the 112 cities and townships in the Detroit metropolitan area over five-year periods from 1977 to 1992. The five-year increments were chosen to allow for substantial change in the observed use of incentives and to coincide with the availability of census data. The specific incentives included in the study were property tax abatements, downtown development authorities (DDAs), tax increment finance authorities (TIFAs), and industrial development bonds (IDBs). (IDBs will not be discussed here because their use has been severely limited by the Tax Reform Act of 1986.) With a DDA, the city legislative body designates the boundaries of one downtown district over which the authority is allowed to implement a development plan. The DDA has the power of eminent domain within the district, the authority to levy a local property tax of up to 1 percent for development, and may also use tax increment financing. A TIFA may be established by municipalities for issuing debt to finance an economic development project. Only one TIFA can be established in a municipality but its borders can be modified at any time. The bonds issued by the TIFA are secured and repaid by future property tax revenue streams on improvements captured by the authority.

Anderson and Wassmer used multiple regression models to determine the impact of these policies or incentives on the communities. Virtually all of the incentives have some impact (positive or negative). For example, the use of a TIFA was associated with increased use of property tax abatements; a DDA was associated with a rise in the value of commercial property, an increase in employment and population, and a decrease in the local poverty rate.

Although the brief preceding discussion hardly summarizes the diverse literature on the political science and economics approaches to local economic development, it does indicate differing interests and cultures. Political scientists want to know why things are the way they are. Economists want to know if things work the way they are supposed to.

The Evolution of Development Policies

The locus of local economic development policy over the past twenty-five years has clearly shifted from the federal government to the states, and finally to local governments. When we talk about the locus of economic development, this does not refer to the level of government doing the work, for that has always been the task of local government. We are talking about power—about who calls the shots. The federal government did so twenty years ago, when the dominant economic development tool, beyond IDBs, was the Urban Development Action Grant (UDAG).

The Urban Development Action Grant

The UDAG program was a real estate development program, although it never exactly targeted real estate. It was the heart of President Jimmy Carter's urban policy, enacted into law in 1977. The purpose of this discretionary grant program was to alleviate central city decay in the nation's most economically depressed urban areas by means of the strategic use of direct capital subsidies (Stephenson 1987). Federal grants were targeted to communities with the greatest need for economic and physical revitalization by stimulating private investment in specific development projects. A formula measuring urban distress was used to determine eligibility for the program. A city could apply for a grant if it met either the program standards for distress or had a "pocket of poverty." Staff at the Department of Housing and Urban Development (HUD) reviewed applications, not only for eligibility requirements but also for other program goals. An applicant had to meet the minimum requirement for firm public and private commitments; have a ratio of private investment to UDAG funds of at least 2.5 to 1; and satisfy the requirement that the project would not be feasible without UDAG funds (Gatons and Brintnall 1984).

The San Antonio, Texas, Hyatt Regency project gives the flavor of typical UDAG projects. The goal of the Hyatt project was to initiate a comprehensive revitalization of about six city blocks in the heart of San Antonio's historic downtown commercial area. A major component of the project was a riverwalk linkage—a multilevel pedestrian walkway at both the San Antonio River and street levels to connect the Alamo Plaza with the river.

The heart of the project was a 600-room luxury convention hotel, the Hyatt Regency, located on the banks of the San Antonio River. The lowest level of the hotel is a part of the riverwalk, providing sidewalk dining, entertainment, and shopping. Other components of the project included a small commercial shopping mall, a 500-car parking garage, including about 7,500 square feet of retail space, and a major restoration of the facades of historic buildings facing the Alamo. The project met its stated goals, generating about 690 new jobs and about $2.1 million in new property taxes (in 1984). About $37 million in private funds were invested in the hotel, with another $14 million used to restore ten historic properties (Bingham 1998, 91–92).

The UDAG program no longer exists, despite the fact that it was extremely popular. President Carter started the program in 1977 with an initial authorization of $400 million per year for the first three years. When UDAG was reauthorized for another three years in 1980, Congress increased appropriations to $675 million annually. When Ronald Reagan became president, in 1981, he had different ideas. He was opposed to direct subsidy programs like UDAG and worked to have it terminated. Although he was not successful in ending the program, he did manage to reduce its size. By 1988, UDAG appropriations were down to $216 million. In the end, it was Congress that killed UDAG. In the budget deliberations of 1989, Congress faced the choice of funding a space station for NASA or funding UDAG. Congress zeroed out UDAG.

What did UDAG accomplish? The program awarded $4.6 billion to communities for physical redevelopment over its twelve-year existence. It was responsible for about 3,000 projects in more than 1,200 cities during its lifetime and generated more than $30 billion in private investment in American cities (Rich 1992). But UDAG did something more. It taught city development officials about real estate development—what it takes to make a project work financially. It also taught both the public and private sectors about public-private partnerships. Cities learned that they could successfully partner with developers, and developers learned that they could partner with cities.

Enterprise Zones

Ronald Reagan may have opposed UDAG, but that did not mean he opposed economic development or all federal economic development efforts. One idea he did champion was enterprise zones. The zone concept was introduced to America from England by Stuart Butler's *Enterprise Zones: Greenlining the Inner City* (1981). It was introduced to American politics by Jack Kemp, a former U.S. representative who was secretary of the Department of Housing and Urban Development from 1989 to 1993. During the 1980s more than thirty federal enterprise zone bills were introduced in Congress, but none ever passed.

In his 1991 State of the Union address, President George H. W. Bush proposed establishing an enterprise zone program, and more bills were introduced, but with the same result. It was not until empowerment zones (EZs) and enterprise communities (ECs) were authorized in 1993, during the Clinton–Gore administration, that the federal government gave support to something like enterprise zones.

The states, however, had become enamored with the concept much earlier. Between 1981 and 1993, when the federal EZs/ECs were authorized, forty states enacted some type of zone program. These state programs have two important similarities: "First, enterprise zone programs target economically distressed areas. Second, enterprise zone programs offer special incentives and benefits to the targeted areas in an effort to spur new investment and job creation" (Dabney 1991, 327). However, these programs differ dramatically from one state to another. "They are urban, rural, and suburban. The number of zones ranges from one in Michigan to 1,422 in Louisiana. State zone programs vary in terms of their incentives, criteria designation, objectives, coordination of resources, and management styles" (Mossberger 1999, 14). But the heart of all zone programs is the idea that cutting taxes and reducing government regulations would regenerate distressed urban areas through the invisible hand of the market. This, of course, is what appealed to President Reagan so much.

The 1980s were the perfect time for zone development. Zones are an important product of four interrelated trends. First, a growing body of scholars, policy analysts, and politicians were expressing dissatisfaction with government solutions to urban decline and instead championing the free market, deregulation, and privatization as solutions to urban redevelopment. Second, the courts and legislatures demonstrated a broader appreciation of the concepts of public use (eminent domain) and public purpose (taxation) in the context of urban development. Third, the development and use of innovative financial instruments, such as tax increment financing (TIFs), were supporting public-private partnerships. Finally, the federal fiscal presence had lessened. Reagan's new federalism diminished the federal contributions to states and localities, forcing them to become more innovative (Wolf 1990, 123–125).

Although enterprise zones are quite diverse, the program in Louisville, Kentucky, is representative. The city has one of the oldest and largest EZs in the United States, introduced in 1982 when Kentucky authorized zones. The Louisville EZ is managed by the Office for Economic Development, a joint agency of the City of Louisville and Jefferson County governments. (This is typical of EZs, which are authorized by the state but are operated by urban governments.) Kentucky zone legislation authorizes the use of state sales tax exemptions, real estate value assessment freezes, property tax waivers on vehicles, and building permit fee waivers and discounts to companies that hire workers living in an impoverished area and/or invest in buildings and equipment.

The zone,

originally defined in 1982 to include 3.75 square miles west of and south of Louisville's central business district, was expanded in 1984 and 1986 as city and state officials sought to include the city's main airport, a large Ford Motor Company plant, a chemical manufacturing region, a greenfield industrial park along the Ohio River, and some older residential areas to the east of downtown. To maintain required physical contiguity between disparate neighborhoods, the entire University of Louisville campus was also included in the EZ. After the 1986 expansion, the EZ included nearly 46 square miles and 60 census tracts. (Lambert and Coomes 2001, 170)

Lambert and Coomes found it extremely difficult to evaluate the impact of the zone because of other development programs.

For example, Kentucky state government spent $60 million to fund a major expansion of the Louisville airport—this within the second definition of the zone. The state dollars were used to leverage more than $500 million in federal dollars to plan, acquire land, demolish houses, and construct a new runway and other facilities. The state investment in new infrastructure prompted United Parcel Service (UPS), the state's largest employer, to greatly expand its international freight hub there. Most of the EZ benefits claimed by proponents are linked to the airport expansion. UPS and other airport-related firms did take advantage of EZ tax advantages; however, it would be far-fetched to claim that the EZ program caused the local economic benefits. (p. 169)

There is certainly no consensus that other EZ programs have had much of an impact on their regions' economies. Approximately forty evaluations of EZ programs have been completed to date, and one would be hard-pressed to conclude that they stimulated economic development beyond what would have occurred anyway (for example, see Dabney 1991; Dowall 1996; Greenbaum and Engberg 2000). In fact, many firms located in EZs have not taken advantage of the EZ benefits. State EZs were a noble experiment, but one that cannot conclusively be said to spur economic development.

Tax Increment Financing

The current craze in urban economic development is tax increment financing (TIF), an economic development tool now available to municipalities in forty-eight states. What distinguishes TIF from earlier economic development tools is the lack of subsidy from higher levels of government. UDAG was funded by the federal government, and most of the tax and regulatory relief available to firms in enterprise zones came from the state. TIF district expenditures are financed from incremental property tax revenues. TIFs do have one thing in common with UDAG and EZs, which is that most TIF districts must be considered "blighted."

TIFs are now the most popular form of economic development financing in many major metropolitan areas. Although they have been around for years, they are just now gaining popularity. For example, the majority of Chicago's TIF districts were established between 1996 and 1999. By 1999, about 10 percent of Chicago's tax base was in TIFs (covering 13,000 acres).

A TIF is very much a local financing tool in that it is derived from property taxes (the most important own-source revenue of local governments). A city formally designates a specific geographic area for improvement and then designates it a TIF district. Any future growth in property tax revenues is used to pay for initial and ongoing economic development. Once the district has been formally designated, the initial assessed property valuation is held constant for a specified period, typically twenty years or more. The city, or a separate TIF authority, depending on the state, uses its power of land assembly and sale, site clearance, relocation, utility installation, and street construction and repair to improve the district and offers subsidized financing to businesses and developers. As private investment is attracted to the area, the assessed value of property and its taxes are expected to rise. The difference between the taxes on the base value (property when the TIF district was established) and the new assessed value is the tax increment. Instead of the increment revenues going into the city's general fund and to other taxing bodies with jurisdictions over the area (for example, the school district and/or county), the increments go back into the TIF to pay for debt issued to pay for the improvements (Weber n.d., 9).

A TIF district can raise revenue in two ways. First, the district can pay for improvements as they go, using the tax increment from each year. This usually means that development is very slow, since it can occur only at a gradual pace congruent with the growth in the tax increment for any given year. The more common financing method is the issuance of general obligation bonds, which provide immediate financing for the TIF project. Bonds are typically issued for a period of ten to twenty-five years and are retired by using the tax increment generated by the TIF district. Once the project is completed and the debt retired, the TIF district goes out of business and the tax increment reverts to traditional purposes (Paetsch and Dahlstrom 1990, 83–84).

Figure 10-1 illustrates how a TIF might work. Let us assume a 10 percent property tax rate, with about one-third of the tax going to the city government, one-third to county government, and one-third to the school district. We also assume that the value of the property before development was $40 million. Thus, before development, the three units of government would split $4 million in property taxes annually. As development begins, the TIF issues bonds in the amount of $60 million, to be paid back over the twelve-year life of the TIF (plus interest). Once development is completed (in year four), the property is now worth $120 million and pays $12 million annually in taxes. The TIF keeps $8 million, which it uses to pay off bonds, and the three units of local government continue to split $4 million. When the TIF's life has expired at the end of the twelve years (and the bonds have been paid off), the three units of local government now split the $12 million in tax revenue, and each collects $4 million.

The major advantage of TIFs is flexibility. In general, the only restrictions on them are those imposed by the states concerning geography and project terms. In most cases, TIFs can be applied to any area meeting broad statutory standards and to any project proposal demonstrating financial feasibility. The TIF process can be initiated any time a development opportunity presents itself. A TIF can be used with other funding mechanisms, or it can be designed to provide 100 percent of the funding necessary for the project.

A second advantage of TIFs is their political popularity, based on the inherent presumption that a TIF redevelopment project will pay for itself when properly planned

Figure 10-1   Example of Revenue Changes in Urban Governments following TIF Adoption

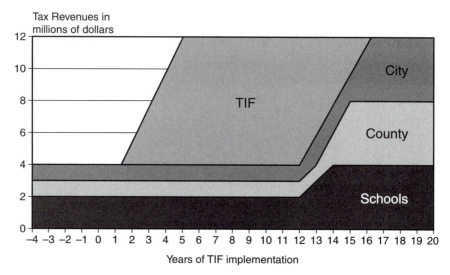

and executed and will have no effect on the overall real estate tax burden of the community.

When compared with typical grants, however, a TIF project can be extremely complex. Its development and execution can be a formidable financial exercise, with many opportunities for error or misjudgment (Paetsch and Dahlstrom 1990, 92–94).

Also, speculating on property tax increases requires cities to collaborate closely with private businesses. As Weber states, TIF districts "typically begin as coalitions of land-based elites, particularly real estate developers, banks, retailers, and firms with considerable investment in the city. These 'growth coalitions' plan for their district's redevelopment and then seek public funds and regulatory and developmental capacity to realize those plans.... The TIF process is conducive to the establishment of these ephemeral growth coalitions, which are less visible than the formal infrastructure of a budgetary process; (p. 23). For some, this means that the private sector is just out for other subsidies; thus the flip side of flexibility is accountability.

Finally, critics complain that TIFs force other units of government beyond municipalities to contribute to economic development projects without their consent. A TIF is popular with city governments precisely because it enables them to evade responsibilities and shift part of the cost of financing development to other jurisdictions. The taxes on any increase in the assessed property values of the TIF district go into a separate fund to pay for TIF activities. Meanwhile, taxes on the base value of the properties remain the same for the designated life span of the TIF and continue to be paid to the different local taxing bodies. Much of the tax revenue forgone by freezing the value of properties in the TIF districts would have been paid to county governments, or to the school, library, or other special districts with jurisdiction over property in the TIF (Weber n. d., p. 30).

TIFs complete the current cycle. The process of local economic development has truly become localized.

Conclusion

In his review of the literature on the politics of urban economic development, Wolman with Spitzley (1996) sets out an agenda for research on this subject. First, he suggests that it is necessary to develop new operational measures of the extent of local economic development activity, to collect appropriate data, and to examine in some relatively flawless way what factors are associated with varying levels of economic development activity.

Similarly, more empirical research needs to be undertaken concerning the attitudes of local decision makers in the economic development arena. Rubin's (1988) work is still the classic, although it is now more than fifteen years old.

Finally, Wolman recommends research on the distributional outcomes of local economic development policy. What are the differential effects of economic development activity and the outcomes of that activity, based on class, ethnicity, race, and gender?

But that may be jumping the gun. Before we examine levels of development activities or other political questions, it behooves us to know if urban economic development policies work. This is exactly what happened with enterprise zones. Social scientists of all persuasions, using widely different methodologies, studied the economic impacts of enterprise zones. Clearly this type of work is needed for tax abatements, TIFs, and other local development policies. In fact, there is some suggestion that property values in communities using TIFs do not grow as fast as they do in communities with no TIFs (Dye and Merriman 1999). So let us first concentrate on outcomes. Once we know if program outcomes are what was intended, we can then concentrate on the political questions.

Suggested Readings

Bartik, Timothy J. 1991. *Who Benefits from State and Local Economic Development Policies?* Kalamazoo, Mich.: Upjohn Institute. The first contemporary detailed study of the impacts of economic development incentives.

Bingham, Richard D., and Robert Mier, eds. 1993. *Theories of Local Economic Development: Perspectives from Across the Disciplines.* Newbury Park, Calif.: Sage. More than fifty theories of economic development, from a wide variety of academic disciplines, are described.

Fisher, Peter S., and Alan H. Peters. 1998. *Industrial Incentives: Competition Among American States and Cities.* Kalamazoo, Mich.: Upjohn Institute. An examination of the impact of industrial incentives on firms in a variety of industries.

Reese, Laura A. 1997. *Local Economic Development Policy: The U.S. and Canada.* New York: Garland. A good example of the political science approach to the study of economic development.

Wolman, Harold, with David Spitzley. 1996. "The Politics of Local Economic Development." *Economic Development Quarterly* 10 (May): 115–150. An excellent review and critique of political science research on economic development.

References

American Economic Development Council (AEDC). 1984. *Development Today.* Chicago: AEDC.

Anderson, John E., and Robert W. Wassmer. 2000. *Bidding for Business: The Efficacy of Local Economic Development Incentives in a Metropolitan Area.* Kalamazoo, Mich.: Upjohn Institute.

Bartik, Timothy J. 1991. *Who Benefits From State and Local Economic Development Policies?* Kalamazoo, Mich.: Upjohn Institute.

Bingham, Richard D. 1998. *Industrial Policy American Style: From Hamilton to HDTV.* Armonk, N.Y.: M. E. Sharpe.

Bingham, Richard D., and Robert Mier, eds. 1993. *Theories of Local Economic Development: Perspectives from Across the Disciplines.* Newbury Park, Calif.: Sage.

Birch, David L. 1978. *The Job Generation Process.* Cambridge: MIT Press.

Blair, John P., Rudy H. Fictenbaum, and James A. Swaney. 1984. "The Market for Jobs: Locational Decisions and the Competition for Economic Development." *Urban Affairs Quarterly* 20 (September): 64–77.

Bowman, Ann O'M. 1987a. *The Visible Hand: Major Issues in City Economic Policy.* Washington, D.C.: National League of Cities.

——— 1987b. *Tools and Targets: The Mechanics of City Economic Development.* Washington, D.C.: National League of Cities.

Butler, Stuart M. 1981. *Enterprise Zones: Greenlining the Inner City.* New York: Universe Books.

Dabney, Dan Y. 1991. "Do Enterprise Zone Incentives Affect Business Location Decisions?" *Economic Development Quarterly* 5 (November): 325–334.

Dowall, David E. 1996. "An Evaluation of California's Enterprise Zone Programs." *Economic Development Quarterly* 10 (November): 352–368.

Dye, Richard F., and David F. Merriman. 1999. "The Effects of Tax Increment Financing on Economic Development." University of Illinois, Chicago, unpublished paper, September.

Fisher, Peter S., and Alan H. Peters. 1998. *Industrial Incentives: Competition Among American States and Cities.* Kalamazoo, Mich.: Upjohn Institute.

Furdell, Phylis A. 1994. *Poverty and Economic Development: Views of City Hall.* Washington, D.C.: National League of Cities.

Gatons, Paul, and Michael Brintnall. 1984. "Competitive Grants: The UDAG Approach." In *Urban Economic Development,* ed. Richard D. Bingham and John P. Blair, 115–140. Beverly Hills, Calif.: Sage.

Greenbaum, Robert, and John Engberg. 2000. "An Evaluation of State Enterprise Zone Policies." *Policy Studies Review* 13 (summer–autumn): 29.

Haider, Donald. 1989. "Economic Development: Changing Practices in a Changing US Economy." *Environment and Planning* 7 (November): 451–469.

Jones, Brian D., and Lynn W. Bachelor. 1993. *The Sustaining Hand.* 2d ed. Lawrence: University Press of Kansas.

Lambert, Thomas E., and Paul A. Coomes. 2001. "An Evaluation of the Effectiveness of Louisville's Enterprise Zone." *Economic Development Quarterly* 15 (May): 168–180.

Logan, John R., and Harvey L. Molotch. 1987. *Urban Fortunes: The Political Economy of Place.* Berkeley: University of California Press.

Mier, Robert, and Joan Fitzgerald. 1991. "Managing Economic Development." *Economic Development Quarterly* 5 (August): 268–279.

Molotch, Harvey. 1976. "The City as a Growth Machine." *American Journal of Sociology* 82 (September): 309–331.

Mossberger, Karen. 1999. "State-Federal Diffusion and Policy Learning: From Enterprise Zones to Empowerment Zones." *Publius* 29 (summer): 13–31.

Paetsch, James R., and Roger K. Dahlstrom. 1990. "Tax Increment Financing: What It Is and How It Works." In *Financing Economic Development,* ed. Richard D. Bingham, Edward W. Hill, and Sammis B. White, 82–98. Newbury Park, Calif.: Sage.

Pagano, Michael A., and Ann O'M. Bowman. 1995. *Cityscapes and Capital.* Baltimore: Johns Hopkins University Press.

Peterson, Paul E. 1981. *City Limits.* Chicago: University of Chicago Press.

Reese, Laura A. 1997. *Local Economic Development Policy: The U.S. and Canada.* New York: Garland.

Rich, Michael J. 1992. "UDAG, Economic Development, and the Death and Life of American Cities." *Economic Development Quarterly* 6 (May): 150–172.

Rubin, Herbert J. 1988. "Shoot Anything That Flies, Claim Anything That Falls: Conversations with Economic Development Practitioners." *Economic Development Quarterly* 2 (August): 236–251.

Rubin, Irene S., and Herbert J. Rubin. 1987. "Economic Development Incentives: The Poor (Cities) Pay More." *Urban Affairs Quarterly* 23 (September): 37–62.

Stephenson, Max O., Jr. 1987. "The Policy and Premises of Urban Development Action Grant Program Implementation: A Comprehensive Analysis of the Carter and Reagan Presidencies." *Journal of Urban Affairs* 9 (winter): 19–35.

Stone, Clarence M. 1989. *Regime Politics: Governing Atlanta.* Lawrence: University Press of Kansas.

Swanstrom, Todd. 1985. *The Crisis of Growth Politics: Cleveland, Kucinich and the Challenge of Urban Populism.* Philadelphia: Temple University Press.

Weber, Rachel. n.d. "Scaling Down: Fiscal Enclaves in the Entrepreneurial City." University of Illinois, Chicago, unpublished paper.

Wolf, Michael Allan. 1990. "Enterprise Zones: A Decade of Diversity." In *Financing Economic Development,* ed. Richard D. Bingham, Edward W. Hill, and Sammis B. White, 123–141. Newbury Park, Calif.: Sage.

Wolman, Harold, with David Spitzley. 1996. "The Politics of Local Economic Development." *Economic Development Quarterly* 10 (May): 115–150.

11 Urban Services

David N. Ammons

Developments in urban service research and practice over the past century, or even more recently, cannot be summarized easily. Clearly, however, the intense focus on efficiency in the delivery of urban services that was so prevalent—even dominant—in the research and writings of the first half of the twentieth century dimmed somewhat by midcentury but never receded entirely, as other dimensions of service delivery gained prominence. Much of the work on urban services in more recent years has focused on patterns of service delivery and on efforts to improve the quality, responsiveness, and effectiveness, as well as the efficiency, of local government services.[1]

Urban services are policy outputs in the urban political system. The term "urban services" covers everything from police and fire protection to refuse collection, street and sidewalk maintenance, parks and recreation, water and sewer services, and much more. Among the policy outcomes of the urban political system are the effects produced by these services, including their impact on the lives of city residents.

Part of the research focusing on urban services has illuminated trends in the scope and quality of services provided to urban populations and the techniques used to produce or manage these services, sometimes linking political and demographic factors to variations. Other works have examined the efficacy of alternate strategies or techniques of service delivery. These areas of emphasis in research and publication may be categorized as follows:

1. *Inventories of service delivery systems.* This category includes a host of surveys conducted by local government professional associations and scholars that explore the nature and quality of urban services or the prevalence of selected approaches for managing or delivering these services. For example, the International City/County Management Association (ICMA) conducts periodic surveys exploring the practice of contracting for service delivery by local governments (Miranda and Andersen 1994; Morley 1989).
2. *Political or sociological studies of service delivery patterns.* These studies advance urban service inventories to the next level of academic inquiry, typically focusing on the relevance of politics, local government structure, leadership characteristics, or community demographics to urban services and the manner in

which they are delivered. For example, studies have linked council-manager government to a tendency to contract for a few specific types of services, such as public health and public transit, despite the general conclusion that the form of government has little bearing on overall contracting patterns (Ferris and Graddy 1986; McGuire, Ohsfeldt, and van Cott 1987). Another example of such research is the discovery that turnover in the office of mayor appears to increase the likelihood of contracting for some services, while turnover of city managers seems to have the opposite effect for others (Clingermayer and Feiock 1997).

3. *Analysis of the mechanics of managing service delivery.* This category includes works that provide a detailed examination of various tools thought to be useful for service delivery itself or for the evaluation of services. Reports that offer carefully developed advice on process reengineering, total quality management, performance measurement, managed competition, intergovernmental cooperation, or volunteerism are examples.

4. *Evaluation of the efficacy of service delivery strategies.* Research in this category assesses alternate organizational and management strategies for their effects on important dimensions of service delivery, principally costs and quality. Analyses of the effectiveness of routine police patrols, the cost and service quality ramifications of contract services, or the possible economy-of-scale advantages of large service delivery units are examples (Hirsch 1968; Institute for Local Self Government 1977; Kelling, Pate, Dieckman, and Brown 1974; Savas 1977a, 1977b; Stevens 1984).

Research products in each of these categories have illuminated efforts to improve urban services. Over the years, such efforts have led to the introduction of business techniques, structural reform, and greater professionalism in local government. They also have prompted the adoption of service delivery alternatives and new strategies for achieving greater performance.

Professionalization of Service Delivery

Rampant corruption in government near the close of the nineteenth century inspired a reform movement lasting more than thirty years. Reformers of the Progressive Era, extending approximately from 1887 to 1920, directed their attention to governmental corruption, political patronage, and the problems of government waste and inefficiency. Their focus on the prize of greater efficiency was so intense that government from 1906 to 1937 earned the label "Government by the Efficient" (Mosher 1968).

Scientific management, a concept that encouraged systematic analysis of work processes and the design of efficient production methods, was introduced during this period. Within a short time, scientific management became a worldwide phenomenon. Its originator, Frederick Taylor, is proudly claimed as the father of industrial engineering and was warmly embraced for a time by the fledgling field of public administration. Public administration, however, eventually distanced itself from scientific management, alleging that Taylor's methods were cold and compassionless, altogether lacking in sensitivity to the well-being of employees and the importance of positive human interaction in supervisory relations. Modern scholarship has begun to challenge this harsh judgment, suggesting that Taylor and his methods have been misrepresented, his words taken out of context, and his concern for workers understated (Nyland 1989; Schachter 1989).

Efforts to make the operations of government more businesslike were accompanied by Progressive Era efforts to make the structure of local government more businesslike as well. First, the commission form, introduced in 1900, and soon the council-manager form of government, introduced in 1908, were proclaimed by reformers as structures that could reduce undue political influence on administration and increase the efficiency of local government.

The council-manager form became the favorite of the reformers, endorsed by the National Municipal League as early as 1915. This form of government, featuring the appointment by the city council of a professionally trained city manager to supervise the operations of the municipality and to advise the council on policy matters, is now found in more than half of all U.S. cities with populations of 5,000 or greater (ICMA 2001, xii). The popularity of the council-manager form signaled an expanding belief that local government services could be improved under the direction of professionals—not only in the position of city manager but in departmental offices as well.

Urban service delivery through the twentieth century was increasingly influenced by professionalism—not only in cities with the council-manager form but also in those having other forms and choosing to appoint professionally trained managers and technical specialists to various administrative posts. The influence of professionalism has been felt in the recruitment of employees with more extensive preparation and specialized knowledge, the application of formal standards and informal professional norms affecting operating procedures and service quality, and interest in professional certification or accreditation in some fields of specialization. Increased professionalism often has contributed to enhanced services and innovativeness; however, it has not guaranteed creativity and open-mindedness to new ideas. Professional groups are not always friendly toward innovation. Borins (1998, 67, 288) found opposition when professions that normally have little interaction are required to work together; when new tasks or responsibilities lie outside what members of the profession believe to be the proper scope of their work; or when a given initiative calls for the use of volunteers or paraprofessionals.

Urban Service Improvements and Reforms

Proponents of service improvement have offered an assortment of plans for lifting the performance of local governments. Some perhaps could qualify as "grand strategies," designed to alter service responsibilities dramatically or replace a staid, bureaucratic orientation with a new culture of productivity. Other plans, however, have been more limited in scope and promise, mere tactical steps offered as a means of achieving service improvements in one department, program, or task at a time. In most cases, the scale at which a given idea is applied determines whether the plan is aptly characterized as a grand strategy or a tactical move. A plan to consolidate operations of a city and county, for example, might be characterized one way if the plan involves a fundamental merger of two governments and another way if it is more limited, perhaps involving the maintenance of county equipment by the city garage or the assignment of all parks and recreation responsibilities to the county government. A plan to privatize virtually all city services might be labeled a grand strategy, whereas a plan to introduce competition through more selective contracting, managed competition, or benchmarking would be regarded as tactical.

Consolidation

Many metropolitan areas have large numbers of small local governments and layers of overlapping special districts. Critics have charged that such fragmentation impedes the formulation and adoption of important plans and public policies, robs the area's central government of adequate resources, and leads to service duplication (Bollens and Schmandt 1975; Lyons and Lowery 1989; Lyons and Scheb 1998; Rusk 1995). Often their proposed solution is to consolidate governments into a smaller number, perhaps consolidating the county and its cities or merging cities, in pursuit of coordinated decision making and presumed economies of scale.

Persons who attack fragmentation, critics charge, rarely do so on the strength of persuasive evidence of the inefficiencies or service duplications they allege.

Supporters of metropolitan consolidation . . . rarely cite evidence beyond supplying a list of the number of local governments servicing a metropolitan area. This is like listing the numbers of local grocery stores as evidence to support massive campaigns to eliminate many of those stores. (Ostrom, Bish, and Ostrom 1988, 139)

Vincent Ostrom, Robert Bish, and Elinor Ostrom contend that hard evidence refutes popular assumptions regarding high levels of service duplication, showing instead that multiple service producers in a single metropolitan area typically divide service delivery responsibilities among themselves systematically. Rarely were two or more local governments found actually duplicating services for the same collective consumption unit (p. 140).

Arguments about presumed inefficiencies attributable to the effects of overlapping responsibilities of governments in the United States and in other countries more often than not have been based on anecdotes rather than credible quantitative analysis (Brown 1994). Although consolidation campaigns customarily have emphasized opportunities for presumed efficiencies, empirical studies rarely have confirmed such gains.

Proponents of small local governments challenge the criticisms of fragmentation by pointing to a set of benefits. They contend that the existence of multiple local governments increases citizens' choices of tax and service packages, expands opportunities for political participation, and enhances government's responsiveness to citizen needs and preferences (Adrian 1961; Ostrom, Tiebout, and Warren 1961). Furthermore, R. J. Oakerson and R. B. Parks have found that some fragmented local governments have used intergovernmental agreements to secure many of the benefits of a more unified system, including economies of scale, without sacrificing the advantages of smallness (Oakerson and Parks 1988; Parks and Oakerson 1989).

Whatever the merits of the competing sides of the debate, relatively few consolidation initiatives have succeeded with the voters—and rarely have these involved urban areas with populations of more than 250,000 (Harrigan and Vogel 2000, 352).

Other Service Consolidations

Short of full-fledged city-county consolidation or city-city merger, other service delivery arrangements that involve the combining of service zones or the merging of functions are possible. The term "functional consolidation" refers to an arrangement in which two local governments, often a city and a county, agree to have selected services delivered to their combined territories by one government or the other, by a newly constituted department formed from the two preexisting departments, or by a third party, perhaps a private contractor. Examples of services sometimes involved in functional consolidations include planning, building inspections, emergency communications, and recreation. Some such arrangements are long standing. Charlotte and Mecklenburg County, North Carolina, for instance, have cooperated in the delivery of selected services to their combined citizenry since the 1940s (Mead 2000).

The consolidation of disparate functions within a single local government is also a choice some units have made. Some cities, for example, have merged their police and fire departments into a public safety department with cross-trained public safety officers. Among the cities that have adopted such an arrangement are Kalamazoo, Michigan; Palm Springs, Florida; Spartanburg, South Carolina; Sunnyvale, California; and Texarkana, Arkansas.

Economies of Scale

Politicians and politically attuned citizens often speak comfortably about economies of scale in the provision of local government services. Sometimes they can be heard to argue that merger, annexation, population growth, or service expansion to include the territory of a neighboring jurisdiction makes sense, because such a move would allow service costs to be spread across a greater number of recipients, thereby reducing unit costs and achieving economies of scale. Or, if on the other side of the political debate, they argue that losses of autonomy, identity, control, and small-town values resulting from proposed growth or merger outweigh the presumed—and commonly accepted—gains in economies of scale. It is too bad that the research on economies of scale is not as clear cut as the rhetoric.

When higher volumes of service production yield lower unit costs—that is, lower costs per unit of service—the production function is said to benefit from economies of scale. Increasing the number of households receiving refuse collection services is likely to increase the total cost of that service. However, if increasing the number of households reduces the *cost per household* for refuse collection service, economies of scale are present.

Local government services sometimes enjoy economies of scale for one or more of the following reasons:

- *Technical efficiencies* may occur for some services in a manner roughly equivalent to the advantages that large manufacturing facilities have over smaller plants. The larger plant benefits from long production runs and the ability to make major capital investments and spread the capital costs across a larger number of customers. A large water treatment plant, a large library, or a large jail, for instance, conceivably could derive similar technical efficiencies.
- The addition of service units may result in *more complete utilization* of equipment and infrastructure. If excess capacity is available, expanding production to tap that reserve will reduce unit costs.
- The greater size of an operation could justify acquisition of *advanced expertise or sophisticated equipment*—or result in more complete utilization of the talent and equipment already on hand. Some small local governments cannot justify the expense of hiring the top talent in a given field or purchasing the best equipment, even when that talent and equipment might bring new efficiencies to the operation. The price is simply too high, given the small number of customers to be served. A larger operation could spread the additional cost across its large customer base and bring the efficiency advantages of greater expertise and sophisticated equipment at a more modest cost per customer.
- Greater size brings the advantages of *volume purchasing* and access to better *investment options*.

The research on economies of scale in local government service delivery has yielded helpful insights in a few notable cases but, on the whole, may be characterized as ambiguous. Although some studies have been conducted with care and have guided local government decisions, other analyses have been less helpful and have been criticized by George Boyne (1995, 213–222) for the following:

- *The use of population as a proxy for outputs.* Many studies simply divide total expenditures by population to arrive at unit costs; however, population could misrepresent the units of service actually being produced. Having a larger population might or might not generate a proportionately greater demand for outputs of a given service.
- *Cost accounting weaknesses.* Too many studies are based on figures that do not follow consistent cost accounting rules across organizations, some including a given category of cost and others excluding it.
- *Insensitivity to quality of service differences.* If a given local government is larger than others and spends less per unit for a particular service, the lower expenditure might be evidence of economies of scale or it might simply reflect poorer quality of service.
- *Ignoring differences in plant size.* A large city might operate three water plants, have five independently operated refuse collection zones, and have four semi-independent police districts, each with its own headquarters. That city has operations of different scale for various service functions and, in studies of economies of scale, should not be treated simply as one unit with outputs equal to its total population.

Despite the presence of these shortcomings in various combinations in much of the research on economies of scale, some studies have been sufficiently rigorous to yield informative, though sometimes inconsistent, results. The landmark work of Werner Hirsch (1964, 1965, 1968) explored size economies in several local government functions. Hirsch concluded that most local government services are horizontally integrated, which means that they provide services by using multiple production plants at the same stage of the production process. Neighborhood fire stations and recreation centers, police precinct stations, branch libraries, and neighborhood schools are examples. Although typically coordinated by central offices, each station, center, or branch operates with a degree of independence. Therefore, the scale of the operation, at least insofar as scale economies are concerned, is more accurately reflected by the size of an individual branch or its service zone than it is by the combined total of all branches. Unlike vertically integrated services, such as large-scale water and wastewater treatment plants, horizontally integrated services were judged unlikely to yield appreciable economies of scale (Hirsch 1968).

Intermittent research since the 1960s has explored the relevance of economies of scale in the production of various local government services—for example, fire services, libraries, police, refuse collection, and roads (Ahlbrandt 1973; DeBoer 1992; Deller, Chicoine, and Walzer 1988; Duncombe and Yinger 1993; Gyimah-Brempong 1987; Hirsch 1965; Kitchen 1976; Walzer 1972). In their review of data on police, fire, and solid waste collection, Ostrom, Bish, and Ostrom (1961, 157–161, 184) found little evidence to support the popular assumption that larger scale would always produce better, more efficient services. Although economies of scale were evident when the number of recipients of solid waste collection service increased to more than 15,000, economies of scale were less pronounced for police and fire services. Modest cost advantages for large police operations were offset by evidence that officers in these departments were stretched thin, with higher ratios of population served per officer on the street, potentially jeopardizing service quality.

Economies of scale have been detected in the performance of property tax assessments, with cost-of-service advantages for larger assessment offices up to those appraising 100,000 parcels (Sjoquist and Walker 1999). Beyond 100,000 parcels, economies of scale have been exhausted.

Findings and conclusions reached across studies of economies of scale are mixed and often contradictory. Some of this ambiguity is attributable to differences in the nature of local government services that not surprisingly yield different evidence on this issue. Part of the ambiguity is attributable to the analytic weaknesses in many of the studies, as noted previously. Examining a large number of studies in search of overarching economy-of-scale lessons can be a daunting task. Nevertheless, when Fox reviewed forty-five studies of economies of scale in education, fire protection, police protection, refuse collection, roads, and water and sewer, he found a pattern showing greater potential for size economies in capital-intensive services than in labor-intensive services (Fox 1980). Although size economies were found for each of the services examined, some diseconomies for large sizes were also detected.

Not merely daunting, the task of drawing lessons from multiple studies can also be frustrating. Consider, for example, the obvious dismay in the words of one researcher following a 1982 review of seventy-three studies focusing on economies of scale in British local governments:

We can conclude with confidence that, under certain not well understood circumstances, it may, or may not, be more, or less, economical to have larger, or smaller, local authorities. (Newton 1982, 193).

Other efforts to combine the findings of various studies have yielded similarly ambiguous conclusions (Travers, Jones, and Burnham 1993).

Researchers and local government decision makers seeking definitive answers are likely to be frustrated, for the evidence is rarely unequivocal. However, by focusing on the most meticulous analyses in a selected local government function, tendencies that have sufficient strength or regularity to support service delivery decisions can sometimes be detected. Many cities, for instance, adjusted the size of their refuse collection zones and considered alternative service delivery arrangements following E. S. Savas's discovery of economies of scale for refuse collection up to 50,000 population, but few economies beyond that scale (Savas 1977a, 1977b).

Privatization

Proponents of contracting out local government services—the most common form of privatization in cities and counties[2]—contend that private companies operating under contract can deliver services more cheaply and often at higher quality than can the government itself, despite the companies' additional requirements to turn a profit and pay taxes and their inability to borrow money at interest rates as low as those typically secured by local governments. Some of the staunchest advocates of privatization argue simply that private companies are better managed and offer a superior service delivery mechanism. Other proponents are less zealous in their advocacy and offer a variety of explanations for the tendency of contractors to be able to produce more favorable results: greater opportunities for economies of scale because they are less restricted by jurisdiction limits, superior purchasing power for equipment and supplies through volume purchases, fewer managerial regulations and operating restrictions, greater flexibility in personnel management, lower costs for unskilled and semiskilled labor outside of government, and the power of competition.

The last mentioned factor—the power of competition—most frequently gets the credit for privatization's successes. Public choice theorists contend that competition among potential service producers yields advantages that are unlikely to exist when a local government enjoys monopoly status (Blais and Dion 1992; Downs 1967; Jackson 1982; McMaster and Sawkins 1996; Mueller 1989; Niskanen 1968, 1971; Savas 1974). When city and county departments enjoy a captive market and no threats to their market dominance, they may become complacent in their service delivery routines, with oversupply and inefficient service production the unfortunate but likely results. Competition leads to the adoption of practices that improve services, cut costs, or both. Compared with their public-sector counterparts, private companies are more likely to have fewer layers of management, adopt cost-saving technologies, and use their personnel with greater flexibility (Berenyi and Stevens 1988, 11–20; Stevens 1984).

The evidence from surveys of local government officials and empirical studies is mixed, but most of it appears to confirm in general the cost advantages of contracting. That is not to say that contracting is always less expensive than in-house operations for a given level of service, but only that it tends to be. A particularly well-managed in-house operation might be less costly than services from available contractors.

Surveys and other studies have counted cost savings, as well as service quality improvements and expanded access to services, among the benefits of contracting for local government services (Keane, Marx, and Ricci 2001). In a 1995 survey of the 100 largest U.S. cities, respondents reported average estimated savings of 20.7 percent for contracted work in public works/transportation, 17.3 percent in health and human services, 16.6 percent in parks and recreation, 16.3 percent in public safety, and 16.1 percent in support services (Dilger, Moffett, and Struyk 1997, 21–26). Gains in service quality reportedly averaged 27.6 percent for contracted work in public safety, 27.2 percent in support services, 25.7 percent in parks and recreation, 24.6 percent in health and human services, and 24.2 percent in public works/transportation. More than three-quarters of the municipal finance officers responding to a 1996 National League of Cities survey cited "dollar savings to the city" as a very significant factor motivating their city's privatization decisions (Stone, Bell, and Poole 1997).

Empirical analyses, based on the facts and figures of urban service delivery, tend to corroborate the advantages of contracting noted in surveys. Based on extensive empirical research on the cost ramifications of contract refuse collection services, Savas (1977a) found that contracting decreased the cost of sanitation services by 29 to 37 percent. Studies of contracting for other functions have yielded similar results. Some, for example, have focused on Rural/Metro Corporation, which has produced fire services under contract for the city of Scottsdale, Arizona, since its municipal incorporation in 1952. Privatization enthusiasts have praised the arrangement for encouraging operational innovations (for instance, the use of no-frills fire equipment, the deployment of cross-trained employees from other municipal departments to supplement station-based firefighters, and the championing of stringent sprinkler requirements) and for remarkable performance efficiencies. One notable study compared Scottsdale with three other suburban Phoenix municipalities and found that Scottsdale's fire service effectiveness on five measures was comparable to that of the others, but its contracted service achieved these results at about half the cost (Institute for Local Self Government 1977).

In a study of selected services in the five-county Los Angeles metropolitan area, Barbara Stevens (1984) found no appreciable differences in the quality of service produced by municipal departments and by contractors for any of the eight services examined—residential refuse collection, asphalt overlay, street cleaning, traffic signal maintenance, street tree maintenance, turf maintenance, janitorial service, and payroll preparation. Cost-of-service advantages, however, were discovered for contract operations in seven of the eight services (Stevens 1984; Berenyi and Stevens 1988). The cost disparity in these seven services was least in street tree maintenance, where the cost of municipal operation was 37 percent greater than it was for contract services, and greatest for asphalt overlay, where municipal operations were 96 percent more costly than contract services. Only the payroll preparation function showed no cost advantage for contract production.

These are only a few of the many empirical studies that have compared in-house and contract production of local government services (for others, see Table 11-1). Reviews of such studies in combination generally have concluded that the bulk of evidence lies in support of greater efficiencies when contractors produce these services (Boyne 1998; Kiewiet 1991; Siegel 1999; Stein 1990).

Cost advantages are the most frequently cited reason for contracting out, but not the only reason. Additionally, local governments can acquire by contract special expertise to address a given problem or meet a particular service demand that they might be unable to justify or afford as a required skill in a full-time employee. Furthermore, contracting can reduce start-up costs and neutralize wage disadvantages (Siegel 1999).

The range of possibilities for contracting is great. In practice, the extent of contracting varies from function to function, but "contracts have been used for every service local governments provide" (Miranda and Andersen 1994, 28). In fact, some cities operate using the Lakewood Plan and contract for most or all of their services, usually contracting with other governments or a combination of governments and private companies.

The Lakewood Plan derives its name from Lakewood, California, which was incorporated as a municipality in 1954 but chose to secure virtually all of its services by means of contracts, principally with Los Angeles County. Today, more than 100 "contract cities" in California provide most municipal services by means of contract with other local government producers or private firms (Lavery 1999, 1).

Use of the Lakewood Plan is not confined to California. Taylorsville, Utah, for example, has a population of 60,000 but only twelve municipal employees (Osborne and Plastrik 2000, 188). Only planning and permitting are handled in house; everything else is produced through intergovernmental agreements or contracted out. Where small cities contract for services with larger city or county governments, they are able to secure the advantages of more sophisticated facilities—for example, more advanced emergency dispatch facilities, crime labs, and fire training centers—without having to incur major capital expenses themselves. Furthermore, they typically enjoy the flexibility of tapping additional service delivery resources—equipment and personnel—when a local event or crisis warrants extraordinary response, without making a permanent investment in crisis-level equipment and staffing.

But not all services are equally conducive to contracting. Stein (1990) observed that city governments are inclined to retain responsibilities in house for services that resemble collective and common property goods, while being more receptive to alternative arrangements for services resembling toll goods and private goods. In the

Table 11-1   Evaluative Studies of Local Government Contracting for Selected Services

Urban Services	Findings
Fire Protection	
Ahlbrandt (1973, 1974); Moore (1994)	Municipal fire department costs per capita (Seattle) 39 percent to 88 percent higher than contract fire service (Scottsdale, Ariz.).
Poole (1976); Smith (1983)	Switching to private contract fire fighting reduces costs by 20 percent to 50 percent.
Institute for Local Self Government (1977)	Cost of fire service by contract in Scottsdale, Ariz., approximately one-half the cost for equivalent protection in three comparison cities with municipal fire departments.
Kristensen (1983)	Cost of private fire service in Denmark 65 percent lower than for government service.
Motor Vehicle Maintenance	
Pommerehne and Schneider (1985)	West German study found private costs to be 50 percent lower than public costs for auto repairs.
Stolzenberg and Berry (1985)	Contracting saved approximately 17 percent; cost reductions of more than 40 percent were achieved when in-house operators won contract in managed competition.
Campbell (1988)	Contractor costs were 1 percent to 38 percent lower than municipal costs for equivalent or higher levels of service.

late 1990s, vehicle towing and solid waste collection were among the services most commonly contracted out to private for-profit companies (Table 11-2). The operation of homeless shelters was among the services frequently contracted out to non-profit organizations.

From a management perspective, the best candidates for contracting are services having clear objectives and those that are easily specified, measured, and monitored (Donahue 1989). The availability of multiple service producers contending for the contract is also a factor contributing to immediate and long-term success.

Table 11-1   (continued)

Refuse Collection

Savas (1974, 1977a, 1980); Stevens and Savas (1977); Edwards and Stevens (1976)	Public service was found to be 40 percent to 60 percent more expensive than contract service.
Collins and Downes (1977)	No significant cost differences between in-house and contract service in St. Louis area.
Petrovic and Jaffee (1977)	Cost of municipal collection in midwestern cities was 15 percent higher than contract collection.
Stevens (1978)	Open competition (free market) is 10 percent to 25 percent more expensive than public delivery and 25 percent to 50 percent more expensive than municipal contracting.
Stevens (1984)	Cost savings of 22 percent for competitive contracting versus in-house service.
Savas (1987)	Findings from nine studies conducted over a decade indicate that municipal collection costs exceed contract collection by about 35 percent.

Sources: John C. Hilke, Competition in Government-Financed Services (New York: Quorum Books, 1992), 69–94; Rowan A. Miranda, "Privatizing City Government" Ph.D. dissertation, University of Chicago, Harris Graduate School of Public Policy Studies, 1992, 81–82; Gilbert B. Siegel, "Where Are We on Local Government Service Contracting?" *Public Productivity and Management Review* 22 (March 1999): 375–383.

Despite the apparent advantages and widespread use of contracting, many observers and critics recommend caution. Some insist that contracting opens new opportunities for corruption, that without true competition too many contractors become local monopolies, and that the importance and burden of contract monitoring are often overlooked or underestimated. Some question the appropriateness of contracting critical or sensitive local government services. For example, in a survey of directors of local health departments, respondents expressed reluctance to privatize communicable disease services. Researchers detected a "pervasive concern that by contracting out services, health departments can lose the capacity to respond to dis-

Table 11-2   Local Government Services Most Frequently Contracted Out

Contracts with Private For-Profit Companies	Contracts with Private Nonprofit Organizations
Vehicle towing and storage, 79%	
Commercial solid waste collection, 60%	Operation of homeless shelters, 61%
Gas operations, 57%	
Legal services, 51%	
Residential solid waste collection, 49%	
Operation of daycare facilities, 48%	
Electric utility operations, 40%	
Solid waste disposal, 40%	Operation of museums, 39%
Hazardous materials disposal, 37%	
Hospital operations, 36%	Cultural and arts programs, 36%
Tree trimming, 36%	Hospital operations, 36%
Street repair, 34%	Drug and alcohol treatment programs, 35%
Maintenance of emergency vehicles, 34%	
Maintenance of heavy equipment, 33%	
General fleet maintenance, 32%	Daycare facilities, 31%

Source: Excerpted with permission from Lawrence L. Martin, *Contracting for Service Delivery: Local Government Choices* (Washington, D.C.: International City/County Management Association, 1999): 6–8.

Note: Percentages are for respondents who reported contracts in 1997.

ease outbreaks and other crises" (Keane, Marx, and Ricci 2001).[3] Other observers worry about loss of control and accountability, as well as service inequities, when local governments no longer produce the services themselves (Donahue 1989, Halachmi and Holzer 1993, Hilke 1992, Kettl 1993, Morgan and England 1988, Voytek 1991, Wilson 1989).[4]

Managed Competition

Managed competition leads to privatization only when private companies outbid local government departments for the privilege of producing a given service. In managed competition, the local government is one of the bidders.

This approach to the selection of service producers is popular among local government decision makers who are receptive to privatization but believe that the key to getting the best product or service at the best price is *competition*—not simply securing a service producer from the private sector. If the local government department can use its advantages (for example, no taxes and no profit requirement) to produce a competitive bid, these officials are pleased to retain the service in house. Among the city governments often noted for their managed competition programs are Phoenix, Indianapolis, Charlotte, Cleveland, and New York City.

The city credited with being the first to experiment with managed competition is Phoenix, which began engaging its own departments in competitive bidding with private contractors in 1979. By 1995, Phoenix had used this competitive process to make fifty-six service delivery decisions affecting thirteen functions, ranging from refuse collection to public defender services; city departments were selected twenty-two times and private contractors thirty-four times. The competitive process yielded documented savings of more than $27 million and notable gains in service quality as well. For example, the percentage of ambulances responding to emergencies within ten minutes improved from 48 percent at the beginning of that service's entry into the competitive process in 1984 to 95 percent by 1995 (Flanagan and Perkins 1995).

Indianapolis entered the arena of managed competition in the wake of a successful mayoral campaign actually waged on a privatization platform. Once in office, Mayor Stephen Goldsmith came to believe that the key to achieving favorable cost and quality of local government services was competition rather than privatization. Managed competition was credited with huge savings in Indianapolis, but critics contended that many of the savings were illusory, that claims of success often were "sleight of hand," and that the case of Indianapolis was "more an example of good marketing than good government" (Thompson and Epstein 2001, B1).

Even if some of the claims were inflated, the documented benefits of managed competition appear to be real and substantial in magnitude. A key to these benefits among the local governments most often named as exemplars in this process was the engagement of their own departments as serious competitors that could either craft a winning bid themselves or force outside firms to submit an excellent offer. Typically, these governments prepared their employees to compete effectively. Phoenix, Indianapolis, and others analyzed current procedures, equipment, and staffing and attempted to streamline their operations before preparing the municipal bid, sometimes employing consultants in that endeavor (Martin 1999b). Charlotte conducted training classes entitled "Competition 101" for its employees.

Competitive government was a key value in the movement to reinvent government, introduced in the 1990s. Managed competition was an important strategy in that movement. "The issue is not public versus private," say reinventors. "It is competition versus monopoly" (Osborne and Gaebler 1992, 76).

Competitive Service Delivery Arrangements

Yet another variation that draws on the benefits of privatization is an arrangement that relies on competition at the service delivery stage—not simply competition in the bidding process. Cities that divide their service districts and allow some territories to be handled by private contractors and others by their own municipal forces enjoy the benefits of competition without relinquishing the service delivery role altogether. Nor do these cities relinquish the expertise in a given service that accompanies hands-on experience in actually delivering that service. Although studies have shown that private-sector service producers in such arrangements are somewhat more efficient than their municipal counterparts, both parties tend to be better performers in cost and service quality than they would have been without the competitive pressure of having an alternative producer in the district next door (Ammons and Hill 1995; Savas 1981).

Miscellaneous Initiatives to Improve Service Delivery

Over the years a variety of initiatives beyond structural reform, professionalism, consolidation, and assorted forms of competition have been advanced as strategies or techniques for improving urban services. Among these initiatives have been the movement to replace centralized authority for some functions with decentralized, grass-roots control (Lawrence and Lorsch 1967; Mintzberg 1989; White 1999); the drive to introduce and subsequently to strengthen performance measurement in local government operations, partially as a means to ensure accountability and partially for management feedback, analysis, and operations improvements (for example, Ammons 2001; Hatry 1999; Hatry, Blair, Fisk, Greiner, Hall, and Schaenman 1992); and various quality-of-service efforts, including quality circles, total quality management, and methods for securing citizen or customer feedback (for example, Miller and Miller 1991).[5]

In some cases, the findings from field research have challenged and helped reshape prevailing thought on service delivery strategies. A prime example is the landmark study known as the Kansas City preventive patrol experiment. This year-long experiment, which began in 1972 under the sponsorship of the Police Foundation, tested the effectiveness of routine police patrols in Kansas City, Missouri (Kelling, Pate, Dieckman, and Brown 1974; Henig, Lineberry, and Milner 1977). The findings challenged conventional wisdom regarding the value of police patrol as a means of reducing crime and increasing citizens' feelings of security.

For purposes of experimentation, Kansas City was divided into areas with three different deployment strategies. In one area, police units responded to calls but engaged in no routine patrols whatsoever. In the second area, police patrols were intensified far beyond the norm. In the third area, the "control group," patrol activities continued unchanged from their previous levels. Researchers detected no statistically significant differences among the three areas in burglaries, auto thefts, larcenies involving auto accessories, robberies, or vandalism—the types of crimes presumed to be deterred by visible patrol. Similarly, there were no appreciable differences among the areas in the rates at which citizens reported crime, citizen satisfaction with police, or fear of crime. Years later, proponents of community-oriented policing would argue that just increasing routine patrol or police presence was not enough, urging instead a more focused or targeted deployment of police resources within selected neighborhoods.

Also in the 1970s, a study of one- versus two-officer patrol cars in San Diego challenged conventional wisdom on safety and effectiveness, if not efficiency (Boydstun, Sherry, and Moelter 1977). One-officer cars were found to be safe, more efficient, and just as effective as two-officer units.

Some communities have improved service efficiency through the use of task systems that reward employees for their diligence (Frazier and Lewis 1981, 4). Some have experimented with process reengineering, which entails the complete rethinking of a process—perhaps starting from scratch—to achieve a design that produces dramatically enhanced results (for example, lower costs, higher quality, speedier production). Others have engaged in benchmarking, comparing their own performance with that of outstanding counterparts or relevant standards and seeking "best practices" (Ammons 2001; Keehley, Medlin, MacBride, and Longmire 1997).

Reinventing Government

American government is no stranger to high-profile initiatives designed to achieve major administrative reform. Scientific management, merit systems, the federal Taft commission of 1911 and the subsequent efficiency commissions formed at state and local levels, the Brownlow committee in 1937, the Hoover commissions, civil service reform, the Winter commission, the Volcker commission, and others have influenced local practices, whether or not local government was their principal focus. Near the close of the twentieth century came yet another reform initiative—this one labeled *reinventing government.*

In a movement both pervasive in its influence on public sector management and surprising in the depth of its popular appeal, the drive for reinvention swept the nation following the 1992 publication of *Reinventing Government,* written by David Osborne and Ted Gaebler. Their book extolled the virtues of governments that were market oriented, customer driven, and focused on results and government officials who favored decentralization, community empowerment, and participative, team-oriented systems. With subsequent coauthor Peter Plastrik, Osborne later refined the formula for reinventing government to encompass five strategies (Osborne and Plastrik 2000; 1997):

- *The core strategy,* which tightens an organization's focus on its fundamental mission, concentrating its essential efforts on that mission and perhaps shedding some of its less important duties.
- *The consequences strategy,* which calls for performance-based rewards and penalties through such devices as managed competition, fee-for-service revenue structures, and incentives for reaching performance targets.

- *The customer strategy,* which takes into account the needs and wishes of service recipients and strives to meet their expectations.
- *The control strategy,* which insists on accountability for results while decentralizing decision-making authority.
- *The culture strategy,* which seeks to change the attitude of public-sector employees from a bureaucratic mind-set to a culture that embraces high performance standards and innovation.

The principles of government reinvention were widely heralded by politicians, local government managers, and the public. Perhaps part of the appeal for local officials was that so many of the reinvention principles were "developed and applied first in local government settings" (Kearney, Feldman, and Scavo 2000, 537). Most city managers responding to a 1998 ICMA survey agreed with the principles of reinvention and reported having already recommended initiatives in their community consistent with these principles (Rivera, Streib, and Willoughby 2000). Survey responses from human resource administrators in 1996 indicated that "public agencies that have engaged in reinvention see themselves as better, faster, stronger—that is, as organizations with improved processes, more ability to handle tasks efficiently, and greater effectiveness" (Durst and Newell 1999, 74).

Among the most popular of all the programs publicized under the banner of government reinvention is the law enforcement initiative known as community-oriented policing (COP). Despite roots anchored in police innovations that actually predate the reinvention movement, such as problem-oriented policing and team policing, COP was quickly adopted as a poster child of reinventing government (Gianakis and Davis 1998; Turner and Wiatrowski 1995). The essential elements of community policing include police consultation with the community regarding security needs, focused problem solving to remedy the conditions that contribute to crime, cooperation among police and nonpolice agencies, and command devolution for service delivery decisions (Bayley 1994). Some of these essentials appear to be at odds with the "hierarchical, military model [of traditional police departments], which has been largely closed to public participation" and "an organizational structure that may be antithetical to [the] basic precepts" of community policing (Gianakis and Davis 1998, 486–487).

Some observers have questioned the practical feasibility of COP programs and the depth of commitment to the principles and philosophy of community policing among self-proclaimed COP adopters (Buerger 1994; Klockars 1991; Moore 1994; Roberg 1994). Adoption studies have noted resistance among police supervisors to command devolution, as well as little evidence of police departments willing to open themselves to meaningful citizen involvement and community empowerment (Gianakis and Davis 1998). Nevertheless, by the mid-1990s, 42 percent of the police departments serving 50,000 residents or more claimed to have adopted some aspect of community policing (Trojanowicz 1994). A study of COP adoptions in Florida, however, suggests that adopters sometimes exaggerate the extent of structural changes being made, the degree of decentralization actually occurring, and the depth of community involvement beyond intelligence gathering for crime investigation and prevention purposes (Gianakis and Davis 1998). Still, many departments have at least decentralized patrol functions to substations, added specialized community policing units to their existing patrol operations, or sensitized patrol officers to the principles of community policing and the importance of positive community relations.

Despite the warm embrace of politicians, local government managers, and the public, as well as the popularity of programs such as community-oriented policing that were often associated with reinventing government, the movement and the book at its center received a mixed reception from scholars—some praising the book and others pointing out its shortcomings. Critics complained of conceptual weaknesses and inconsistencies (Fox 1996; Goodsell 1993; Kellough 1998); weak, anecdotal scholarship, yielding inconsistent recommendations that ignored history (Williams 2000); incessant "bashing of the bureaucracy" and only modest concern with "matters of justice and fairness" (Frederickson 1996); ill-advised calls for entrepreneurial behavior in the public sector, introducing adventurousness and a willingness to bend the rules (DeLeon and Denhardt 2000; Goodsell 1993; Terry 1998); and an insistence on converting citizens to customers (Carroll 1995; Frederickson 1996).

Those who praised the book and the movement it spawned offered a perspective that differed sharply from that of the critics. For instance, they saw *Reinventing Government* not as an attack on bureaucrats but instead as a book that "acknowledged the contributions of public managers . . . , a welcome contrast to aggressive bashings delivered by other parties" (Rivera, Streib, and Willoughby 2000, 121). They argued that calculated risk taking had produced important public-sector gains (Behn 1998) and that the systematic study of recognized innovators revealed nothing to validate the worst fears of the critics of entrepreneurial government (Borins 2000). Furthermore, they suggested that the argument about the *citizen* and *customer* labels was overblown.

Although proponents of a customer service orientation for local government accord high status to the citizen as customer, critics perceive it otherwise. Citizen involvement is primarily passive in the customer model, with little action beyond intermittent complaints or occasional participation in satisfaction surveys (Frederickson 1994, 9). Critics prefer an alternate model that focuses on citizens as the owners of government. Although the owner model clearly is appropriate in a conceptual sense, in practice it would demand that citizens recognize "a duty to get involved in city affairs and instruct politicians and public administrators in 'shareholder' demands" (Schachter 1995, 530; also see Frederickson 1992, 13). The unwillingness of most citizens to be so involved may undermine this model.[6]

If the customer label implies diminished status, it is unintentional. Nothing in the published comments of practicing local government officials who are enthusiastic about customer service suggests a lower regard for customers than for citizens (Mc-Clendon 2000). Kettl suggests that the roles of citizen and customer are not incompatible and that in most instances citizens can be treated as owners *and* customers, thereby giving government the opportunity to benefit from the "genuine value in the customer service approach" (1994, 34).

The books by Osborne, Gaebler, and Plastrik on which government reinvention is based are more journalistic than analytic, with principles drawn primarily from anecdotal rather than systematic evidence. Many of the reinvention principles that are most controversial among scholars have not been adequately tested. Treating them as hypotheses and testing their validity would be a worthy endeavor for urban service researchers and analysts.

The State of Urban Service Research

A review of articles published in *Public Administration Review* from 1979 to 1989 led Watson and Montjoy (1991) to conclude that local government was well represented as a topic of inquiry, with 30.9 percent of all articles devoted partially or fully to local government. Furthermore, most of these articles were catalogued as being directed toward management topics (for example, finance and budgeting, general management, and personnel management) and therefore were said to be focused on "nuts and bolts questions" rather than "broader, social issues."

With so much research devoted to topics of local government management and, as noted in this chapter, to urban services, why do public administration scholars continue to hear complaints that their work is irrelevant from so many of those who practice public administration? Why do practitioners call much of it "too academic"? Why do employers complain that although recent graduates of some public administration programs might possess considerable knowledge, they *cannot do anything*? A clue might be discovered in the categories of urban service research outlined at the beginning of this chapter. These categories are as follows:

1. Inventories of service delivery systems.
2. Political or sociological studies of service delivery patterns.
3. Analysis of the mechanics of managing service delivery.
4. Evaluation of the efficacy of service delivery strategies.

The first two categories identify urban service patterns and analyze them in an effort to understand what they mean and why they exist. Research of this kind produces excellent material for seminars and is likely to be of interest to students of urban affairs. But to a practicing local government official this kind of research is likely to seem relevant mostly to classroom discussions and, all in all, not too helpful as the basis for practical decision making. Telling a city manager that various percentages of cities conduct citizen surveys, measure performance, contract for service, or use automated refuse collection equipment, and that the tendency to adopt any of these practices is linked to particular community characteristics, forms of government, managerial tenure, or the extent of unionization, provides neither justification for doing so in this manager's city nor instructions for ensuring effective implementation. Many of the factors of interest to the researcher—for example, population, region, per capita income, fiscal stress, and even form of government—are perceived by the practitioner as being beyond management control. Hence, "too academic."

The practicing manager's interests tend to lie in the third and fourth categories. Consider the topic of citizen feedback. Telling a city manager how to avoid survey pitfalls and derive useful information (category 3) or demonstrating empirically the documentable value of citizen surveys (category 4) are more practical and valuable services than merely reporting the number or percentage of cities conducting surveys (category 1). However, even the third and fourth categories have weaknesses that make some managers uncomfortable. The third category is sometimes the domain of writers who may be characterized as true believers—advocates of particular strategies and techniques simply because they make sense to their proponent, not because their value has been demonstrated empirically or even anecdotally on a sufficiently consistent basis. The fourth category, potentially the most relevant and valuable of all to practitioners, includes some excellent studies based on rigorous analysis of facts and figures that are pertinent to the management of urban services and address choices that are controllable by local initiative. But not every entry in this category would elicit practitioner accolades, for the category is diluted by impressionistic studies that record what survey respondents merely say they *think* is the effect of one management initiative or another.

This assessment differs from that of critics who say that public administration research in general lacks sufficient methodological rigor to compare favorably with the research of mainstream social science disciplines such as economics, political science, sociology, and psychology (Perry and Kraemer 1986; White 1986; Stallings and Ferris 1988; Houston and Delevan 1990). Although greater rigor and methodological sophistication would in many cases strengthen the quality and value of public administration research, the greater issue, from a practitioner's perspective, is the purpose of the research and the relevance of the questions being asked. As noted by Richard Box, it is inappropriate to compare the research and research methods of practice-oriented fields like law, planning, architecture, education, and business or public administration with the research and research methods of disciplines that are more inclined to value knowledge strictly for its own sake (Box 1992). If the purpose of research in the applied or professional fields differs somewhat from the purpose of research in the mainstream social sciences, it should not be too surprising if the relevant research questions and the methods suitable for answering them differ as well.

Unquestionably, some issues related to urban services are matters of politics, sociology, or law. Nevertheless, to an extent greater than for most other aspects of urban government, issues of service delivery tend to be pragmatic and managerial. For these issues, the most relevant research questions are similarly pragmatic and managerial.

To assume that a study deemed "too academic" is simply too sophisticated methodologically for a given practitioner audience is perhaps incorrect. Most local government officials are accustomed to taking professional advice from specialists in disciplines other than their own, often based on techniques that are sometimes quite sophisticated. More often than not, being labeled "too academic" means that the research is simply considered not relevant to the decision process.

Consider, for example, the literature on the monitoring of service contracts by local governments. Surveys that indicate the percentage of cities claiming to monitor contractor performance (category 1) and studies that associate greater monitoring tendencies with cities of a given population range or government form (category 2) provide an interesting discussion point for a conference speaker or a graduate seminar but are likely to be dismissed by a local government practitioner as irrelevant to decisions regarding contract monitoring in that practitioner's community. Specific advice on the mechanics of monitoring particular types of service contracts (category 3) would be more helpful. Best of all would be research that demonstrates empirically the value of various types and levels of contract monitoring (category 4). Ironically, this final category of research tests the academic skills of the researcher to a greater extent than any of the others do; yet this category is less likely than the general surveys or correlation studies to be labeled by practitioners as "too academic."

Conclusion

The focus on efficiency that dominated the writings on urban services in the first half of the twentieth century broadened by midcentury to include patterns of service delivery and the quality, responsiveness, and effectiveness, as well as the efficiency, of urban services. Research on urban services has been extensive. However, a substantial portion of this work, although of interest in the *study* of urban systems, has been of limited value to the *practice* of urban management. Studies that catalog patterns of service delivery, describe trends in the adoption of various management techniques, or correlate service patterns and community characteristics have been far more plentiful than the more managerially valuable studies that systematically analyze management and service delivery tactics or evaluate the efficacy of service delivery strategies. The interests of urban service practitioners and service recipients would be better addressed by shifting greater research attention to the latter.

Suggested Readings

Gargan, John J., ed. 1997. *Handbook of Local Government Administration.* New York: Marcel Dekker. This book includes several chapters on urban services written by distinguished scholars.

Kemp, Roger L. 1997. *Managing America's Cities: A Handbook for Local Government Productivity.* Jefferson, N.C.: McFarland. The author describes the major service functions performed by local governments, provides operational details, and notes recent trends in service delivery.

Morgan, David R., and Robert E. England. 1999. *Managing Urban America.* 5th ed. New York: Chatham House. The authors incorporate urban research throughout this volume and devote individual chapters to "Analysis for Urban Decisions," "Urban Service Delivery," and "Improving Productivity."

Whelan, Robert K. 1999. "Public Administration—The State of the Discipline: A View from the Urban and Local Management Literature." *Public Administration Quarterly* (spring): 46–64. This article offers insightful commentary on recent research in urban administration.

References

Adrian, Charles R. 1961. "A Metropology: Folklore and Field Research." *Public Administration Review* 21 (summer): 148–157.

Ahlbrandt, Jr. Roger S. 1973. "Efficiency in the Provision of Fire Services." *Public Choice* 16 (fall): 1–15.

——— 1974. "Implications of Contracting for Public Service." *Urban Affairs Quarterly,* 9 (March): 337–358.

Ammons, David N. 2001. *Municipal Benchmarks: Assessing Local Performance and Establishing Community Standards.* 2d ed. Thousand Oaks, Calif.: Sage.

Ammons, David N., and Debra J. Hill. 1995. "The Viability of Public-Private Competition as a Long-Term Service Delivery Strategy." *Public Productivity and Management Review* 19 (September): 12–24.

Antunes, George, and Kenneth Mladenka. 1976. "The Politics of Local Services and Service Distribution." In *The New Urban Politics,* ed. Louis Masotti and Robert Lineberry, 147–164. Cambridge, Mass.: Ballinger.

Bayley, David H. 1994. "International Differences in Community Policing." In *The Challenge of Community Policing,* ed. Dennis P. Rosenbaum, 278–281. Thousand Oaks, Calif.: Sage.

Behn, Robert. 1998. "What Right Do Public Managers Have to Lead?" *Public Administration Review* 58: 209–224.

Berenyi, Eileen Brettler, and Barbara J. Stevens. 1988. "Does Privatization Work? A Study of the Delivery of Eight Local Services." *State and Local Government Review* 20 (winter): 11–20.

Blais, Andre, and Stephane Dion, eds. 1992. *The Budget-Maximizing Bureaucrat.* Pittsburgh: University of Pittsburgh Press.

Bollens, John C., and Henry J. Schmandt. 1975. *The Metropolis: Its People, Politics and Economic Life*. 3d ed. New York: Harper and Row.

Borins, Sandford. 1998. *Innovating with Integrity: How Local Heroes Are Transforming American Government*. Washington, D.C.: Georgetown University Press.

——— 2000. "Loose Cannons and Rule Breakers, or Enterprising Leaders? Some Evidence about Innovative Public Managers." *Public Administration Review* 60 (November–December): 498–507.

Box, Richard C. 1992. "An Examination of the Debate over Research in Public Administration." *Public Administration Review* 52 (January–February): 62–69.

Boydstun, John, Michael E. Sherry, and Nicholas P. Moelter. 1977. *Patrol Staffing in San Diego: One- or Two-Officer Units*. Washington, D.C.: Police Foundation.

Boyne, George A. 1995. "Population Size and Economies of Scale in Local Government." *Policy and Politics* 23 (July): 213–222.

——— 1998. "Bureaucratic Theory Meets Reality: Public Choice and Service Contracting in U.S. Local Government." *Public Administration Review* 58 (November–December): 474–484.

Brown, Gordon R. 1994. "Canadian Federal-Provincial Overlap and Presumed Government Inefficiency." *Publius* 24 (winter): 21–37.

Buerger, Michael E. 1994. "The Limits of Community." In *The Challenge of Community Policing*, ed. Dennis P. Rosenbaum, 270–273. Thousand Oaks, Calif.: Sage.

Campbell, A. 1988. "Private Delivery of Public Services: Sorting Out the Policy and Management Issues," *Public Management* 68 (December): 3–5.

Carroll, J. D. 1995. "The Rhetoric of Reform and Political Reality in the National Performance Review." *Public Administration Review* 55 (May–June): 302–310.

Clingermayer, James C., and Richard C. Feiock. 1997. "Leadership Turnover, Transaction Costs, and External City Service Delivery." *Public Administration Review* 57 (May–June): 231–239.

Collins, John N., and Bryant T. Downes. 1977. "The Effects of Size on the Provision of Public Services: The Case of Solid Waste Collection in Smaller Cities," *Urban Affairs Quarterly* 12 (March): 333–334.

DeBoer, Larry. 1992. "Economies of Scale and Input Substitution in Public Libraries." *Journal of Urban Economics* 32 (September): 257–268.

DeLeon, Linda, and Robert B. Denhardt. 2000. "The Political Theory of Reinvention." *Public Administration Review* 60 (March–April): 89–97.

Deller, Steven C., David L. Chicoine, and Norman Walzer. 1988. "Economics of Size and Scope in Rural Low-Volume Roads." *Review of Economics and Statistics* 70 (August): 459–465.

Dilger, Robert Jay, Randolph R. Moffett, and Linda Struyk. 1997. "Privatization of Municipal Services in America's Largest Cities." *Public Administration Review* 57 (January–February): 21–26.

Donahue, John D. 1989. *The Privatization Decision*. New York: Basic Books.

Downs, Anthony. 1967. *Inside Bureaucracy*. Boston: Little, Brown.

Duncombe, William, and John Yinger. 1993. "An Analysis of Returns to Scale in Public Production, with an Application to Fire Protection." *Journal of Public Economics* 52 (August): 49–72.

Durst, Samantha L., and Charldean Newell. 1999. "Better, Faster, Stronger: Government Reinvention in the 1990s." *American Review of Public Administration* 29 (March): 61–76.

Edwards, Franklin R., and Barbara J. Stevens. 1976. "Relative Efficiency of Alternative Institutional Arrangements for Collecting Refuse: Collective Action vs. the Free Market," New York: Columbia University Graduate School of Business, Research Paper No. 151.

Ferris, James, and Elizabeth Graddy. 1986. "Contracting Out: For What? With Whom?" *Public Administration Review* 46 (July–August): 332–344.

Flanagan, Jim, and Susan Perkins. 1995. "Public/Private Competition in the City of Phoenix, Arizona." *Government Finance Review* 11 (June): 7–12.

Fox, C. J. 1996. "Reinventing Government as Postmodern Symbolic Politics." *Public Administration Review* 56 (May–June): 256–262.

Fox, William F. 1980. *Size Economies in Local Government Services: A Review.* Washington, D.C.: U.S. Department of Agriculture, Economic Development Division, Economics, Statistics, and Cooperatives Service. Rural Development Research Report No. 22.

Frazier, Mark, and Jim Lewis. 1981. "Some American Communities 'Privatize' to Cut Costs." *Transatlantic Perspective* 5 (July): 4–5.

Frederickson, H. George. 1992. "Painting Bull's-Eyes Around Bullet Holes." *Governing* 6 (October): 13.

————— 1994. "George and the Case of Government Reinventors." *PA Times* 17 (January): 9.

————— 1996. "Comparing the Reinventing Government Movement with the New Public Administration." *Public Administration Review* 56 (May–June): 263–270.

Gianakis, Gerasimos A., and G. John Davis III. 1998. "Reinventing or Repackaging Public Services? The Case of Community-Oriented Policing." *Public Administration Review* 58 (November–December): 485–498.

Goodsell, Charles T. 1993. "Reinvent Government or Rediscover It?" *Public Administration Review* 53 (January–February): 85–87.

Gyimah-Brempong, Kwabana. 1987. "Economies of Scale in Municipal Police Departments: The Case of Florida." *Review of Economics and Statistics* 69 (May): 352–356.

Harrigan, John J., and Ronald K. Vogel. 2000. *Political Change in the Metropolis.* 6th ed. New York: Longman.

Hatry, Harry P., Louis H. Blair, Donald M. Fisk, John M. Greiner, John R. Hall Jr., and Philip S. Schaenman. 1992. *How Effective Are Your Community Services?* Washington, D.C.: Urban Institute and International City/County Management Association.

Hatry, Harry P. 1999. *Performance Measurement: Getting Results.* Washington, D.C.: Urban Institute Press.

Henig, Jeffrey, Robert L. Lineberry, and Neal A. Milner. 1977. "The Policy Impact of Policy Evaluation: Some Implications of the Kansas City Patrol Experiment." In *Public Law and Public Policy,* ed. John A. Gardiner, 225–241. New York: Praeger.

Herzog, Richard J., and Ronald G. Claunch. 1997. "Stories Citizens Tell and How Administrators Use Types of Knowledge." *Public Administration Review* 57 (September–October): 374–379.

Hilke, John C. 1992. *Competition in Government-Financial Services.* New York: Quorum.

Hirsch, Werner Z. 1964. "Local vs. Areawide Urban Government Services." *National Tax Journal* 17 (December): 331–339.

————— 1965. "Cost Functions of an Urban Government Service: Refuse Collection." *Review of Economics and Statistics* 47: 87–93.

————— 1968. "The Supply of Urban Public Services." *Issues in Urban Economics.* Baltimore: Johns Hopkins University Press.

Houston, David J., and Sybil M. Delevan. 1990. "Public Administration Research: An Assessment of Journal Publications." *Public Administration Review* 50 (November–December): 674–681.

ICMA. 2001. *The Municipal Year Book: 2001.* Washington, D.C.: International City/County Management Association.

Institute for Local Self Government. 1977. *Alternatives to Traditional Public Safety Delivery Systems.* Berkeley, Calif.: ILSG.

Jackson, P. 1982. *The Political Economy of Bureaucracy.* London: Phillip Allen.

Keane, Christopher, John Marx, and Edmund Ricci. 2001. "Perceived Outcomes of Public Health Privatization: A National Survey of Local Health Department Directors." *Milbank Quarterly* 79: 115–137.

Kearney, Richard C., Barry M. Feldman, and Carmine P. F. Scavo. 2000. "Reinventing Government: City Manager Attitudes and Actions." *Public Administration Review* 60 (November–December): 537.

Keehley, Patricia, Steven Medlin, Sue MacBride, and Laura Longmire. 1997. *Benchmarking for Best Practices in the Public Sector.* San Francisco: Jossey-Bass.

Kelling, George L., Tony Pate, Duane Dieckman, and Charles E. Brown. 1974. *The Kansas City Preventive Patrol Experiment: A Technical Report.* Washington, D.C.: Police Foundation.

Kellough, J. Edward. 1998. "The Reinventing Government Movement: A Review and Critique." *Public Administration Quarterly* 22 (spring): 6–20.

Kettl, Donald F. 1993. *Sharing Power.* Washington, D.C.: Brookings Institution.

——— 1994. *Reinventing Government? Appraising the National Performance Review.* Washington, D.C.: Brookings Institution.

Kiewiet, D. Roderick. 1991. "Bureaucrats and Budgetary Outcomes: Quantitative Analyses." In *The Budget Maximizing Bureaucrat,* ed. Andre Blais and Stephane Dion. Pittsburgh: University of Pittsburgh Press.

Kitchen, Harry. 1976 "A Statistical Estimation of an Operating Cost Function for Municipal Refuse Collection." *Public Finance Quarterly* 4 (January): 56–76.

Klockars, Carl B. 1991. "The Rhetoric of Community Policing." In *Community Policing: Rhetoric or Reality,* ed. Jack R. Greene and Stephen D. Mastrofski, 239–258. New York: Praeger.

Kristensen, Ole. 1983. "Public Versus Private Provision of Government Services: The Case of Danish Fire Protection Services." *Urban Studies* 20(1): 1–9.

Lavery, Kevin. 1999. *Smart Contracting for Local Government Services.* Westport, Conn.: Praeger.

Lawrence, P. R., and J. W. Lorsch. 1967. *Organization and Environment.* Cambridge: Harvard University Press.

Levy, Frank, Arnold Meltsner, and Aaron Wildavsky. 1974. *Urban Outcomes: Schools, Streets, and Libraries.* Berkeley: University of California Press.

Lineberry, Robert L. 1975. "Equality, Public Policy and Public Services: The Under-Class Hypothesis and the Limits to Equality." *Policy and Politics* 4 (December): 67–84.

——— 1977. *Equality and Urban Policy: The Distribution of Municipal Public Services.* Beverly Hills, Calif.: Sage.

Lyons, W. E., and David Lowery. 1989. "Governmental Fragmentation Versus Consolidation: Five Public Choice Myths About How to Create Informed, Involved and Happy Citizens." *Public Administration Review* 49 (November–December): 533–542.

Lyons, William, and John M. Scheb II. 1998. "Saying 'No' One More Time: The Rejection of Consolidated Government in Knox County, Tennessee." *State and Local Government Review* 30 (spring): 92–105.

Martin, Lawrence L. 1999a. *Contracting for Service Delivery: Local Government Choices.* Washington, D.C.: International City/County Management Association.

——— 1999b. "Public-Private Competition: A Public Employee Alternative to Privatization." *Review of Public Personnel Administration* 19 (winter): 59–70.

McClendon, Bruce. 2000. "Taking Customer Service to the Next Level," *Public Management* 82 (December): 12–17.

McGuire, R. A., R. L. Ohsfeldt, and T. N. van Cott. 1987. "The Determinants of the Choice between Public and Private Production of a Publicly Funded Service." *Public Choice* 54 (August): 211–230.

McMaster, R., and J. Sawkins. 1996. "The Contract State, Trust Distortion and Efficiency." *Review of Social Economy* 54 (summer): 145–167.

Mead, Timothy D. 2000. "Governing Charlotte-Mecklenburg." *State and Local Government Review* 32 (fall): 192–197.

Melkers, Julia, and John Clayton Thomas. 1998. "What Do Administrators Think Citizens Think? Administrator Predictions as an Adjunct to Citizen Surveys." *Public Administration Review* 58 (July–August): 327–334.

Miller, Thomas I., and Michelle A. Miller. 1991. "Standards of Excellence: U.S. Residents' Evaluations of Local Government Services." *Public Administration Review* 51 (November–December): 503–513.

Mintzberg, Henry. 1989. *Mintzberg on Management.* New York: Free Press.

Miranda, Rowan. 1992. *Privatizing City Government.* Chicago: Doctoral Dissertation, University of Chicago, Harris Graduate School of Public Policy.

Miranda, R., and K. Andersen. 1994. "Alternative Service Delivery in Local Government, 1982–1992." In *The Municipal Year Book 1994,* 26–35. Washington, D.C.: International City/County Management Association.

Mladenka, Kenneth R. 1981. "Citizen Demands and Urban Services: The Distribution of Bureaucratic Response in Chicago and Houston." *American Journal of Political Science* 25 (November): 693–714.

Moore, Mark H. 1994. "Research Synthesis and Policy Implications." In *The Challenge of Community Policing: Testing the Promises,* ed. Dennis P. Rosenbaum, 285–299. Thousand Oaks, Calif.: Sage.

Morgan, David, and Robert England. 1988. "The Two Faces of Privatization." *Public Administration Review* 48 (November–December): 979–987.

Morley, Elaine. 1989. "Patterns in the Use of Alternative Service Delivery Approaches." In *The Municipal Yearbook 1989,* 33–44. Washington, D.C.: International City/County Management Association.

Mosher, F. C. 1968. *Democracy and the Public Service.* New York: Oxford University Press.

Mueller, D. 1989. *Public Choice II.* Cambridge: Cambridge University Press.

The Municipal Year Book. 2000. Washington, D.C.: International City/County Management Association.

Newton, K. 1982. "Is Small Really So Beautiful? Is Big Really So Ugly? Size, Effectiveness, and Democracy in Local Government." *Political Studies* 30 (June): 190–206.

Niskanen, William A. 1968. "The Peculiar Economics of Bureaucracy." *American Economic Review* 58 (May): 293–305.

——— 1971. *Bureaucracy and Representative Government.* Chicago: Aldine-Altherton.

Nyland, C. 1989. *Reduced Worktime and the Management of Production.* New York: Cambridge University Press.

Oakerson, R. J., and R. B. Parks. 1988. "Citizen Voice and Public Entrepreneurship: The Organizational Dynamic of a Complex Metropolitan County." *Publius* 18 (fall): 91–112.

Osborne, David, and Ted Gaebler. 1992. *Reinventing Government: How the Entrepreneurial Spirit Is Transforming the Public Sector.* Reading, Mass.: Addison-Wesley.

Osborne, David, and Peter Plastrik. 1997. *Banishing Bureaucracy.* Reading, Mass.: Addison-Wesley.

——— 2000. *The Reinventor's Fieldbook.* San Francisco: Jossey-Bass.

Ostrom, Vincent, Charles M. Tiebout, and Robert Warren. 1961. "The Organization of Government in Metropolitan Areas: A Theoretical Inquiry." *American Political Science Review* 55 (December): 831–842.

Ostrom, Vincent, Robert Bish, and Elinor Ostrom. 1988. *Local Government in the United States.* San Francisco: Institute for Contemporary Studies.

Parks, R. B., and R. J. Oakerson. 1989. "St. Louis: The ACIR Study." *Intergovernmental Perspective* 15 (winter): 9–11.

Perry, James L., and Kenneth L. Kraemer. 1986. "Research Methodology in the *Public Administration Review,* 1975–1984." *Public Administration Review* 46 (May–June): 215–226.

Petrovic, W. M., and B. L. Jaffe. 1977. "Aspects of the Generation and Collection of Household Refuse in Urban Areas." Bloomington: Indiana University.

Pommerehne, Werner W., and Friedrich Schneider. 1985. *Private or Public Production: A European Perspective.* Aarhus, Denmark: University of Aarhus.

Rivera, Mark D., Gregory Streib, and Katherine G. Willoughby. 2000. "Reinventing Government in Council-Manager Cities: Examining the Role of City Managers." *Public Performance and Management Review* 24 (December): 121–132.

Roberg, Roy R. 1994. "Can Today's Police Organization Effectively Implement Community Policing?" In *The Challenge of Community Policing*, ed. Dennis P. Rosenbaum, 249–257. Thousand Oaks, Calif.: Sage.

Rusk, David. 1995. *Cities Without Suburbs*. 2d ed. Baltimore: Johns Hopkins University Press.

Savas, E. S. 1987. *Privatization: The Key to Better Government*. Chatham: Chatham House.

Savas, E. S. 1974. "Municipal Monopolies versus Competition in Delivering Urban Services." In *Improving the Quality of Urban Management*, ed. W. Hawley and D. Rogers, 473–500. Beverly Hills, Calif.: Sage.

———— 1977. *The Organization and Efficiency of Solid Waste Collection*. Lexington, Mass.: Lexington Books.

———— 1977. "An Empirical Study of Competition in Municipal Service Delivery." *Public Administration Review* 37 (November–December): 717–724.

———— 1981. "Intracity Competition between Public and Private Service Delivery." *Public Administration Review* 41 (January–February): 46–52.

Schachter, Hindy Lauer. 1989. *Frederick Taylor and the Public Administration Community: A Reevaluation*. Albany: State University of New York Press.

———— 1995. "Reinventing Government or Reinventing Ourselves: Two Models for Improving Government Performance." *Public Administration Review* 55 (November–December): 530–537.

Siegel, Gilbert B. 1999. "Where Are We on Local Government Service Contracting?" *Public Productivity and Management Review* 22 (March): 365–388.

Sjoquist, David L., and Mary Beth Walker. 1999. "Economies of Scale in Property Tax Assessment." *National Tax Journal* 52 (June): 207–220.

Smith, Gerald E., and Carole A. Huntsman. 1997. "Reframing the Metaphor of the Citizen-Government Relationship: A Value-Centered Perspective." *Public Administration Review* 57 (July–August): 309–318.

Stallings, Robert A., and James M. Ferris. 1988. "Public Administration Research: Work in PAR, 1940–1984." *Public Administration Review* 48 (January–February): 580–587.

Stein, Robert M. 1990. *Urban Alternatives*. Pittsburgh: University of Pittsburgh Press.

Stevens, Barbara J., ed. 1984. *Delivering Municipal Services Efficiently: A Comparison of Municipal and Private Service Delivery*. New York: Ecodata.

Stevens, Barbara J. 1978. "Scale, Market Structure, and the Cost of Refuse Collection." *Review of Economics and Statistics* 60 (August): 438–448.

Stevens, Barbara J., and E. S. Savas. 1977. "The Cost of Residential Refuse Collection and the Effect of Service Arrangements," *The Municipal Year Book: 1977*, vol. 44, 200–205.

Stolzenberg, Ross M., and Sandra Berry. 1985. *A Pilot Study of the Impact of OMB Circular A-76 on Motor Vehicle Maintenance Cost and Quality in the U.S. Air Force*. Santa Barbara: Rand Corporation.

Stone, Mary N., Amy K. Bell, and James Brandon Poole. 1997. *Perspectives on Privatization by Municipal Governments*. Washington, D.C.: National League of Cities.

Terry, Larry D. 1998. "Administrative Leadership, Neo-Managerialism, and the Public Management Movement." *Public Administration Review* 58 (May–June): 194–200.

Thompson, Neal, and Gady A. Epstein. 2001. "City Budget Savings Claimed in Midwest." *Baltimore Sun*, April 19, B1.

Travers, Tony, George Jones, and June Burnham. 1993. *The Impact of Population Size on Local Authority Costs and Effectiveness*. York, England: Joseph Rowntree Foundation.

Trojanowicz, Robert C. 1994. *Community Policing: A Survey of Police Departments in the United States*. Lansing: National Center for Community Policing, Michigan State University.

Tullock, Gordon. 1965. *The Politics of Bureaucracy*. Washington, D.C.: Public Affairs Press.

Turner, Robyne, and Michael B. Wiatrowski. 1995. "Community Policing and Community Innovation: The New 'Institutionalism' in American Government." In *Issues in Community Policing*, ed. Peter C. Kratcoski and Duane Dukes, 261–270. Cincinnati: Anderson.

U.S. Advisory Commission on Intergovernmental Relations (ACIR). 1987. *The Organization of Local Public Economies.* Washington, D.C.: ACIR.

Voytek, K. 1991. "Privatizing Government Service Delivery: Theory, Evidence and Implications." *Government and Policy* 9 (May): 155–171.

Walzer, Norman. 1972. "Economies of Scale and Municipal Police Services: The Illinois Experience." *Review of Economics and Statistics* 54 (November): 431–438.

Watson, Douglas J., and Robert S. Montjoy. 1991. "Research on Local Government in *Public Administration Review.*" *Public Administration Review* 51 (March–April): 166–170.

White, Richard D., Jr. 1999. "More Than an Analytical Tool: Examining the Ideological Role of Efficiency." *Public Productivity and Management Review* 23 (September): 8–23.

White, Jay D. 1986. "Dissertations and Publication in Public Administration." *Public Administration Review* 46 (May–June): 227–234.

Williams, Daniel W. 2000. "Reinventing the Proverbs of Government." *Public Administration Review* 60 (November–December): 522–534.

Wilson, James Q. 1989. *Bureaucracy.* New York: Basic Books.

Notes

1. Another major thrust of service delivery research in the 1970s and 1980s addressed the equity of local government services. For example, see Antunes and Mladenka 1976; Levy, Meltsner, and Wildavsky 1974; Lineberry 1975, 1977; and Mladenka 1981. Although important in its own right and carried forward by a few current scholars, this line of research in local government functions other than public education has been overshadowed by the more abundant work on service quality, effectiveness, and efficiency—the focus of this chapter.

2. Other forms of privatization include the granting of service franchises and the government's abandonment of a field of service altogether, relying on the private market to meet service demands.

3. Concern among health directors about maintaining in-house operations for some functions should not be misconstrued as general opposition to contracting in this field. Almost three-quarters of the nation's local health departments report having privatized at least some of their services (Keane, Marx, and Ricci 2001).

4. On the other hand, proponents of contracting for local government services note that private companies are less encumbered by regulations that often restrict government operations. This flexibility, coupled with a desire to ensure continuation of their contract, can sometimes produce a service delivery partner that public managers find to be more responsive and "easier to deal with than their own bureaucracies" (Osborne and Plastrik 2000). From this perspective, control is greater, not less.

5. Citizen assessments of the quality of local government services, as revealed through surveys, have been shown in some cases to be more favorable than administrators in these governments had anticipated (Melkers and Thomas 1998). Recent research has attempted to identify categories of knowledge that may be gleaned from responses to open-ended survey questions and to observe managerial responses to these categories of knowledge (Herzog and Claunch 1997).

6. A third model, labeled a "value-centered model," engages citizens as co-investors with government on issues and services that are dearest to these citizens, drawing on their time and personal resources for programs that address recreation, education, crime reduction, or other matters of concern, but requiring less involvement than that required by the owner model. The value-centered model depicts citizens as shareholders and the government as "trustee, steward, and manager of the enterprise's assets, programs, and services that deliver value to its citizen investors" (Smith and Huntsman 1997).

12 The New Politics of Urban Schools

Kenneth K. Wong

Research in urban school politics is substantially shaped by the central concerns in political science. In his seminal article in the *American Political Science Review* that marked the beginning of the field of school politics, Thomas Eliot (1959) developed a research agenda for the "continuing analysis of how the schools are run and who runs them" (p. 1032). Studies at the local level, according to Eliot, would include "structural analysis" of how districts are organized, "behavioral analysis" that examines the impact of professional and citizen leadership and interest-group activities on policy decisions, and voting analysis on elections and bond issues. Since then, generations of political analysts have conducted systematic investigations of these issues, which form the base of knowledge on the "authoritative allocation of values" in the educational policy arena (Easton 1965). In other words, scholarship in the politics of education directs our attention to the way educational governance is organized, the distribution of power in the decision-making process, the nature and management of conflict, and the outcomes and impact of policy decisions.

The urban setting provides a particularly rich context for the political analysis of educational issues. From a systems approach, urban school politics illuminates a policymaking system in which demand makers influence governmental decisions. In the 1950s and the 1960s, for example, urban schools were under enormous pressure to integrate minority students and to equalize resource allocation. Since the 1990s, urban school districts have increasingly focused on productivity, particularly student performance. For this reason, much of the current literature centers on reform, an issue I will discuss later in this chapter. My goal is to clarify one of the central foci of this chapter, reform, and connect it to the broader discourse.

To be sure, the scope and quality of policy responses are subject to various constraints, as suggested in socioeconomic trends. In recent years, many urban districts experienced enrollment decline while maintaining a higher concentration of students from minority and low-income backgrounds. As middle-class families relocate in suburban communities, large urban systems lose their political influence in the state capital. At the same time, teachers' unions continue to place budgetary demands on the district. In other words, policymakers and educators in urban districts confront a host of political and social challenges that are embedded in the broader societal structure—residential choice, locational density, suburbanization of political power, and socioeconomic characteristics of the school population.

This chapter examines how the current political and policy demands reshape the governance of public schools in the urban context. It begins with an overview of local school governance, which can be largely characterized by an elected school board and an appointed, strong professional superintendent as the chief executive. Then, synthesizing the current literature on how urban schools respond to competing demands for reform, I differentiate four strands of reform in terms of their relative focus on performance-based accountability and system-wide restructuring. The chapter concludes with a brief discussion of the future research agenda in urban school politics.

The Local Character of School Politics

In American public education, local control prevails. From a constitutional-legalistic view, localities are merely political subdivisions of the state, and local powers can be granted only with the consent of the state legislature. In reality, once their legal status has been established, local governments enjoy control over critical resources that can be used to sustain their existence. Localities can select their own political representatives, decide on fiscal policies, and choose the scope of their services.

Historically, states moved toward district consolidation to provide more uniform educational services in a more economical manner. Smaller districts often experience difficulties in recruiting qualified teachers, upgrading physical facilities, and maintaining an enriched curriculum. As of 1997, there were approximately 13,700 local school boards (see Table 12-1). Nationwide, school boards oversee over 90,000 schools. In the 1940s, there were almost 109,000 school districts. School district consolidation occurred at a much faster pace than that of the local governments overall. Although school boards constituted 70 percent of all local governmental bodies in 1942, they accounted for only 16 percent in the late 1990s. Although four out of five school boards are responsible for fewer than 3,000 students, the average size of districts has grown over the years. Today about a third of the boards are located in five states: California, Texas, Illinois, Nebraska, and New York.

While the number of school districts has changed significantly over the years, district governance and administration have remained remarkably stable. The dominant mode for the selection of school board members is a nonpartisan election held in an off year or off month from the local general election. Board members can be elected from subdistricts or district-wide (at large). Term limits are not usually placed on board membership. These elections are rarely contested and usually involve very low voter turnout. Even fewer voters are likely to attend board meetings, which are often

Table 12-1 Change in the Number of Public School Districts

	1942	1962	1982	1997
Total number of school districts	108,579	34,678	14,851	13,726
Total number of local governments	155,067	91,186	81,780	87,453
Percentage of school districts to number of local governments	70.0%	38.0%	18.2%	15.7%

Source: U.S. Census Bureau, *Census of Governments, Government Organization, Series (GC(1)-1),* (Washington, D.C., U.S. Government Printing Office, various years.)

held on a monthly basis. Given the low political interest in school board politics, many researchers note the dominance of civic elites and interest groups in these elections. However, a few exceptions are found in major cities. Although an overwhelming majority of school boards are popularly elected, those in Baltimore, Boston, Chicago, Cleveland, Oakland, Philadelphia, Trenton, and several other cities are appointed either by the mayor or jointly by the mayor and the governor.

Table 12-2 provides examples of the wide range of methods used to select urban school boards and their taxing authority. Listing thirty members of the Council of Great City Schools, the table shows that twenty-three districts have a popularly elected school board. Only seven districts have an appointed board: Atlanta, Baltimore, Boston, Chicago, Cleveland, the District of Columbia, and New York City. With regard to the taxing authority, nineteen districts enjoy fiscal autonomy from the general political system. In five districts, however, the school board needs budgetary approval from city hall: Anchorage, Baltimore, Boston, Memphis, and Nashville.

The state constitution grants substantial authority to the local school boards. Thomas Shannon (1992), former executive director of the National School Boards Association, has argued that school boards serve several indispensable functions on behalf of the common good. They draw the attendance boundary for each school, develop strategic plans, oversee the operation of the system, comply with federal and state laws, evaluate educational programs, arbitrate complaints from citizens and employees, and represent the collective interests of the entire district. The boards also negotiate contracts with teachers' unions and serve as managerial buffers between individual schools and state and federal agencies. Above all, the board hires (and fires) the top executive or the school superintendent to lead the school bureaucracy. In other words, local school boards make a "non-nationalized" educational system functional.

Table 12-2   Formal Governance in Selected Large School Districts

School District	Board Membership	Taxing Autonomy
Albuquerque Public Schools	7 members elected for 4-year staggered terms	Budget adopted by school board
Anchorage School District	7 members elected for 3-year staggered terms	Budget approved by Anchorage assembly
Atlanta Public Schools	9 members elected for 4-year terms	Independent
Austin Independent School District	9 members elected for 4-year terms, with half of members up for reelection biennially	Independent
Baltimore City Schools	9 voting members and 1 nonvoting student jointly appointed by Baltimore mayor and Maryland governor	School board budget one part of city hall budget
Boston Public Schools	7 members appointed by mayor to serve 4-year staggered terms	Budget approved first by mayor and then by city council
Buffalo City School District	9 members elected	Independent
Chicago Public Schools	7 members appointed by mayor	Budget approved by school board
Cleveland Municipal School District	9 members appointed by mayor	Independent
Dallas Independent School District	9 members elected for 3-year staggered terms	Independent
Denver Public Schools	9 members elected for 4-year staggered terms	Budget adopted by board of education
Des Moines Independent Community School District	7 members elected for 3-year terms	Granted authority to certify the budget prepared by superintendent
District of Columbia Public Schools	5 elected members, 4 members appointed by mayor, and 2 student representatives	Independent
Fort Worth Independent School District	9 members elected for 4-year terms	Independent
Fresno Unified School District	7 members elected for 4-year staggered terms	Independent

Table 12-2   (continued)

Houston Independent School District	9 members elected for 4-year staggered terms	Independent
Los Angeles Unified School District	7 members elected	Budget adopted by school board, then sent to superintendent
Memphis City Public Schools	9 members elected for 4-year terms	Budget approved by city council
Miami–Dade County Public Schools	9 members elected for 4-year staggered terms	Independent
Milwaukee Public Schools	9 members elected for 4-year terms	Independent
Nashville–Davidson Metropolitan Public Schools	9 members elected for 4-year staggered terms	Budget approved by city council and then by mayor
New York City Board of Education	8 members appointed by mayor, 5 parent-members appointed by the presidents of 5 boroughs, budget approved by the school board	Independent
Oklahoma City Public Schools	8 members elected for 4-year terms	Independent
Portland Public Schools	7 members elected for 4-year terms	Independent
Richmond Public Schools	9 members elected for 2-year terms	Independent
Salt Lake City School District	7 members elected	Independent
San Diego City Schools	5 members elected for 4-year staggered terms	Independent
San Francisco Unified School District	7 members elected	Independent
Seattle Public Schools	7 members elected for 4-year terms	Independent
Toledo Public Schools	5 members elected for 4-year terms	Independent

Source: Council of the Great City Schools, www.cgcs.org/about/member.cfm, May 2002.

To be sure, the daily operation of the school system relies heavily on a functional school bureaucracy, often referred to as the central office. The growth of a district-level bureaucracy throughout much of this century has contributed to a strong professional management model in the urban district (Tyack 1974). At the top of the central bureaucracy is the school superintendent, who assumes educational, managerial, and fiscal responsibilities for the entire district. To provide daily services to a large number of students, the school system tends to adopt a bureaucratic structure—centralization of decision making, routinization of task performance, and standardization of resource generation and allocation. The urban district resembles a complex hierarchical structure, with centralized authority and line departments. The organization's insiders enjoy autonomy from outsiders' influence because the former possesses expertise and information on how the system operates. External pressures from state and federal government are largely accommodated through an internal division of labor, which is characterized by specialized bureaus in which program administrators are insulated from one another. When allocating resources, the lay school board largely follows the recommendations made by professional administrators (Danzberger, Kirst, and Usdan 1992).

The superintendent and his or her central office staff also exercise a great deal of influence on the schools. In most districts, the school board and the superintendent recruit and replace the school principals. Teacher recruitment, with a few exceptions, is generally processed at the central office. Most schools lack discretion over their own budgetary allocation. At the same time, the centralized bureaucratic model has served several important functions in the public school system: it manages competing political demands, routinizes service delivery, distributes comparable resources to schools across neighborhoods, enforces national and state mandates on academic standards and equity issues, and, above all, provides organizational stability to a complex operation that serves a diverse clientele (Wong 1992).

An independent school district that is free from general governmental control is consistent with the American ethos. An autonomous school system reflects strongly held public beliefs in democratic, nonpartisan control over public education. The public has traditionally equated local control with an elected board that enjoys district-wide authority in the constitutional-legal framework of educational governance. In contrasting private and public schools, Chubb and Moe (1990) characterized public school governance as "direct democratic control."

From an economic perspective, the presence of multiple school systems resembles a quasi-market arrangement that can be cost efficient for consumers. States and localities with multiple suppliers of services promise a better fit between consumer-taxpayers' preferences and the level and quality of local services. As Tiebout's (1956) classic work suggested, taxpayers make residential decisions on the basis of maximizing the benefits they expect to obtain from public services and minimizing the level of taxes they have to pay for those services. In particular, middle-class tax-payers who can afford to spend more on goods and services are keenly concerned about the quality of basic services such as schools. As Hirschman (1971) argued, they are more inclined to exit when they perceive a decline in municipal services that they value. Studies of district-level performance in metropolitan areas suggest that inter-district competition can improve service quality (Hoxby 1998). The migration of middle-class families to suburban school districts seems to provide the empirical support for this line of argument. The recent establishment of quasi-public boards that oversee charter schools also indicates the increasing popularity of parental choice when neighborhood schools are failing (Hill 1997).

Reform in Governance: Some Typologies

From a systems approach, the political insulation of the school system is far from complete. External political and economic forces constantly shape leadership succession, conflict management, and resource allocation, among others. In the urban context, competing visions of how schools should be governed have emerged in recent years. Political efforts to reconfigure governance and management have provided a rich empirical basis for a more systematic understanding of the new politics of urban schools.

Despite its historic and contemporary accomplishments, the central school board and its bureaucracy are increasingly viewed with skepticism with regard to their effectiveness in the changing urban context. First, an oversized central bureaucracy may result in cost inefficiency. In their study of New York City, Ravitch and Viteritti (1997) observed, "Most of the necessary functions are over administered and under supervised." Substantial resources are used to support central services instead of being allotted to the schools themselves. In New York City, the board's own analysis showed that only 42 percent of the budget was spent on classroom instruction during 1995–1996. Making matters worse were audit inconsistencies in the Division of School Safety, which hired 3,000 security officers, and in the Bureau of Supplies, which controlled a $160 million budget for purchases. Although New York's problems may be unique, virtually all urban districts have to face the question of whether some of the centralized functions can be better performed (and at a lower cost) by the individual schools and private vendors.

A second concern is accountability. Centralized authority has been criticized for its lack of responsiveness to community needs. Since the 1960s, civic and community-based organizations have directed their efforts to diversify the makeup of the school leadership, which presumably would improve policy responsiveness. However, in

1998, only 5 percent of the nation's superintendents were minorities and only 12 percent were women. In response to constituent politics, urban districts have instituted various mechanisms to improve district–school communication and collaboration. I will discuss the "shared" arrangement later in the chapter.

A third concern with the centralized model is its lack of demonstrable effects on student performance. In an increasingly technologically oriented global economy, policy makers, business leaders, and parents often blame the central bureaucracy for the decline in student performance in the United States. Will high school graduates acquire adequate skills to compete with their peers in other countries? Does the projected shortage in the labor force mean that employers will have to hire the less skilled in the future? Can the new work force perform well in a technologically complex world? The public seems uncertain that bureaucratized school organizations are effective in meeting these challenges. To be sure, the causes of performance decline are complex, as socioeconomic factors and other cultural barriers continue to constrain teaching and learning. Nevertheless, the public's perception of bureaucratic ineffectiveness is often reinforced by various accounts of low student performance in standardized tests in urban areas. For example, the 1997 state report card on New York City showed that 89 percent of all its elementary schools failed to reach the state's expectations on reading performance. These and other indicators of student achievement are particularly frustrating in that the United States spends a great deal more on education than other Western countries do (Hanushek 1994). The Third International Mathematics and Science Study in 1999, for example, ranked American eighth graders around the middle in comparison with their peers in all industrialized nations.

The rise of accountability-based school politics challenges our current understanding of how politics shapes educational issues. Accountability has created new demands for popularly elected political leaders such as mayors and governors to exercise more direct control over the central bureaucracy in education. The new focus also raises questions as to whether interest groups are able to conduct business as usual without losing credibility and public support. An increasing number of parents, particularly in low-income minority neighborhoods, support choice-based programs that promote competition in the educational sector. In other words, we have entered a phase of institutional transition, where politics of the status quo is subject to mounting pressure to incorporate the new demand for accountability.

Table 12-3 synthesizes the literature on the politics of school reform and identifies four major models for restructuring school governance in the urban setting. Although reform models are not mutually exclusive and are often implemented simultaneously within a district, an analytical scheme will clarify the political conditions that shape a particular strand of school reform. The four models vary along two conceptual dimensions. First, reforms can be differentiated in terms of the level of

Table 12-3   A Typology of the Politics of Urban School Reform

Level of Analysis	Accountability Focus of Governing Paradigm	
	Accountability in Policymaking Process	*Performance-based Accountability*
Systemwide	Institutional power and authorities redefined **(A)**	Mayor-led integrated governance reform **(C)**
School–Community	Shared governance or site-based empowerment **(B)**	Consumer-driven programs (for example, vouchers and charter schools) **(D)**

analysis, that is, whether they empower the capacity of system-wide institutions or shift power to the school and community level. Second, governing paradigms can be conceptualized in terms of their relative focus on accountability. Some reforms are designed to improve accountability in the policymaking process, whereas others focus on higher student performance.

More specifically, within the arena of process-oriented accountability, one strand of reform consists of multiple efforts to redefine the power and authorities of key system-wide institutions, such as the school board and the central school bureaucracy (cell A in Table 12-3). Another strand of process-oriented reform can be labeled "shared governance," which allows site-level decisions on hiring and resource allocation (cell B). Likewise, two kinds of reform politics are differentiated, focusing on performance-based accountability. Mayor-led "integrated governance" focuses on raising outcome-based performance (cell C), whereas consumer-driven programs such as state-funded vouchers and charter schools are designed to rely on market-like efficiency to improve student performance (cell D). The following sections will discuss the nature and scope of each strand of reforms. I will also consider the model's effectiveness in improving political access, school quality, and student performance.

Governance Accountability as the Focus of System-wide Reform

As the public increases its demands for policy access and performance-based accountability in public schools, the quality of district-level governance is called into question. The Report of the Twentieth Century Fund Task Force on School Governance (Twentieth Century Fund 1992) observed that school boards "are facing a serious crisis of legitimacy and relevance." According to a survey of school board members in 128 districts in sixteen states, even they perceived themselves as least effective in "the core elements of governance—leadership, planning and goal setting, involving parents and the community, influence on others, policy oversight, board operations, and board development" (Danzberger, Kirst, and Usden 1982). For example, the survey indicated that boards used inconsistent performance measures to evaluate their superintendents. Furthermore, due to the Progressive Era's efforts during the first half of the twentieth century to take politics out of schools, school boards are largely isolated from other lateral institutions that affect the well-being of children (for example, housing and health care agencies).

The public's declining confidence in school board leadership seems salient in urban districts. Based on a 1998 survey, the National School Boards Foundation reported, "There is a consistent, significant difference in perception between urban school board members and the urban public on a number of key issues" (NSBF 1999, 12). While 67 percent of the urban board members rated schools in A and B categories, only 49 percent of the urban public did. Three out of four board members rated the teachers as excellent or good, whereas only 54 percent of the public did so. The public seemed half as likely as the board members to agree that the schools were "doing a good job" in the following areas: preparing students for college, keeping violence and drugs out of schools, maintaining discipline among students, and teaching children who don't speak English. Subsequently, the National School Boards Foundation called upon urban leaders to sharpen the focus on community engagement and student performance.

Racial Politics in Schools

Political reforms have been instituted to improve accountability in the policymaking process at the system-wide level. One type of reform is associated with racial succession on school boards. Many analysts observe that the predominantly white power structure seems less ready to respond to the minority and low-income constituency in urban schools. According to this view, a shift in racial control over governmental institutions would improve school quality and promote student performance. However, this conventional expectation is not empirically supported by a study of school reform in four black-led cities: Atlanta, Baltimore, Detroit, and the District of Columbia (Henig, Hula, Orr and Pedescleaux 1999). None of these cities were able to produce any measurable educational progress for minority students. The authors found that "racialized politics" has contributed to the ineffectiveness of governance in both direct and indirect ways. Particularly important is the extent to which local stakeholders are affected by "fears, suspicions, expectations, loyalties, tactics, and habits related to race" (p. 7). Multiple aspects of racialized politics are illuminated by the authors' careful analysis of interviews with hundreds of actors both outside and inside the formal governmental institutions, including influential persons (for example, city council members and business leaders), community advocates, and education specialists.

The four cities provide ample evidence of how racial concerns have constrained the collective behaviors of both black and white elites. For example, black community activists are reluctant to criticize black city officials, because they want to preserve the reputation of black institutions in general. Likewise, white business elites tend to refrain from criticizing black-controlled school system, fearing that their actions may be seen in racial terms. In other words, race complicates coalition building, because it "continues to affect perceptions, calculations, loyalties, and concerns in ways that tug at the thread of collaboration and erode civic capacity to undertake meaningful and sustained reform" (Henig, Hula, Orr, and Pedescleaux 1999, 212). Consequently, black leaders become complacent, and white business elites are risk averse in black-led cities. Interracial trust and confidence become so limited that civic capacity lacks a solid foundation.

Civic Capacity and Schools

This study of black-led cities by Henig, Hula, Orr, and Pedescleaux constitutes a conceptual subset of a larger effort to rethink institutional arrangements. Headed by Clarence Stone, the Civic Capacity and Urban Education Project assembled a team of political scientists to study school politics in eleven cities (Stone, Henig, Jones, and Pierannunzi 2001). To improve the quality of school governance, Stone and his associates called for various sectors, both public and private, to work together, system-wide, on human development issues. "Civic capacity," argued Stone and his associates, "involves mobilization by a broader array of community interests to remove policy-making authority from subperforming policy subsystems" (p. 7). However, none of the eleven cities attained a systemic level of civic mobilization. Among the structural barriers were functional insulation of the school administration from other policy domains, a culture of preserving jobs in the context of "employment regimes," and distributive politics reinforced by union power.

Efforts to build civic capacity are likely to be affected by the way interest groups are articulated and organized. In this regard, the analytical lens that differentiates "materialist" and "post-materialist" values is useful in understanding the political tension on accountability issues (Inglehart 1990). Although interest-group politics is central to our pluralist system, "materialist-oriented" organized interests can become autonomous power centers that undermine the organizational capacity of the school system. A major "materialist-oriented" interest group is the teachers' union. Grimshaw's (1979) study of Chicago's teachers' union suggested that the union has undergone two phases in its relationship with the city and school administration. During the formative years, the union largely cooperated with the administration (and the mayor) in return for a legitimate role in the policymaking process. In the second phase, which Grimshaw characterized as "union rule," the union became independent of either the local political machine or the reform factions. Instead, it looked to the national union leadership for guidance and engaged in tough bargaining with the administration over better compensation and working conditions. Consequently, according to Grimshaw, policymakers "no longer are able to set policy unless the policy is consistent with the union's objectives" (p. 150). The aging of union organizations, in Cooper's (2000) view, has led to the problems of "mature institutions," with union leaders having to mediate trade-offs between quality and supply. Seeing a new trend in school competition, Johnson (2001) observed the need for replacing "collective bargaining" with "reform bargaining."

Countering the materialist values are the post-materialist politics that have emerged in American cities. Clark and his associates note the rise of the "new political culture" in city hall and argue that hierarchical structures, such as the traditional patronage-based political machinery, no longer play a key role in mobilizing citizen concerns (Clark and Hoffmann-Martinot 1998; Wong, Jain, and Clark 1997). In urban centers, union membership in the manufacturing and service sectors has declined. Ideologically based groups, both left and right, seem to have lost much of their credibility in city council, state legislature, and the nation's capital (Berry 1999). Instead, citizen actions are increasingly realigned in terms of post-materialist concerns. They have become more focused on quality-of-life issues such as lower crime rate and better schooling and park services, less organized along rigid class cleavages, and more pragmatic about governmental and market solutions to address educational and social problems at the local level. To the extent that the post-materialist regime persists, racial and class categories will become less predictive of how citizens view and decide on educational policy issues.

Given the broadening and direct involvement of civic and political leaders in educational reform, there is a challenge to develop a framework for measuring the performance of a wide range of institutional actors. Although student performance serves as a useful indicator of the overall performance of a school system, its aggregated character falls short of specifying the link between the roles and responsibilities of the institutional players and the process that raises school performance. In other words, there is a need to develop indicators of institutional effectiveness to assess the new governance regime. Toward this goal, Wong and Moulton (1998) developed an institutional "report card" on various state and local actors, including the governor, mayor, legislature, and school board. Using survey responses from members of the broad policy community in Illinois and Chicago, Wong and Moulton found that the school board and the central administration in Chicago have significantly improved their institutional rating following the mayor's taking control of the schools (see also Wong and Jain 1999b).

In short, district-level governance is in transition in the era of accountability. While many communities maintain their tradition of nonpartisan, popularly elected school boards, urban districts that are perceived as low performing are under multiple pressures to improve the quality of governance. Though political and civic leaders have yet to fully mobilize broad-based support for human development issues, reformers have achieved varying degrees of success in improving the management and accountability of the school bureaucracy. I will now turn to three other reform models and discuss how they are designed to respond to public demands to improve accountability.

Shared Governance: Enabling Site-Based Decisions

Giving more power to parents and professionals in school operation and budget allocation represents one major reform strand to reduce centralized control. Decentralized reforms are directed at reallocating power between the central authority and the schools within the public school system. Not surprisingly, the specific arrangements that enable schools to make decisions to address their particular needs vary widely across districts as well as among schools within a district. By the 1990s, virtually all urban districts had some form of shared governance, with parents and community representatives participating in the decision-making structure at the school sites. Examples of these arrangements include the New York–style community board; site-based management in Dade County, Florida, Rochester, and Salt Lake City; and, in Chicago, a locally elected parent council in each school.

Decentralization has changed the social and organizational relations in the school community. In New York, according to one study, decentralization has improved social relations among low-income minority parents, teachers, and pupils by creating a climate of trust and understanding that fosters staff morale and student aspirations and enhances parental support for teachers' work (Rogers and Chung 1983). At the same time, decentralization has its limitations. Based on a study of forty-four schools in eleven districts in the United States and Canada, Wohlstetter and associates (1997, 204) found that decentralization has not been effective in stimulating "self-improving" conditions that improve student performance. Many decentralized arrangements were far from complete, in that schools were given partial control over the nonpersonnel budget, but they did not have access to high-quality professional development (Wong 1994). Because of the incremental nature of granting power to the school sites in most districts, the principal of each school continues to define educational priority and management issues.

The most extensive effort to ensure that parents are indeed the key decision makers was the local school council (LSC) reform in Chicago in 1989 and 1995. Even when the mayor was given control over the schools in 1995, the LSC remained in operation at the school sites. The 1988 Chicago Reform Act was guided by the belief that parent and citizen empowerment through local school councils would improve educational performance. The act was designed to restore public confidence by granting parents substantial "ownership" of schools. In this regard, the LSC can be seen as an experiment in "political redistribution," creating new governing rules that enable parents in predominantly low-income minority neighborhoods to exercise allocative decision making (Katznelson 1981). Such a redistribution of power was facilitated by several factors in Chicago during the late 1980s. Harold Washington, Chicago's first black, reform-oriented mayor, created a process that legitimized community input early in the "mobilization phase." Despite Washington's death in 1987, the participatory process retained a fair representation of both the business elites and the city's public school clientele, which is predominantly low income and minorities. Consequently, the participatory process resulted in a set of policy agreements that formed the basis for the legislative proposal to establish 550 LSCs throughout the district.

To enhance accountability, the central office decentralized policymaking by turning it over to the LSC and the principal at each school site. Each eleven-member council consists of six elected parents (the majority), two community representatives, two teachers, and the principal. There is also one student member at the high school level. Members of each local council are given substantial authority; they can hire and fire the principal (no longer a tenured position as a result of the 1988 act), allocate lump sums from a state compensatory fund, and develop school improvement plans. According to the most liberal assessment, about one-third of all the elementary schools have a local school council that is in good operational standing after several years of reform (Consortium on Chicago School Research 1993). Consistent with the expectation of those who supported the redistribution of power, the LSCs have a direct impact on the selection of principals. During the seven years when the LSC model dominated Chicago school governance, the selection of principals often reflected the racial and ethnic makeup of the LSCs and their neighborhood constituencies (Wong and Moulton 1996). Between 1989 and 1994, the number of principals who were black increased from 37 percent to 50 percent, and the number who were Latino increased from 7 percent to 11 percent. Principals who were white decreased from 56 percent to 39 percent during the five-year period.

Although the LSCs seemed to exercise their appointive power fairly visibly throughout the school system, their electoral base shrank during the period of decentralization. After the first LSC election in 1989, voter turnout declined significantly, falling by 55 percent between 1989 and 1993 (Wong and Moulton 1996). Indeed, the decline was even more dramatic when measured just in terms of parents and community residents (not including teachers, staff, and students). Turnout of parents and community residents plunged by 68 percent in a five-year period. While overall turnout improved somewhat during 1996 and 1998, there was a 53 percent drop in parental turnout between 1989 and 1998. As voter turnout declined, fewer candidates ran for LSC offices. Between 1989 and 1993, the number of candidates declined from 3.18 to 1.36 per seat. By 1993, one out of every three schools in Chicago lacked a full slate of candidates. Clearly, these trends pose a challenge for maintaining the facilitating conditions for large-scale reform.

Turning to the issue of school effectiveness, the evidence in Chicago's LSC reform has been inconclusive. Although in standardized tests the school-by-school trends in reading showed a fairly sharp decline, math and writing performance did not worsen between 1989 and 1995 (Bryk, Kerbow, and Rollow 1997). These trend-line analyses, however, did not include data prior to the implementation of the 1989 reform. Furthermore, based on a selective sample of elementary students, a longitudinal analysis revealed that achievement gains were uneven in subject areas, grade levels, and length of time students were enrolled in school (Bryk, Kerbow, and Rollow 1997). This study did not include the 30 percent of elementary students who moved from school to school during an academic year. Nor did the reform improve academic performance at the high school level. From an institutional perspective, one may argue that the unsatisfactory student performance is due to the uneven capacity of the LSCs. However, if the LSCs failed to build up their governing capacity in a seven-year period—a fairly reasonable time frame in which to expect organizational improvement—one has to question whether the LSC is an effective model for improving schools system-wide. After all, only one-fourth of the elementary school teachers perceived that decentralized reform had a positive impact on the quality of student academic performance (Sebring, Bryk, and Easton 1995). In light of these concerns, in 1995 a bipartisan legislative coalition in Chicago adopted a comprehensive reform proposal that created "integrated governance."

Mayor-Led Integrated Governance to Improve Student Performance

Mayor-led integrated governance is a reform model designed to integrate political accountability and educational performance at the system-wide level (Wong 1999). In several large districts, the mayor assumes control of schools with an appointed school board and a superintendent. Currently, twenty-four states have passed legislation authorizing the management of school districts by either state officials or mayors. Mayoral takeovers have occurred in Chicago, Boston, Cleveland, Detroit, and Washington, D.C., among others. Since becoming mayor of New York City at the beginning of

2002, Michael Bloomberg has sought legislative support to appoint the school board. "The public, through the mayor, must control the school system," he said in his inaugural address.

In this regard, mayoral leadership in education occurs in a policy context wherein years of decentralized reform alone have not produced system-wide improvement in student performance in big-city schools. Reform advocates who pushed for site-based strategies may have overestimated the capacity of the school community to raise academic standards. Decentralized reforms are directed at reallocating power between the system-wide authority and the individual school sites. However, decentralized initiatives often fail to give full consideration to powerful demand makers in the system, such as the teachers' union and other organized interests. Decisions made at the school site are constrained by collective bargaining agreements. In addition, decentralization may widen the gap between schools with access to external capital (such as parental organizational skills and grants from foundations) and those that receive limited support from these sources. In response to these concerns, integrated governance enables the mayor to rely on system-wide standards to hold schools and student accountable for their performance. Failing schools and students are subject to sanctions while being given additional support (Wong 2001).

Mayoral control of school districts does not necessarily reach the full potential of the integrated governance reform model. Mayors may choose not to focus on educational improvement. Given the presence of competing interests, mayors are known to mediate and seek compromise (Peterson 1976). Some mayors may treat employment in the school district as their "spoils" to support a patronage-based machinery (Rich 1996). Others may withhold their political capital in public education. Still other mayors are reluctant to take direct intervention to turn around low-performing schools.

These political and programmatic variations exist in four cities, where the mayor exercises more complete control over the school system: Boston, Chicago, Cleveland, and Detroit (see Wong and Jain 1999a).

Boston. The Boston school community was highly polarized during the bussing controversy in the 1970s. Since then, the district's racial composition has changed dramatically, going from about 50 percent white to greater than 80 percent minority in the 1990s. Boston still retains some very prestigious schools, such as Boston Latin, but overall the school system has been widely perceived as "too politicized," with declining quality. In this challenging context, Mayor Ray Flynn in 1989 supported passage of a referendum that gave the mayor direct control over the school system. It was approved by a very narrow margin, 50.8 to 49.2 percent. As a result, Boston's mayor appoints a seven-member board, as opposed to a thirteen-member elected board in the past.

Mayor Thomas Menino, Flynn's successor, was among a new group of mayors who have successfully reformed the management practices in city agencies. He viewed educational reform as an important strategy for retaining middle-class residents in the city. In 1992 Menino appointed the seven members to the first postreform school board and proclaimed himself an education mayor. His strong educational platform gained voters' approval in 1996, when 54 percent of the electorate opposed the referendum that called for a shift to an elected school board. The 1996 election saw an unusually high turnout of 68 percent, in sharp contrast to the 32 percent turnout in 1989 when the reform was adopted.

In his 1996 State of the City speech, Mayor Menino tied his political future to the success of the school system, urging Boston resident to "judge me harshly" if goals for schools were not realized. The mayor invested financially in the schools as well, adjusting the city's entire budget to ensure that educational reforms have priority. Since Menino took office, the School Department's operating budget has increased by $60 million. Its capital budget increased by $43.2 million, or 255 percent. In 1995 Menino appointed Thomas Payzant, former U.S. assistant secretary of elementary and secondary education, as school superintendent. Payzant worked closely with Menino on the first five-year reform plan and, after seven years on the job, is one of the longest-serving urban district superintendents. Menino's school board also voted to end bussing and returned the schools to a neighborhood-based system.

Menino saw the promise of policy coherence as he exercised direct authority over the public school system. The business community strongly supported the mayor, and although the teachers' union initially opposed the move, its leadership gradually came round to support Menino. Among the mayor's first accomplishments was a five-year contract with the teachers' union. Several neighborhood and minority groups complained that they were not adequately represented as a result of mayoral control and continued to oppose his authority. During his tenure, Menino focused on the implementation of learning standards and standards-based student assessments. His administration launched a five-year plan, with strong accountability at the classroom and school levels. The mayor also initiated a high school restructuring plan. Overall, Menino was among the most involved mayors in terms of making educational policy.

Chicago. The Chicago School Reform Amendatory Act, which took effect in July 1995, reverses the trend toward decentralization of authority over school operations and redesigns the governance arrangement so that power and authority are now integrated. The 1995 law suspended the power of the School Finance Authority, eliminated the School Board Nominating Commission, and diminished the ability of the local school councils to operate independently of board policy. Mayor Richard Daley sought greater control of schools, as he considers education to be one of the essential services that will keep middle-class residents in the city. A strong public school system, in his view, can also attract businesses to Chicago.

Integrated governance in Chicago is characterized by (1) a reduction of competing authorities (such as the School Board Nominating Commission) and a coordination of activities in support of system-wide goals and standards; (2) mayoral appointment of school board members and selection of top administrators; and (3) powers granted to the school board to hold local school councils accountable to system-wide standards in professional conduct.

The 1995 legislation left intact some features of the previous decentralized arrangements, but it reduced competing institutional authority and recentralized administrative authority. As a result of the 1995 reform, appointment decisions emanating from the mayor's office closely link the board, top administration, and the mayor's office. The fifteen-member board was decreased to five, and the mayor was given the authority to appoint the board's president and its members and the chief executive officer in charge of the schools. Daley picked Paul Vallas, his former budget director, to serve as the chief executive officer from 1995 to 2001. The top appointments in the central office made between July 1995 and February 1998 reflect a diversity of expertise, with over 40 percent of the appointees coming from the private sector, nonprofit organizations, and city agencies. In areas not directly related to educational services, such as finance and purchasing, over 60 percent of the appointees came from outside of the school system.

A particularly important feature of the 1995 reform law was an eighteen-month moratorium on teachers' strikes. The Chicago Teachers' Union has been an assertive demand maker since the late 1960s, when it obtained the right to collective bargaining. Since 1970, strikes have often resulted in school closings. For example, eleven school days were lost in 1970, ten days in 1980, two days in 1985, and nineteen days in 1990. Using both the threat of a strike and the strike itself, the teachers' union has been able to obtain multiyear contracts with terms that favorably preserved their work conditions (Wong 1999). Under the new political conditions following the 1995 reform, Mayor Daley sought and succeeded in getting labor peace.

The Vallas administration seemed to have turned around the school system. The CEO and his team restored public confidence and gained strong support from the media, businesses, and civic groups (Wong 2001). Since the mayor took over the schools, social promotion was eliminated and standardized test performance has steadily improved every year at both the elementary and the high school level. The mayor's board has signed two four-year teachers' contracts that sustain labor peace, and the Vallas administration has begun to implement a more rigorous academic curriculum in the high schools. Because of Chicago's academic success, President Bill Clinton praised the district two years in a row in his State of the Union messages.

Cleveland. Cleveland is a unique case. The state took over the school district administration in 1995, when the federal district court withdrew the powers of governance from the locally elected board of education and placed those powers in the hands of the state superintendent of public instruction. The Cleveland school district was in a "crisis situation." Of all the students from the 1990–1991 eighth-grade classes, only 33 percent graduated from high school in 1995, and only 7 percent of them performed at grade level. Concerned about poor school performance early in his tenure, Mayor Michael White had used his office to support school board candidates and sought broader support from the business community.

Cleveland regained local administrative powers in 1998, when the federal court lifted the previous orders. An Advisory Committee on Governance of the Cleveland Summit on Education proposed a bill in 1997 that gave control of the district to the mayor. Influenced by Chicago's success, Mayor White negotiated with a Republican governor and a Republican legislature to gain control of the schools in 1998. He appointed Barbara Byrd-Bennett, an educator from New York City, as CEO and appointed a nine-member school board. This leadership team was able to raise $800 millions in school construction bonds and improved student achievement.

Detroit.   Mayor Dennis Archer strongly opposed a state remedy to take over the Detroit school district, which Republican governor John Engler had proposed in 1997. The governor was dissatisfied with the city's low-performing schools and the school district's consumption of a major part of the state budget. Detroit public schools received 64 percent of its revenue from the state (compared with an average of 47 percent for the ten school districts) and 11 percent from the federal government. The state share and Detroit's education expenses were expected to increase under Michigan's restructured school finance system equalizing funding across school districts. The school system was widely perceived as being in crisis: only half of Detroit's high school students graduated. Most basic supplies—from textbooks to toilet paper—somehow had trouble making it into schools. Teachers routinely walked out on strike. In Mayor Archer's view, the city's decades-long flight of middle-class residents could not be reversed unless the schools improved.

In 1998, Archer offered to participate in a local reform plan that would have engaged a broad spectrum of the Detroit community, but the elected school board tabled the proposal. Seeing Chicago as a success story, the mayor negotiated with Governor Engler to gain greater control over the school system. The governor and the Republican legislature granted him control in 1999, whereupon the mayor appointed six board members in April of that year. The seventh member is the state superintendent. The board then appointed a former president of Wayne State University, David Adamany, to serve as the schools' chief executive officer. Detroit's initial experience in mayoral control seems highly contentious. Business leaders supported the mayor, but the teachers' union opposed him. The local community groups and civil rights groups were split, with the Detroit NAACP opposing mayoral control but the Detroit Urban League supporting it. Mayor Archer also negotiated several performance-based accountability measures with the state legislature, among them a proposal for reduced class size, mandatory summer school, substantive after-school programs, and technical training for teachers.

Mayor-led integrated governance in Boston, Chicago, Cleveland, and Detroit has been facilitated by the following factors: (1) mayoral vision on performance-based accountability; (2) broad public dissatisfaction with school performance for several years preceding integrated governance; (3) state leadership dominated by Republicans willing to empower the mayoral office to address school problems; (4) strong business support that has translated into the adoption of corporate management practices to address complex bureaucratic problems in school districts; and (5) weakened legitimacy of traditionally powerful service provider groups (unions) and service demand groups (racial and neighborhood-based groups). Further research is needed to determine whether the early success of this model in Boston and Chicago can be replicated in other districts.

Consumer-driven Model and the Promise of Performance-based Accountability

Dissatisfied with low performance in public schools, an increasing number of policymakers and reformers are focusing on market-like competition as the driving force to raise student performance (Hirschman 1971). Three major types of choice programs exist in urban districts. They vary in terms of the degree to which parents can choose schools outside of the existing public schools. The most established type is the magnet school, which offers parents a choice of specialty programs in public schools outside their neighborhood. Practically every urban district operates programs of this type. Charter schools offer another type of parental choice. In the past ten years, about two-thirds of the states have passed legislation on charter schools. These schools are often developed and operated by the broader business and civic community. Although usually granted substantial autonomy from central office direction, charter schools are subject to standards-based accountability in the public school sector. The more radical type of parental choice is the state-funded voucher program, in experimental use in Milwaukee and Cleveland. These voucher programs allow parents to choose nonpublic schools, including religious schools.

Public School Choice.   Choice in public schools, including the recent charter school movement, serves the function of a political buffer. They are policy mechanisms to enable schools to meet public demands at a particular time. Magnet programs can be traced back to the desegregation era of the 1960s, when they served as a strategy to stem white flight. Charter schools of the 1990s are designed to circumscribe institutional constraints such as union power. By relaxing school admissions policy on student selection, choice programs are designed to keep parents satisfied with the public schools instead of opting for nonpublic schools (see Raywid 1985; Wong 1992).

Since at least the 1960s, middle-class parents have exited urban public schools for various reasons, including dissatisfaction with their declining quality, concerns over mandatory racial desegregation programs, and residential choice in the suburbs. In the 1990s, parental concern over schools' lack of accountability became a key factor. Public schools are not designed to meet the new expectations on performance, according to Chubb and Moe (1990). Using the High School and Beyond surveys for 1982 and 1984 and the Administrator and Teacher Survey data for 1984, Chubb and Moe found that the market-oriented nonpublic schools were far more likely to produce what they described as effective organizations. These high-performing schools, mostly nonpublic, can be distinguished from low-performing schools (mostly urban public). As the two authors observed, "Their goals are clearer and more academically ambitious, their principals are stronger educational leaders, their teachers are more professional and harmonious, their course work is more academically rigorous, and their classrooms are more orderly and less bureaucratic" (p. 99). Consequently, Chubb and Moe suggested parental choice in education as a way of eliminating the constraining effects of interest-group politics and governmental regulation.

The Chubb and Moe recommendation to transform public education into a marketplace has been controversial. Opposition to choice has been based on concerns over equal educational opportunities and self-selection. Choice programs are likely to "cream off" better students and take other resources out of neighborhood schools. Local residents may perceive that the conversion of their neighborhood school to a choice program deprives them of direct access to their community-based service institution. Questions have been raised about the implementation of a system-wide choice plan, with regard to distribution of school information to all parents, transportation costs, and compliance with civil rights provisions. In short, choice programs may come into conflict with other restructuring efforts in public schools and may destabilize school governance.

The concern over lack of information for all parents was the focus of a study of public school choice. Based on an extensive survey of about 1,600 parents in two districts with choice programs and two comparable districts without programs, serving as "controls," Schneider, Teske, and Marschall (2000) identified the critical role of a small group of well-informed "marginal consumers" who actively exercised their schooling choice. Their presence, according to the study, seemed sufficient in explaining the quality and performance of the schools. Consequently, the authors concluded, "[M]arginal consumers do increase the efficiency of education outcomes for everyone" and not just for themselves (p. 184).

Although charter schools are labeled as public schools, they are distinctive in several major aspects. The school's charter or contract explicitly states the conditions and expectations for outcome-based performance (Bierlein 1997; Hill 1997). The authorizing agency can be the local school board or other legal entities such as universities. Once established, charter schools enjoy substantial autonomy in setting teacher salaries and work conditions, although they are bound by state regulations regarding safety, health, dismissal, and civil rights. School funding follows students to the charter schools, which are operated on a multiyear renewable contract. Thirty-six states and the District of Columbia have passed laws providing for the creation of charter schools. In the 1999–2000 academic year, 1,689 charter schools were in operation, and an additional 305 were approved to open in 2000–2001. At least one district in California has converted to a system of charter (or contract) schools. Enrollment in charter schools increased to about 2.5 percent of the nation's public school student population in 1999–2000. In Arizona, California, and Michigan, charter enrollment figures are much higher.

Do charter schools create a competitive environment that causes regular public schools to make greater efforts to raise their performance? The rationale of competition has been widely cited, but there is a need to determine whether evidence exists to support such a claim. The literature, not surprisingly, is split on this issue. This section will highlight lessons learned about the nature of competitive effects (see Wong and Shen 2001).

Competitive effects are constrained by legislative compromise. Based on interviews and policy/legal analysis in four states, Bryan Hassel (1999) found that legislative compromise has played a significant role in reducing the competitive impact of charter schools. Laws that cap the number of charter schools, cushion the financial blow to traditional district schools, or reduce the autonomy of charter schools all contribute to reducing the impact a charter school can make. In a study of five urban districts, Teske and his associates (2001) attributed the modest effects of competition to several factors. The effects of charter school competition are lessened by financial cushioning and by a lack of school-level penalties for losing students to charter schools. Growing student populations may also reduce the competitive effects; even though traditional public schools are losing relative market share, the absolute number of their students remains constant. In districts where charter schools did have an impact, piecemeal rather than system-wide changes were made, mostly concerned with expanding the school day by offering new add-on programs.

The strong presence of charter schools tends to have a greater effect on districts.   In a survey of teachers in Nevada and Arizona, Maranto, Milliman, Hess, Gresham (1999) examined changes in traditional public schools in three types of districts, namely, those with no competition, the threat of competition, and strong competition. The study concluded that charter school competition tends to have a slight to moderate impact on public school changes. In a nationwide sample of teachers, students and parents, Finn et al. (2000) found that middle-size and small districts are more responsive to market-like competition.

Systemic improvement may not result from charter reform alone. In Minnesota— host to the longest-running experiment in charter schools—their impact on system-wide reform is still inconclusive (Center for Applied Reserach and Educational Improvement, 1998). The report, while not dealing explicitly with the competition question, argued that starting charter schools is very difficult work and may take a significant amount of time and commitment before producing measurable, system-wide impacts on Minnesota school districts. Similarly, a study conducted by Amy Stuart Wells (2000) on seventeen charter schools in ten districts across the state of California found limited evidence to support the notion that charter competition spurred improvement at the system-wide level. This general lack of significant response to competition suggests a time lag in school districts' ability to adopt policy change (Rofes 1998).

Competition produces mixed results for low-performing schools. A few studies suggest that charter schools provide better schooling opportunities for students with special needs. Basing their observations on a nationwide survey, Finn, Manno, and Vanourek (2000) found that charter schools function as "havens," where programs are designed to serve nontraditional student groups (such as school dropouts with drug and substance abuse). This finding is echoed in Hassel (1999), who viewed charter schools as most effective in situations where they can rectify the district's failure to provide adequate educational services for students with special needs. However, the results are largely mixed in terms of academic performance in low-performing schools. From an extensive study of the educational system in New Zealand, which has had ten years of autonomous schools operating in a competitive environment, Fiske and Ladd (2000) found that a competitive environment created uneven results. Although a large number of regular schools and their students continued to perform well, they also found that "autonomy and competition cannot and will not, in and of themselves, solve the problems of troubled urban schools." In short, given the mixed evidence on academic outcomes, there is a need for more research on what works and what does not work in charter schools as a system-wide reform.

Voucher Experiments in Milwaukee and Cleveland. An unusual kind of political alliance has emerged to address the growing concerns with failing public schools in the inner city. This new alliance consists of two core segments of the Republican and Democratic Parties. Frustrated with the low quality of schooling opportunities for their constituencies, lawmakers and religious and community leaders in African American neighborhoods (a traditional core of the Democratic Party) have parted company with the teachers' union (another Democratic core) and supported a more radical solution to the crisis in urban education. In Milwaukee, Polly Williams, a black state lawmaker, and Howard Fuller, a black activist and former superintendent, became the most outspoken supporters of the state-funded voucher program, which began in 1990. In Cleveland, Fannie Lewis, a Democratic member of the city council, spearheaded the 1994 passage of the choice program in the Ohio legislature. Joining the Democratic core were Republican governors and their business allies who saw choice as a mechanism not only to improve school performance and market efficiency but also to weaken the influence of the teachers' union. In both Milwaukee and Cleveland, this unique alliance was gradually broadened to include the Catholic Church and a wide range of business interest groups. Seeing a broadening of support, key proponents of choice have attempted to increase the demand and supply of choice programs. For example, Milwaukee's mayor, John Norquist, favored raising the income ceiling on eligibility. Advocacy groups that favor choice, such as the Heartland Institute in Chicago, continue to play an active role in organizing lobbying efforts in state capitals.

Evaluation of the Milwaukee choice program, the first one in a major city, has received national attention. To be sure, assessment of this pilot program was controversial, fueled by charges and countercharges made by two teams of researchers. On one side was the Witte team at the University of Wisconsin, which cautioned against generalizing the positive effects of the experiment. Witte (1991) showed that the choice program encountered a great deal of confusion and implementation problems during the start-up phase. Reviewing the program's fourth-year data, Witte, Thorn, Pritchard, and Claibourn (1994) concluded that "in terms of achievement test scores . . . students perform approximately the same as students [in the Milwaukee Public Schools]" (p. 28; see also Witte 2000, chap. 6). The report did recognize that the choice students maintained higher attendance rates and that their parents were highly satisfied with the selected schools. Looking back at the Milwaukee voucher experience, Witte (2000) observed a political push to expand the "targeted program" to "universal vouchers" that give middle-class parents a state subsidy for private school choice. Witte's analysis of the student enrollment pattern in 1998 indicates that public school parents, who were predominantly low income and minority, were not the major beneficiaries of the program. He pointed out that "only 23 percent of the total in Choice were transfer students" from the Milwaukee public schools (p. 188). Two-thirds of these students were already attending religious schools. Witte's findings imply that choice has a modest impact on improving the life opportunities for those who were attending low-performing public schools in Milwaukee.

On the other side of the debate is the Peterson team at Harvard University's Kennedy School of Government. Peterson and Noyes (1997) found that students made significant gains by the third and fourth years of their enrollment in the choice program. Comparing student applicants who were not selected for the choice programs with students who were, Peterson's research team found that the latter were, on the average, five percentile points higher than the former in math in the third year and more than eleven points higher in the fourth year. In reading, choice participants were nearly five percentile points higher than their comparison group after four years. These positive patterns led Peterson to conclude: "If duplicated nationwide, they would reduce the current difference between white and minority test score performance by at least one third and perhaps by more than one half" (p. 145). Encouraged by the results in Milwaukee, Peterson is leading similar evaluation research on the state-funded choice program in Cleveland and on the privately funded scholarship program in New York City, Dayton, and other cities.

The Cleveland voucher program was equally contentious. The program started in the fall of 1996 and was immediately challenged by the federal lower court for violating the "Establishment Clause," as students were allowed to choose religious schools. The program was restricted to lower elementary grades during the initial phase. In its first year, about two-thirds of the nearly 2,000 participants enrolled in kindergarten or first grade, and about 25 percent had attended private schools in previous years. In 2000, 96 percent of the 3,700 students in the program attended religious institutions. The Cleveland program is likely to expand following the Supreme Court's 5–4 decision in June 2002. In *Zelman v. Simmons-Harris,* the majority of the Court upheld the use of vouchers for enrollment in religious schools. The majority ruled that the Ohio program "is entirely neutral with respect to religion. . . . The program is therefore a program of true private choice."

Like the Milwaukee choice evaluation, the Peterson team backed the experiment, while criticisms came from another team of researchers, this time from Indiana University. The first evaluation was conducted by the Harvard team, which found significant test score gains among the 263 students attending the two newly created choice schools (known as Hope schools) (Greene, Howell, and Peterson 1997). Then researchers at Indiana University assessed third-grade performance and found no effect from the voucher program (Metcalf et al. 1998). In response, the Harvard team reanalyzed and expanded the data used in the Indiana University study. Not surprisingly, the second Harvard report concluded positive program effects in language skills and science (Peterson, Greene, and Howell 1998). Clearly, the policy challenge is whether student gains in pilot choice projects, such as in Milwaukee and Cleveland, can be sustained when they are scaled to the system-wide level.

Conclusion

The 1990s can be characterized as the beginning of accountability-based politics in urban public education. The public, policymakers, and organized interests have increased their demands for improvement in district-level governance as well as student performance. These demands, coupled with various institutional responses, have gradually redefined the politics of education at the local level. The new politics of accountability comprises a hybrid of choice, standards, sanctions, and incentives. This new politics has gradually replaced the existing paradigms that rely on a strong central bureaucracy or "materialist oriented" interest-group politics. Instead, various types of reform politics have emerged to move districts to rearrange power and authority both at the system-wide and school site levels. At the system-wide level, reformers have tried to mobilize and engage a broad coalition to promote human development issues. At the site level, schools' sense of "ownership" is seen as a viable force to improve performance. The parental empowerment experiment in Chicago is arguably the most extensive decentralized reform in the United States. In the past few years, a different kind of centralized model has come into vogue, which we label mayor-led integrated governance. Unlike the traditional bureaucratic model, integrated governance, as exemplified in Chicago since 1995, focuses on student outcomes, policy coherence, and greater accountability. As a greater number of urban school boards are likely to be appointed by mayors, it is important to sharpen our understanding on measuring this particular strand of reform and its performance. Just as the public school system is becoming more concerned with performance-based accountability, different types of parental choice programs, both in and out of the public sector, are gaining public support, particularly in inner cities, where school performance is low. The Supreme Court's favorable ruling on the Cleveland voucher program will enhance the legitimacy of similar programs across the states. In sum, variation in governing structures—not only within the public sector but also involving the nonpublic sector—will continue to shape our understanding of school politics in the urban setting.

Suggested Readings

Chubb, John, and Terry Moe. 1990. *Politics, Markets, and America's Schools.* Washington, D.C.: Brookings Institution Press. This book argues that low school performance is closely related to the governance structure in the public school system.

Orfield, Gary, and Carol Ashkinaze. 1991. *The Closing Door: Conservative Policy and Black Opportunity*. Chicago: University of Chicago Press. An extensive study of equal opportunities in education, jobs, and housing in metropolitan Atlanta.

Peterson, Paul E. 1976. *School Politics Chicago Style*. Chicago: University of Chicago Press. A classic in the politics of education that examines mayoral influence and reform conflict during Mayor Richard J. Daley's tenure in Chicago.

Tyack, David, and Larry Cuban. 1995. *Tinkering Toward Utopia: A Century of Public School Reform*. Cambridge: Harvard University Press. A historical perspective on the challenge of implementing reform in the American educational policy system.

Wong, Kenneth K. 1999. *Funding Public Schools: Politics and Policy*. Lawrence: University Press of Kansas. An overview on the politics of allocating school resources in U.S. federalism.

References

Berry, Jeffrey. 1999. *The New Liberalism*. Washington, D.C.: Brookings Institution Press.

Bierlein, Louann A. 1997. "The Charter School Movement." In *New Schools for a New Century*, ed. Diane Ravitch and Joseph Viteritti, 37–60. New Haven: Yale University Press.

Bryk, Anthony, David Kerbow, and Sharon Rollow. 1997. "Chicago School Reform." In *New Schools for a New Century*, ed. Diane Ravitch and Joseph Viteritti. New Haven: Yale University Press, 164–200.

Center for Applied Research and Educational Improvement, College of Education and Human Development, University of Minnesota. 1998. *Charter Schools Evaluation: Final Report 1998*. Online at http://education.umn.edu/CAREI/Reports/charter/default.html.

Chubb, John, and Terry Moe. 1990. *Politics, Markets and America's Schools*. Washington D.C.: Brookings Institution Press.

Clark, Terry N., and Vincent Hoffman-Martinot, eds. 1998. *The New Political Culture*. Boulder: Westview Press.

Consortium on Chicago School Research. 1993. *A View from the Elementary Schools: The State of Reform in Chicago*. Chicago: Consortium on Chicago School Research.

Cooper, Bruce S. 2000. "An International Perspective on Teachers Unions." In *Conflicting Missions? Teachers Unions and Educational Reform*, ed. Tom Loveless, 240–280. Washington, D.C.: Brookings Institution Press.

Danzberger, Jacqueline, Michael Kirst, and Michael Usdan. 1992. *Governing Public Schools: New Times, New Requirements*. Washington, D.C.: Institute for Educational Leadership.

Easton, David. 1965. *A Systems Analysis of Political Life*. Chicago: University of Chicago Press.

Eliot, Thomas H. 1959. "Toward an Understanding of Public School Politics." *American Political Science Review* 53 (December): 1032–1051.

Finn, Chester E., Bruno V. Manno, and Greg Vanourek. 2000. *Charter Schools in Action: Renewing Public Education*. Princeton: Princeton University Press.

Fiske, Edward B., and Helen F. Ladd. 2000. *When Schools Compete: A Cautionary Tale*. Washington, D.C.: Brookings Institution Press.

Greene, Jay, William Howell, and Paul E. Peterson. 1997. "An Evaluation of the Cleveland Scholarship Program." Occasional Paper, Program on Educational Policy and Governance, Harvard University.

Grimshaw, William. 1979. *Union Rule in the Schools*. Lexington, Mass.: Heath.

Hanushek, Eric. 1994. *Making Schools Work: Improving Performance and Controlling Costs*. Washington, D.C.: Brookings Institution Press.

Hassel, Bryan M. 1999. *The Charter School Challenge: Avoiding the Pitfalls, Fulfilling the Promise*. Washington, D.C.: Brookings Institution Press.

Henig, Jeffrey, Richard Hula, Marion Orr, and Desiree Pedescleaux. 1999. *The Color of School Reform: Race, Politics, and the Challenge of Urban Education.* Princeton: Princeton University Press.

Hill, Paul. 1997. "Contracting in Public Education." In *New Schools for a New Century,* ed. Diane Ravitch and Joseph Viteritti. New Haven: Yale University Press, 61–85.

Hirschman, Albert. 1971. *Exit, Voice and Loyalty.* Cambridge: Harvard University Press.

Hoxby, Caroline. 1998. "What Do America's 'Traditional' Forms of School Choice Teach Us about School Choice Reform?" *Economic Policy Review* 4 (March): 47–59.

Inglehart, Richard. 1990. *Culture Shift.* Princeton: Princeton University Press.

Johnson, Susan Moore. 2001. "Reform Bargaining and Its Promise for School Improvement." In Tom Loveless, ed., *Conflicting Missions? Teachers Unions and Education Reform,* ed. Tom Loveless, 7–46. Washington, D.C.: Brookings Institution Press.

Katznelson, Ira. 1981. *City Trenches.* New York: Pantheon.

Maranto, Robert, Scott Milliman, Frederick Hess, and April Gresham, eds. 1999. "Do Charter Schools Improve District Schools?" In *School Choice in the Real World: Lessons from Arizona Charter Schools.* Boulder: Westview Press.

Metcalf, Kim, William Boone, Frances Stage, Todd Chilton, Patty Muller, and Polly Tait. 1998. "A Comparative Evaluation of the Cleveland Scholarship and Tutoring Grant Program: Year One: 1996–97." Bloomington: Smith Research Center, School of Education, Indiana University.

National School Boards Foundation. 1999. *Leadership Matters: Transforming Urban School Boards.* Alexandria, Va.: National School Boards Foundation.

Peterson, Paul E. 1976. *School Politics Chicago Style.* Chicago: University of Chicago Press.

Peterson Paul E., Jay Greene, and William Howell. 1998. "New Findings from the Cleveland Scholarship Program: A Reanalysis of Data from the Indiana University School of Education Evaluation." Occasional Paper, Program on Education Policy and Governance, Harvard University.

Peterson, Paul E., and Chad Noyes. 1997. "School Choice in Milwaukee." In *New Schools for a New Century,* ed. Diane Ravitch and Joseph Viteritti, 123–146. New Haven: Yale University Press.

Ravitch, Diane, and Joseph Viteritti. 1997. "New York: The Obsolete Factory." In *New Schools for a New Century,* ed. Diane Ravitch and Joseph Viteritti, 17–36. New Haven: Yale University Press.

Raywide, Mary Ann. 1985. "Family Choice Arrangements in Public Schools: A Review of Literature." *Review of Educational Research* 55 (4) (winter): 435–467.

Rich, Wilbur C. 1996. *Black Mayors and School Politics.* New York: Garland.

Rofes, Eric. 1998. "How Are School Districts Responding to Charter Laws and Charter Schools?" Berkeley: Policy Analysis for California Education (PACE).

Rogers, David, and Norman Chung. 1983. *110 Livingston Street Revisited.* New York: New York University Press.

Schneider, Mark, Paul Teske, and Melissa Marschall. 2000. *Choosing Schools: Consumer Choice and the Quality of American Schools.* Princeton: Princeton University Press.

Sebring, Penny, Anthony Bryk, and John Easton. 1995. *Charting Reform: Chicago Teachers Take Stock.* Chicago: Consortium on Chicago School Research.

Shannon, Thomas. 1992. "Local Control and Organizacratz." In *School Boards: Changing Local Control,* ed. Patricia First and Herbert Walberg. Berkeley: McCutchan.

Stone, Clarence N. Jeffrey R. Henig, Bryan D. Jones, and Carol Pierannunzi. 2001. *Building Civic Capacity: The Politics of Reforming Urban Schools.* Lawrence: University Press of Kansas.

Teske, Paul, Mark Schneider, Jack Buckley, and Sara Clark. 2001. "Can Charter Schools Change Traditional Public Schools?" In *Charters Vouchers, and Public Education,* ed. Paul E. Peterson and David Campbell. Washington D.C.: Brookings Institution Press, 188–214.

Tiebout, Charles. 1956. "A Pure Theory of Local Expenditures." *Journal of Political Economy* 64 (October): 416–424.

Twentieth Century Fund. 1992. "Facing the Challenge: The Report of the Twentieth Century Fund Task Force on School Governance" (with a background paper by Jacqueline P. Danzberger). New York: Twentieth Century Fund.

Tyack, David. 1974. *The One Best System.* Cambridge: Harvard University Press.

Wells, Amy S. 2000. "Beyond the Rhetoric of Charter School Reform: A Study of Ten California School Districts." Los Angeles: UCLA Charter School Study 6–7.

Witte, John. 2000. *The Market Approach to Education.* Princeton: Princeton University Press.

——— 1991. *First Year Report: Milwaukee Parental Choice Program.* Madison: La Follette Institute of Public Affairs, University of Wisconsin–Madison.

Witte, John, Christopher Thorn, Kim Pritchard, and Michelle Claibourn. 1994. *Fourth Year Report: Milwaukee Parental Choice Program.* Madison: University of Wisconsin.

Wohlstetter, Priscilla, Susan Albers Mohrman, and Peter Robertson. 1997. "Successful School-Based Management: A Lesson for Restructuring Urban Schools." In *New Schools for a New Century,* ed. D. Ravitch and J. Viteritti, 201–225. New Haven: Yale University Press.

Wong, Kenneth K. 1992. "The Politics of Urban Education as a Field of Study: An Interpretive Analysis." In *The Politics of Urban Education in the United States,* ed. J. Cibulka, R. Reed, and K. Wong, 3–26. London: Falmer Press.

——— 1994. "Linking Governance Reform to Schooling Opportunities for the Disadvantaged." *Educational Administration Quarterly* 30 (May): 153–177.

——— 1999. *Funding Public Schools: Politics and Policy.* Lawrence: University Press of Kansas.

——— 2001. "Integrated Governance in Chicago and Birmingham (UK)." In *School Choice or Best Systems,* ed. Margaret C. Wang and Herbert Walberg, 161–212. Mahwah, N.J.: Lawrence Erlbaum.

Wong, Kenneth K., and Pushpam Jain. 1999. "Mayors and Schools: Integrated Governance and Educational Accountability." Paper presented at the annual meeting of the American Political Science Association, Boston.

——— 1999. "Newspapers as Policy Actors in Urban School Systems: The Chicago Story." *Urban Affairs Review* 35 (November): 210–246.

Wong, Kenneth K., Pushpam Jain, and Terry N. Clark. 1997. "Mayoral Leadership in the 1990s and Beyond: Fiscally Responsible and Outcome Oriented." Paper presented at the annual meeting of the Association for Public Policy Analysis and Management, Washington, D.C.

Wong, Kenneth K., and Mark Moulton. 1996. "Developing Institutional Performance Indicators for Chicago Schools: Conceptual and Methodological Issues Considered." In *Advances in Educational Policy: Rethinking School Reform in Chicago,* vol. 2, ed. K. Wong, 57–89. Greenwich, Conn.: JAI Press.

——— 1998. "Governance Report Cards: Accountability in the Chicago Public School System." *Education and Urban Society* 30 (August): 459–478.

Wong, Kenneth K., and Francis Shen. 2001. "Institutional Effects of Charter Schools: Innovation and Stratification." Paper presented at the annual meeting of the American Educational Research Association, Seattle.

13 Suburban and Metropolitan Politics

J. Eric Oliver

Over the past fifty years, America has become a nation of suburbs. In 1950, most Americans lived either in large central cities or rural areas, and only about a quarter lived in areas that could be called suburban, that is, places outside of a large central city but still within a metropolitan area. Today a suburb is home to one in two Americans. In most instances, these suburbs are far different from their urban or rural counterparts. Central cities often are noted for their size, density, and heterogeneity (Wirth 1938), whereas suburbs are typically thought of as small, spacious, and homogeneous (Baldassare 1992). And while rural places are socially and economically self-contained, most suburbanites travel to other places for work, shopping, or leisure. Arguably, suburbanization was one of the biggest changes in American society in the twentieth century, altering the way Americans relate to their family, friends, and greater communities.

Despite the enormity of this change, we know very little about how suburbanization is shaping American political life, particularly at the local level. Although some sociological aspects of suburbanization, such as racial segregation and urban sprawl, are well documented (see Massey and Denton 1993; Calthorpe 1993), many of its political implications are not well understood. Most commentary on the suburbs comes largely from journalistic speculation, architectural criticism, or popular impressions in books and movies rather than from empirical research. In these critiques, suburbs typically are lambasted as overly privatized, alienating landscapes, with residents who are parochial in their political concerns and xenophobic regarding the greater metropolis (see Mumford 1961; Jacobs 1961; Jackson 1985; Ehrenhalt 1996; Kunstler 1993; Langdon 1993). Suburbs are anticommunitarian, we are told, and their residents are putatively angry, withdrawn, and hostile toward government (Whyte 1956; Suarez 1999). Suburbs resist tax increases, fiercely defend their zoning autonomy, and focus primarily on a NIMBY-style politics (McKenzie 1994). Suburbanites are Republican and conservative, nurturing a right-wing political agenda (McGirr 2001). According to some writers (Putnam 2000; Suarez 1999), the ennui and alienation of suburban life are detriments to the community, as well as to the health and well-being of the American citizenry. There are, however, three problems with these indictments of suburban life.

First, most studies are very unclear about what a suburb really is. According to census definitions, a suburb is any place within a metropolitan area that is not a central city. This usage is not very helpful, as it conflates localities that vary widely in size, age, land use, and racial and economic composition. For example, if we simply divide metropolitan places into the categories of cities and suburbs, then Yonkers, Scarsdale, and Bayshore, New York, are all one kind of place (suburb), and New York City another (city). Yet it is hard to imagine that local politics in multiethnic Yonkers is the same as it is in affluent Scarsdale or middle-class Bayshore, and that all are categorically different from New York. Given the diversity of localities within metropolitan areas, such crude taxonomies do more to obfuscate than clarify the reality of suburbanization. For example, it makes little sense to say that suburbs foster conservative politics or Republicanism, given the great diversity of places that fall under the suburban heading. (Such arguments mistakenly conflate the contextual effects of suburban residence with the fact that more conservatives or Republicans may simply choose to live outside of central cities.) In other words, how can one generalize about the distinctive politics of a place if one cannot say what exactly makes that place distinctive in the first place?

Second, there are few theories that explain the dynamics of suburban politics. The politics of suburbia can be manifested at the national level, at the metropolitan level, or in the locality. Yet at all three levels, our knowledge of how suburbanization shapes political life is not well developed. Take, for example, local politics in suburbia. Most theories of local politics are derived from the studies of relatively large and diverse communities. These works focused on topics such as the role of elites and growth regimes (Banfield 1961; Dahl 1961; Polsby 1963; Stone 1989; Wolfinger 1974), the limits on local government in the face of municipal competition (Peterson 1981; Teibout 1956), and the potential of minority empowerment (Browning, Marshall and Tabb 1997; Karnig and Welch 1981; Welch and Bledsoe 1988). Considering the variety of suburban places, it is unclear how well suited any of these theories are for explaining suburban politics as a whole or the political life of an individual community. Beyond the topic of exclusionary zoning (Danielson 1976; Plotkin 1991) and political participation (Oliver 2001), political scientists have not explored in any systematic way the functioning of suburban institutions or the mass behavior of suburbanites. Consequently, we have few analytical frameworks for explaining how or why suburban political processes operate as they do at the national, metropolitan, or local levels.

Third, there has been little empirical research focusing specifically on suburban politics, particularly during the past thirty years. Previous research on suburbs largely consists of ethnographies of particular places, most of which were conducted in the 1950s and 1960s (Berger 1960; Gans 1967; Seeley, Sim, and Loosley 1958; Whyte 1956; Williams, Herman, Liebmann, and Dye 1965), or surveys that crudely dichotomize residents of cities and suburbs (Verba and Nie 1972; Wirt, Walter, Rabinowitz, and Hensler 1972). Although these works often provide interesting descriptions of individual localities, they do not reveal whether any of their observations can serve to generalize for suburbs as a whole. In other words, it is impossible to know whether the behaviors observed in one place are particular to that community or are applicable to all suburbs. Meanwhile, most studies that employ wider range data to study communities or their residents (Fischer 1982; Verba and Nie 1972; Wirt et al. 1972) either sample from only a small number of places or rely on relative crude classifications for places. Although a few recent studies have begun to reexamine suburban politics (Gainsborough 2001; Oliver 2001), suburbs remain a very understudied aspect of the American political scene.

In sum, even though America may now be a suburban nation, political science has lagged in explaining how it may be affecting our democratic processes. The systems model could be used to increase our understanding of political and policy processes in the suburban environment, but it has seldom been done. For example, we still do not know whether party affiliation, vote choice, and the distribution of power operate differently in suburban places than they do in central cities and how these differences may be caused by the suburban context. In this chapter, I analyze what we do know about suburban politics and identify topics that are ripe for future research. But rather than simply summarize a literature and speak to research needs, I will offer a new framework for understanding metropolitan places. I believe a new conceptualization of suburbs is necessary before we can grasp the dynamics of political life in America's metropolitan areas. Thus our first step in exploring suburban politics is to reconsider the idea of a suburb.

What Is a Suburb?

Most people think of suburbs in terms of conceptions popularized on television shows and movies that began to appear in the 1950s and continue today. It is an image of ranch homes, soccer moms, weekend cookouts, shopping malls, and quiet streets. The reality of the suburbs, not surprisingly, is a lot more complicated than the popular stereotypes. Suburbanization has really been a number of different processes that have been going on for over a century. Some places, like Concord, Massachusetts, started as rural towns and then became engulfed by an expanding metropolis. Other places, like Lakewood, California, were collections of houses that were incorporated by developers to lower their tax rates, establish zoning autonomy, and enhance property values. Still others are planned communities, like Celebration, Florida, or retirement villages, like Lakeway, Texas, that are designed to be unique. The rapid growth of suburbs over the past fifty years has created a tremendous variety of localities within the metropolis. We now have exurbs, postsuburbs, edge cities, inner- and outer-ring suburbs, middle-class suburbs, working-class suburbs, elderly suburbs, African American suburbs, and so forth (Baldassare 1992; Harrigan and Vogel 2000). Such a wide range of labels creates a tremendous challenge for anyone trying to determine what is meant by suburb.[1]

In trying to make sense of all the different definitions and conceptions of what makes a suburb, two important factors should be kept in mind. First, suburbs must be understood less in subordinate relation to central cities and more as independent units that are equivalent to cities. Suburbs were once defined in terms of their dependence on cities (the term suburb means literally *sub,* "beneath or inferior to," and *urb,* "city"), whereas today suburbs and cities have outgrown their old hierarchical relationship. More people commute from one suburb to another than to a central city, and a significant number of central city residents go to suburbs to work, shop, and play. Given the greater degree of social, economic, and cultural mutuality between cities and suburbs, all metropolitan places should be considered more equivalent as units of analysis rather than in some superordinate or subordinate position.

Second, the other key aspect of suburbanization is political fragmentation in the metropolitan area (Lewis 1996). Suburbanization is, as Michael Danielson (1976) noted, primarily "a political phenomenon." Institutional autonomy is the essence of suburbanization and the basis of suburban politics. Without different local political boundaries, it would be impossible to tell where New York City ends and Yonkers begins. Municipal and special district boundaries, by dividing a metropolitan population into separate political jurisdictions, also create communities of distinct political interests, interests that are often in conflict with one another. The key to understanding suburban politics, whether it is the politics of the metropolis or of the particular place, is first to appreciate the social and political by-products of this institutional division. At one level, fragmentation creates distinct political jurisdictions that may be in conflict or competition with one another. At another level, political fragmentation fosters tremendous social differentiation among places. Suburbs use tax measures, zoning autonomy, and other policies to foster communities that are very narrow in their social composition. There are now places that are composed of only the wealthy, of only homes, or of only whites, often within a larger and diverse metropolitan area. The most important political aspect within metropolitan areas is not whether a locality is a central city or a bedroom suburb, but rather its level of political fragmentation and the social and political distinctiveness that arises from its political autonomy.

Given these two factors—the equivalence of cities and suburbs and the importance of political jurisdictions—I would argue for a new framework for characterizing metropolitan places, as illustrated in Table 13-1. On one side is the traditional view, where metropolitan places are considered either as central city or suburb. Most studies of urban politics focused on central cities (which were distinguished by their regional

Table 13.1 Classification Schemes of Places in U.S. Metropolitan Areas

Traditional Characterization	New Characterization
Central cities (large, poor, nonwhite)	Differentiate metropolitan areas by degree of fragmentation
Suburbs (small, white, affluent)	Differentiate incorporated metropolitan places by
	Population size
	Economic composition
	Racial composition
	Types of government
	Land usage
	Unincorporated Areas

differences or whether they had reform-style political institutions), while suburbs were typically lumped together as a single category of place. On the other side is the new characterization. It differentiates metropolitan areas by their degree of fragmentation. Metropolitan areas vary, ranging from those that are subdivided by a large number of local governments to those that are under the control of a small number of political authorities. The new characterization also treats all incorporated places within a metropolis as similar units of analysis; as a category, they are differentiated only from unincorporated areas within a metropolis. (Unincorporated areas may have their own style of politics; see Burns 1994.) Among the incorporated metropolitan places, where the vast majority of Americans live, we can differentiate localities on the basis of five major characteristics: population size, economic composition, racial composition, land use, and type of governing structure. As America has suburbanized, its metropolitan places have become more differentiated along these five dimensions.

Population Size

In 1950, over 75 percent of Americans lived either in rural areas or cities with populations of over 100,000. Fifty years ago, America was a country mostly of farms and big cities. Today less than 50 percent of Americans live in such places. The majority of Americans now live in localities with a population under 100,000 that are part of a metropolitan area. Population size differentiates places that were once considered both central cities and suburbs. Among places the U.S. Census Bureau characterizes as central cities, population size varies, from New York (pop. 8,008,278) to Enid,

Oklahoma (pop. 47,045). Suburban places range from tiny communities of under 200 residents, like Tavistock, New Jersey, to places as large as Sterling Heights, Michigan, with a population above 100,000.

Economic Composition

America's metropolitan places are highly differentiated by their economic composition. The common stereotype is that central cities are disproportionately poor, whereas suburbs are generally affluent or middle class. This view distorts the economic diversity of metropolitan places. On average, larger cities have lower median household incomes than smaller places do, but the latter have a much larger range of income levels. Most larger cities have a median household income somewhere between $25,000 and $35,000. Smaller localities (most of which are commonly known as suburbs) have median household incomes that can fall below $20,000 a year (for example, East St. Louis, Missouri) or rise to over $120,000 (Kennilworth, Illinois). Most interestingly, suburbanization has led to the emergence of places that are economically homogeneous. Before suburbanization, most places had a wide variety of economic groups within their borders. Rich and poor lived within the same communities. Today we have places that are composed of only the rich (Scarsdale, New York) or only the poor (Camden, New Jersey).

Racial Composition

A similar pattern has occurred with respect to the racial composition of America's metropolitan places. During the 1960s, as large numbers of whites moved to the suburbs, a traditional view emerged that central cities were composed of large minority populations, while suburbs were overwhelmingly white. And, to a large extent, this was true. In 1970, over 97 percent of suburbs were almost entirely white, while most large cities had a high proportion of minorities. Today larger cities continue to have a higher proportion of nonwhites (and smaller cities a disproportionately high percentage of whites), but racial diversification has begun to occur within smaller places as well. One in four African Americans now lives in a suburb, and the fast-growing Latino and Asian American populations are increasingly suburbanizing. But many of the patterns of racial segregation that occur within large cities continue to be replicated in smaller communities. Rather than see minorities, particularly African Americans, integrate into predominantly white places, suburbanization has fostered the creation of smaller localities that are predominantly black, such as Prince George's County, Maryland, and Willingboro, New Jersey. In other words, African Americans are becoming more suburbanized, but they are moving mostly to black suburbs rather than integrating into white suburbs. Nevertheless, as more minorities migrate outward in the metropolis, suburbs are no longer the solely white enclaves they once were.

Land Use

American metropolitan places are becoming increasingly differentiated by their land usage. Traditionally it was thought that America's large central cities, the products themselves of commercial and industrial forces, were distinguishable from suburbs on the basis of their mixed land usage. Large cities had shopping areas and industrial zones, whereas small suburbs were predominantly residential or "bedroom" communities with a high percentage of home owners. Over the past thirty years, however, this pattern has changed. With the expansion of economic activity outward into the greater metropolis, smaller suburban localities are becoming more varied in their land use. Edge cities like Arlington, Virginia, and Stamford, Connecticut, have become mini-downtowns, with millions of feet of commercial office space. Others, like Industry, California, have manufacturing centers. But size does not necessarily mean diversity. Some predominantly residential places like Garland, Texas, or Livonia, Michigan, have very little commercial or industrial property but have over 100,000 residents—populations that make them among the larger places in the country. The diversity of land uses that were once the sole characteristic of big cities is now evident in many suburban areas.

Political Institutions

Finally, we can also distinguish metropolitan places by the types of political institutions that governed them. The traditional view is that central cities were the home of machine-style politics and their accompanying institutions—mayor-council forms of government, district elections, and partisan ballots. Suburbs were the home of reform-style governments, characterized by council-manager leadership, at-large elections, and nonpartisan ballots. The expansion of metropolitan areas, particularly in the Sun Belt, has blurred this distinction. Many large central cities now have reform-style political practices such as nonpartisan elections or council-manager governments, while many smaller suburban places, especially in the Northeast, have older style political institutions such as partisan elections and mayoral governments. Although the majority of medium-size cities continue to have council-manager governments and most larger cities have mayors, cities and suburbs are no longer so neatly divided along institutional lines.

In sum, our attempts to understand suburban politics depend heavily on how we conceptualize the suburb. At one level, we must characterize metropolitan areas by the degree to which they are divided among different political jurisdictions. And to explain the politics within these jurisdictions, we need to move away from simply characterizing a place as being either a central city or a suburb. Rather, it is more accurate to analyze local politics in contemporary metropolitan areas by counting all localities (both central city and suburb) as similar units of analysis that are differentiated by these major social characteristics. Instead of making generalizations about "suburban" politics that would apply to all places, it is more useful to look at how characteristics such as population size, economic and racial differentiation, or land use affect local politics and then examine where any particular community sits. Politics in a small, homogeneous, and residential place differs greatly from what it is in a small, heterogeneous place with a variety of land uses. Any generalizations we want to make about metropolitan politics will revolve around the larger issues of political fragmentation that allow this great social differentiation to occur in the first place. Our next step is to ascertain how well existing theories of local politics apply to localities that are so highly differentiated.

Theories of Suburban Politics

Currently we do not have any overarching theories of suburban politics. As noted above, this is largely because of the tremendous diversity in places called suburbs, which makes it quite difficult to generalize about suburban politics. For example, Robert Wood (1959) tried to describe the suburban political experience but ended up finding a series of contradictions. Suburbanites appeared to be simultaneously fulfilling the dream of a Jeffersonian democracy while at the same time disengaging from local affairs. Other observers of suburban politics similarly have run aground on the fact that suburbs seem to have so many opposing political processes happening at once: suburbanites are parochial yet disinterested in local affairs, apathetic yet fiercely defensive of local zoning prerogatives, conservative yet at the vanguard of progressive national politics (Colman 1975; Kramer 1972; Schwartz 1976; Thomas 1998; Wirt et al. 1972). How do we make sense of all these contradictions? What can we say about how democracy operates in suburbs when the term suburb means so many different things?

To answer these questions, it makes sense to think about suburban and metropolitan politics on three levels. At one level are the effects of suburbs on national politics. To what extent has suburbanization shaped the electoral patterns, party politics, and legislative agenda at the national level? At another level is the macropolitics caused by political fragmentation across the metropolitan area. How does the extent to which a metropolis is either unified under one political authority or divided between different municipalities and special district governments affect the way resources are distributed and political battles are defined? Finally, at the smallest level, is the internal micropolitics occurring within each municipality, school district, or other local governmental unit. In other words, how does the social and economic composition of a place, as well as its political institutions, shape the political contests that occur within its borders? With respect to all three levels of analysis, existing theories within political science can offer many important insights for explaining the dynamics of democratic life.

Politics at the National Level: The Consequence of Suburbanization for American Politics

Writing in a cover story for the *Atlantic Monthly*, William Schneider (1989) argued that 1992 was the beginning of the suburban century in American politics, because this was the year that suburbanites came to constitute a majority of American voters. Democrats, Schneider warned, would have to alter their strategies to appeal to this new constituency, lest they become a minority party. Some even attributed Bill Clinton's electoral success and the later Republican capturing of Congress in 1994 to their ability to win the hearts and minds of suburban voters (Thomas 1998). But is this correct? Can we say that suburbanites have a distinct agenda with respect to national politics that differentiates them from city dwellers or rural residents? What possible unifying factors about the suburban context could shape a set of national opinions?

The first answer to these questions that emerged in the 1950s was that suburbanization made Americans more conservative and Republican. The electoral success of Dwight D. Eisenhower and the Republicans in the 1950s was often attributed to the ways suburbs changed voters. Moving to a suburb, it was thought, led citizens to abandon the ethnically rooted identification with the Democrats and the New Deal that had characterized urban life in the 1930s and 1940s. Yet scholars who researched this topic in the 1960s found little evidence that suburbanites were any different from other parts of their states in voting behavior or political attitudes (Zikmund 1967, 1968). Studies comparing the political attitudes of city dwellers and suburbanites generally concluded that whatever differences arose generally came from the individual characteristics of the people living in such places (such as race, education, or age) and not from any contextual effects from their surroundings (Wirt et al. 1972).

More recent scholarship, however, suggests that a distinctive type of suburban politics may be finally emerging. Analyzing data from the National Election Studies between 1952 and 1992, Juliet Gainsborough (2001) argues that a distinct political agenda has crystallized in the attitudes and preferences of suburban residents, particularly since the 1970s. Suburban residents are more likely to vote for and identify with Republicans than people in central cities do, irrespective of their age, income, education, or other individual factors. According to Gainsborough, the social and political conditions of most suburbs make their residents disinterested in the problems of large cities (and their policy solutions) and more interested in moderate political issues—a sentiment echoed by other analysts of suburban voting behavior (Thomas 1998). But unlike earlier scholars, Gainsborough does not just compare city and suburban residents. She also considers the demographic composition of the entire metropolitan area and finds that those with greater racial diversity and less stratification between cities and suburbs are less likely to support Republican candidates and more likely to support welfare and other social benefits programs.

In short, the hints of suburban national political agenda seem to be materializing, although this is greatly dependent upon the social conditions of the metropolitan area. In those areas where suburban residents are most removed from the social conditions of central cities, such as poverty and a degraded public infrastructure, they are less supportive of policies that promote urban revitalization. Suburbanites who reside closer to urban areas or live in a more diverse metropolis exhibit less of this distinctive type of suburban attitude. These effects, however, are still rather small, and individual demographic differences are still much greater predictors of political attitudes. Nevertheless, suburban residence does seem to have a minor impact on national political orientations. Whether these trends continue, and how the political parties orient their platforms in response to suburban voters, remains to be seen.

Politics at the Macrolevel: The Costs and Benefits of Metropolitan Fragmentation

The second factor that may cause suburbanization to have an impact on politics concerns the metropolitan area. Here the impact of suburbanization is partly a story of the role of institutions and the political cleavages they define. If the essence of suburbanization is the political fragmentation of a metropolis into various subunits, then a central part of suburban politics is what type of political dynamic that fragmentation creates. The flip side of this story is the attempt to unify metropolitan areas under one government. In looking at the literature over the past fifty years, political scientists are generally split about what impact political fragmentation has on the functioning of local democratic politics.

On one side are the critics of fragmentation. According to this view, the separation of metropolitan populations into various governmental units has several negative consequences, including high levels of economic and racial segregation (Danielson 1976; Rusk 1993; Weiher 1991), giving certain economic interests disproportionate political power (Burns 1994), hindering growth management and control (Catlin 1997), promoting inefficiencies and replication in the distribution of public services (Wood 1958), and exacerbating the social problems of metropolitan areas, including urban sprawl, traffic congestion, and concentrations of poverty (Dreier, Swanstrom, and Mollenkopf 2001). For example, a metropolis that includes fifty suburbs will have to finance fifty separate police stations, fire stations, city halls, and so forth, instead of just one. This replication of services putatively loses economies of scale and also inhibits coordination across units (Gullick 1962).

Moreover, fragmentation is alleged to have social costs as well. More often than not, fragmentation leaves central cities with a disproportionate number of the poor, who require more social services and provide less of a tax base to fund them. Through exclusionary zoning techniques (such as minimum lot sizes, banning multifamily dwellings, and minimum sizes on single-family homes), high- and middle-income citizens can effectively exclude the poor from their communities (Danielson 1976). This economic segregation (and the racial segregation that typically accompanies it) generates inequalities in services, tax burdens, and school financing (Rusk 1993). One of the biggest policy consequences of political fragmentation in metropolitan areas is the increasing level of racial segregation in schools. By having schools administered by suburban municipalities or having separate suburban school districts, political fragmentation creates tremendous differences in educational environments based on race. Nearly fifty years after the Supreme Court's opinion declaring racially segregated schools unconstitutional, most American schoolchildren remain in schools that are either predominantly white or predominantly minority. For example, 64 percent of African American children attend schools that have a black majority; 30 percent attend schools that are over 90 percent black (Orfield, Eaton, and Jones 1997). David Rusk (1993) argues that the solution to this problem is to allow central cities greater powers in annexing their surroundings. In his analysis of America's metropolitan areas, Rusk argues that those places with "elastic" central cities (cities with the ability to annex surrounding developed areas) have lower levels of racial and economic segregation and enjoy better fiscal health than their "inelastic" counterparts. Elastic cities like Houston, Atlanta, and Orlando are able to incorporate suburbs into their borders and are less constrained both fiscally and socially than are inelastic cities like Boston, Cleveland, or Chicago, which are effectively hemmed in by suburbs.

On the other side are those who see benefits from fragmentation (Ostrom, Bish, and Ostrom 1988; Schneider 1989). Most of these thinkers subscribe to a "public choice" view of local politics, an analytical framework derived from the field of economics. As first articulated by Tiebout (1956) in his seminal article, public choice theorists begin with the assumption that individuals are "rational actors," that all human actions derive from individuals seeking to maximize the utility of their actions for their own personal gains. Using this assumption, public choice theorists speculate that citizens will seek to maximize the returns to their tax expenditures by choosing locales with a combination of the lowest tax rate and the highest level of services. In other words, citizens basically act as consumers of public services—senior citizens will seek towns with low taxes and senior centers, parents will move to places with better schools, businesses will seek towns with lower service fees, and so forth. In the public choice world of high mobility and information, citizens "vote with their feet" for services and apply pressure to local leaders by threatening to leave. Local governments, eager to attract "ratables"—those who will pay more in taxes than they require in services, such as businesses or wealthy residents—will seek efficiencies between their revenues and expenditures.

The political implications of fragmentation from a public choice perspective are well developed in Paul Peterson's *City Limits* (1981). Peterson begins his analysis with the assumption that local governments are interested in local growth and are in competition with one another for taxable property. To attract these groups, Peterson suggests that localities will seek to cuts taxes by minimizing "redistributive" expenditures—the policies that transfer payments to groups who provide little in tax revenue, such as the poor. Since most cities cannot maintain the high taxes necessary to finance redistributive policies such as welfare or housing assistance without losing their tax base to a nearby community, they will minimize such welfare spending. In short, suburban political fragmentation will cause a "race to the bottom," as communities compete for ideal taxpaying residents. Peterson later comments on the importance of federal institutions (which can control the flow of labor and capital) to provide such redistributive services.

Although both analyses of fragmentation offer compelling logic, neither can offer empirical certainty. On the one hand, political consolidation might, in theory, eliminate much of the exclusionary zoning, racial and economic segregation, and fiscal inequalities that exist across metropolitan areas, but, in practice, researchers have not found any proof that consolidation does promote greater political or economic equality or provide greater economies of scale in the delivery of services (Keating 1995). Indeed, one problem with having a large unified government for an entire metropolis is that it further distances citizens from government (Berry, Portney, and Thomson 1993; Oliver 2001). Under such a situation, the dynamics of big-city politics, where wealthy groups exercise disproportionate power because of their small numbers and greater organizational capacity (Stone 1989), may hold. Political consolidation may eliminate the fragmentation that allows for high levels of economic and racial segregation, but it does not necessarily ensure greater equality in public services.

On the other hand, one may criticize the public choice celebrations of fragmentation. The public choice framework makes heroic assumptions about citizen mobility or information about localities and generally discounts the political process as an important determinant of policy. It is very unlikely that citizens act solely in the consumerist way that public choice theorists describe. Most citizens choose their residence because of work or family considerations and less because of some optimizing calculation between tax rates and municipal services. Moreover, local leaders, especially in many suburban areas, are not simply concerned with growth or reducing taxes, particularly if their community has other amenities. There is mixed evidence that competition for localities actually provides more efficient local governments (Keating 1995).

Irrespective of whether one believes that fragmentation is harmful or beneficial, few metropolitan areas have succeeded in establishing more unified governments. Some metropolitan areas, like Phoenix, Arizona, are under one jurisdiction simply because they are dominated by an elastic central city that has been able to annex its surrounding areas. In most metropolitan areas, however, there are few formal institutions with significant governing power over the entire urban area. Outside of Miami–Dade County, Florida; Portland, Oregon; and Minneapolis–St. Paul, Minnesota, there are no metropolitan-area governments with the ability to tax, zone, administer a range of services, and perform many of the same functions that municipalities do. But does this mean America's metropolitan areas are simply collections of independent municipalities in fierce competition with one another? Not necessarily. Although metropolitan area governments may be very rare, in many of these areas alternative institutions have arisen to tackle their problems.

The most common form of metropolitan coordination is a council of government (COG). Arising largely from federal incentives for metropolitan planning that were introduced in the 1960s, COGs are voluntary associations composed of local governments, including municipalities, counties, and special districts. These intergovernmental associations work to coordinate service delivery such as sewage and solid waste disposal, roads, and water supplies across the municipalities in the same region. Although COGs are useful in helping municipalities communicate and develop long-term plans, they are very weak as governments. Much like the United Nations, COGs depend upon the voluntary participation of their constituent members. Consequently, COGs rarely can impose decisions that would have adverse effects on any particular member, as that municipality would then leave. For example, if the Houston area COG decided to impose growth controls that would limit the ability of a suburb like Katy to develop its land, it is likely that Katy would simply remove itself from the COG and continue to do what it pleases. As institutions, COGs do little to actually govern a metropolitan area.

One aspect of metropolitan area living, transportation, has become so important that a new type of regional institution has been created—the metropolitan planning organization (MPO). Federal legislation in the early 1990s required urban areas to create boards to design regional transportation plans and administer federal highway grants. Since regions that do not establish these MPOs risk losing federal support for highways and transportation, most metropolitan areas have been quick to form them. But, like the COGs, the MPOs have little power to determine what is actually done by the cities and counties within their jurisdiction. Compliance among localities is voluntary, and MPOs do not have the power to tax or zone or enforce compliance with the plans they derive. Given the experience with COGs, one might think that MPOs are nothing but paper tigers and that real metropolitan governance is an illusory goal.

But as the case of Portland, Oregon, demonstrates, simply having an organization dedicated to addressing metropolitan area issues is an important first step for the development of real institutions of metropolitan governance. Portland's Metro government, which evolved from a COG and a special district government, coordinates zoning across all municipalities within the region, enforces a growth boundary that limits suburban sprawl, encourages urban redevelopment within the downtown, and coordinates transportation, solid waste disposal, and other vital services. What makes Metro unique is its ability to raise its own revenues through fees and voter-approved taxes and its independent authority to enforce land-use planning. With its regionally elected board, it is truly a metropolitan area government.

In sum, the dynamics of metropolitan politics are determined by the extent to which its population is subdivided into separate governments. Metropolitan areas with less fragmentation or that are unified under a single metropolitan government are more likely to have political battles resembling those of larger cities, with a single institution being the focus of political struggle. The question of whether this style of governance is beneficial or harmful to the ideal practice of democratic governance remains open to debate. Metropolitan areas that are more politically divided among a large number of municipalities will experience a wider range of political conflicts spread over a larger number of sites. In these places, the focus of local politics will be more on minibattles within each community. How such political battles play out is the focus of the smallest level of analysis.

Politics at the Microlevel: The Dynamics of Local Politics in the Fractured Metropolis

At the smallest level, suburban politics is also about the internal conflicts that occur within a particular community. Here the evidence from political science is much less direct. Over the past forty years, the study of local politics in the United States has focused mostly on large cities and the traditional question of "Who governs?" Few studies have examined the internal dynamics of politics within suburbs. The question remains, therefore, as to whether the same groups and processes that typically dominate big-city politics also rule in suburban areas. Before answering this question, it is useful to quickly reexamine the dominant perspectives in urban politics.

In examining the power structure of big cities, social scientists historically divide into two camps. On one side are those who see local politics as controlled by a power elite of social and economic notables (Hunter 1953; Mills 1956). In this model, a handful of elites make all the important decisions that occur within city government on issues ranging from housing redevelopment to education to zoning. On the other side are the so-called pluralists, who argue that different groups have varying degrees of power in local government, depending on the particular issue and policy arena

(Dahl 1961; Polsby 1963; Wolfinger 1974). Pluralists see power not as concentrated in a few hands but dispersed asymmetrically over a wide range of issues. Local politics does not consist of permanent cleavages but rather of various groups and individuals either conflicting or coming together in temporary coalitions, depending on the salience of a particular policy or measure.

More contemporary scholars have tried to reconcile these camps by focusing on the land-oriented character of local politics and the challenges of forming governing coalitions. Most notable has been the work of Logan and Molotch (1987) and Clarence Stone (1989). For example, one complaint about the pluralist model is that it cannot make consistent predictions of who is likely to be involved in local affairs. In response, Logan and Molotch offer a compelling explanation of why some types of citizens are more interested than others in local politics. According to Logan and Molotch, citizens have one of two relationships to land: either they seek nonmonetary use value from their property (shelter, safety, and enjoyment) or they seek exchange value (rent or property development and speculation). Those landlords who seek much of their income from the rents they can extract or property values they can increase have great incentives to be involved in local politics. Not surprisingly, local politics is typically focused on land issues, specifically the promotion of economic growth, and often draws people with professional interests in land, such as developers, real estate agents, and bankers. Clearly, not all interest in local politics will come from this relationship to land. Ethnic and racial considerations as well as machine politics and patronage are also important determinants of local political activity (Wolfinger 1974). Nevertheless, across a broad range of places, those with commercial interests in land will continue to be important groups in local politics. In this view, local politics is largely about the contests over how to increase property values.

Yet the difficulty with Logan and Molotch's theory, as well as both elite and pluralist theory, is that they cannot account for why some groups are more successful than others in reaching their political goals. Clarence Stone's (1989) theory of regime politics outlines the conditions that enable groups to form successful governing coalitions. In Stone's view, public leaders and private developers often form a symbiotic relationship: economic luminaries provide the commercial endeavors and campaign financing that help local leaders retain power, and local leaders make zoning decisions and direct public priorities toward sustaining economic development. The small size and tight social networks of those in office and those seeking high exchange values enable these reciprocal, informal, and long-lasting governing arrangements to take hold. It is not simply being a large commercial interest that gives power, but the ability to work consistently with local leaders in a mutually beneficial way. The key to understanding power is to grasp who is a good partner in a governing coalition and how well positioned that person or group is in the social and economic circles of a particular community. But while these theories of local power are quite useful for explaining the political dynamics in large cities with ample commercial interests, their suitability for explaining suburban politics is questionable. Most theories of urban politics basically assume that a plurality of interests exists within a particular community and that communities are under pressure for economic growth. With these assumptions, most theories then strive to ascertain how well any one set of interests is represented or how much the growth pressure shapes the policymaking process. However, for suburban politics, the presumption of either a difference in interests or of growth pressure is debatable, particularly in a community that is socially homogeneous or predominantly residential. In a place made up of only affluent, white home owners or only poor minorities, we might expect less competition between interest groups and few arenas for developers to weave their political schemes. The question then arises, How well do these theories explain the dynamics of politics in suburban areas?

The answer to this question depends, in large part, on the social and institutional characteristics of the place, as delineated in Table 13-1. Take, for example, population size. Most larger places are typically more racially and economically diverse and are likely to have more mixed land use. Consequently, we should expect localities with more than 100,000 in population to mimic the politics of larger cities, with the same types of political patterns: pressure for economic growth and development, concerted efforts of economic interests, especially those focused on commercial properties, and electoral politics centered on partisan or racial cues.[2] Similarly, in places that are small but have either mixed land use or greater economic or racially diversity, we should find similar types of political dynamics that often occur in the urban politics literature. In short, if larger suburbs resemble large cities in their diversity, the patterns of democratic politics should be quite similar. In these instances, the politics surrounding growth regimes, mentioned in the research of Logan and Molotch and Stone, will be evident.

Increasingly, however, suburban places of all sizes are becoming more distinguishable from large cities. The traits that make suburban places distinctive can have a large impact on their politics. For example, one important trait is the singularity of their land usage, specifically in places that are largely composed of homes. In residentially predominant bedroom suburbs, pressures for growth and economic development will be less acute. With fewer commercial interests seeking to extract rents from properties, the growth-oriented regimes often present in larger cities will not be evident. The question remains as to what exactly does shape politics in these homogeneous places. We currently have no theories to explain the dynamics of politics in places with solely residential land usage.

Nor do we understand how other traits that distinguish suburban places, such as their racial and economic homogeneity, also affect local politics. Oliver (2001) finds that the economic and racial composition of a community is an important determinant of whether people involve themselves in local affairs. Residents of places that are very affluent or economically and racially homogeneous are far less likely to participate in local civic activities than are people in more diverse communities. Just as community diversity affects political participation, we might also expect that it will be important for shaping local politics. In localities that are economically and racially homogeneous, residents are more likely to have a relatively high degree of uniformity in their political interests. As long as no threat was made to the parameters along which the community is defined, local politics could be characterized as nonconfrontational, with citizens less engaged and basically avoiding conflict. In such homogeneous places, local conflict may tend to be about the personal disagreements of a small class of locally involved citizens rather than any major clashes among large groups.

In more economically and racially diverse places, however, we should expect to see more widespread conflict. Residents in these places tend to be more interested in local affairs (Oliver 1999), more likely to organize into interest groups to advance their electoral goals (Leighley 1996), use group-based heuristics to shape their vote choice (Terkildson 1993), have different views on the role of government, or have specific issues that animate their decisions. Thus, for example, it is likely that voters will be information seekers and make informed choices (Lupia and McCubbins 1998) when the economic composition is more diverse, as a greater variety of interest groups will be contesting fiscal policy. Similarly, in places with greater percentages of minorities, political conflicts are more likely to be defined along ethnic or racial lines.

In sum, the key to understanding the dynamics of politics within a suburban place is first to identify the social composition of that community. If it resembles a large city, presumably many of the existing theories developed in the urban politics literature will be applicable. But in places that are small or homogeneous or with unvaried land usage, the internal dynamics of suburban politics remains unknown. We should not expect the same types of growth machines to exert political power or the same types of pluralistic political pressures that are found in large cities. How political conflict emerges in such places is a topic needing future research.

Directions for Future Research

For the most part, scholars of local politics have not kept up with the changing demographics of the United States. Although most Americans now live in suburban areas, most political scientists concerned with local affairs continue to focus on the politics of large central cities. As a result, our knowledge of suburban politics is far behind what it should be. But at the same time suburbanization is a prime topic for future research. The social, economic, and political diversity of suburban areas offers the conditions of a natural experiment to gain understanding of what shapes the dynamics of local politics, particularly as America grows into the twenty-first century. Pressing questions exist for each of the three political arenas listed above: national, metropolitan, and local.

In the realm of national politics, for example, recent research suggests that suburban social contexts can shape the political views of their residents (Gainsborough 2001), but the question remains as to whether this is a temporal effect or a trend that will continue. As the major political parties orient themselves toward a suburban electorate, will suburban voters continue to divide along partisan lines? What also remains to be seen is how the suburban character of the electorate will change the political agenda within Congress. Will there be more legislation aimed at suburban interests in Congress? Will this come at the expense of rural or urban areas?

Similarly, the impact of political fragmentation in the metropolitan area is also a topic needing further investigation. Many commentators argue for greater consolidation of cities and suburbs (Rusk 1993), but the politics of such consolidations is still uncertain. The political conditions under which such consolidation can occur are quite rare, as resistance comes from both suburbanites wanting to protect their political autonomy and minorities in central cities afraid of losing political power (Owen and Wilburn 1985). Even smaller scale changes, such as efforts to mandate "fair-share" low-income housing in affluent suburbs, meet fierce opposition (Kirp, Dwyer, and Rosenthal 1995). The question remains as to how and where central cities and suburbs can coordinate more effectively and adopt mutually beneficial governing arrangements, even without adopting formal institutional mechanisms of metropolitan governance.

Finally, little is known about the internal politics of suburban places that do not have the size or diversity of a large city. We still have little knowledge of how the basic mechanisms of democratic governance operate in most homogeneous suburban places. What differentiates people in a community where everyone has the same race, economic status, and land tenure? Are political battles in such a place the same as they are in a more diverse setting? Under what conditions are policy changes adopted in places that seem dedicated to preserving the status quo?

In answering these questions, we need to reexamine many of the traditional arenas of political contestation that political scientists focus on the national and state level and see how they operate in localities. One example is voting in local elections. Almost all of our knowledge about how people vote is based on research concerning national elections. We know almost nothing about how and why people vote in local contests, particularly outside of central cities. Most research on local voting behavior derives either from case studies of individual locales (Ferman 1985; Hero and Beatty 1989; Kleppner 1985; Mollenkopf 1994; Shefter 1985; Sonenshein 1993), aggregate level analyses of voter turnout (Alford and Lee 1968; Monroe 1977), or focuses on the representation of women and minorities on local councils (Darcy, Welch, and Clark 1987; Engstrom and McDonald 1982; Svara 1991; Welch 1990). Our current research is very unclear about what shapes citizens' preferences in most local elections. This is partly because the tremendous diversity in localities across America, as well as the timing, structure, and organization of their elections, makes it difficult to formulate generalizations. Another reason is that theories of electoral behavior and public opinion developed from individual-level research on the national level (for example, Campbell, Miller, and Converse 1959; Miller and Shanks 1996) largely ignore social contexts. Consequently, many important questions remain unanswered. Do suburban voters really behave as consumers of public services, as some theorists suggest (Tiebout 1956; Schneider 1989), or do other factors shape their political views? Do residents of more homogeneous locations have a different view about the role and function of government than do those in more diverse locales? We might expect that in homogeneous communities voters would be less interested in local politics, would base their vote choice less on particular issues and more on personal connections or social ties to candidates, and probably would be more hostile to governmental units that accommodate more diverse sets of interests, that is, regional, state, or national governments (Baldassare 1992). But this claim is unsubstantiated.

The key aspect of researching local politics in suburban areas is to prioritize the social and institutional composition of a locality as a primary determinant of citizen attitudes and behavior. Individual differences in age, education, race, and gender are important in shaping local as well as national political attitudes, but they cannot fully explain how Americans understand local political life. The tremendous differentiation in places that has been the by-product of suburbanization means that social contexts are becoming more important as determinants of citizen behavior. New studies of suburban politics need to focus on how social segregation and institutional arrangements reduce the capacity of municipal government for adjudicating conflict.[3]

Conclusion

The transformation of the United States into a suburban nation offers many exciting challenges and opportunities for scholars of American politics. Suburbanization is changing the character of politics at the national, metropolitan, and local levels. How these changes are occurring and what they mean for American democracy, however, remain unclear. In short, with respect to suburban politics, there is a lot more that we do not know than what we do know. Much of our ignorance is due to the conceptual roadblocks presented by the diversity within suburban forms. It is impossible to determine what influence suburbs might have on national elections or how suburban voters might differ from city dwellers when so many different types of places get lumped together in one category. But this diversity need not be an impediment to understanding political life in the twenty-first-century metropolis. Suburbanization has created a greater systematic differentiation in American places, particularly with respect to their economic and racial composition and their land use. The key to understanding suburban politics remains in measuring how these differences affect the basic workings of democratic governance. Only when we compare how processes like voting, political participation, and policy formation differ in places composed of only one social class or one type of land use and in places that are more diverse can we begin to understand how the process of suburbanization is shaping the practice of American democracy.

Suggested Readings

Dreier, Peter, Todd Swanstrom, and John M. Mollenkopf. 2001. *Place Matters: Metropolitics for the Twenty-first Century.* Lawrence: University Press of Kansas. A thorough study of the ill effects of economic segregation in metropolitan areas.

Gainsborough, Juliet. 2001. *Fenced Off: The Suburbanization of American Politics.* Washington, D.C.: Georgetown University Press. An important new study of the impact of suburban growth on national politics.

Jackson, Kenneth. 1985. *Crabgrass Frontier: The Suburbanization of the United States.* New York: Oxford University Press. A classic history of the growth of suburbs and their impact on American society.

Oliver, J. Eric. 2001. *Democracy in Suburbia.* Princeton: Princeton University Press. An empirical examination of how suburbs shape political participation and community involvement.

Orfield, Gary, Susan Eaton, and Elaine Jones. 1997. *Dismantling Desegregation: The Quiet Reversal of Brown versus Board of Education.* New York: New Press. Using illustrative maps, this book offers a convincing argument that the fate of cities and suburbs is highly linked.

References

Alford, Robert R., and Eugene C. Lee. 1968. "Voting Turnout in American Cities." *American Political Science Review* 62 (September): 796–813.

Baldassare, Mark. 1992. "Suburban Communities." *Annual Review of Sociology* 18: 475–494.

Banfield, Edward C. 1961. *Political Influence.* New York: Free Press.

Berger, Bennett. 1960. *Working Class Suburb.* Berkeley: University of California Press.

Berry, Jeffrey M., Kent E. Portney, and Ken Thomson. 1993. *The Rebirth of Urban Democracy.* Washington D.C.: Brookings Institution.

Browning, Rufus, Dale Rogers Marshall, and David H. Tabb. eds. 1997. *Racial Politics in American Cities,* 2d ed. New York: Longman.

Burns, Nancy. 1994. *The Formation of American Local Governments.* New York: Oxford University Press.

Caitlin, Robert. 1997. *Land Use Planning, Environmental Protection, and Growth Management.* Chelsea, Mich.: Ann Arbor Press.

Calthorpe, Peter. 1993. *The Next American Metropolis.* New York: Princeton Architectural Press.

Campbell, Angus, Warren E. Miller, and Philip Converse. 1959. *The American Voter.* Chicago: University of Chicago Press.

Colman, William G. 1975. *Cities, Suburbs, and States.* New York: Free Press.

Dahl, Robert A. 1961. *Who Governs? Democracy and Power in an American City.* New Haven: Yale University Press.

Danielson, Michael. 1976. *The Politics of Exclusion.* New York: Columbia University Press.

Darcy, Robert, Susan Welch, and Janet Clark. 1987. *Women, Elections, and Representation.* New York: Longman.

Dreier, Peter, Todd Swanstrom, and John H. Mallenkopf. 2001. *Place Matters: Metropolitics for the Twenty-first Century.* Lawrence: University Press of Kansas.

Ehrenhalt, Alan. 1996. *The Lost City: Discovering the Forgotten Virtues of Community in the Chicago of the 1950s.* New York: Basic Books.

Engstrom, Richard, and Michael McDonald. 1982. "The Underrepresentation of Blacks on City Councils." *Journal of Politics* 44 (November): 1088–1099.

Ferman, Barbara. 1985. *Governing the Ungovernable City: Political Skill, Leadership, and the Modern Mayor.* Philadelphia: Temple University Press.

Fischer, Claude. 1982. *To Dwell Among Friends: Personal Networks in Town and City.* Chicago: University of Chicago Press.

Gainsborough, Juliet. 2001. *Fenced Off: The Suburbanization of American Politics.* Washington, D.C.: Georgetown University Press.

Gans, Herbert J. 1967. *The Levittowners.* New York: Pantheon Books.

Gullick, Luther. 1962. *The Metropolitan Problem and American Ideas.* New York: Knopf.

Harrigan, John J., and Ronald K. Vogel. 2000. *Political Change in the Metropolis.* New York: Longman.

Hero, Rodney, and Kathleen Beatty. 1989. "The Elections of Federico Pena as Mayor of Denver: Analysis and Implications." *Social Science Quarterly* 70 (June): 300–310.

Hunter, Floyd. 1953. *Community Power Structure: A Study of Decision Makers.* Chapel Hill: University of North Carolina Press.

Jackson, Kenneth. 1985. *Crabgrass Frontier: The Suburbanization of the United States.* New York: Oxford University Press.

Jacobs, Jane. 1961. *The Death and Life of Great American Cities.* New York: Vintage Books.

Karnig, Albert, and Susan Welch. 1981. *Black Representation and Urban Policy.* Chicago: University of Chicago Press.

Keating, Michael. 1995. "Size, Efficiency, and Democracy: Consolidation, Fragmentation, and Public Choice." In David Judge, Gerry Stoker, and Harold Wolman, eds. *Theories of Urban Politics,* 117–134. Thousand Oaks, Calif.: Sage.

Kirp, David, John Dwyer, and Larry Rosenthal. 1995. *Our Town: Race, Housing, and the Soul of Suburbia.* New Brunswick: Rutgers University Press.

Kleppner, Paul. 1985. *Chicago Divided: The Making of a Black Mayor.* DeKalb: Northern Illinois University Press.

Kramer, John, ed. 1972. *North American Suburbs: Politics, Diversity, Change.* Berkeley: Glendessary.

Kunstler, James Howard. 1993. *The Geography of Nowhere: The Rise and Decline of America's Man-made Landscape.* New York: Simon and Schuster.

Langdon, Phillip. 1993. *A Better Place to Live: Reshaping the American Suburb.* Amherst: University of Massachusetts Press.

Leighley, Jan. 1996. "Group Membership and the Mobilization of Political Participation." *Journal of Politics* 58 (May): 447–463.

Lewis, Paul. 1996. *Shaping Suburbia: How Political Institutions Organize Urban Development.* Pittsburgh: University of Pittsburgh Press.

Logan, John, and Harvey Molotch. 1987. *Urban Fortunes: The Political Economy of Place.* Berkeley and Los Angeles: University of California Press.

Lupia, Arthur, and Matthew McCubbins. 1998. *The Democratic Dilemma: Can Citizens Learn What They Need to Know?* New York: Cambridge University Press.

Massey, Douglas, and Nancy Denton. 1993. *American Apartheid: Segregation and the Making of the Underclass.* Cambridge: Harvard University Press.

McGirr, Lisa. 2001. *Suburban Warriors: The Origins of the New American Right.* Princeton: Princeton University Press.

McKenzie, Evan. 1994. *Privatopia: Homeowner Associations and the Rise of Residential Private Government.* New Haven: Yale University Press, 1994.

Miller, Warren, and Merrill Shanks. 1996. *The New American Voter.* Cambridge: Harvard University Press.

Mills, C. Wright. 1956. *The Power Elite.* Oxford: Oxford University Press.

Mollenkopf, John. 1994. *A Phoenix in the Ashes: The Rise and Fall of the Koch Coalition in New York City Politics.* Princeton: Princeton University Press.

Monroe, Alan D. 1977. "Urbanism and Voter Turnout: A Note on Some Unexpected Findings." *American Journal of Political Science* 21 (February): 71–78.

Mumford, Lewis. 1961. *The City in History.* New York: Harcourt Brace and World.

Oliver, J. Eric. 1999. "The Effects of Metropolitan Economic Segregation on Local Civic Participation." *American Journal of Political Science* 43 (January): 186–212.

———— 2001. *Democracy in Suburbia.* Princeton: Princeton University Press.

Orfield, Gary, Susan Eaton, and Elaine Jones. 1997. *Dismantling Desegregation: The Quiet Reversal of Brown versus Board of Education.* New York: New Press.

Ostrom, Vincent, Robert Bish, and Elinor Ostrom. 1988. *Local Government in the United States.* San Francisco: Institute for Contemporary Studies.

Owen, C. James, and York Wilburn. 1985. *Governing Metropolitan Indianapolis: The Politics of Unigov.* Berkeley: University of California Press.

Peterson, Paul. 1981. *City Limits.* Chicago: University of Chicago Press.

Plotkin, Sidney. 1991. *Keep Out: The Struggle for Land Use Control.* Berkeley: University of California Press.

Polsby, Nelson W. 1963. *Community Power and Political Theory.* New Haven: Yale University Press.

Putnam, Robert. 2000. *Bowling Alone.* New York: Simon and Schuster.

Rusk, David. 1993. *Cities without Suburbs.* Washington, D.C.: Woodrow Wilson Center Press.

Schneider, Mark. 1989. *The Competitive City: The Political Economy of Suburbia.* Pittsburgh: University of Pittsburgh Press.

Schwartz, Barry, ed. 1976. *The Changing Face of the Suburbs.* Chicago: University of Chicago Press.

Seeley, John, Alexander Sim, and Elizabeth Loosley. 1958. *Crestwood Heights: The Culture of Suburban Life.* New York: Basic Books.

Shefter, Martin. 1985. *Political Crisis/Fiscal Crisis: The Collapse and Revival of New York City.* New York: Basic Books.

Sonenshein, Raphael. 1993. *Politics in Black and White: Race and Power in Los Angeles.* Princeton: Princeton University Press.

Stone, Clarence. 1989. *Regime Politics: Governing Atlanta, 1946–1988.* Lawrence: University Press of Kansas.

Suarez, Ray. 1999. *The Old Neighborhood: What We Lost in the Great Suburban Migration, 1966–1999.* New York: Free Press.

Svara, James. 1991. *A Survey of America's City Councils: Continuity and Change.* Washington: National League of Cities.

Terkildsen, Nayda. 1993. "When White Voters Evaluate Black Candidates: The Processing Implications of Candidate Skin Color, Prejudice, and Self-Monitoring." *American Journal of Political Science* 37 (November): 1032–1053.

Thomas, G. Scott. 1998. *The United States of Suburbia*. Amherst, N.Y.: Prometheus Books.

Tiebout, Charles M. 1956. "A Pure Theory of Local Expenditures." *Journal of Political Economy* 64 (October): 416–424.

Verba, Sidney, and Norman H. Nie. 1972. *Participation in America: Political Democracy and Social Equality*. Chicago: University of Chicago Press.

Weiher, Gregory. 1991. *The Fractured Metropolis: Political Fragmentation and Metropolitan Segregation*. Albany: SUNY Press.

Welch, Susan. 1990. "The Impact of At-Large Elections on the Representation of Blacks and Hispanics." *Journal of Politics* 52 (November): 1050–1076.

Welch, Susan, and Timothy Bledsoe. 1988. *Urban Reform and Its Consequences: A Study in Representation*. Chicago: University of Chicago Press.

Whyte, William. 1956. *The Organization Man*. New York: Simon and Schuster.

Williams, Oliver, Harold Herman, Charles S. Liebmann, and Thomas Dye. 1965. *Suburban Differences and Metropolitan Politics: A Philadelphia Story*. Philadelphia: University of Pennsylvania Press.

Wirt, Frederick, Benjamin Walter, Francine F. Rabinowitz, and Deborah R. Hensler. 1972. *On the City's Rim: Politics and Policy in Suburbia*. Lexington, Mass.: D. C. Heath.

Wirth, Louis. 1938. "Urbanism As a Way of Life." *American Journal of Sociology* 44 (July): 1–24.

Wolfinger, Raymond E. 1974. *The Politics of Progress*. Englewood Cliffs, N.J.: Prentice-Hall.

Wood, Robert C. 1958. *Suburbia: Its People and Their Politics*. Boston: Houghton Mifflin.

Zikmund, Joseph II. 1967. "A Comparison of Political Attitude and Activity Patterns in Central Cities and Suburbs." *Public Opinion Quarterly* 31 (spring): 69–75.

———— 1968. "Suburban Voting in Presidential Elections." *Midwest Journal of Political Science* 12 (May): 239–258.

Notes

1. Unfortunately, even the classification scheme provided by the U.S. Census Bureau is not very helpful. Although the census does not formally define any places as suburbs per se, it does informally designate some places by default. The census divides localities between those in metropolitan areas and those in nonmetropolitan or rural areas. As of the 2000 census, there are officially 280 consolidated metropolitan statistical areas or metropolitan statistical areas in the United States (metropolitan area being defined as a central city of at least 50,000 residents and the surrounding counties that have a high degree of social and economic integration with that nucleus). The metropolitan areas range in size from the greater New York area (which includes northern New Jersey and Connecticut), with 21,199,865 people, to Enid, Oklahoma, with only 57,813 residents. Within metropolitan areas, the census categorizes places as being either the central or the noncentral city. By default, a suburb is any part of a metropolitan area that cannot be counted as the central city. As noted earlier, this type of definition does little to offer us much leverage in understanding the systematic differences across suburban places.

2. This might not always be the case, particularly as more residential places like Garland, Texas, or Livonia, Michigan, reach large population sizes.

3. What remains needed, however, are data to thoroughly test these assertions. In most research, there is no way to examine whether the extent of political conflict in a locality directly shapes citizens' perceptions about the role and function of local government or their specific

choices in local elections. Nor are there any appropriately geocoded survey data that sample from enough suburban locales. Most national level data either do not have enough respondents from suburbs or do not have proper geographic identifications. Most locally constructed surveys tend to be of large cities and do not have enough questions about issues, all vote choices, or the role of government. One of the biggest challenges for researchers will be collecting data from a wide variety of locales that are easily comparable.

Index